Krishna Bihari

The Indian Mirror

Volume 19

Krishna Bihari

The Indian Mirror
Volume 19

ISBN/EAN: 9783741170799

Manufactured in Europe, USA, Canada, Australia, Japa

Cover: Foto ©Thomas Meinert / pixelio.de

Manufactured and distributed by brebook publishing software
(www.brebook.com)

Krishna Bihari

The Indian Mirror

The Indian Mirror

EDITED BY KRISHNA BIHARI SEN, M. A.]

SUNDAY EDITION

[REGISTERED AT THE
GENERAL POST OFFICE.]

VOL. XIX.   CALCUTTA, OCTOBER 5, 1879.   NO. 104.

CONTENTS.

Telegraphic Intelligence.

FROM THE PRESS COMMIS-SIONER.

THE ENGAGEMENT NEAR SHUTUR GURDAN.

SIMLA, 4TH OCTOBER.

The column under General Roberts was to march to Zahidabad on the 3rd. Great difficulties about transport. No certain information of the attitude of troops in and about Cabul. They are apparently in want of leaders. On the 2nd, the Ghilzais assembled in great force on the ridge about Shutur Gurdan. They were attacked and driven off with a loss of thirty killed. Our casualties were Major Griffiths, 3rd Sikhs, and a Sergeant of the 67th of signalling party. Both slightly wounded, also three men of the 3rd Sikhs. The affair will have a good effect all over the country. On the 3rd, Colonel Jenkins, with guides, cavalry, and a detachment of the 9th Foot, reconnoitred Peahbolak.

Editorial Notes.

LORD AND SIR HENRY LAWRENCE were descendants by their mother's side of John Knox.

ONE of the most eminent temperance preachers is Mr. J. B Gough. He is now in England, is in his sixty-second year, has travelled about 420,000 miles, and delivered nearly 8,000 lectures within the last thirty-seven years, and yet, says a contemporary, he has not been in bed a whole day from illness since 1846.

WE approve the resolution of the Band of Hope Committee upon the advisability of opening a temperance column in the Indian Mirror. The space at our disposal is unfortunately limited. We shall try our best, however, to meet the views of our young friends. For the present, a Temperance column will appear in the Sunday Edition once every month.

THE death is announced of the Rev. Dr. Joseph Mullens, for many years belonging to the London Missionary Society at Bhowanipore. The lamented deceased was lately called to work in Madagascar. His death occurred in Africa, where he had gone to organise the Society's Missionary operations round Lake Tanganika. Dr. Mullens is, therefore, another victim to the tropical climate of Africa. His fate is mourned by a large circle of friends and admirers. In India, his memory is still cherished with affection and respect.

HERBERT SPENCER gives the following definition of Evolution :—"Evolution is a change from an indefinite, incoherent homogeneity to a definite, coherent heterogeneity, through continuous differentiations and integrations. The mathematician Kirkman translates the definition into plain English :—"Evolution is a change from a nohowish, untalkaboutable, all-alikeness to a somehowish and in-general-talk-aboutable not-all-alikeness, by continuous somethingelsifications and stick-togetherations." Both definitions are equally intelligible.

THE last anniversary of the death of Auguste Comte, the founder of Positivism, was celebrated by a special service at the Positivist Chapel, Holborn. Dr. Congreve delivered an address, in which he maintained that positivism was essentially religion, because it inculcated religious culture apart from morality or right action. It appealed, not to the intellect, but to the heart and feelings, and it was pre-eminently the religion of women, because it was based on tenderness and sympathy. Of all things in the world, the Positivist's declamations in favor of religion and devotional culture, seem to us to be the most wildly incoherent and incomprehensible.

THE retirement of Dr. Cumming is an event of pretty good significance in the Christian church in England. Some years ago, his utterances were eagerly watched for, and much importance was attached to his expositions of scripture, and especially to his interpretations of prophecy. As with many others, he became prophet instead of remaining interpreter, and his power waned in proportion as his predictions proved to be untrue. We think that Dr. Cumming's utterances have done more to damage people's faith in prophecies than the bitterest arguments ever advanced by anti-Christians on the subject.

THE Bishop of Manchester, in consecrating a church, lately, at Bolton, referred to Dr. Allman's presidential address, and said that, a few years ago, Professor Tyndall startled the world by speaking of matter as containing the promise and potency of every form of life. They were now told by Dr. Allman

that what was meant was mere physical or material life ; protoplasm was not the author of our will, affection, reverence or faith. Therefore, it would not help him much to fight the battle of life against wickedness and sin. Perhaps, in that great and unreachable region, which lay beyond the farthest reach of our physical investigation, there might be something which was not matter or force, and there might be room for God and the human soul, and in these two beings they had the elements concentrated of the Christian religion.

MR. GLADSTONE attributes the general spread of unbelief in France and Italy to Roman Catholicism. It is no secret, he says, that among the educated men of France and Italy, with the exception of a few individuals, the Christian dogma has ceased to hold an authoritative sway over either intellect or life. It is not this or that tenet which they doubt ; the whole basis has crumbled, the whole superstructure fallen to the ground ; and what even in this day moves some of them when they come to England is, astonishment at the large number of believers. There can be no doubt about the general infidelity; but whether this is owing to Roman Catholicism is more than we can say. We are of opinion that the falling-off of national vigour in France is contemporaneous with scepticism and unbelief.

FIRST Pagan, then Christian—this is the text which the Calcutta comic paper preaches to its fellow-religionists. Read the following :—

> Soldiers, yours the work of vengeance,
> Show to spare and swift to slay
> Be your arms when next the Afghan
> Shall confront you in the fray,
> Let your father Viking's fierceless
> Quell all thoughts of mercy, say
> To the dotards who would stop ye.
> We are Odin's men to-day.
> Thor and Odin against Mahomet
> Till the accursed walls are flat;
> Till our comrades' bones are rescued—
> We'll be Christian after that.

If our readers refer to the file of Punch during the time Russophobia was raging in England, they will understand the vast difference between the moral atmosphere of Great Britain and that of India.

A MAN who has taken to the cultivation of religion is constantly required to look to two things about him: (1) that his faith in God remains unshaken, and (2) that his moral nature continues unspotted. It behoves him also to see that there is no divorce between these two. We have often found men intensely religious, whose moral nature is not quite enviable, and moral men whose faith in God is not vivid and strong. In many souls, there is a struggle going on between these, We should prevent either of them gaining the mastery over our nature,

In India, the divorce of religion from morality is the chief characteristic of many sects. This is the result chiefly of an undue cultivation of the emotional nature. To all people who boast of their spiritual attainments one test may be applied. Are they moral? If the question be answered in the negative, you may be sure it is not the right sort of devotion that they are indulging in.

---:o:---

THE *Sheffield Telegraph* publishes a clever "Lament of Bathybius." Those among our readers to whom Bathybius may not be quite a familiar name, will be good enough to read the following after reading our article headed Concessions of Science :—

HUXLEY (*log.*) :
"Whether you are in yourself the essence—
Potential essence of life to be—
Or merely expressed the amorphous presence
Of calcic sulphate, is dark to me.
I know not whether you are or are not ;
I only know that you seem to be.
I must puzzle, though others care not,
Yet puzzle is vain—I am all at sea."

DISCIPLE (*resp.*) :
Broken my rest ; and torn with strange emotion
I toss in rhyme,
For a non-proven, questionable notion
In " deep-sea slime,"
Time was I worshipped, almost a fanatic,
Before his shrine ;
Invoked his aid in language truly Attic—
" Bathybius, mine ! "
But now I find this vaunted protoplasm
Excites a smile,
A doubtful kind of passing facial spasm—
And I revile !

Exit " reviling."

---:o:---

AT a meeting of the commission of the General Assembly of the Free Church of Scotland, Dr. Begg moved and carried this resolution :—"The Commission, taking into consideration the threatening aspect of God's Holy Providence, particularly in the general and long-continued depression of trade and commerce, above all, with reference to the gloomy prospect of the harvest, resolve to call upon the rulers of the nation to set apart a special time for becoming exercises, and to invite all classes to humble themselves under the hand of God, making confession of sin, and imploring His mercy." Upon this the *Spectator* observes :—" It is really a problem why teachers calling themselves Christians—as does Dr. Begg—so often assume that every trouble a community undergoes, is a sign of divine displeasure. Lord Bacon said that while prosperity is the blessing of the Old Testament, adversity is the blessing of the New ; and even that is hardly true, for one of the Psalmists says, Blessed is the man whom Thou chastenest." This must be the view of all sober reasoners. Our relations with God should be distinctly spiritual. Prayers for material things interfere with faith, in the first place, because we are ignorant of the physical laws of the universe. Events apparently injurious may be ultimately good. In the second place, such prayers are not always answered, in which case people's faith in Providence is sure to be undermined.

THE EDUCATION OF NATIVE YOUTHS IN ENGLAND.

---o---

A CONTROVERSY is going on between two contemporaries as to whether young Native Civilians should be compelled to pass a few years in England. We need not interpose our voice between the two combatants. But this subject is important, and we hope to be permitted to say a word or two on the subject of England-going in general. We are ourselves satisfied that a visit to England is necessary for good education, and that travel is the first thing needed to broaden the sympathies of the Bengali heart. But while saying so, we must not be blind to the many disadvantages of a prolonged stay in a foreign country, to a young man not under any sort of guardianship, to whom the temptations of London civilised life may be a veritable ruin. Many of the youths who go to England escape from their homes, and having no introduction letters to respectable people, they are dragged headlong into the whirlwind of fashionable society, the attractions of which prove pretty often destructive to their best interests. No wonder that very few of those who have returned from England have been able to attract the esteem and admiration of their countrymen. Clad in their outlandish costume and carrying their affectation of English manners to a ridiculous extent, they repel and seldom attract those of their friends who would fain learn from them the bright side of civilised life. There is nothing of that high tone and general elevation of character which would wring admiration and respect. The bad that they had in them, while here, is rendered worse by their stay in a foreign country, while the good that they have to show is not so good after all as to encourage others to send their sons to England. The reason is not far to seek. Young men who have lived from their birth under the roof of their parents, find themselves suddenly freed from control when they inhale the free air of England. They place themselves immediately upon the footing of independent gentlemen, receive and return visits, live, dance and flirt as any Englishmen. We do not think that such a life can be at all favorable to moral growth. Boys of the same age in England are placed under the control of well-managed households or institutions, while the sweet and chastening influence of the English home, bears upon their life in a manner not conceivable to the poor, exiled, forlorn Indian youth. The best friends of India in England have often shown their anxiety for the education of these youngsters. But the complaint with which they accompany this expression of their concern is to the effect that our young men are unwilling to place themselves under control. Two or three of the most eminent statesmen who had been to India were consulted on the subject. But they told the same tale. Under the circumstances it behoves our countrymen to ponder well the situation which the action of our young friends has forced upon them. We perfectly sympathise with those parents who, enlightened themselves, would not object to England-going on principle, and yet have a mortal fear that a stay in a foreign country might tend to corrupt the morals of their sons. Why should we, say they, send our sons to England, when we are convinced that we shall not get them back, that they will be anglicised and willingly exclude themselves from Native Society? Such is the general tenour of the objections urged on this head. Is it not time that an earnest effort should be made to remove the objections? We think it is too late to suppress the spirit of travelling which has developed itself among our youngmen. The best thing ought to be to place them under good guardianship in England. If that be impracticable, the next best thing, we regret to say, is to discourage England going as much as possible. For our part we are inclined to advocate the establishment of an institution like the proposed Indian Institute at Oxford, the management of which might keep itself in close correspondence with guardians in India.

THE CONCESSIONS OF SCIENCE.

---o---

DR. ALLMAN, extracts from whose speech at the British Association we reproduced in these pages on Sunday last, has done a signal service to the cause of science by drawing a broad line of demarcation between the physical and the spiritual side of the question of the origin of life. In that exhaustive address he gave a summary of the properties of that mysterious substance which philosophers call protoplasm, and described, in clear terms, the history of the attempts hitherto made to verify that substance. Dr. Allman agreed with many scientists as to the identity of all forms of physical life, and agreed also in referring them to the same mysterious substance. But having said so far, he stopped. He would not follow his brother scientists where they would transcend this physical life, and bridge the gulf that separates it from the mental or spiritual. He said that our physical organism might be the same as the lowest forms of living matter, but refused to admit that thought was a property of protoplasm. Here is a concession of no ordinary importance made by science. We believe the re-action is coming against the wildest flights of the scientist's imagination. Some of the doctrines which have recently startled the world have been carefully examined by Pandits, and it has begun to be generally asserted that there is no scientific basis for any one of them. We alluded recently to the controversy between Professor Haeckel, the maddest by far of all known evolutionists, and the learned Dr. Virchow, and we observed how the latter candidly conceded that, so far as science was concerned, none of those doctrines were proved. Dr. Virchow's opinion is ably maintained by Dr. Allman. But we need not stop here. Mr. Joseph Cook, one of the most popular lecturers of America, has clearly summarised the concessions which scientific men have made in respect of their own theories. We are indebted to a correspondent of the *Bombay Guardian* for specimens of them reproduced from Mr. Cook's Monday lectures. We extract them here :—

Haeckel concedes :—
That the theory of man's descent from apes is, according to the admission of the wholesale evolutionists, deductive and not inductive—a result of speculation and not of observation.
That it probably can never be established by the inductive, that is by the most strictly scientific method.

Huxley concedes :—
That *spontaneous generation* must have occurred, on the doctrine of evolution as held by him and his school cannot be true.
That spontaneous generation has never been known to occur.
That it is against all the ascertained analogy of nature to suppose that it ever has occurred.
That if spontaneous generation has not occurred, it must be admitted that a *supernatural* act originated life in the primordial cell or cells.

Kant has said :—
"Give me matter only, and I cannot explain the formation of a caterpillar."

Dana said :—
That no remains of fossil man bear evidence to less perfect creatness of structure than in civilised man or to any nearer approach to the man-ape in essential characteristics. The existing man-apes belong to lines that reached up to them as their ultimatum, but, at that line which is supposed to have reached upward to man met the first link below the lowest level of existing man has yet been found. This is the more extraordinary in view of the fact that, from the lowest limits in existing

man, there are all possible gradations up to the highest; while below that limit, there is an abrupt fall to the ape-level, in which the cubic capacity of the brain is one-half less. If the links ever existed, their annihilation without trace **is so extremely improbable that it may be pronounced impossible : *until some are found, science cannot assert that they ever existed.***

Darwin now admits that:—

"After reading the essay of Nageli on plants, and the remarks by various authors with respect to animals, in the earlier editions of my origin of species I, probably, attributed too much to the action of natural selection or survival of the fittest. I had not formerly sufficiently considered the existence of many structures which appear to be, as far as we can judge, neither beneficial nor injurious ; and this I believe to be one of the greatest oversights as yet detected in my works."

It was the haughty claim of Huxley, Bärnum and Hæckel:—

That Bathybius is an organism without organs. That it performs the acts of nutrition and propagation.

That with other organisms like itself, it stands at the head of the terrestrial history of the development of life.

That it spans the chasm between the living and not living.

But Bathybius has been discovered by the ship *Challenger* to be a sulphate of lime which, when dissolved, crystallises as gypsum !

With regard to the pretensions of this last, we may allude to what Professor Huxley said in reply to Dr. Allman at the meeting of the British Association. In thanking the President, the learned Professor said :—

The President had alluded to a certain thing to which he (Professor Huxley) had given the name of "Bathybius," and it was said, with perfect justice, he had brought Bathybius into notice. At any rate, he had christened it, and he was in a certain sense its earliest friend. A number of admirable persons had taken the little thing in hand, and made much of it. He had hoped, indeed, that his young friend Bathybius would turn out a credit to him, but he was sorry to say as times had gone on Bathybius had not verified the promise of his youth. In the first place, he could not be found when he was wanted ; and in the second place, when he was found, all sorts of things were said about him. However, his own mind was perfectly at ease about young Bathybius ; for, whatever else could be said about men of science, it could not be said that they endeavoured to conceal one another's mistakes. He had the utmost confidence, therefore, that if Bathybius happened to be a blunder, it would be carefully exposed by somebody. Up to the present time that had not been done.

Now, whatever be the nature of Bathybius, whether it be a real thing or not, we must admit that it cannot be the origin of thought, or rather that thought cannot be one of its properties. Taking these concessions into consideration, we may reasonably hope that the time will soon come when scientific men, laying due stress upon the nature and functions of science, will come round and make knowledge once more subserve the purposes of true religion.

THE CHURCH OF GOD.

We said in our last issue that theism is a necessity of the world, and that, say what others may, it is the only system of belief which is capable of furnishing a panacea for the evils to which humanity is a prey. In the pages of history we recognise the voice of God calling upon man at repeated intervals to do worship unto Him ; but the deep marks of blood which disfigure almost every page of it and the signs of jealousy, disunion, discord and unbelief which are visible everywhere, tell us that that voice has ever been disobeyed, and its ring not so much as able to produce the least appreciable influence upon the stolid human heart. Humanity,

indeed, has ever been struggling to rise upwards to heavens ; but its weaknesses have been the greatest obstacles to the attainment of that end. The Judaic dispensation is a standing monument of the will of God on this earth ; and if, in spite of it, Christ became indispensable, it was because, standing as it did upon grounds purely national, that religion became too much exclusive, fanatical and addicted to the letter to be of permanent use to men. Worship, if anything, must be sweet, and the worship of the loving and dear Merciful God must be the sweetest of all sweet things. The Jews never recognised this element of religion, and the result was that mankind pined and groped for more light. They thirsted for nectar, and lo! stones were given them instead. Christ was, therefore, a necessity and right nobly did he discharge his mission. He was the greatest preacher of theism, and both by life and precepts gave men a real picture of the High Being who sent him. But, as we have said, human weaknesses came to stand in the way, and behold the Father was eclipsed by the glory of His son. Christianity has doubtless sweetened religion, given it, indeed, the very thing the world wished for in place of the dry and exclusive literalism of the Jewish faith. But, then, it is not the worship of God, but of God as exhibiting Himself entirely in man. Once more, therefore, did the course of nature deviate from its intended path, and mankind was made to cry for the invisible Being. Yes, the world cries for God, our own India cries for Him. This country, the home of idolatry and abject superstitions, raises its suppliant voice to heaven, and piteously invokes Divine blessings upon itself. If we were asked how we came to interpret the wishes of our nation, we should ask every one to peruse history, and mark therein page after page recording the soul's innermost struggles for light. Again and again has the national intellect striven to free itself from the tyranny of priesthood ; again and again has monotheism been preached to the people. Alas ! the griping hand of despotism has as often strangled the new-born faith, and given instead a monster horn of Idolatry. In Wilson's Sects of the Hindus many creeds are to be found that, monotheistic at first, degenerated into polytheism afterwards. Sects rise in rapid succession in this country, and most of them are protests against the tyranny of spiritual despotism. The Brahmo Somaj seems to us to be the chosen instrument in the hands of God to fight with and overcome this hydra-headed monster. It is, if we may say so, the only organisation which in modern times has been raised to inculcate the worship of the one only God. Individuals there may be, and are, in abundance who devoutly cultivate the theistic faith. But nowhere before the advent of the Brahmo Somaj was monotheistic worship organised into a church. Unique in its nature, laws and constitution, the Brahmo Somaj has shown that it can satisfy the spiritual cravings of man, and make the heart capable of infinite progress towards God. It has raised the aspirations of the Hindu intellect and purified its moral tone ; and it may be said, without fear of contradiction,that had it not been for it, the infidelity of the present century would have thrown the educated community into a pit unfathomable of sin and corruption. Our church is a Godsend to the country, and it will be the blessed means of liberating the land from the thraldom of its many evils. It has been said that theism in itself, without the aids and appliances of a supernatural revelation, is in-

competent to influence mankind. We beg to reply it is this very mixture of supernaturalism and mediatorial faith which theism is destined to demolish. The Brahmo Somaj will allow no medium to interpose between God and man. Its aim is to understand the missions of the greatest prophets, those prophets that came to preach the unity of the Godhead ; its work is to fall at the feet of Christ and other masters, and devoutly learn from them the glorious truths of monotheism. The Brahmo Somaj glorifies Christ, because he has taught the world the nature and worship of God. We are thus ready to understand the prophets, to profit by them, to assimilate their spirit with our flesh and blood, and,through and in accordance with their directions, find our way to the heavenly throne. Surely, they come from God, and their words we're inspired from heaven. They were the messengers of a Loving Father ever ready to save humanity from sin. They were commissioned to reveal Him to the world. Should we not hear them, should we not obey them, should we not greet them in our heart of hearts and eagerly listen to their messages of peace ? It is one of the most glorious birthrights of our church that it has been accorded the task of recognising His voice in every religious prophet that came to preach. Let not, then, Brahmos utter one word more in depreciation of Christ and the prophets. To say that they are unworthy of our love would be to blaspheme God, because to say so would be to proclaim one's disbelief in a living providence. We have before us the volume of nature every letter of which displays the loving hand of God. We have science ministering to us and revealing His wisdom. We have in the prophets the best of friends, whose duty it is to remove the veil which hides His face. Lastly, we have our own conscience through which we hear His still small voice. These are the various means whereby our faith in an invisible Being becomes strong, and we can assure our brethren that the more these multiply, the better will be our faith in the long run. Do not speak of this means or that only for the attainment of heavenly knowledge. No, the world is at our disposal. Whatever things are pure and of good report, whatever men are God-seeking and God-inspired, are ours. The narrow bounds of utility and the selfish demands of an exclusive nationalism are not ours. We spurn limits. How glorious the heritage ; how beautiful the revelation in our life's scriptures ! May we be worthy of the dispensation that has brought us together in an ever expanding and expansive church.

Brahmo Somaj.

THE *Theistic Quarterly Review* for October is just out. We hope to notice it soon.

BABU GOUR GOVIND ROY has gone to Lucknow to celebrate the anniversary of the local Brahmo Somaj.

BABU PROTAP CHUNDER MOZOOMDAR will go to Lahore soon to conduct the anniversary of the Punjab Brahmo Somaj.

THEOLOGICAL INSTITUTION.

BABU KESHUB CHUNDER SEN delivered a lecture on "Character" at the Theological Institution on Saturday, the 20th September, 1879.

The lecturer said :—There are four departments in which we realize the voice of God. The spiritually-minded hear the voice of God in the various laws of their physical, intellectual, moral and spiritual nature. Some people say it is the laws of nature which govern and regulate our bodily health ; but we say it is the voice of God which controls our physical nature. We cannot break the laws of health with impunity. The commandment of God that "Thou shalt obey the laws of health" is written upon every muscle and nerve in the physical organism. We hear the voice of God in the laws of health as the ancient *Rishis*, Moses, Isaiah, and other prophets heard it in other matters. I discharge a religious duty when I satiate my hunger or thirst, because thereby I execute God's commandment. The voice of God in our physical nature is the gospel of health or hygiene. Through our hunger God thus commands us ;—"Go and eat." Enjoined by God we eat, and through His prohibition we refrain from eating when there is no hunger in us.

(2) Intellect hungers and thirsts just as body hungers and thirsts. As man must eat something, so he must read something. Every man is psychologically constituted to seek and enjoy truth. Information of some kind man must have. This curiosity or thirst for truth is another expression for God's voice which says :—"Go and be wise."

(3) In the third department, namely, our moral nature, the voice of God which we hear is the gospel of character. Character is a thing which we cannot form or mould, unless we believe in the doctrine of God's voice. It is conscience or God's voice within which helps to mould our character. It is this which makes it incumbent upon us to form our character. Why should we be honest? Because God commands us to be so. Whatever God says is right and absolutely moral. It is not for expediency or utility that honesty is the best policy. Go straight to the altar of God, and God says :—"Thou shalt speak the truth. Sacrifice your life for India." We cannot take benevolence in our hand and weigh it in the scales of utility. God says :—"Give every one what is due to him." That is duty. This sense is ingrained in our moral nature. We are so constituted as to hear the voice of God in the development of our moral nature. The doctrine of the day of final judgment is not natural. God is judging us every moment. If I disobey Him in any department of my nature, physical, intellectual, moral or spiritual, He chastises me. There is a stinging wasp which makes rest impossible. God makes this world too hot for him who fails to do His will. The smarting consciousness of sin haunts the sinner wherever he goes. An intolerable uneasiness follows him. It ruffles the mind, perturbs the whole spirit. The sinner may administer opium to get rid of the agonies of penitence ; but the vengeance of God's retribution is upon him. Such is the constitution of nature that he cannot feel happy after having done some villainous act. So long as man is not beast, this voice of God is heard—"Thou shalt do this, or Thou shalt not do that." Whenever I commit something wrong, the voice of God, in spite of myself, says :—"You do wrong." There is remorse or compunction in me. The Heavenly Judge chastizes me, seated upon the throne of conscience. Those who are strictly obedient to His voice are men of character or heroic souls. They are destined to enter the pleasant haven of righteousness. Inspiration is the highest development of the voice of God.

THEOLOGICAL INSTITUTION.

THE FINE ARTS.

BABU PROTAP CHUNDER MOZOOMDAR delivered a lecture on Fine Arts at the Theological Institution on the 30th August last, the following is a summary of the lecture :—

The subject of the Fine Arts is an educational one. Unfortunately in this country, the Fine Arts are not considered a part of liberal education. The University here think that a certain amount of intellectual culture is all that is required for the faculties of the young. In Europe, no man is considered educated, who does not understand the Fine Arts. The man who could not appreciate a celebrated piece of painting, would very likely be taken as a clown. One who had no eye for the beauty and grandeur of the noble structures of European architecture, such as the Cathedral of St. Peter at Rome, the marble Cathedral of Milan, or that of the German city of Cologne, could not take an intelligent part in enlightened conversation. A man not understanding Greek statues or Roman culture, is not an educated man. So in Europe the cultivation of Fine Arts is an indispensable element in education. The lecturer, therefore, advised his hearers to try to understand them as much as possible.

What are the Fine Arts? In Greece, they worshipped the Muses. All the poets, since then, (not excepting even Puritanic, Protestant Milton) invoked their aid, when they undertook to sing something great or noble. The Muses presided over the temples, over the mountains and bays, over peace and prosperity, over love and joy. They were modest virgins who always concealed themselves only to manifest their powers, when required. They were the geniuses of the Fine Arts. The fact is, they were the personification of the Arts, beautiful and divinely inspired figures, lovely forms of thought and feeling, constituting the pantheon of wisdom and grace, and æsthetic godliness. They were supposed by them to be the daughters of Jupiter, they inhabited the waterfalls and woodlands, the romantic mountain solitudes, and the clear unfathomable blue of the heavens. But Rome and Greece are emptied of the classical genius, Olympus is deserted, the Capitol desecrated, and Europe has turned Christian. Philosophy and science have disenchanted the earth and sky, yet there is still a nominal adherence to the Muses.

In his former lecture the lecturer had spoken of the perception of beauty in the universe by the soul. The mind in man perceived a mind in the universe, the soul perceived a mysterious soul of beauty, grandeur, exactness, symmetry and harmony in creation. Impressions of such a nature were so deep that they struggled to find expression. They addressed us so deeply and truly, stirred and roused the mind of man so unavoidably and so violently that the percipient mind wanted to express it in its fulness. The winds sighing, the birds singing, the flowers blooming, the streams rushing, the thunder roaring, the sea rolling, women singing, children playing, the trees growing, the moon rising in the gloom, flooding the whole horizon with a strange light, made such a deep impression in the mind that it moved man to respond to what it perceived. The sea is sometimes destructive, the winds make havoc, the children make trouble, and the women quarrel oftener than they sing ; still the combination in the universe strikes a chord of human nature, and it must respond. In going to make that response, it tries to express what it feels. This is the origin of the Fine Arts. When the breezes blow and the streams murmur, man instinctively strains his voice to a song—even men who have the most dissonant and discordant of voices, who sing so badly that we do not know whether they bray or sing. We cannot help singing. Music possesses human nature, overmasters it. Man is a slave to the goddess of music. Shakespeare says the man who has no music in him, is fit for treason. All the Fine Arts have their origin in the hidden harmonies of man's mind. Michael Angelo on the mountains finds an unspeakable adaptation between his susceptibilities and thoughts and the magnificent structures of nature, eternally snow-crowned crests, the sun rising and setting behind them, the dome-shaped summits, the turrets of ice, the caves, precipices, broad green valleys amid all the noble beauties of a mountain scenery. The mind is raised to sublimity, aspirations rise, ideals present themselves, vast structures are planned and piled, noble temples are built, grand cathedrals and mighty fortresses rise to touch the sky. And standing on the Cathedral of Milan, one might see, on the one hand, the white Alpine heights and, on the other, the blue waters of the Adriatic. Clouds and mountains must have suggested human architecture.

Music, poetry, architecture, sculpture and painting have different objects, but all have the same root. Michael Angelo once met a stone-mason with a piece of unhewn marble. He told him to polish certain parts of it, and leave others unpolished. The man did it and found a beautifully-formed human face. Such is the penetration of genius. Man lisps in poetry, and a poet is said to be born, not made.

We are apt to think that the Fine Arts have no connection with religion. Some religions forbid painting, some forbid music. But the grandest singing is religious singing, and the noblest paintings glorify religion. These are the most wonderful frescoes in old churches like that of St. Mark at Venice, or St. Peter at Rome. The best paintings of Europe are, as a rule, religious. The heads of Christ, the forms and face of the Madonna, the crucifixion of Jesus, the Martyrdom of saints, the Last supper, and the great Agony furnish subjects for the greatest paintings. Architecture is always religious in India. Our ancient temples are the only relics of the artistic culture of our forefathers. The frescoes, carvings and the various other artistic executions at the sacred edifices in Southern and Western India, the monasteries and topes and cave temples of the Buddhists, show that, in ancient India, the arts formed the province of religion. The best and noblest European music comes from Germany. Handel, Mozart, Beethoven composed only religious pieces, and did not fritter away their time in love-songs. Handel's Oratorio, illustrating some of the events of the Old Testament, are heard by thousands in London. Thousands of pilgrims assemble every year on Easterday for the grand music from the orchestra of the Roman Catholic Church of St. Peter at Rome. On Thursday night, before 12 o'clock, the whole Church is covered with funeral gloom, and the orchestra plays deep and melancholy notes. Just as the bells of the Church solemnly toll out 12 o'clock, the gloom is suddenly taken off, thousands of gas-jets are at once lit up, and the organ peals out notes of joy, and ten thousand voices join them with songs of gladness. In India, too, the most celebrated pieces of music are all religious. The Dhrupads and Rags only glorify God. What is the best poetry we have got? The Hymns of the Rig Veda, the Upanishads, the Gita and the Bhagavat, the Gathas of Zend, the Psalms of David. When is Shakespeare most profound? When he describes the motives, intricacies and relations of human nature. Milton's poetry has shaped the Christianity of the day. The simple unmixed esthetical vitality, in grandeur, sublimity, sweetness, pathos, harmony, purity, depth, creates the Fine Arts, when the pent-up soul tries to speak the unspeakable. If the soul of artistic excellence, be the excellence of the ideal within, what can supply such ideals better than religion? What can transcend the sublimity, greatness, depth and pathos of human faith and human suffering? A pure face, untainted with sin, blooming in peace and love to God, defieth all the beauty of the flowers. A noble and manly faith in God's love has in it a depth and pathos that furnishes the grandest subjects to the artist. Hence the subservience of the arts to religion. Progress in religion means progress in artistic culture.

Why have we so little artistic culture in India to-day? Because we have not much development of religious truth. When that will be the Brahmo Somaj will blossom out in a thousand forms of beauty. How Chaitanya created a new school of music! The old *rags* and *raginis* do not move half so much as those sweet hymns called *Sankirtans*. Why? Because they try to express greater feeling, faith, resignation and love. The man who composed these could never find words to utter all that they felt. Why are Rammohun Roy's hymns so much prized? Because they present a deep life within them. The feelings of faith and devotion act as wonderful impulses in the heart. They develope everything. What marvellous beauty is there in those few distiches of which Hafiz scratched on pieces of brick. The inspiration of religion is the soul of the Fine Arts. It is God's breath that swells a man's soul. Centuries have rolled, and nations have risen and fallen, but the soul of Christ still lives and fires Tennyson and Wordsworth and Longfellow, and is displayed in the grand cathedrals of Italy and Germany. If we wish that painting should rise, that poetry should flow out of our hearts, if we hope to compete with the artists of Europe, we must cultivate religion, try to behold in our hearts the light of divine beauty and majesty. The Egyptians raised their Pyramids, the Greeks their pantheon, the ancient Hindus their pagodas; are the modern Hindus to build nothing?

Let India first raise in her heart the cathedral of faith and truth, and cathedrals will rise without. David sang, Dante sang, Milton sang, Rishis sang, the Rig Veda, the Upanishads, and the Brahmins sang in India in the past; shall India remain dumb to-day?

Correspondence.

[We do not hold ourselves in any way responsible for the opinions of our correspondents.—ED., I. M.]

THE BAND OF HOPE.

TO THE EDITOR OF THE "INDIAN MIRROR."

SIR,—I am desired by the Executive Council of the Band of Hope to lay before you the following resolution, passed at their last meeting, and to request you kindly to accede to their wishes : --

"That the Executive Council of the Band of Hope have noticed with regret the absence in Bengal of any Periodical -- either weekly, monthly or quarterly -- published solely with the object of advocating the cause of Total Abstinence ; and, in the present financial condition of the Band, they are also painfully conscious of their inability to undertake that noble enterprise themselves. Under such circumstances, the Council believe it expedient to request the Editor of the *Indian Mirror* (Sunday Edition,) to open a Temperance column in his journal, and thereby supply the whole community with informations, local and foreign, on the question."

I sincerely hope and trust that you will be good enough to take the matter into your serious consideration and do the needful.

Yours &c.,
NALIN BEHARI SIRCAR,
Honorary Secretary.
Band of Hope, 2nd October 1879.

---0---

OUR YOUNG MEN.

---0---

TO THE EDITOR OF THE "INDIAN MIRROR."

SIR,--In your issue of the 17th August last, you make certain queries as to the conduct of young men of the present generation in comparison with that of their predecessors. You say "they are not liberally better" as regards moral excellence; but I am sorry to maintain that being myself a student, and one who has to mix with all classes of young men, I have observed that the case is just the reverse. One young men are in no way better than their predecessors ; of course, there are exceptions as exceptions there are to every rule: but to take a general view, it is so. They are immoral; the number of those who resort to bad places is considerably less ; but they treat each other in such a manner, eat such immoral jokes that one would blush to talk to them.

It would not be out of place here to mention something of the discipline which our young men care to undergo. Our school boys are independent ; they never hesitate to speak in the face of their superiors ; they care little for what the teachers order them to do. In a word, they are very disobedient.

On the subject of intoxication, I may say that few of our young men are seen to imbibe *ganja* or *charas.* The vice of drunkenness, I think, has increased of late among young men; but there is every prospect of its gradual decrease.

As for truthfulness and honesty, nothing can be known as certain. My impression is that students are more truthful now-a-days ; but I am sorry to say that they have not that courage or rashness which is essential to that virtue : they often shrink from speaking the truth in cases of emergency.

Yours &c.,
PRIYO NATH MULLICK.

THE LECTURE AT SIMLA.

---0---

TO THE EDITOR OF THE "INDIAN MIRROR."

SIR,--Your issue of 14th September, in which you were good enough to insert a report of a lecture which I delivered in Simla, reached me somewhat late. May I trouble you to insert one or two corrections of the report, though rather tardy in appearance.

1. In the second paragraph of the introduction, the first of those views which debate the uniqueness of Christ should be *pantheism,* not *tradition.*

2. In the first paragraph of part 1, one of my chief points was missed; *viz.,* the specific analogy between nature and the moral (not outer) world by which we may test true greatness. In the physical universe, the greatness of bodies is tested by their power of attraction : and similarly in the moral world the greatness of man is measured by his power of attraction, and consolation, &c., forming others into a society of which his own personality is the centre and binding power.

3. In the fourth paragraph of part 3, the point is not "who first preached the true religion in the Christian religion," but "who first preached and universal toleration ?" None of the nations of antiquity, nor their philosophers. These all maintained a proud exclusiveness. But Paul, the narrow-minded Pharisaic Jew, was so changed by the power of Christ that he recognised the one humanity amid all national and social distinctions, and the Christian Church has always followed his leading.

Any of your readers who may have been interested in the subject of the lecture on Christ and Great men, have doubtless been able to make other minor corrections themselves.

Yours &c.,
H. U. WEITBRECHT.
The 29th September 1879.

EXPLANATIONS.

---0---

TO THE EDITOR OF THE "INDIAN MIRROR."

SIR,--I fully admit the force of Dr. Tyssen's remarks in reference to my argument from the Greek original of Luke 18.19 ; and I entirely withdraw the sentence in which it occurs. The interpretation I suggested remains, I consider, true.

I am surprised that your correspondent " D" should not have understood that I spoke of unity *as applied to Godhead,* when I asked him to find the word in the Bible. The argument from the omission of a particular modern term is to my mind quite worthless in itself. But " D" thought it good as against Christian teaching; so I thought it well to remind him it would apply rather severely against Unitarian teaching.

His other main line of argument--*viz.,* the difficulty of understanding the co-existence of opposite sets of attributes in Jesus Christ--is, I conceive, absolutely fatal to any sort of Theism. This I hope to shew in the course of a short series of letters which I began in your last issue.

I further to trespass further on your space, and, therefore, reserve my second letter on theism for your next issue.

Your &c.
LUKE RIVINGTON.
Indore, September 1879.

P. S.--For the sake of any Christian readers of your paper, I feel bound to say that I always spell the personal or possessive pronoun, when it refers to Jesus Christ, with a capital letter at the beginning--as also the word "Son"--but that your printer expresses his opinion by changing it to a small letter, although he, like yourself, is not responsible for the opinions of correspondents whether expressed by words or capital letters.

☞ We beg to assure Father Rivington that the omission of the capital letter is not deliberate.--ED, *I. M.*

THE GOSPEL OF ST. JOHN.

---0---

TO THE EDITOR OF THE "INDIAN MIRROR."

SIR,--Your correspondent Mr. Rivington has addressed a third letter to you on the subject of the fourth gospel. This time he argues in favor of its authenticity by saying that the first gospel, which in many points depicts Jesus as a man, in some points depicts him as a God. My answer is that I never said it didn't. It narrates that he was miraculously conceived, that his mother was betrothed at the time, but proceeded to solemnize her marriage without bequeathing her intended husband of the condition she was in, and that the husband was afterwards enlightened in a dream. It narrates that Jesus multiplied provisions, that he stilled a tempest, performed miraculous cures, gave sight to the blind, walked on water, and raised the dead to life. It narrates that many people were possessed with devils, and that Jesus cast out many of these devils, some of which would depart on being spoken at even by his disciples, while others would not depart unless the exorciser had previously eaten less than was good for him. (Mathew xvii, 21). Does Mr. Rivington suppose that I believe a word of all this, and does he expect your readers to believe it? Surely, the fact that the first gospel contains many episodes depicting Jesus as an ordinary man shows that the supernatural stories about him are untrue. Mr. Rivington does not deny humanity, but says that he was both God and man. To my mind that is equivalent to saying that he was both God and not God ; a contradiction in terms in fact. The only reasonable explanation of the contradictions in the Gospels is this : that the real Jesus was a man in all respects, and that his followers gradually altered their conception of him into that of a God, and the writers of the gospels have put together some authentic records respecting him,

and some later stories which were invented concerning him, being in some cases ordinary events distorted in a supernatural light, in other cases allegorical stories afterwards narrated as material facts, and, in some cases absolute inventions. I believe myself that the relations of God to man have always been the same as they are now, and that the devil and all devils have always been as absolutely non-existent as they are now, being merely the creatures of human imagination. I may add that I believe that the same Divine spirit or influence which inspired Jesus to proclaim that the sole essential point in the Law and the Prophets, was this, " Thou shalt love the Lord thy God with all thy heart, and thy neighbour as thyself," inspires all theists to say the same of the rites, ceremonies, and dogmas, of the various forms of religion, Christian, Hindu and the rest, which exist in the world at the present day. Those are the true followers of Jesus who call upon men to rely, not on faith in the writer of the New Testament; not on faith in any one or more of the organisations called Churches, for teaching religion ; not on faith in the divinity of the person, or authority of the recorded teaching of Jesus; but on faith in the Creater of the Universe, in which we find ourselves placed, and in the author of the minds with which we find ourselves endowed. But to return once more to Mr. Rivington's letter. He makes another attempt to take advantage of your readers' ignorance of Greek. He says [" I and my Father are one"--not one person, one original will not bear that), but one in power, one in substance, one in essence.] I place his words between square brackets. Now let me distinctly say that the Greek words correspond exactly to the English ones, "I and my Father are one," and will bear just as much, and necessarily imply just as little as the English ones will. There is nothing whatever to be got out of them. The word 'one' is in the neuter in the Greek, but that merely indicates the general idea expressed in English by the word "one" not followed by any noun. If Mr. Rivington means that this text should be read in the same sense as others in the same book, in which the same expression occurs, I willingly accept his argument. Thus in John xvii, 11, 20, 21, 22, we find Jesus praying to God for his disciples, "that they may be one, as we are." Here 'one' is in the neuter in the Greek, and the phrase merely means 'united in purpose and opinion.' Then the whole argument, based on this text, that Jesus represented himself as God, not as a man, falls to the ground. I still maintain that the statement in the fourth Gospel is worthless to prove that Jesus even uttered these words; but, if he did, then it may be argued, from the same Gospel, that he did not intend by them to advance any claim to God.

Your brother Theist,
AMHERST D. TYSEN.

WAS JESUS AN ECLECTIC !

---0---

TO THE EDITOR OF THE "INDIAN MIRROR."

SIR,--That Rammohun Roy was an eclectic, there can be no manner of doubt. He spared no pains, no mental labor, no daily and nightly search or study, that could help him to the best thoughts of the best thinkers, of all creeds and of all ages, on the life of God for the soul of man : godlikeness, godliness, religion. It is saddening to look around the central city of Indian mentality, the Athens of British India, Calcutta, and strain one's eyes in vain to discover a follower of Rammohun, a Brahmo, who practically emulates The Founder in this respect. Where is there such a student as he was of Hebrew, Greek, Latin, English, Persian, Arabic, Sanskrit? Where is the man, on Indian soil, who aims to be such a tireless hunter and captor of the highest and loveliest truths of all religions? Long will thou hold thy place, oh great Rammohun,--as the Indian Prince of seekers ; the King of Bengali enquirers and publishers; the crown of our most genuine eclecticism! --All eclecticism, of course, is that of thought and work, choosing the best ; the best out of the good things, found and only to be found, by years of search and struggle : by a life-long industry, and eternal vigilance. All true knowledge is eclectic ; and no man can preach or write, who is not a faithful *chooser* of thoughts and of words. All practical life is eclectic ; the artist choosing his colors ; the builder his materials ; the doctor his medicines ; the scholar his books. Let none discredit eclecticism, because God has made it the law of true *thought* and of right *action,* and not the law of the heart's love or of the soul's worship. All love is one love, if it be God's love in us, and *here* is no eclecticism. All worship one, if it be simple, child-like trust in God. No child can be an eclectic, but only a man. "Come, know what you worship," is the call of Jesus as an eclectic. "In malice be ye children, but in understanding be men," is the cry of Paul the eclectic; and he crowns his eclecticism with the very law of it, "Prove all things, hold fast (only) that which is good"; that which God gives you to see is good; you and not another. Now, if this law of a manly religious life be endangered by some Brahmos, through the exclusive love and devotion of their *Yoga and Bhakti* (though few have *enough* even of this love and faith) it is miserably evident that

"Wisdom finds a narrow path
With here and there a traveller,"

in the God-commanded ways of Divine eclecticism, whether in the Christian or in the non-Christian world. Of course, to their own "environment," all who dare to be electics are,—as Jesus was, "deceivers," insurgents, revolutionists. They are mad; they are infidels, they are blasphemous. They should be crushed with stones, or burned with fire. "He hath a devil and is mad, why hear ye him?" It is not worth while to take note of the splendid eclecticism of Jesus, to which the reverence of the Christian church (good in its way, but partial) has so long shut the eyes of its disciples. Charles Beard said the other day in Manchester,—(and I, for one hear Jesus, by his word and work, saying the same thing,)—"The world is growing too old, knowledge too broad, humanity too conscious of its unity to find satisfaction in race-religions":—that is God's life, as reflected in the highest experience of any one race, cannot long be accepted as complete and catholic,—or as absolute and final. All religions must grow; and grow in unison. They must meet as friends in council, and distil out of their individual revelations the only true religion. God speed that family meeting, that codification, of all theistic truths into one 'Brahmoism,' that will be nearest to God, and grandest of all, because simplest of all. The knowledge of true religion is yet to come. Love we have. Trust we have. The highest and broadest reach of the eclecticism of Jesus, we have not. Nor can it ever be ours, unless we open our eyes and our ears to it; and accept it from all points of the compass, north and south, east and west, as he did. But how does this appear? Does it come out in the four gospels? No: certainly not to the superficial reader of them.—Nor have we time to show, to-day, except by a hint or two, how, year by year,—improving history and geography and the study of the life of Jesus *in situ*,—proves the grandeur of his eclecticism; and shows hidden there—the secret of his power and of his success;—and of his doing more than any other man,—through twenty centuries,—to feed the growing thought and strength of many nations. Two unquestioned facts—which we have not space here to draw out,—but to which we earnestly call attention, are these:—First the fact that he,—Jesus,—received as a birth-gift, the quintessence of the religious wisdom of India, of Persia and of Egypt,—through the protracted captivities of his people, the Hebrews; to whom God gave centuries of study in Asia and Africa under teachers of the world's then most highly developed religions. All these helped Jesus to his childhood's faith. He took them in, with his mother's milk. That is one thing to remember and study out. Another fact is this;—Jesus was not born in Jerusalem. His thinking began at Nazareth. And where is Nazareth? On the southern slope of the Lebanon hills, that border Palestine on the north. Through this glorious valley still runs the commerce of "oldest city in the world," Damascus. It goes thus down to the sea, and thence to Alexandria and Rome, and the cities of the Mediterranean. By the door of Jesus the mountain boy, passed,—for thirty years continually,—before he opened his mouth as a teacher—the great caravan of merchants (with their interpreters) exchanging with Europe the richest saleable products of Bengal, of China, of Persia, of Babylonia; and so on....Did the God-given soul and mind of Jesus use these rare opportunities? Surely yes. And thus was he taught of God. Thus did he suck the honey of truth with a divine eclecticism.

Yours &c.,
D.

Literary and Scientific.

A NEW dramatic story entitled "Psyche," by Dr. George Macdonald, will shortly be published.

THE eighteen hundredth anniversary of the destruction of Pompii was to have been solemnly observed by Italian Archæologists on the 25th of September last.

THE story is told that the editor of the witty but abusive Richmond *Christian Advocate* consulted his physician not long ago. The doctor examined him, and after a moment's reflection said: "Brother Lafferty, you have a very bad tongue."

THE proposed observatory on Mount Etna, at a height of 9,652 ft. will be the second highest building of its kind, the most lofty observatory in the world being situated at Pike's Peak, Colorado, at an elevation of 14,336 ft. above the sea level.

DR. BARNARDO, in the current number of *Night and Day* states that he has found the Chicago specific against intemperance—red Peruvian bark—exceedingly useful in dealing with drunkards who wish to reform, especially, if they have been accustomed to spirits.

TENNYSON completed his seventieth year, August 5th. He has been recognized now forty years as a great poet, and has enjoyed better health, more riches, and wider popularity during his life than has ever been the lot of any other British poet.

THE House of Lords now musters 507 members, ranging from the Prince of Wales, who sits as Duke of Cornwall, to the Junior Baron Charles Bowyer, Lord Norton. The roll includes 4 Royal Dukes, 2 Archbishops, 22 Dukes, 19 Marquises, 134 Earls, 32 Viscounts, 24 Bishops and 262 Barons, some of the Peers, however, being numbered twice by reason of their different offices.

AN English spelling Reform Association has been established, attached to no special scheme of reform, but bent on advocating the broad principle of improvement in spelling. The Association has grown out of a movement inaugurated some time since amongst various School Boards, who memorialized the Duke of Richmond for a Royal Commission to report on changes in spelling in the interests of educational progress.

IN *Macmillan* for September is published an article on "An Editor's Troubles" by Mr. W. Minto. In it we read of the difficulties which the late Mr. Macvey Napier, Editor of the *Edinburgh* from 1829 to 1847, had with his contributors, particularly Brougham and Macaulay, each of whom seems to have entertained the most contemptuous estimate of the other, which,—in strict confidence, of course,—was duly communicated to their common editor.

THE Poet Laureate's elder brother inherited Grasby Hall and some neighbouring farms many years back, and for the sake of the £1,000 or £2,000 a year, which they yielded he entirely dropped the Tennyson and became the Rev. Charles Turner, a name which stands on the title-page of his book of sonnets. He died a few months ago, living no issue, and his wife followed him to the grave within a few weeks. The next heir is the Laureate, but according to *Truth*, he will not accept the condition which rigorously enforces the entire suppression of the Tennyson.

WE noticed in these columns, sometime ago, the discovery of a new method of taking instantaneous photographs by the use of gelatine dry plates. We now learn from the *Graphic* that some new and admirable photos of Her Majesty and the Princess Beatrice have been taken at Windsor Castle by Mr. Arthur Melhuish, F. R. A. S., by means of that method. The chief advantage of this new system is that the time of exposure for a portrait becomes, at least, six times as speedy as by other methods. Thus it may be said that instantaneous photography can now be achieved, consequently it is no longer difficult to photograph a smile in sharp clear definition.

SOME years ago, the Duke de Luynes brought the sarcophagus of the King of Sidon from the East, and presented it to the French Government. M. Roller has recently deciphered the inscription on the sarcophagus now deposited at the Louvre. Part of it runs thus:—"A curse is pronounced against royal persons or others who should open this tomb, or lift the tomb which contains me, or transport me in this tomb. They shall not be buried with the dead, they shall not lie in a tomb, they shall not leave any descendants, and the holy gods will deliver them into the hands of their enemies, who will chase them from their country." The *Jewish World* notes, as a curious coincidence in regard to this curse, that the Duke de Luynes, who bought the sarcophagus, and presented it to the French Government, and his son met their deaths in the Papal War, in Italy, in 1859. Again, it was through the instrumentality of the Emperor Napoleon III, that it was brought to Paris, and deposited in the Louvre. He was routed at Sedan, and his body reposes on foreign soil. His son met with an untimely death, far away from his home, and at the hand of his enemies. There is not a descendant left of Napoleon III, or the Duke de Luynes.

Latest News.

—THE *Englishman* has received the following telegram, dated Zargun Shahr, 3rd October:—"The force left Kushi yesterday, and has reached here safely. Fighting is probable soon. Yakub is still in camp, but anxious to return to Cabul. Wali Mohammed has met the General here. The principal people have left Cabul. The force is in splendid condition for fighting.

"At the Shutar Gurdan yesterday the enemy lost thirty killed and many wounded; we only two wounded. We advance again to-day. There are very great difficulties about transport, which, however, will not delay the advance. It is expected to be in Cabul on Sunday."

[FROM THE PRESS COMMISSIONER.]

—A VERY interesting report has been received from Mr. Baber, H. M's Consul, Chung Ching, on the proposed opening of that place to foreign trade. Mr. Baber states that the high range which at Wu-Shan Hsien bisects the breadth of China with mathematical precision, and forms the well-known gorges of the Yangtse, is the natural boundary line between the Eastern and Western Divisions of the Empire. The hundred and tenth meridian which passes through it, defines with accuracy throughout its length from Mongolia to Hainan even the administrative limits of the eastern and western provinces, and separates the great plain from the mountainous interior. Ssuchuan is the only region west of that demarcation, which is really populous and productive, and the city of Chung Ching is the focus and sole outlet of its trade.

Salt and silk are chiefly reckoned as composing three-tenths of the resources of Ssuchuan—opium is not generally included in the enumeration, being regarded as an extra, and the remaining products are drugs, white wax, sung oil, sugar, tobacco, safflower, rhubarb, grass-cloth, hemp, tea, and a great number of miscellanea, conspicuous among which is timber. Of all these, silk alone is likely to interest foreign trade directly, though a demand for tobacco may arise to a greater extent, and for some of the numerous articles classed under the head of drugs. The mineral wealth of the province which principally lies in the District of Chienchang (Ning-Yuan-Fu) and its confines, is regarded by the Ssuchuanese rather as Yunan produce, its locality, however, is too remote from water communication, and too difficult of access for it to be much affected by any opening of ports on the Yangtse to foreign commercial intercourse. There is an abundance of iron and coal, and widely distributed; but they do not form matter of export. Thirty-six million Tels may be accepted as a rude approximation to the export trade of the province, some two-thirds of which passes Chung Ching.

As regards cotton, Mr. Baber states that "the one weak point in the complacency of the Ssuchuanese is the want of cotton, though even that is grown to no small extent in the country round Sui-ting-fu. I have no means of ascertaining the annual return. It is reputed to be warmer than the cotton of Eastern China, but is not of good color, and is, therefore, used for wadding winter clothing, and for weaving into fabrics for rough wear. Its fibre is more silky, and a coverlet made of it weighs less for equal warmth than the eastern variety, two statements which amount to much the same thing. It sells for a higher price than imported cotton. Twenty years ago the production was greater than at present, although, during the last three years, it has somewhat increased; it is admitted, however, that the cultivation succeeds but poorly; the plants seem to run to wood instead of flower and to grow too tall; whether from being planted too closely together, or from want of skilled tending, or from poorness of soil, is a moot point among cultivators.

"Cotton, therefore, in one form or another, is the principal want and the principal import, and Chung Ching is its emporium for nearly the whole province. My inquiries give the total import at something more than 200,000 bales of from 150 to 160 catties each, a quantity which appears to have varied little during the last ten years. I cannot learn that any considerable supply goes directly to Sü-chou-fu, or that the Shensi trade is of much importance, but my information, on the latter point, is not quite satisfactory. When it is remembered how much cotton is used by the Chinese for wadding clothes, quilts and mattresses, it is clear that an import even double, or a great deal more than double this amount, would be insufficient. The deficit is made up by cotton cloth imported from the Eastern provinces, by Tibetan wollens, and by the products of European and American looms.

"The imported raw material is woven into cloth not in any special manufacturing town or district, but in the farms and country houses where the industry forms the principal occupation of the women. When it is remarked that the rude loom costs about 3,000 cash, or say twelve shillings; that the spinning wheels and other appertenances cost next to nothing or are home-made; that, at least, half the labor devoted to weaving costs nothing at all, since the women of the family, who undertake it, would be unoccupied without it; and again that the cloth thus produced is far more durable, much warmer and practically much cheaper than any foreign imported cotton fabric superior, in short, in every respect but appearance. It may be judged how little chance foreign goods have of contending advantageously with it. The Shangai Deligates speak very expositely on the hopelessness of the conflict.' As the people count nothing for their time or labor, anything which the cotton cloth realises over the cost of the raw material is reckoned profit. This is doubtless a considerable obstacle to the more extensive introduction of foreign cotton goods, for the foreign manufacturer competes at a disadvantage with the amateur weivers of Sszchuans, who are able to put their goods on the market on terms somewhat analogous to those on which the elegant productions of gratuitous labor are sold at ladies' bazars. These remarks are sufficient to dispose of the strange fallacy so often met with in one form or another, that so many million Chinamen require so many million coats and trowsers, and that, *therefore*, they must buy foreign manufactures. It cannot be too often repeated that the webs of Manchester are unsuited to the rough field-work of the Chinese, and that foreign imports are a luxury and not a necessity. This condition is most especially true of western China.

"There is no question here of the oversizing or filling of certain cotton goods, of which so much has lately been said. The Sszchuanese, himself a manufacturer, is an excellent judge of the quality of cotton fabrics, and if the wares are of an inferior character, they simply fetch an inferior price; there is no intention of fraud on the one side, nor apprehension of it on the other. I am told by natives engaged in the trade that the quality of imported cottons has somewhat deteriorated of late years, but that on the other hand they are cheaper, and that if purchasers require a superior kind, they can have it by paying for it all which is the crudest common sense and the simple answer to the charge of falsification. Native usages and habits create a demand for a poor class of goods. For instance, the Chinese spend profuse sums on funerals, and a great many mourners attend them, not necessarily to follow the coffin, but to enjoy the two or three days feasting which the proceedings include. It is etiquette for the bereaved family to present the guests with mourning apparel, which in China is white, and, of course, the cheapest shirtings are bought for the purpose. Again foreign cottons being eminently fashionable, the large class of needy but pretentious persons, who aspire to be well dressed on small means buy the very cheapest article they can find; so long as it is foreign cloth they are satisfied. A ludicrous proof of the estimation in which such goods are held, was furnished me in a village near the Sifan border, where a street fight had occurred between the villagers and a party of Sifans who were passing. On enquiring the cause of the quarrel I was told that one of the Sifans carried an umbrella covered with foreign cotton, and that such pretention was insufferable."

With regard to woollen goods Mr. Baber states:—"To turn to woollen imports: the Shanghai Delegates write: 'The demand for woollen goods is a criterion of prosperity in China; in Sszchuan we find that woollens, as compared with cottons, are more extensively used than in any other part of the country, and the Prussian traveller is of much the same opinion. In no province is the taste for these so conspicuous as in Sszchuan. Broadcloth is highly appreciated and much in demand, not for protection against the cold, but on account of *its outward appearance* and *because it is not within reach of every body*." I underline the latter words, because they indicate the same demand for cheap and showy articles as in the case of cotton piece goods; thus an excellent Russian broadcloth, too good for the market, which comes in through Shensi, finds very little sale except in Chingtu and even there its consumers are for the most part strangers from the north eastern provinces; in purely Sszchuanese markets, it retreats before inferior but less costly imports.

"As in the case of piece-goods again, we find that where woollens become indispensable, namely, in the cold elevated western region, English goods are not a necessary; the necessary want is already supplied. It is a little surprising to discover that the Lhassa territory is a manufacturing country, and a rival of England in a Chinese market; but it is not the less true that the woollen clothing worn in that part of Sszchuan and Yunnan which lies, speaking broadly, west of the meridian of Chiating-fu, and north of Tali-fu, is manufactured in Lhassa and its dependencies. These imports consist of various descriptions of stout serge, known among Sibetans and Chinese as Pu-lu, and of a coarse blanket stuff, named Mu-tze by the Chinese and Lawa by the Tibetans. The chief markets for such goods are Sachienlu and the great fair Yueh Fai of Tali-fu. The best quality of Pu-lu (or Pelo) is called Sich-pi-iron-skin by the Chinese, and is in demand at points so distant from Lhassa as Yunnan-fu and Chung Ching; but these are about the limits of its export.

"That goods of so remote an origin find eager demand among so poor a population as the mountaineers of western Sszchuan holds out good promise of success to the native woollen manufacture which is now being set on foot at Lan-chow-fu in Kansu. If the promoters turn their attention more especially to the production of cheap and substantial frieze and the like, they will probably make short work of Tibetan competition in Chinese and Mongolian markets, but it is far less likely that in so inaccessible and isolated a situation they will be able to manufacture goods capable of contending with English woollens. The scheme appears to be directed more particularly against Russian trade on the north-western frontier."

Owing to the region of Sszchuan being difficult for the purposes of transport, because of its being surrounded with mountains, and interspersed with mountain streams, Mr. Baber has come to the conclusion that under these circumstances, the prospect of establishing a foreign trade with Chung Ching would be attended with little or no advantage to British trades; but that if it be supplemented by a provision declaring all the upper waters, not the Yangtse only below Chung Ching free to steam navigation, such a course is advisable as a means of inviting and facilitating the access of steam transport.

Calcutta.

WE are requested to announce that the next general meeting of the Band of Hope will be held at the Albert Hall, on Wednesday next, at 5P. M., when Revd. K. S. Macdonald, M. A., will deliver a lecture on "Law, Love and Liberty in reference to liquor." Babu Keshub Chunder Sen, the President of the Band, will take the chair.

FROM the monthly Report of the Charity Section of the Indian Association in September, we learn that the sum of Rs. 74-1-3 was spent in the maintenance of two respectable women, and in liquidating their debts; Rs. 13-8 was spent for the support of eight poor families; Rs. 6 for that of seven widows; Rs. 3-4 was given to the blind, lame and incurables, four in all; Rs. 14-13 was spent in supporting fourteen students; Rs. 2 was the total amount of daily charities; Rs. 19 was spent in doctor's fees and medicines; Rs. 3 was the sum spent in defraying the travelling expenses of some destitude persons in their journey home; Re. 1-3 was for small repairs of buildings; Re. 1-13-3 for small charities; and Rs. 2-6-1 for contingent expenses.

Selections.

PRIESTS AND DOCTORS

(*Christian World.*)

ALL the great mysteries are suggested by the two words at the head of this article; and none perhaps could be found illustrating more pointedly what it is that renders the greatest mysteries perplexing and almost irritating—namely, their perfect familiarity combined with their abysmal difficulty. What the soul is, what the body is; what mind is, what matter is; what life is, what death is; whether the free-thinker is right who believes neither in angel nor in spirit, or the orthodox who believes in both; whether man is a law as to himself or whether he is responsible to a Divine Law-giver; whether all suffering, all joy and all duty end in the grave or whether time is a seed-bed in which nurselings are reared for eternity;—such are a few of the questions suggested by the words "soul and body."

The interest of such questions is plainly inexhaustible, and it is a very notable sign of our times—whatever may be its ultimate meaning—that the conductors of the most popular reviews, magazines, and newspapers evidently consider articles in which they are discussed with any considerable measure of ability, only less popular than the most captivating fiction. The discussions generally go deep, and not a few persons are afraid that, one by one, all our cherished beliefs will be cut down by the remorseless axe of science. Even our respected and influential contemporary, the *Lancet*, has been startled by the spread of atheistic materialism among medical men, and has published an earnest protest against "that spirit of restless antagonism to the claims of religion which has unhappily obtained fuller expression in a small section" of the profession "during the last few years." Be the cause what it may, the proportion of unbelievers among doctors has lately increased—increased, we fear, in a higher ratio than can be alleged of any other profession. We agree with the *Lancet* that if the public became convinced that atheism was widely prevalent among medical men the most disastrous consequences to the profession would ensue. Distrusting extremes in all things, the average Englishman distrusts the extreme of irreligion as well as the extreme of one-sided, narrow, or superstitious religion. It is a persuasion, rooted with the grip of an instinct, in the general English mind, that priestism on the one hand, and atheism on the other, debase and enfeeble the moral fibre. The priest, who has no proper respect for himself and his fellow-men, no rational, manly hold on the things of this world, and the atheist, who has no fear of God, no sense of responsibility except to himself and the Statute-book, are alike suspected of moral slipperiness, and thought to be likely to give way under circumstances of great temptation. John Bull has invincible and almost ferocious repugnance to a confessional priest at his wife's ear or an atheist doctor in her bedchamber. Acknowledging with all clearness and emphasis that morally stable and high-minded priests and atheists are to be found, we yet own our belief that in application to priests and atheists in the mass, the English instinct in question is sound. Even when the idea of positive immorality is excluded, it may be insisted on that the habit of ignoring the spiritual in man, and admitting no existence in the universe but matter, produces a coarseness of mind, a callousness of sensibility, which render a man an undesirable associate, particularly for wives, for sisters and for daughters. We have been credibly informed of a French dissecting doctor who fed his dog on human bodies. The hideous and infamous atrocities—of which it is impossible for any person of right human sensibility to hear or read without positive anguish—practised by vivisecting professors in France and Italy are, we cannot doubt, viewed with reprehension by the great body of medical men in England; but their repudiation and condemnation of those fiendish tormentors have certainly been less conspicuous than could be wished. We do not for a moment grant that there is cause to doubt that the medical profession, as distinguished from the legal and military, is the refuge, on the whole, of kind hearts and gentle natures. This is our own firm belief; but, among the public, this opinion has of late been somewhat shaken, and perhaps the most powerful of the reasons why medical men are regarded with less confident feeling than formerly is the extent to which atheistic materialism has made inroads into their ranks.

MEETING OF THE BRITISH ASSOCIATION. —PROFESSOR ST. GEORGE MIVART ON HUMAN AND ANIMAL INTELLIGENCE.

THE obvious difference between the highest powers of man and animals has led the common sense of mankind to consider them to be of radically distinct kinds, and the question which naturalists now profess to investigate is whether this is so or no. It may be affirmed that no animal but man has yet been shown to exhibit true concerted action, or to express by external signs distinct intellectual conceptions, processes of which all men are normally capable. But just as some plants simulate the sense, perception, voluntary motions and instincts of animals without there being a real identity between the activities thus superficially similar, so there may well be in animals actions simulating the intellectual apprehensions, ratiocinations and volitions of man without there being any necessary identity between the activities so superficially alike. More than this, it is certain a priori that there must be no such resemblance since one organization is similar to that of animals and since sensations are, at least, indispensable antecedents to the exercise of our intellectual activity. He has no wish to ignore the marvellous powers of animals or the resemblances of their actions to those of man. No one could reasonably deny that many of them have feelings, emotions and sense of perceptions similar to our own; that they exercise voluntary motion and perform actions grouped in complex ways for definite ends; that they, to a certain extent, learn by experience, and can combine perceptions and reminiscences so as to draw practical inferences, directly apprehending objects standing in different relations one to another, so that, in a sense, they may be said to apprehend relations. They will show hesitation, ending apparently, after a conflict of desires, with what looks like choice or volition, and such animals as the dog will not only exhibit the most marvellous fidelity and affection, but will also manifest evident signs of shame, which may seem the outcome and indication of incipient moral perceptions. It is no great wonder, then, that so many persons, little given to patient and careful introspection, should fail to perceive any radical distinctions between a nature thus gifted and the intellectual nature of man. But unless he was greatly mistaken, the question could never be answered by our observations of animals, unless we bore in mind the distinctions between our own higher and lower faculties. Animals, it was noticed, noted in ways in which they would not act had they reason; while all they did was explicable by the association of sensations, imaginations, and emotions such as occurred in our own lower faculties. Apes (like dogs and cats) warm themselves with pleasure at deserted fires; yet, though they see wood burning and other wood lying by, though they have arms and hands as we have, and the same sentient faculties, they have never been recorded to have added fuel to maintain their comfort. Swallows will continue to build on

a house which they see has begun to be pulled down, and no animal can be shown to have made use of attendant experience to intentionally improve upon the past. If, on the other hand, animals were capable of deliberately acting to concert, the effects would soon make themselves known to an so forcibly as to prevent the possibility of mistake.

At the close of the discourse, Professor Allman moved a vote of thanks to the President of the section for his address. He said that Professor Mivart had very judiciously and with great care brought forward certain phenomena connected with the psychology of the lower animals, and he had quite correctly maintained that there was not a mere difference in degree, but that there was no actual difference in kind between the psychological power of the lower orders of animals and men. Setting aside the faculty of speech, which placed a wide gulf between the animal and man, a most remarkable difference was the absolute want in the lower animals of design, of drawing or of modelling. No lower animal exhibited the slightest tendency to represent another object by imitative design. Many had great powers of imitating gesture and sound, but they could not imitate form; but when they looked to the early days of man, they found evidence that there was the natural love for drawing. We have on the bones of the mammoth representations of the mammoth himself, and there were traces of this power at the very dawn of humanity. Sir J. Lubbock, in seconding the motion, said he could not concur in all the views expressed by his two friends, who had preceded him. He could not help thinking that the difference between the intelligence of man and the lower animals was one not altogether of kind, but one of degree, although he admitted that there was an enormous gap between them. It was said there was no indication in the lower animals of any idea of right and wrong. He would not inquire whether there might not be some races of men who were in the same condition. (Laughter.) Great stress had been laid on the power of speech; but there was one good reason, why his favorite insects could not speak, and that was because they did not breathe through their mouths; they breathed through holes down their sides. (Laughter.) He would tell them what some of his ants did the other day. He killed a blue-bottle fly and pinned it down. An ant pulled at it for about 20 minutes, and then went to the nest some yards off, and brought out a party of ten other ants, who joined in the attempt to carry off the fly. He thought it only fair to withdraw the pin, and the ants then carried the fly off in triumph to their nest. That might not be a proof, but it was impossible for any one to communicate more obviously with his friends than did these ants. (Hear.) He could not but think that the difference which existed between them and men was one rather of extreme degree than of radical distinction itself. It must be remembered that many of these animals seemed only for a short time, and the section, he believed, would scarcely care to have the intelligence of man measured by that of a child a year old.

The motion having been put and carried.

The President acknowledged the compliment, and said he had no difficulty in admitting the fact stated by Sir J. Lubbock, but they did not touch his point.

Advertisements.

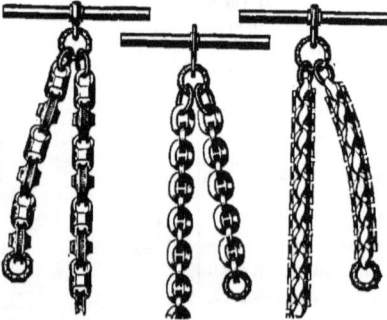

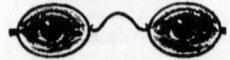

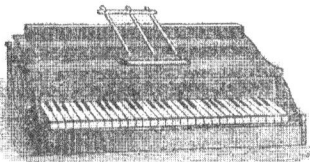

The Indian Mirror

EDITED BY KRISHNA BIHARI SEN, M. A.]

SUNDAY EDITION

[REGISTERED AT THE
GENERAL POST OFFICE.]

VOL. XIX.   CALCUTTA, OCTOBER 12, 1879.   NO. 243.

Telegraphic Intelligence.

FROM THE PRESS COMMISSIONER.

A DETERMINATION TO SIMLA, 11TH OCTOBER FIGHT.

From Shutur Gurdan it is stated that the bearer of the last message from General Roberts said that Mahomed Kurim Khan and Gholam Hyder Khan, with the three Herati regiments, had shut themselves up in Bala Hissar and intended to die fighting. Bala Hissar is said to have two large breeches in the walls.

NEWS FROM GENERAL ROBERTS' CAMP.

SIMLA, 11TH OCTOBER.

General Roberts telegraphs from outside Cabul on the 8th October. Hearing that troops from Kohistan were entrenching themselves on the high hill beyond Bala Hissar and immediately overlooking Cabul city, General Roberts sent General Massey with eight squadrons of Cavalry round by the north of the City to watch the roads. Leaving Bamian and Kohistan and having cut off their retreat simultaneously, General Baker was sent to attack the enemy from the high hills above Bala Hissar. By sunset General Massey had reached Alliabad on Bamian road. He found the Sherpur Cantonment deserted and in it seventy-eight guns. At sunset, General Baker was about to attack the enemy's position. General Macpherson rejoined General Roberts on the evening of the 8th with stores and reserve ammunition. Information having been received that the regiments from Ghuzni were trying to join the force opposed to General Baker, General Macpherson was sent with a force to strengthen General Baker. It has been ascertained that large numbers of Ghilzais were assembled to join the force opposed to us on the 6th, but arrived too late. Some have returned to their homes.

THE REMOVAL OF THE BRITISH RESIDENCY FROM MANDALAY.

From Thayetmyo Mr. St. Barbe reports that he reached the frontier on the 10th. His departure from Mandalay took place as arranged without opposition. A number of people have left Mandalay, and all the flotilla steamers have come away accompanying Mr. St. Barbe.

HER MAJESTY'S MESSAGE TO THE ARMY.

By order of the Queen Empress, the Viceroy has requested the Commander-in-Chief to convey to General Roberts and the troops engaged under his command the expression of Her Majesty's warm satisfaction with their noble conduct in the very successful and important action at Charasiah which the Viceroy lost no time in reporting to Her Majesty. The Queen-Empress desires to express to her gallant troops her sorrow for those of their comrades, who fell in this action and in the recent brilliant exploit at Shutur Gurdan, and the Viceroy is commanded to make known to the Commander-in-Chief Her Majesty's anxiety for further information as to the condition of the wounded.

Editorial Notes.

THE *Independent* says :—" The *Christian Intelligencer* calls Keshub Chunder Sen a positivist, which he is not at all ; and then a man who is trying to be an infidel.' Our readers know better."

——:o:——

A UNITARIAN Minister lately delivered a lecture in connection with the British Association meeting, on the subject " Science, of course. What then ?" Among those present were, we notice, Sir George and Lady Campbell. Is Sir George among the prophets too ?

——:o:——

ON Tuesday next at 4·30 P. M. Babu Keshub Chunder Sen will address on open air gathering in College Square. He will take up the following subject :—"Is it true that God exists ?" As all the Native schools and colleges close on the above day, it is to be hoped that there will be a large concourse on the occasion.

——:o:——

THE following curious story comes from Paris:—"In the belief that an era of religious persecution is at hand, a number of Catholics and Royalists have united in a scheme for seeking liberty to uphold the Catholic faith by fleeing to the island of Papua, where they contemplate establishing a Monarchy, under M. de Breuil, the Marquis de Rays."

——:o:——

DEAN STANLEY, says the *Cincinnati Commercial*, was not equal to his opportunities when he performed the marriage ceremony for Prof. Tyndall. The Dean should have asked the groom : " Do you take this autonopoid to be your co-ordinate, to love with your nerve centers, to cherish with your whole cellular tissue, until a final molecular disturbance shall resolve its organism into its primitive atoms ?"

——:o:——

THE Archbishop of Canterbury, presiding at the Annual Meeting of the Church Missionary Society at Dover, said that it was a remarkable fact that, amongst the missionaries of the Roman Catholic body throughout the world, the greatest supply came from France, the least religious country in Europe. The sight of infidelity and wickedness at home no doubt stirred the hearts of thoughtful men more truly to appreciate the blessings of the gospel of Christ.

——:o:——

THE effect of perfume on the human character has been tried by an Italian professor, who has educated 78 girls under the influence of various scents, at least so says the *New York Times*. The rose produced an amiable and prudish damsel ; those brought up in an odour of violets were gentle and religious ; geranium produced decision of character ; musk, amiability, langour, and a taste for dress ; and patchouli had the worst effect on the moral character.

——:o:——

A HINDU temple at Gonda was sometime ago struck by lightning, and the officiating priest was killed thereby. The other day, a Christian church in Switzerland crowded with worshippers was struck by lightning, a little girl was killed on the spot and many others dangerously injured. A contemporary associates both these occurrences with the wrath of God. The Hindu and the Roman Catholic are both punished for idolatry. Will our contemporary kindly state if no Protestant church was ever been struck by lighting ?

——:o:——

CAN you tell me, O brother, what you think to be the most beautiful picture under the sun ? Surely enough, we think it is the face of a true devotee in prayers. Often have we, in the midst of our congregational worship, opened our eyes to watch a devotee's countenance. We are sure we speak the truth when we say that the beauty of that countenance surpasses that of the moon in her varied phases. How heavenly! There he laughs, anon he weeps; he is in flames now; melted in tears again. How often have our hearts been moved by the heavenly sight.

——:o:——

BROTHER Theist, give up sentimental non-sense. Cultivate reality. Your mock profession of piety do not deceive us. It is life we want ; it is character, faith and sterling honesty that we expect. You may close your eyes for hours, and yet you may be a humbug. But let there be honesty in your frame, and your very eyes will look love. There are two things which you should cultivate above all—sincere prayer and a desire to be good. Piety and morality—yes, these are twin brothers in the family of God

——:o:——

A WAR with Cabul and an impending war with Burmah pretty well denote the enviable position we are in. The latter calamity, we must say, is not brought about by our own

Government. It is the result of the heartless policy of the young barbarian who now wields the sceptre over Burmah. Whatever the cause, devout men in India and England ought to pray that the calamity might be withhold from us. We hear of prayers for fine weather; why should not the church raise its voice against the impiety and wickedness of war?

—:o:—

The *Jewish World* quotes from a German Jewish periodical a series of arguments in favor of the theory that the Zulus are the descendants of Israel. Their high consideration for their chiefs, their pastoral life, the purchase of wives, their peculiar ornaments, their observance of a sort of Feast of First Fruits, many of their traditions which appear to be perversions of Old Testament stories, all seem to point to Hebrew descent. The chief of one of their most influential tribes is called Moschesch, and Abram is a common name. All the animals declared impure by the Mosaic Law are impure for Kaffirs, who detest pork. The same laws respecting individual purity prevail as those prescribed in Leviticus, and circumcision is generally practised, if not obligatory.

—:o:—

A meeting of the Band of Hope was held on Wednesday last when Mr. Macdonald delivered a lecture on "Law, Love and Liberty in Liquor." There was a good audience, and the young men seemed to be benefited by the address. The President, Babu Keshub Chunder Sen, closed the meeting by a suggestion which, we hope, will be carried out. He said that there was in England a Humane Society which awarded medals to persons who had saved people from drowning, and recommended that there should be a Humane Society in India for rewarding persons, who would rescue others from a watery grave in the bottle. Young men might go on making their friends sign the pledges and they might succeed in reclaiming drunkards. A man who will get, say, 500 pledges signed, or one who will save at least one confirmed drunkard, should be rewarded with a medal from the Band of Hope. In this way virtue should be rewarded, and honest efforts in a good cause gratefully recognised.

—:o:—

A correspondent of the *Pioneer* ventures to sit in judgment upon Mr. Austin's letter to the *Times* upon Simla morality. We conceive that there are two ways of manifesting one's dissatisfaction with the letter in question. One is the indignant mode, and the other the cynical. We are familiar with the former in the writings of the *Bombay Gazette*, whose utterances we respect; but the half-cynical, half concessive language of the letter can find its fitting place only in one journal, and that is the *Pioneer*. The correspondent says coolly enough :—"Perhaps, our morals, so far as they differ from other people's morals, are the morals of the future." That is good. But here is some thing better :— "Anglo-Indian society's conditions, says Mr. Austin in conclusion, must always be lax as compared with the British standard. So much the better for Anglo-Indian society. The British standard is a very stupid one." This is cynicism with a vengeance.

—:o:—

Mr. Tracy Turnerelli prepared a golden wreath for the Prime Minister and collected 52,000 pennies as the people's tribute. The wreath, as is well known, was refused, and it remains a psychological puzzle how or in what cunning ways an admiration so strong

could give way to detestation so hearty. But Mr. Turnerelli remains a hero-worshipper all the same, with this difference that before the presentation of the wreath he worshipped Lord Beaconsfield as god; now the same worship is offered to him as the devil. He explained in a lecture why he revered the Premier; it was because of his satanic qualities. For a struggle with a Power like Russia, Mr. Gladstone was too kind and too good. "It wanted a man with the heart of the Devil himself, and Lord Beaconsfield does not stand at trifles." What prevents Mr. Turnerelli from placing the wreath upon his own head?

—:o:—

A year or so ago, says the *Bombay Guardian*, "a young gentleman of Ahmedabad, of the Jain religion, perusing his studies of the ancient Jain Shastras, was surprised to find that they contained nothing to justify the idolatry that now so markedly characterizes the Jain worship of Western India. The young man made haste to communicate his discovery to others, and the consequence was that a considerable number of persons in Ahmedabad agreed together to worship God without the use of idols, or visible representations. We understand that a decree of ex-communication has lately been fulminated against these reformers, and that the greater part of them have ceased to take part in the theistic services." For the Jains to worship God would, we think, be to renounce Jainism. Beginning with something like the atheism of the Buddhists, this system has fallen into idolatry, and if it ever retraces its steps, it can be carried only to the primitive unbelief. It would be a pity if the new movement in favor of theism were allowed to collapse through persecution.

—:o:—

The *Lucknow Witness* may be right in his estimate of Christian as opposed to Hindu morality, and may, on the strength of this opinion, base his advocacy of the larger employment of Christians in the administration of this empire. But let our contemporary observe that it is a question of justice as between two races that is involved, and it would not do to dismiss the question by a sweeping assertion of the superiority of one race over the other. Trait for trait the educated Hindu should be proved to be actually inferior to the European. Now, when the *Times'* correspondent insinuates that the path to promotion is rendered marvellously smooth in the case of certain officials who happen to possess pretty wives, are we to suppose that the supposed inferiority of the Hindu has any reference to this particular defect? The charge which the *Times'* correspondent prefers points to a condition of things so shamelessly bad that, unless contradicted, its effect upon the Native mind would be one not likely to be easily removed. We think it would be better, on the whole, if our contemporary could manage to argue the question in detail, in order that it might be discussed to the satisfaction of every one.

—:o:—

The spiritual enthusiasm among the more advanced Brahmos, which we lately noticed in these columns is, we are glad to observe, rapidly growing into an organized form. It is proposed to organize a missionary expedition during the approaching holidays, to be composed of the Singing Missionary as the head and a considerable number of devout Brahmos including the minister and several missionaries, one of whom will act as general Secretary and receiver of alms. The expedition will probably start as soon as the holidays

commence; but will continue to advance even after the offices have re-opened. The object of this arrangement is to enable our lay brethren to avail themselves of the annual recess to join the party and leave it at convenience. The party propose to take the East Indian Railway route, calling probably at Hughly, Burdwan, Rampore Hat, Bankipore and other places to be determined upon hereafter. There will be a complete singing staff, and also lecturers and preachers, who will give addresses in English, Hindi and Bengali, as the occasion may require. Those who wish to join the mission are requested to send their names to the Mission Office. Friends in provincial stations, who may welcome the mission, are also requested to put themselves in communication with the above office without delay. We wish the expedition God-speed.

—:o:—

Some 57 out of 80 representatives at the Congress of German societies for Prevention of Cruelty to Animals have voted for a proposal to seek the legislative restriction of the practice of vivisection throughout Germany. This is carried to a cruel excess in both Germany and France. The progress of materialism, we have no doubt, is the cause of all the torments inflicted upon poor animals in the cause of science. Good-natured people have made the doctrine of evolution the ground upon which they base their appeals on behalf of animals. It may appear strange to them that, on the contrary, it has the effect of lessening our regard for suffering, both human and animal. One acute vivisectionist is said to take delight in feeding his dogs with the flesh of human carcases brought for dissection. Well, when scientists have proceeded so far, we do not know what is to prevent them from extending their experiments from the lower animal to man. For aught we know it may be the turn for savages and the aboriginal tribes next. And why put forth the pretext of benevolence and the desire to benefit humanity? Sir Philip Francis, the worthy co-adjutor of Warren Hastings, found money-making a profession as good and honorable as vivisection. When asked how he could fleece the Native so well, he replied—"Yes, if money were his blood, I would feel no compunction in opening his veins."

—:o:—

If a little amount of silly talk and harmless nonsense could bring upon our countrymen the Vernacular Press Act, we do not know if a Gatling gun would suffice to repress the open-mouthed sedition of the Irish Press. The Cabul tragedy seems to have thrilled the hearts of Irish patriots with a sort of unaccountable joy, and this they have taken to expressing in a variety of ways. The *Irishman*, in a leading article, headed "Crimson Cabul," says : "As the English did in Zululand, so were they done by in Cabul. They were forced by the burning mass of the conflagration to rush from the flames upon the bayonets of the people whom they had foully robbed of their freedom." The Irish Patriot asks "if there is an honest man that does not feel with satisfaction that British greed for territory has received a great, if somewhat tardy cheek?"—The *Flag of Ireland* says "The massacre of Cabul will be regretted in England, but the rest of the world will hold the Cabulese blameless if not wholly justified. The invasion was wanton, wicked, atrocious, and unprovoked save by the demon of greed. The Amir is a cunning Asiatic, and he may have played well his part. Were he a Pole, and had done such deeds to the damage of Russia, the English would proclaim him a patriot. Therefore, what is righteous at Warsaw is not unrighteous at Cabul."—The *Weekly News* says, " John Bull will rue the day he ever set foot in Afghanistan, for he must either run out of it in confusion and incur the contempt of Asia, or, taking possession of it, bring himself under the terrible swing of the Russians."

THE NEW WINE.

LIKE new wine, genuine religion creates a ferment in the mind. The test of spirituality is uncommon conduct. When God touches the heart, He touches it with new and unexpected aspirations. A religion that is fond of repetition is of the earth earthly. Apostles of the true stamp are original men, rather wild, somewhat foolish, according to the current and atheistic definition of folly. Wordly proprieties are the exact contraries of the regenerate freedom of the spirit. A spiritual man is born a gentleman, the incarnation of social grace and personal loveliness; but he scorns to be bound by the petty conventionalities which make the code of worldly amiability. The spirit of piety is an ardent fire that kindles up the whole nature. Where there is no kindling, there is no faith. Personal ambition may kindle, the selfish desire of glory may kindle, the love of money may kindle, but nothing kindles human nature so much as the ardent love of God and truth. When does a man show to his best? When does a man yield more than he is thought capable of? When does he speak best, act best? When his heart kindles. When his heart is cold and inert, sick and slothful, then the ablest man becomes like a clod of earth. Blessed is the man whose heart is kindled by the love of God, who, in the name of his Father, feels a new stir in him, and is led forth to enterprise and achievements unattempted before. Blessed is the man who is calm amidst obloquy and danger in the service of his Master. He depends upon the reality of Divine help for the successful accomplishment of his mission. And he receives the help that never fails him at the hour of need. Brahmos, and especially Brahmo Missionaries, be full of the new wine of genuine spirituality. Let fiery enthusiasm guide your steps in all that you do for the spread and for the establishment of your religion. Let your faith be unto the world a new dispensation for saving sinners, and reconciling God's children to their Father. First know what gospel to carry to the waiting world, then utter that gospel with the strength and assurance of men who deeply believe what they say. Is God more real to you than any thing else in the world? Do you believe God has called you, and commands you to go forth on His work? Find out what that work is, and do it like men who are under a new influence. Faith is a marvellous power. He that has a mustard seed of it will yet revolutionize the world.

POETIC GENIUS.

A NATION's poetry shapes its character. We, Hindus, know it to our cost. It will require some centuries more to purify our literature and our national imagination from the taint of Sanskrit drama. And what is true of Indian poetry is true of English poetry. We believe there is a movement afoot, headed by the present Premier, to raise a monument to Lord Byron. Perhaps, there is no doubt that Byron was a great poet. But the harm which he has done to English poetry, to English

imagination and to English character is incalculable and irremediable. In the month of July, two somewhat striking articles appeared in two English magazines. In *Fraser*, there is an article on Shelly as a Lyric Poet by the Professor of Poetry in the University of Oxford, and in *Macmillan*, there is an article on Wordsworth by Mr. Matthew Arnold. Shelly and Wordsworth were both poetic geniuses, but they were as far apart as the antipodes. Shelly, like Byron, was the child of impulse. And his impulses were all derived from what in plain vernacular would be called unmixed carnality. It is said he had "no conscience;" no moral instinct was ever revealed to him. He did the grossest wrong, was guilty of the most bare-faced immorality; but there is not a throb of manly repentance in the whole course of his subsequent effusions, though they are full of a selfish melancholy and bitterness. "In some of his impulses," says the Professor of Poetry in the University of Oxford, " he was more, in other things essential to goodness he was far less, than other men; a fully developed man he certainly was not. I am inclined to believe that, for his noble impulses and aims, he was in some way deficient in rational and moral sanity. Many of you will remember Hazlitt's somewhat cynical description of him. 'He had a fire in his eye, a fever in his blood, a maggot in his brain, a hectic flutter in his speech, which mark out a philosophical fanatic. He is sanguine-complexioned and shrill-voiced.' Again, ' there runs through his poems a painful taint of supersublimed impurity, of aweless shamelessness which we never can believe came from a mind truly pure. A penetrating taint it is which has evilly affected many of the higher minds who admire him, in a way which Byron's more commonplace licentiousness never could have done." But then for all this, there is a refinement, an ethereal charm, an unearthly music in Shelly's sentiments and verses which few have equalled and none exceeded. On the other hand, Wordsworth is the child of nature, nature in its higher, purer, diviner forms, both in the creation outside, and in the nature of man. His music is solemn, worldwide, and everlasting. He sings to Duty, to the Spirit of the universe, to the wearied soul of man. He is sometimes lost in a Soul of nature, and his utterances remind us of some of the verses in the Upanishads. Shelly will pass away, Byron will pass away, the best and the purest of our race have already banished them from their hearts. But Wordsworth shall grow, is already growing with the growth of goodness and purity among men. Mr. Matthew Arnold concludes his article by quoting Wordsworth's own estimate about his poems :—" They will operate with the benign tendencies in human nature and society, and will, in their degree, be efficacious in making men wiser, better and happier."

MR. VOYSEY'S WORD OF WARNING.

THE last number of the *Theistic Quarterly Review*, which is just out, contains a contribution from the pen of Mr. Voysey. It is headed a " Word of Warning," and in it Mr. Voysey reproduces with greater vehemence his attacks on Christ and our Minister's utterances. It seems to us to be almost impossible to meet him as an antagonist—in the first place, because he is too bitterly hostile to Christ to think soberly of him; in the second place, he

has the weakness of supposing that every theist, who can speak lovingly of Christ, must be insane; and thirdly, because Mr. Voysey is *very* unfair to his opponents. We shall explain ourselves with regard to this third head. An opponent's fairness is tested by the way in which the deals with the arguments of the opposite party. Readers of John Stuart Mill's Examination of Sir William H milton's Philosophy have noticed the scrupulous fairness with which he represents the views of his great rival. Extracts are fully given, and the greatest care is taken to remove the suspicion of unfairness. If we are asked to try Mr. Voysey by this test, we find him sadly wanting. He has not only not taken the means to acquaint himself with his opponent's views, but he actually distorts and misrepresents them. Instances of this we gave on another occasion, when we had the misfortune to criticise him. We need not, therefore, go over the old ground again. In this article we shall point out one or two more instances of Mr. Voysey's unfairness. Mr. Voysey says that, " put what construction you will upon Babu Keshub's words, the Christian Religion, as held by all and in all ages of these Christ (excepting only by the Unitarians) involves a belief in two Gods, a Father and a Son, both co-eternal together and co-equal, not to speak of a third god little worshipped." We should ask our readers to mark the little clause " excepting only by the Unitarians." If Unitarians do not believe in two Gods, where is the difficulty in supposing that the Theists also do not believe in that duality? And why should Mr. Voysey be so careful to tell us, Brahmos, a fact which we know so well regarding this dual divinity? " There is," he says, " no room in the heart of man for *two* gods. One only must reign supreme ; and wherever there has been a mediator or intercessor set up as a refuge or help for the soul, that mediator has displaced and dethroned the one true God." Here, if Mr. Voysey's aim be to insinuate that the Brahmos believe in a mediator, he is sadly mistaken, or he is preaching only a truism. The following passage is altogether of Mr. Voysey's fruitful imagination) that the Brahmos are going to be Christians :—

You would dishonor also yourselves. For many and many a one will suspect your motives for the change, and attribute it to previous insincerity and to a base selfishness. They will say you have renounced Theism for Christianity, because the latter " pays better" than the former, and you were bent on seeking your worldly advancement. If they do not say this, they will say ' your judgment is feeble,' or, in plain language, ' you must be mad.'

Could we be so base as that ? The insinuation, if it be one, is so insulting that we do not deign to notice it. We shall criticise one particular statement. Christ, Mr. Voysey says, "can do you no good. All he could do by the name he has left behind him is to confuse and perplex your minds, to unsettle the authority of your conscience, and to corrupt the instincts of your hearts. He might draw away your soul's have from God, and tempt you to recur to what has been in past times the curse of your country—a dreamy mysticism and lackadaisical contemplation." We say Christ does the very reverse. His life, his precepts, the sacrifice of himself for the world's good and his vivid realisation of God draw us to the Father. We say the more we study Christ, the more we understand the Father; and the more we love him, the more we are drawn to the loving presence of the God that sent him. Do not say, therefore, that Christ lessens our faith. No, no. A blister on our tongue, if we said so. To those among the Brahmos who have been benefited by his teachings, Christ has ever been a great instrument in drawing them to God and in teaching them what He is.

Brahmo Somaj.

THE usual monthly service in the Brahma Mandir takes place this morning. It commences at 7-30 A. M.

THE *Christian Life* has the following :—"Babu Keshub Chunder Sen is being well abused by the Theists for his outspoken reverence for Christ. Mr. Voysey attacks him in England, and an Indian writes in Calcutta : 'To me it appears that the secret of Mr. Sen's extreme love for Christ and blindness to his defects lies in his strong sympathy with him. The saintly soul of Mr. Sen, at whatever distance it may be, finds a response in that of Christ. His merits and infirmities are like those of the prophet of Nazareth. The transcendental effulgence of Christ's pure life bedazzles Mr. Sen, and he falls prostrate at his feet in glowing admiration, and overlooks his defects.'"

THE last number of the *Indian Evangelical Review* contains an article by Mr. K. S. Macdonald, entitled "The Recent History of K. C. Sen's Brahmoism." The concluding paragraph of it is given below :—"As will be seen from our imperfect sketch, Keshub Chunder Sen's Brahmo Somaj is becoming more and more Christianized in certain directions ; while in others it is becoming more Hinduised. This is admitted in Mr. Mazumdar's *Quarterly Review* to which we have referred above, where it is said, 'Christ's life and character are steadily growing to be a ruling power in the Brahmo Somaj of India.' Brahmists believe in their Somaj's 'progressive developments in principle as well as in life and events.' With such a faith and such a growth we leave them to the kind discriminating Christian sympathy of our readers." This expression of sympathy will, we have no doubt, be appreciated. But the article itself is by no means flattering. There are besides many inaccuracies in it which we hope to notice in another issue.

THE BRAHMO'S CREED.

THE Brahmo's Creed has been misunderstood and misrepresented in various ways, of all which we cannot afford to take notice. One point, however, should be explained, though we must say we are sorry there should be any occasion to explain it. Some people have chosen to take a simple statement of principles as an authoritative and formal bond of agreement, without subscribing to which no admission into the Brahmo Somaj is possible. The Brahmo's Creed is what the great majority of Brahmos believe in. The principles are generalized by experience and observation. There may be, very likely there are, a few Brahmos who take exception to one or two of the principles ; but on that account they are no less Brahmos than those who put their faith in the whole creed. Objection, so far as we have been able to ascertain, has been raised on two points. One of these is the mention of Christ as the chief of prophets, and the other is the eminent mention of Keshub Chunder Sen's services as one of the inspired teachers of the Brahmo Somaj. "Inspired" means being directed by the spirit of God which, at different times and in different degrees, fills, fires, and guides the souls of religious leaders. Babu Keshub Chunder Sen is not the only inspired teacher in the Brahmo Somaj. We could have named Babu Devendra Nath Tagore. We could have named Rajah Ram Mohun Roy. Those among our co-religionists, who recognize any distinction between gifted men and their disciples, and who hold that as in other spheres of human thought and life, so in religion, the special blessing of genius is conferred on some men, and not conferred on others, will find it no difficulty to admit the pre-eminent inspiration of Jesus, and his superiority over all other known teachers of religion. But we should not be understood by any one to mean that, without the personal recognition of Christ's claims, there is no salvation, or spiritual light. And if we say this in relation to Christ, we must say it applies much more to the case of Babu Keshub Chunder Sen. Babu Keshub Chunder Sen is neither our mediator nor indispensable for our acceptance with God. Only he has done the Brahmo Somaj incalculable good, and in common gratitude we acknowledge his services and our obligations to him. But there are men in the Brahmo Somaj who, we are sorry to say, can hear the mention of every other name except his name; who cannot bear to see the least credit given to him for anything. And hence they are fiercely angry with the Brahmo's Creed, and circulate all manner of falsehoods in relation to it. Them we do not hope to convince; but to others who want to judge correctly, we may say that we hold some of our leaders in genuine love and honor for what they have taught us, and we want our gratitude should be shared in by every theist here as well as elsewhere. To Babu Keshub Chunder Sen's teachings the Brahmo Somaj is deeply indebted; but it is also indebted to others, and among the latter we may eminently mention Babu Devendra Nath Tagore, and the founder of our church, Rajah Ram Mohun Roy.—*Theistic Quarterly Review.*

Devotional.

Go and proclaim me Mother of India, said the Lord to the disciples gathered round Him.

Many are ready to worship me as their Father. They recognise my kindness mixed with justice. They bow to my stern authority. They also love me as their merciful Father. But they know not that I am their Mother too, tender, indulgent, forbearing and forgiving, always ready to take back the penitent child. Ye shall go forth from city to city and from village to village, singing my mercies and proclaiming unto all men that I am India's Mother. Tell poor and disconsolate India to take comfort in the thought that, though weak and fainting, she is on my lap, and that I am nursing her day and night. She has nothing to fear so long as she is on her Mother's lap. Go, my apostles, and give India hope and comfort. She requires to be roused and cheered by my missionaries. Therefore I send you to preach the glad tidings of the advent of the Good Mother in India to seek and save Her lost children and give salvation to sinners. Do not preach dry theology ; identify not the present dispensation with the reign of a dry Deity. But say to the people of India with loud and earnest voices that their Mother has come to give them light and life. Put me before them as one whom they can easily trust and love, and whose loving-kindness is extremely sweet. Let your behaviour and conversation, preaching and singing be such as may convince those amongst whom you go that you are intoxicated with my sweet dispensation and my sweeter name. You go forth as men almost mad with devotional love, enthusiasm, and joy. Speak and act like self-forgetful devotees lost in God. Show the world that you so love me as your Mother and Friend that you love nothing else, and your only care is to melt the heart of India's children with sweet words about that Motherly kindness which you have so long experienced at my hands. All that ye have freely received from me give ye freely unto others. And while ye preach, take care that you preach your Mother's love and nothing else, and let your hearers feel that you are wholly inebriated with my over-powering affection. Let your words of sweetness and tears of joy convince India that you are my missionaries. And may India, so convinced, come to me and say,—Blessed be Thy name, Sweet Goddess ! We have seen and heard the Supreme Mother's apostles.

Correspondence.

[*We do not hold ourselves in any way responsible for the opinions of our correspondents.*—ED., *I. M.*]

THE DARK SIDE OF THE PICTURE.

TO THE EDITOR OF THE "INDIAN MIRROR."

SIR,—Will you kindly insert the following in your esteemed journal?

I am a young man. This fact, I trust, is a sufficient guarantee that in noticing the defect in the character of the young men of the day, I shall not err on the side of undue severity. The blot in their character that stands out most prominently is their shallowness and pretension. They do not hesitate to discuss the most intricate questions of philosophy and politics. And what is far more reprehensible, as introducing discord and disquiet into the domestic circle, they brook no superior. Persons who, by virtue of relationship, age and experience, are entitled to exercise an authority over them are held as dotards. The feeling of reverence, it would seem, has no place in their heart.

As to their morality it is simply shocking. Their most familiar conversation with one another is a striking proof. It is marked by the utter absence of delicacy and purity. Filthy and vulgar language is what they most delight in using. And, in fact, it is a matter of no marvel that they should be thus morally depraved. They are exposed, from their early boyhood, to all sorts of evil influences. The public schools in which they are placed are hot-beds of immorality. The conversations and examples of their elders at home are anything but edifying. Poor souls! how could they fight against such fearful odds ? The only thing that could have enabled them to withstand these evil influences is moral culture, and of moral culture they receive none. No amount of knowledge can preserve innocence and purity. For that purpose moral force must mount guard.

As a necessary adjunct to their immorality, levity and absence of earnestness form conspicuous traits in their character. They take nothing seriously. Life is given to them for no other end than for its enjoyments. "Eat, drink and be merry" is their motto. Their highest ambition is to become orators. And they make excellent orators indeed ! Modesty they have thrown off as a superfluous part of their nature ; they have enough of brass. They have at their command a large vocabulary of sesquipedalian words. The names of martyrs and patriots flow in torrents from their lips. What more is wanted to make orators ? It is sad, indeed, to find so many young men go away into froth and fume. But this is inevitable. The only cure is "moral thoughtfulness."

One word more, and I shall have done with this disagreeable task. Our young men are singularly wanting in genial and hearty freshness. Even while they are in college, their manners and demeanour savour too much of the world. They are turned men before their time. They lack altogether frankness, simplicity and warmth that are so touching in a youth. For this they shall have to pay dear, when they take their first plunge into the stream of worldly life. Let those who wish to lead a happy and tranquil life, moisten their heart, while it is yet young and soft, with the dew of love and poetry.

Yours &c.,
U. N. G.

The 8th November, 1878.

BIBLICAL INSPIRATION AND INFALLIBILITY,—*XII.*

TO THE EDITOR OF THE "INDIAN MIRROR."

SIR,—When I entered upon the duty of writing a series of letters in the columns of the *Indian Mirror* upon "Biblical Inspiration and Infallibility," I did so with a firm resolve not to allow myself to be diverted from that purpose by anything that might appear in them from any opponent of my views, until, at least, I had completed the series. But in your issue of the 31st ultimo, there is such a temperate letter regarding my "Palpable Contradictions" from the pen of the Rev. Luke Rivington that I too, as he was, "feel drawn" to say something in reply.

Mr. Rivington gives us an explanation of a certain discrepancy that I had pointed out in Letter No. X between Matthew and John. I have carefully reconsidered the Biblical accounts and Mr. R.'s explanation. The latter is not new, and is the only countermove that is made, (and I believe that *can* be made) by orthodox writers to evade the difficulty. But I must say that I am very far from being satisfied with it, and if you will spare me two full columns of your truth-seeking journal, I will endeavour to shew that it is *utterly inadequate*. On the other hand, possibly the good Padri is *not* himself quite satisfied of its adequacy; for he ends his letter thus :—"The truth of the inspiration of the Bible, as commonly understood, would not be vitally affected, if such contradictions could be proved."

(1) "As commonly understood." *What* is that "common" theory or idea of Inspiration to which Mr. R. alludes ? ? Have I not devoted several letters to shew by quotations from the greatest Theologians that there is *no such thing* ? And have I not, in my *very first* letter, shewn that Bishop Harold Browne teaches that *a definite theory of Inspiration is not desirable* and that Bishop Ellicott concurs with him. I will go further : Mr. Rivington has nowhere that I know of given us *his* definition of Biblical Inspiration, yet I will

venture to say that his theory thereon is as *far* removed as *possible* from those of (say) Professor Gaussen, Mr. Burgon, and Canon Ryle.

(2) "The truth of the inspiration of the Bible * * would not be vitally affected if such contradiction could be proved."

By the words "such contradiction" the good Padri, of course, means the "palpable contradictions" with which I charge the Bible, inasmuch as "apparent" contradictions are admitted by all orthodox writers. Does Mr. Rivington really mean to say that a Book may be "*proved*" to contain *palpable contradictions* and *notwithstanding* be the Inspired and Infallible word of Jehovah? Surely, the *least* we have a right to expect in a book of which it is affirmed that it is *inspired* and *infallible*, is that it should be *perfectly free* from all contradictions of fact. If Inspiration does *not* extend to the *facts* of the Bible, *what* becomes of the *doctrines* which all orthodox Theologians tell us are "*based* upon the facts" or "flow from the facts," or "are the necessary results of those facts?"

Yours &c.,
J. T. T.

Simla, the 15th September 1879.

THE FOURTH GOSPEL.

—o—

TO THE EDITOR OF THE "INDIAN MIRROR."

SIR,—A discussion carried on at places so far apart as Delhi and London, cannot, I am afraid, fail to be tedious. I venture, however, to ask you to insert in your next issue a few lines in reply to "Dr. Tyssen's" letter in your number of September 14.

I. With reference to the authenticity of the Fourth Gospel, I heartily concur with "Dr. Tyssen" in hoping that your readers will study this matter for themselves, and, if possible, I will add, in the original authorities. No conviction will result on this side or on that from merely adducing great names. I mentioned the opinions of Professors Ewald, Lightfoot, Westcott and Sanday not as settling the question, but as rebutting Dr. Tyssen's assertion, (which I see he repeats) that "the unhistorical character of the Fourth Gospel can be proved beyond the possibility of a doubt." I may add that should any of your readers determine to investigate this matter for themselves, there is one point, which is very well worth bearing in mind. The decision depends not merely, as is too often thought, on the number of quotations from the Gospel which may be adduced from writers of the second century or on the settlement of various internal difficulties, but on an appreciative study of the rise and whole early history of the church of Jesus Christ. It is quite as much because of the position which I believe it holds with reference to the development of the early Christian Church, as because of the strength of the external authorities in its favor, that I believe St. John to be the author of the book, which goes by his name.

II. The second point on which I ventured to criticize Dr. Tyssen's letter was of yet more transcendent importance. The Christian Church was a numerous society in many lands before the Gospel of St. John was penned. Had its members not believed in the essential divinity of its Founder and their Lord, it may be doubted if it would ever have obtained a footing beyond the land where Christ taught. It was with reference to this fundamental doctrine of the Christian faith that Dr. Tyssen asserted that the Christians of the East learnt it from the West. I ventured to point out that this was nothing more or less than an historical mistake, and I notice that Dr. Tyssen has tacitly abandoned it, and now only states generally that "Christ was a man and that his followers afterwards exalted their conception of him into that of a God." It would be interesting to me as a student of early Christian records, and I have no doubt to others of your readers, too, if Dr. Tyssen would produce contemporary authorities for his original assertion. So complete a change in its view of Jesus Christ cannot have passed over the mind of the early Church without bearing unmistakable traces in its literature.

On the question itself of the divinity of Christ this is not the place to enter in detail. Only I may be allowed to say thus much. The belief of St. Paul did not rest solely on isolated statements of Scripture, however important, but on three great and concentric lines of proof, *first*, the fulfilment in Christ of the hopes of the great Jewish nation; *secondly*, the absolute and unique purity and sinlessness of the life, which was lived in Galilee and Judea; and *thirdly*, the wholly unparalleled fact of the resurrection. He groups these three lines of proof together at the beginning of his most elaborate epistle—see Romans i. 2-4. The evidence which satisfied the mighty intellect of St. Paul, when he considered the claims which Jesus Christ made about himself, will, I believe, as the years go on, and investigation becomes deeper, more thoughtful, and more reverent, satisfy also the mind of India.

Yours &c.,
EDWARD BICKERSTETH,
Cambridge Mission, Delhi.

Kotgarh, 23rd September 1879.

P.S.—I must apologise to Dr. Tyssen for running two of his sentences together. In my manuscript I meant to have placed dots to show that a passage was omitted.

OUR YOUNG MEN.

—o—

TO THE EDITOR OF THE "INDIAN MIRROR."

SIR,—Your Sunday issue of August 17 contains the query:—"Are the young men of the present generation better or worse than their predecessors?" It is rather difficult to answer your query, inasmuch as I cannot quite understand whom to mean by "the young men of the present generation" and whom by "their predecessors." If by the former be meant young men of the age of, say 15 to 20, I must say with you that they are better, so far as morals go. In the first place, rather a large percentage of them does not, I believe, smoke tobacco or drink intoxicating beverages. What a contrast to "their predecessors"! The present writer, who is as it were a connecting link between two generations, has a friend, a few years his junior, high in the public service, who himself says that he smokes tobacco at the rate of—will my young friends believe me?—thirty to fifty *chhilums* a day!! I have somewhere read—I did this about 13 years ago and most probably in a number of the Encyclopædia Britannica—that hard smoking brings on paralysis. In his *Diseases of Modern Life* Dr. Richardson, whose valuable services to the cause of temperance have been noticed in your columns more than once, has enumerated the distempers, including, I believe, weakness of the eyes, to which inveterate tobacco-smokers are liable. As to whether tobacco is or is not a narcotic, it is for the votaries of Æsculapius to say. But I have digressed, and that simply because the question at issue has reference to "moral excellence"; and I have attempted to show that *tamak khao-a* (tobacco-smoking) is, after all, not such an innocent pastime as is supposed by those of our countrymen, who indulge in the ugly habit. As to drinking, there has happily been a revulsion of Native feeling. Young men of the present generation, unlike their predecessors, do not look upon it as a luxury and a so-called civilizing agent. Sons and younger brothers of sots hate the worship of Bacchus with all their heart. I will not allude to *ganja*, *guli*, (*madat*) and *charas* smoking or to opium-eating, as they used to be indulged in by men of an old, by-gone school.

You have named some of the heads into which the subject mooted by you is resolvable. The *second*, (rather the second and third) is:—"Have they (our young men) got a better moral character? Do they resort to bad places and frequent bad companies?" I believe they are better than their predecessors. There are, no doubt, many a youth who sows wild oats; but strike the average, and you will find (as was remarked to me long before you took up the subject, by old men, whose opinion I had invited) that men of the old *regime* were more incontinent than those of the present generation. "It strikes me," so said, about two months ago, an octogenarian with whose name the people of Bengal are rather familiar, "that there are two things for which *Ajkalkar lok* (men of the present age) are remarkable:—1st Truthfulness and 2nd Chastity." He evidently alluded to educated Natives as a class; but his opinion, embodying as it does the result of observations made for upwards sixty years, is certainly favorable to those forming the subject of the present controversy. Speaking of the continency of educated young men, an intelligent old gentleman in Northern Bengal—may his soul be blessed!—thus illustrated his subject in a conversation held with the writer of these lines some years ago:—"Let me state one fact. In this town, formerly, the house of 'a woman of the town' used to be known and identified not so much by the name of the owner as by that of the Babu in whose keeping she was. This is not the case now." "To a man of the old school," an old school master—then a Head Master of a Zillah School—used to say facetiously, "a sink of iniquity is a *maner balish* (mind's pillow!). It is there that, after the day's work, he finds relaxation for his body and for his mind!" Do not our youths—of course there are black sheep among them—form a favorable contrast to this? If my memory be not treacherous, Babu Raj Narain Bose—and I take his name, of course, with feelings of respect—has, in his work, *Akal ar Ekal*, done an injustice to the men of the present *regime* as regards the points raised in your 2nd and 3rd queries. I would, therefore, say a few words more. Those who know even by hearsay and by the probabilities of the case what Bacchanalian orgies are like, must admit that to say that a young man of the present generation hates the "liquid fire" is to say that he is more chaste than the worshippers of the jolly god. Our social organism is somewhat different from that of the English or the French. Therefore decency, or what is called decency, forbids me to state, Montaigne like, a few more facts which admit of no *I-beg-your-pardon*.

Your *fourth* query is:—"Are they more truthful and honest?" I think they are. It is a fact well known to those who live in villages that a couple of generations ago there could be met with in many a village *bhaddra lokes* [respectable (!) persons] who used to support themselves and their families chiefly by fraudulently depriving widows and orphans and such helpless creatures of their property, *e.g.*, lands, gardens &c., But the greatest hater of educated Natives must admit that our young men are angels compared to the class of persons described above. Let us consider another fact-*ghus khana* (bribe-taking.) A time there was when public opinion of a bribe taker was not at all unfavorable to him, provided he could spend his ill-begotten money on the principle:—"Easy come, easy go." How stands the case now? Why, he who takes bribes is hated by educated Natives, and the word *uprimana* (extra-gain) itself has almost come into disuetude. Two generations ago, no one would think of finding an honest man among the ministrial and Police officers. Now, every district in Bengal Proper can boast of, at least, a dozen such officers—Head Clerks, Police Inspectors, Sub-Inspectors, &c., who do not take douceurs. As regards truth-speaking, there are even school boys who are ashamed of telling fibs. A time there was when a class of persons were perjurers and cheats by profession—*gangajalias* and *bebbelias*. The time has come when we meet with a class of persons who are remarkable for their truthfulness—the *Brahmos*.

I should be wanting in gratitude if I were not to say that for this change for the better—and I am not so blind as not to say that there is yet much room for improvement—we are indebted to the British Government—to the education—English education—which they are giving us. Another influence—an outcome of English education—is also at work, though as yet it is like a drop in the vast ocean of Native society—the *Brahmo Somaj*—the (to borrow a word from the Rev. Mr. Dall) "immortal" Theistic movement in India. I stop for the present.

Yours &c.,
TRUTH.

The 25th August.

Literary and Scientific.

SOCIETY in New York is determined in future to be rigidly particular and exclusive. An "*elite* book" has been established, which contains the names of all those who are entitled to enter fashionable circles, and no outsiders whatever are admitted.

THE misuse of English titles and expressions is so general in France, that a special article in a Gallic review is devoted to instructing literary compatriots in the right use and meaning of "Sir" "Miss," "Esqr." "Gentleman," and other common terms.

BUSY people, annoyed by frequent visitors, are recommended to adopt the plan of an ingenious American. This 'cute gentleman keeps a phonograph in his office, and, when he is interrupted in the middle of work, he bids his visitor talk to the instrument, that he may hear the story at his leisure.

A MAN has a fox, a goose, and some corn. He wishes to cross a river. He has to wade, and can only carry one of the three at a time. Now, if he take the fox over first, the goose will eat the corn; if he take the corn first, the fox will eat the goose. How does he manage? Let our young readers try.

M. DE LESSEPS' latest project is to cut the Isthmus of Corinth in order to permit French and Italian vessels to reach Constantinople and the Black Sea, without doubling stormy Cape Matapan, at the extremity of the Morea, and the expense is put at 720,000ℓ. In Austria the project to tunnel the Arlberg is shortly to be brought before the Reichstag. It is suggested to pierce the mountain at a height of 5,281 feet above the sea-level, and to make the tunnel 10,270 metres long.

THE Life and Work of St. Paul in 2 vols. by Canon F. W. Farrar is out. "The existence of a scholarly and yet popular life of St. Paul has been long felt as a pressing want, and is now first supplied by a work which covers in every page the matured and fuller results of a laborious and learned investigation of the whole of what is most trustworthy in the ancient and modern literature of the subject. One of the most charming traits of this very charming work is the minutely picturesque character of the descriptions given of Athens, Rome, Ephesus, Corinth, Antioch, and other remarkable places in the ancient world which were the scenes of St. Paul's labours."

A SAGACIOUS hawk daily accompanies the trains between Meagrigny and Romily near Troyes, on the French Eastern Railway. The small birds in the hedges along the line, frightened by the noise of the engine, fly out as the train rushes by, so the wary hawk hovers high above the locomotive, hidden by the steam, and pounces suddenly upon its prey. If unsuccessful, the hawk returns to its former position, and travels along at the same pace as the engine, unmoved by steam flung by the engineers, and awaiting the next opportunity to catch its dinner. The bird has been known to haunt this line, according to the Paris Globe, for fifteen years, and invariably keeps to the same hunting-ground.

THE Times thus writes of a remarkable clock in America:—There is now on exhibition in Detroit, Michigan, a clock (the work of Mr. Felix Meier, a mechanic), which is said to eclipse the famous clock at Strasburg in complexity and interest. It stands 18ft. in height, and is enclosed in a black walnut frame, elaborately carved and ornamented. The crowning figure is that of "Liberty," on a canopy over the head of Washington, who is seated on a marble dome. The canopy is supported by columns on either side. On niches below, at the four corners of the clock, are four human figures representing "Infancy," "Youth," "Manhood," and "Age"; each has a bell in one hand and a hammer in the other. The dials are supported by angels with fleecy trumpets, and over the centre is the figure of Father Time. At the quarter hour, the figure of the infant strikes its tiny bell; at the half hour, the figure of the youth strikes the bell of louder tone; at the third quarter the man strikes his bell; and at the full hour the grey beard. Then the figure of time steps out and tells the hour, as two small figures throw open doors in the columns on either side of Washington, and a procession of the Presidents of the United States follows. As the procession moves, Washington rises and salutes each figure as it passes, and it in turn salutes him. They move through the door on the other side, and it is then closed behind them. The procession moves to the accompaniment of varied music played by the clock itself. The mechanism also gives the correct movement of the planets round the sun, comprising Mercury, which makes the revolution once in 88 days; Venus, in 224 days; Mars, in 686 days; Vesta, in 1,327 days; Juno, in 1,503 days; Ceres, in 1,681 days; Jupiter, in 4,332 days; Saturn, in 29 years; Uranus, in 84 years. As these movements are altogether too slow to be popularly enjoyed, the inventor has added a device by which he can hasten the machinery to show its working to the public. There are dials which show the hour, minute, &c., in Detroit, Washington, New York, San Francisco, London, Paris, Berlin, Vienna, St. Petersburg, Constantinople, Cairo, Pekin, and Melbourne. The clock also shows the day of the week and month in Detroit, the month and the changes of the year, the changes of the moon, &c. It is said that Mr. Meier has worked on the clock nearly ten years, and for the last four years has devoted his whole time to it.

Latest News.

—LIEUTENANT HERBERT LAWSON has been permitted to volunteer for the Indian Staff Corps under the terms of the Horse Guards General order No. 117 of 1st December 1878.

—THE widow and son of the late Major W. Reynolds, Bombay Staff Corps, killed in action, have been admitted in England to a compassionate allowance of £120 and £30 a year and to gratuities of £292 and £37 respectively.

—CONSEQUENT on the removal to the retired List of Lieutenant-General E. P. Lynch, K.f.S. Bombay Infantry, Major General B. R. Powell, Bombay Infantry, is promoted to the rank of Lieutenant-General, and Col. J. Gordon, Bengal Infantry, is promoted to the rank of Major General.

—IT has been decided by the Home Government to make applicable to India the Royal Warrant of 30th October 1876 fixing new rates of pay for subaltern officers of cavalry and infantry of the British army with retrospective effect from the date of its issue, viz., 1st December 1876. The provisions of this warrant apply to the few officers, and will not permanently increase the established number drawing the higher rate of pay.

—THE Secretary of State has approved of the nomination of Lieutenant G. F. Willis, 34th Foot, as a Probationer for the Bengal Staff Corps.

—A CORRESPONDENCE has recently passed between the India Office and the War Office from which it appears that service as Sub-Lieutenant is not to reckon as part of the five years' service required to qualify a Lieutenant to become a probationer for the Staff Corps.

—THE Secretary of State has approved of the publication of a second edition of the Pay and Promotion Code for India, which will, in future, be considered an official publication.

Calcutta.

THE BAND OF HOPE.

THE following report of the Band's work during the last month, was read at their general meeting, held at the Albert Hall, on last Wednesday afternoon:—

During the last month, 44 young men have joined the Band; the number of those who have signed the pledge is 519 up to date.

We announced at the last meeting that there would be a soiree of the members of the Band last month. But the Council regret to state that as they were unable to procure temperance newspapers, periodicals and illustrated journals, and to make other arrangements essential to the success of the soiree, they thought it proper to postpone it to some future date. Several European gentlemen in the N. W. Provinces have already been written to for temperance publications—both British and American. The Council now hope that before long they will be able to arrange matters, and bring on a successful soiree.

Since we last met, letters have been received from the Secretaries, Students' Association and Students' General Association, Mymensing; Dacca, Krishnagore, and Rungpore Students' Associations; and from the Secretary, Dacca Brahmo Samaj, in reply to the Council's letter to them. They have, sincerely and with much earnestness, responded to our call, and the Council feel thankful to many of them for holding public meetings at their respective places in order to agitate the question of total abstinence, and thereby enlist the sympathy of the people.

The Council have, of late, been impressed with the necessity of publishing a temperance journal in Bengali, and have been contemplating on the best method of carrying it out. But the condition of the Band's finances being not so cheering, the Council thought it advisable for the present to request the Editor, Indian Mirror, (Sunday Edition) to open a temperance column in his journal. They have much pleasure in recording their best thanks to the Editor for having kindly consented to set apart a column in his paper, once a month, for the temperance question. The Council are at present on the look out for a separate fund for the maintenance of the proposed journal, and sincerely hope that before the close of this year, or at the beginning of the next, the Band will have a journal of its own.

NALIN BIHARI SIRCAR,
Honorary Secretary.

The 8th October 1879.

ARRIVAL OF THE OVERLAND MAILS OF THE 19TH SEPTEMBER.

THE P. and O. S. N. Company's S. S. Teheran, Commander A. H. Johnson, arrived in Bombay Harbour on the night of Tuesday last, with the English Mails of the 19th September. The following is the list of passengers:—

From Southampton.—Mr. Johnson, Mr. C. Martin, Mr. W. G. Sharp, Mrs. A. W. Hogg, Mrs. R. Smith and child, Miss A. Selby, Rev. and Mrs. A. G. Lewis, Miss L. Caldraft, Col. and Mrs. E. E. Appleyard, Mrs. Anderson and infant, Mr. and Mrs. Leith and infant, Mrs. C. Leith, Mr. J. Browness, Mrs. Hallam, infant and three children, Mr. J. M. Sheran, Mr. W. A. Smith, Mr. A. Milners, Mrs. Hare, Mr. Appleyard, and Mrs. Wilkinson and child.

From Venice.—Mr. J. Heath, Mr. J. Reid, Mr. J. R. Kipling, Mr. and Mrs. Pout, Mr. Sinclair, Dr. and Mrs. Croaker, Mrs. Cotes, Mr. P. Gyein, Mr. Millick, Mr. W. O. Obson.

From Brindisi.—Mr. W. C. Morgan, Mr. C. Douglas, Dr. Davidson, Major K. Collett, Mr. W. M. Fletcher, Capt. Browning, Col. W. W. Goadfellow, Mr. A. Grant, Dr. Bilcher, Mr. and Mrs. Voght, Dr. Joynt, Mr. J. C. Murray, Mr. C. Taylor, Col. S. J. H. Gordon, Mr. Warrick, Major Blair, Mr. Syed Ali, Dr. Hembery, Mr. J. J. West, Surgeon Gen. Theobalds, Capt. C. A. MacGregor, Lt. Hon'ble Napier, Mr. Fardin, Capt. Massey.

From Aden.—Col. Croggan.

DOMESTIC OCCURRENCES.

—o—

[THE CHARGE FOR NOTIFYING A DOMESTIC OCCURRENCE is ONE RUPEE, AND THE ANNOUNCEMENT MUST BE AUTHENTICATED.]

BIRTH.

SEN.—On Sunday, the 28th September 1879, the wife of Babu Keshub Chunder Sen, of a daughter.

Selections.

THE SURRENDER OF THE ONEIDA COMMUNISTS.

(Independent.)

WE confess to a thorough, genuine, and most delightful surprise. When some years ago, we said that henceforth we did not intend to utter one word against Mormon polygamy without accompanying it with a word more severe, if possible, against the Oneida promiscuity, we did not suppose that the latter evil could be abolished without a long and tedious legal struggle. Since that time we have done our part. The Church has done its part. Public sentiment has been directed against the terrible abomination and legal measures were being prepared. But now, before the campaign was well begun, the Community has itself volunteered to yield to the public opinion about it, and it is announced that it has already given up its system of complex marriage. Henceforth it will conform to the generally recognized moral code.

We are thoroughly glad. We do not stop to inquire closely how far this results from a difference of opinion in the Community, of whom some of the younger generation may not like the promiscuous system. We simply take it as a graceful surrender of the only offensive peculiarity of the body. Mr. J. H. Noyes, the founder of the Community, in his own life-time, proposed the honorable retreat, in these items, which have been adopted:

"I propose

"1. That we give up the practice of complex marriage, not as renouncing belief in the principles and prospective finality of that institution; but in deference to the public sentiment which is evidently rising against it.

"2. That we place ourselves not on the platform of the Shakers, on the one hand, nor of the world, on the other; but on Paul's platform, which allows marriage, but prefers celibacy.

"To carry out this change it will be necessary, first of all, that we should go into a new and earnest study of the 7th chapter of I Corinthians, in which Paul fully defines his position, and also that of the Lord Jesus Christ, in regard to the sexual relations proper for the Church in the presence of worldly institutions.

"If you accept these modifications, the Community will consist of two distinct classes—the married and the celibates—both legitimate; but the last preferred.

"What will remain of our communism after these modifications may be defined thus:

"1. We shall hold our property and businesses in common, as now.

"2. We shall live together in a common household and eat at a common table, as now.

"3. We shall have a common children's department, as now.

"4. We shall have our daily evening meetings and all of our present means of moral and spiritual improvement."

With this change, we pledge to the Oneida community the hearty good will of all Christian people. But for their one immoral feature they would have had it hitherto. We are glad to have them try their experiment of communism, and learn and teach all that can be gotten out of it. We wish them all success in it. We respect their diligence, their conscientiousness and honesty, their business tact, their education of their children, their spirit of careful experiment in social science, their thorough mutual criticism, their deep religious faith and fervour. There has rested on them only one stain and blot. But that has been a terrible one. Their utter rejection of what the world has called marriage, and their substitution for it of a system which made every man the husband of every woman, and any man the father of any woman's child, under the direction of a stirpicultural committee—all this was a menace to the sanctity of all our homes; and the diligence and success of the Community only made them more dangerous, as vice is always dangerous in proportion to its success. This blot removed, and Christianity has no war with the communism which is left, which Christianity, indeed, temporarily adopted, and to which it might conceivably return. But the breach of the law of monogamy Christianity never did allow; and it never will endure it, until the world shall end.

Now, as the Oneida Community has received new light and has conformed itself to the code of Christian ethics, we turn with some hope to the Mormon community, and repeat the hope that it may receive a new revelation. Revelations come in critical times. We trust that our Government will make the times very critical to the Utah polygamists. We trust that the laws be enforced unto the extreme imprisonment allowed by it. Then we may hope for a new Mormon revelation. Already the time is ripe for it. The son of the first prophet is violently opposed to polygamy, and declares that it is a perversion of the faith. The majority of Mormons have but one wife. We have strong hopes that the leaders may see their mistake, may receive some new supernatural light, and may accept the easiest way out of their present peril. Had they always been a law-abiding and mystically pious people, like those at Oneida, we should feel a considerable assurance that new light would break upon them.

INDIAN THEISM,—A NEW PHASE.

(Theistic Quarterly Review.)

THE Theistic Church in India is in a crisis. Even superficial observers have noticed the fact. The external signs are so palpable and striking that none can possibly mistake their nature. They are the premonitory signs of a deep spiritual revival, which recent circumstances have rendered inevitable. They are transparent indications of a spirit of discontent with the old theology, and an earnest struggle to realize a better order of things. As regards the drift and direction of the new tide of thought and sentiment which has set in with almost all the force of a revival movement, there are, of course, differences of opinion. But all classes are agreed that the Brahmos to-day are not what they were yesterday. Their very foundation principles have been shaken. New impulses and new aspirations have taken firm hold of their hearts. A new spirit has touched and enlivened the very centre of their being. They have moved on to an altogether new line of thought. Our remarks apply only to the vanguard of the army, the advanced minds, the elders who mould the lives and character of the rest. And we are speaking only of the centre of the Theistic movement in Calcutta, where Church discipline and Church organization may be said to take their rise. What we mean to say is briefly this. The leading men, in the course of their progressive development, have entered upon a new sphere of spiritual activity, which threatens to revolutionize the whole Church. They have gone, so to say, from the outer into the inner sanctuary of the Lord, where they feel His reality more than they ever did before. The foundations of the Brahmo Church are being laid upon one single point the felt nearness of the Divine Person. Every devotee knows what it is to draw near to the Father and what sentiments such nearness begets. All these sentiments are beginning to manifest themselves one after another among the more devout section of the Brahmo Somaj. Have the public in India and England bestowed sufficient attention upon the peculiar language now-a-days employed by Brahmo devotees? It is wild, it is fiery, it is mystical. It is the language of faith, of vision, of enthusiasm. It reminds us of inspired seers, of Isaiah, and Ezekiel, and Paul, of Wesley, and Swedenborg, of Hafiz, and Kabir, and Ramprasad, of men who saw the spirit-world. If language be, as it truly is, an index to the life within, then it must be concluded that our Church is on the way to that vantage-ground of faith, from where the sights and sounds of the higher world are distinctly seen and heard. Such significant words as these, *seeing, hearing, and touching the Spirit of God*, are becoming quite familiar among advanced Brahmos. Immersion in the deep waters of Divine love and joy, looking joyfully at the perpetual smile on the lips of the Merciful, pressing the sinner's afflicted head on the bosom of the Saviour, the light emanating from the Sun of Holiness reflected on the worshipper's face, the All-Soul and the human soul playing together joyfully, the childlike soul sitting on the lap of the Divine Mother and drinking the milk of inspiration from Her breast, the bird-like spirit that has soared too high in the sky lost in Infinity,—these are some of the many striking metaphors which abound in the devotional literature of the Brahmo Somaj of the present day. There is seemingly a tinge of mysticism in such ideas; at all events they exhibit abundance of sentiment, imagination, and poetry. As was to be expected, such language has created not a few enemies. They see in it, or affect to see in it, nothing but superstition. Superstition indeed! Apply to it scientific tests, and it will be found to represent real faith. The language of faith and inspiration in all theologies is wild and sensational; but it does not follow, therefore, that it is unreal, or based upon fiction. We admit that such sensational language is apt to prove a fertile source of quarrels and wranglings, and may, in the end, lead to error and superstition; and we fully appreciate the warning often given in a friendly spirit that a religion so rational and scientific as Theism ought to use words which are thoroughly exact and perfectly philosophical, and are not likely to mislead. But the critics of the Brahmo Somaj ought to remember that the language complained of is scientifically and philosophically exact, and that it is this very *exactness* which gives rise to discontent and opposition. Take *e. g.* the less thoughtful and devout Theists. Their commonplace devotion does not strike men. Their platitudes, their "Lord, Lord," must always fall flat upon their hearers, and nobody is likely to say aught against them. They are not the grand and original, but the tame and servile imitation. They do not pray, but their lips pray. They read and repeat, but they do not feel. Like praying machines they move as they are made to move. They say what other men prescribe and dictate. Hence their smooth and accurate diction, their round periods, their rich imagery, their superior rhetoric. Theirs is the stereotyped devotion of established theology, all its words being cut and shaped to please mortal ears and not Heaven. But where there is living devotion, it must create its own language, so as to accord with the realities it sees and feels. Were it to rest satisfied with the formal prayers used in churches and the cut-and-dry phrases of popular theology, it would be guilty of lying before God and man. The ordinary worshipper, Hindu, Christian, or Mahomedan, would be justified in saying—Lord Thou hast revealed Thy nature to my understanding. But to the man of faith such expressions would be not only unscientific, but untrue. His position in spirit the world is much higher than that of the ordinary believer. The latter knows, but the former sees; the latter apprehends intellectually or at best emotionally, but the former is brought into the immediate presence of God Almighty, and is so near that he *sees*. It is no fancy, no dreamy mysticism, no hypothesis, no 'I suppose,' but *real vision*. If, then, he says,—Lord, I see Thee and I rejoice in Thy beauty, he says the exact truth. He cannot deny a positive fact; he cannot understate it. He is bound for truth's sake to tell the exact thing, neither exaggerating nor extenuating it. The man who has just commenced to pray does not pretend to receive any response from heaven. He only says but does not care to hear in reply. He, therefore, follows not the voice of God, but his own conscience and judgment enlightened by the Divine spirit. And well he might say in his prayers,—Grant, O Lord, that I may always act according to my best judgment. But such words cannot represent the spirit of the devotee, who has come so close to the throne of the Lord that he cannot look upon conscience apart from Him, and can have no faith in an injunction or command which does not fall from His lips. He would be a maniac, an impostor, if he disbelieved his own senses, or wilfully misrepresented their testimony. He actually *hears* the voice of the Lord instructing him in ethics, and finds no human teacher asserting authority within under the name of 'Conscience.' His devotion must, therefore, of necessity assume some such form as this,—I hear Thy voice guiding me. Blessed Spirit how distinctly and sweetly Thou speakest! Advanced believers cannot but use such language. If they feel nearness to God, they must use expressions which would exactly indicate this spiritual contiguity. If, then, among Indian Theists we hear in these days the peculiar expressions of exalted devotion and faith, let us believe that there is already an upheaval in the Brahmo mind. If the language of reason and logic has given way to the language of faith, let us believe that some, at least, among the leading spirits of our Church have begun to see with the eye of faith, and hear with the ear of faith. Whether the mass will follow the few is problematical; that a mighty struggle will ensue between intellect and faith, between hearsay evidence and vision seems almost inevitable. How the Somaj will pass through the present crisis will be an interesting study to many. If the present crisis be the secession of all Brahmos, who worship the intellect even above the Godhead, the deserted few will have ample consolation in the thought that the whole Hindu nation will consent to be leavened by the leaven of faith, and will not touch the poison of dry rationalism.

Darlington's Pain-Curer has been found to be a certain cure for Pains in the Back, Lumbago, Pains in the Chest, Sore Throats, Coughs, Colds, Tightness of the Chest, Headache, Neuralgia Colics, Rheumatism, Paralysis, Pains in the Groins, Contracted Joints, Gout, Swellings, Old Sores Piles, Ringworm, Pimples, Freckles, & Eruptions on the Skin.

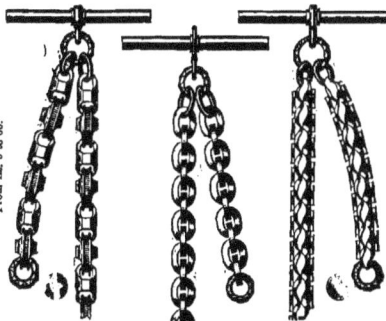

The Indian Mirror

EDITED BY KRISHNA BIHARI SEN, M. A.]

SUNDAY EDITION

[REGISTERED AT THE GENERAL POST OFFICE.]

VOL. XIX.   CALCUTTA, OCTOBER 19, 1879.   NO. 249.

CONTENTS.

Telegraphic Intelligence.

FROM THE PRESS COMMIS- SIONER.

GENERAL ROBERTS' PROCLAMA- TION.

SIMLA, 17TH OCTOBER.

General Roberts, on entering Cabul, issued a proclamation of which the following is the substance. As the inhabitants have pertinaciously opposed the advance after warning, they have become rebels and added to the previous guilt of abetting the murder of British Envoy and companions. Though the British Government could justly totally destroy Cabul, yet in mercy the city will be spared. But a punishment to be remembered is necessary. Therefore the portion of the city which interfere with people or military occupation of the Bala Hissar will be immediately levelled, and a heavy fine will be imposed. Cabul and the surrounding country within a radius of ten miles will be placed under martial law. Military Governor will be appointed. Inhabitants warned to submit to authority. This punishment does not absolve individuals. Searching enquiry into the circumstances of the outbreak will be made and dealt with. Participators carrying arms forbidden in the city and within a radius of five miles. Persons found armed a week from the date of proclamation will be liable to the penalty of death. Articles belonging to the late Embassy to be delivered. Also firearms or ammunition formerly issued to, or seized by, Afghan troops to be produced. Rewards are offered for all rifles brought in. A reward is offered for the surrender of any person concerned in the attack on the Embassy or information leading to capture. Similar rewards are offered for any person also who has fought against the British troops since the 3rd September, and larger rewards are offered for officers of the Afghan army.

SIMLA, 18TH OCTOBER.

The Guide Corps Cavalry and Infantry Wing Ninth Foot Hazara Mountain Battery were to move from Jellalabad to near to Futteabad on the 17th.

Editorial Notes.

OUR readers will be glad to learn that Father Lafont is expected back in India by the middle of next month.

"How can I check anger?" somebody asks. The reply may be as short. "When you strike a servant, can you manage to ask him to pardon you?" The effect upon both would be excellent.

WE learn that the subscribers to the Ram Gopal Ghose Memorial have finally decided to place the bust at the Town Hall, and the picture in the Hall of the British Indian Association.

IN matters spiritual we are allowed to pray with our whole heart to God ; but in matters temporal or physical the best prayer is that uttered by Christ in distress, "Lord, Thy will be done!" This is the only reply we can give to the article of the *Indian Christian Herald* on the subject of prayers for physical good.

SOME one says that one sermon in olden times converted 3,000 sinners, but now it takes 3,000 sermons to convert one sinner. The *Christian Life* suppose he refers to the latest scientific methods of preaching, in which poor science and worse religion get mixed together. We suppose, however, it is Mr. Voysey's sermons that he has specially in view.

THE open air gathering on Tuesday last proved a great and decided a success that some of our friends have recommended that such meetings should be held oftener. The proposal is worthy of consideration. The enthusiasm apparent among our youthful and educated classes is, indeed, a most hopeful sign. This is the time when all preachers and reformers and patriots should zealously co-work to put down infidelity and scepticism.

THE *Rock* having been lately asked "if a heathen could be saved?" made the following cautious reply :—"This is a deep, dark question. The insertion of your letter would flood our columns with correspondence of very dubious value. Our Lord's plain command, 'Preach the Gospel to every creature,' should suffice to stimulate our missionary zeal ; while the caution, 'Judge nothing before the time,' warns us of the danger and folly of hasty conclusions as to the fate of those whom the Gospel may reach." Sweet, but rather evasive.

WE are informed that of late there has been some discussion in the Calcutta Missionary Conference on the question of the present state of High education in India. The view they have generally adopted is, that English teaching in the country, from its connection with Christian missionaries, necessarily partakes of a more or less Christian tone ; and though not always reconstructive in its moral effects, it is useful negatively, as preparing the way for a truer faith by the removal of prejudices and superstitious notions of the people of this country.

EVERY man of faith should keep a diary in which his sins should be carefully recorded, and after every prayer he should ascertain if any of those sins have been removed. It is in this way that faith can be enlarged. We are often uncertain about the exact results of prayer in our life. If statistics be kept of answers to prayers, they will not only be valuable to the struggling soul, but a gain to the world at large. Men are naturally sceptical ; but one sinner reclaimed is a better argument against infidelity than all the volumes of Hamilton and Martineau put together.

THE *Lucknow Witness* complains that people call it the Methodist organ, while the fact is that it is not the organ of any ecclesiastical body. We would advise our contemporary to allow the world to indulge in its own whims. We have ourselves complained of the names people persist in giving us ; but we have seen it is a hopeless task to drive an idea from the world's head, when it has once entered into it. We know of a weekly paper in Calcutta, now defunct, that proclaimed itself to be a European paper ; but the wicked world wouldn't believe it and continued calling it a Native paper. The best philosophy under the circumstances is to maintain a discreet silence and think of Shakespeare's consoling maxim, What's in a name ?

REFERRING to the Rev. Luke Rivington's remarks, in these columns, as to the spelling of personal or possessive pronoun, when it refers to Jesus Christ, with a capital letter at the beginning, the *Bombay Guardian* writes :—"We do not think this to be a valid way of showing deference to the Saviour or to God. Scripture offers no countenance to it. It is confusing, and to be appreciated by the reader needs a measure of attention that would be much better bestowed upon the sense of the passage. We often meet with passages where these capital letters are most punctiliously used, at the same time that what is said is very little to the honor of God or of Christ."

THE Durga Pujah Vacation has commenced. To every person, orthodox or heterodox, except to the trader, the holidays afford intense relief. People are satisfied with their well-earned rest, and they utilise it in a variety of ways. The Press alone is doomed ; it has no holiday to enjoy. We ought to have said we are doomed, for our Native contemporaries have taken leave of their readers. While the country, therefore, is enjoying, we are working. This thought enlivens us. Is not error abroad? Has not hydra-headed superstition caught hold of Bengal within its clutches ? What can be a better, holier occupation than to grapple with this monster? Bengal does need a revival. It is the duty of all earnest patriots to go about convincing the people of the errors of their ways and bringing them to worship the one true God. This is the time when itinerant missionaries should preach and sing the holy Name in villages and towns, when lectures should be delivered, pamphlets written, meetings held, prayers offered and charities instituted for the conversion of misguided people. The best energies one can command should be brought to play, and nothing left undone which should be done to teach the people the sanctity of religion. The Brahmo Somaj has a sacred work to discharge in this season. This is just the time for earnest work. Let us pray, solemnly pray that the Kingdom of God may soon be established in our dear motherland!

We understand that a movement is already set on foot in England by some sincere well-wishers of India, with a view to train up a select number of young Indians of good birth and means, and thus to qualify them to compete for places in the public service with Englishmen on their return to India. A morning contemporary is informed that Lord Northbrook has consented to become the President of a Committee for the purpose, of which Sir H. S. Maine, Sir A. Hobhouse, Sir Barrow Ellis, Sir H. Davis, and Mr. Gerald Fitzgerald will be members, with General Keatinge as Treasurer, and Mr. Frank Wyllie, of the Bombay Civil Service, Secretary. Mr. G. Fitzgerald, son of Sir S. Fitzgerald, is, we learn, the originator of the scheme. Our contemporary says :—"It is proposed that the Committee should act as guardians in England of young Indians of good family, whose character and fitness to come to this country are vouched for by any Indian Civilian of the rank of a Collector; and that the education, morals and manners of the young men should be carefully looked after. Of course, they would not be guaranteed appointments on their return to India ; but their exceptional training would, it is believed, mark them out as eligible subjects for promotion under the new system of nomination which has been introduced for Natives aspiring to high positions in the public service." This is just the movement which we have all along advocated. We are not mistaken, a proposal to the same effect was made sometime ago by Sir W. Muir to Northbrook and the late Lord Lawrence. But the difficulty then, as now, was whether our young men would like to submit to any restraint of the kind.

The Rev. K. S. Macdonald, in his article in the *Indian Evangelical Review*, noticed in our last, portrays our Minister in the following style :—" (Babu Keshub Chunder Sen) was understood to be practising certain forms of asceticism, by walking occasionally barefooted through the streets of Calcutta, cooking his own food, and making roads and visiting the poor while living in a retired villa. But this asceticism was held to be quite consistent with travelling first class by rail, living in style in one of the Calcutta palaces, his own property, being fanned by rich men's sons, wearing the finest broadcloth and Dacca muslin, attending evening parties at Government House, dining in state with friends—always however understanding that he lives a thorough vegetarian." We hope our reverend friend will allow us to put up the following picture by the side of that which he has drawn, and ask the reader to look on that picture and on this :—" Babu

Keshub Chunder Sen is well-known to be practising certain forms of asceticism. From the earliest days of the devotional movement he walked barefooted through the streets of Calcutta on the occasion of the *Nagar Sankirtan*. He used sometimes ago to cook his own food. He made roads in the *Sadhan Kanon*, a garden for devotional exercises, where he retired from time to time. But this asceticism was held to be quite consistent with travelling third class by rail, living in a decent style in a house which was never called a palace, when it was occupied by the Scottish Orphanage, being fanned by servants and surrounded by tag-rag men, called Brahmo Missionaries, who have not a pice in their pocket, wearing the commonest and coarsest *dhuti* usually worn by elderly people, attending evening parties at Government House, eating *muri* with friends—always understanding that he lives a thorough vegetarian."

Mr. Macdonald is eminently unhappy in all his charges against our Minister. He says :—" The Somaj of India has no constitution, no rules, no authorised principles or documents. Keshub has resisted, all these ten years, all efforts to draw up any constitution for the Society and a Trust for the property owned by it. Hence the church built by them is indirectly claimed by Keshub as his own. He has, by various crooked ways, prevented as yet a vote of the members being taken as to its ownership." The bias of the writer is painfully apparent in this passage. As for the constitution, rules, and principles, may we ask if he has enquired that there is such a thing as the Declaration of the Brahma Mandir, quoted by Max Müller in his Science of Religion? And that five years ago the rules of the congregation were clearly laid down at a meeting of the worshippers of the Mandir ? And that fundamental principles of life and conduct were long ago laid down, printed and published for the benefit of the Brahmos? As for the Trust, does Mr. Macdonald know that the Mandir is still indebted, and that when the debt is cleared off, or when the worshippers undertake to clear it off, the Trust also will be forthcoming ? The Brahma Mandir is the property of the public. Neither directly nor indirectly is it, nor can it be, claimed by Babu Keshub as his own. The expenses of its construction were defrayed by public subscriptions; its management is in the hands of the Mission Office, which submits accounts of receipts and disbursements to the Brahmo Somaj of India every year. If in the face of these facts, Mr. Macdonald still persists in saying that the Mandir is the private property of a certain individual, all we can say is that his ideas of property are altogether very strange.

If indications are to be trusted, there is every likelihood of a schism in the Unitarian Church of England. The *Christian Life* admits that there are three parties among the Unitarians. One party acknowledges the divine authority of Jesus Christ and his headship in the Christian Church. Another believes with Theodore Parker that Christ is no Lord or Master, while the third takes its stand under the banners of secularism, agnosticism and the like. We wonder how ministers who declare themselves to be agnostics can conscientiously occupy the pulpit in churches ostensibly erected for the worship of God. We do not clearly understand which of these parties Mr. Martineau heads. So far as we can gather from his published utterances, he is averse to taking a name.

His views on the origin of unitarianism are interesting.

" I cannot but lament, he says, " that Unitarianism had a sceptical origin ; that it began with dissentients from belief, removing successively objects of human veneration and reliance ; and, on the whole, characterised in the eyes of others by its success in proving how few things need be regarded as wonderful and divine. To this spirit, impressed upon our system at first, we are indebted for such accessions of adherents as it receives. The doubters and unbelievers of other and less reasonable churches constitute the new forces of our own ; we grow by men's lapses from their previous convictions ; and thus a critical, cold and untrusting temper becomes silently diffused, unfavorable to high enterprise and deep affections. Moreover, when at length this spirit vanishes, and the genuine sentiments of personal religion acquire power, their effect upon our consolidation as a sect, is the every reverse of their action in orthodox churches. With these who enter or to be no less fatal than the growth of piety inflames sectarian zeal: with us, who attach no terrors to the involuntary mistakes of the sincere, it is otherwise ; the pure perceptions and natural instincts of the pious heart detect and love the good and great in the spirit of other churches ; becoming more devout in mind, we feel ourselves not more, but far less discriminated from the true Christian of every faith ; and our sectarian zeal undergoes inevitable decline. And thus, as a mere theological denomination, we profit by the scepticism of other sects, and lose by the piety of our own."

Mr. Martineau has, therefore, no expectations from any principle of sectarian union or schemes of mechanical organisation. He is for keeping the doors of the Church open to any impressions from outside. From all this it may be inferred that the position of the Unitarian is very unsafe. In the meantime we are told that there is a visible falling-off in the number of adherents and supporters.

THE SPIRIT AND THE LETTER.

We have in previous issues spoken of the true scope and functions of the theistic church in India. The future church of this country, we said, will be one in which God shall be the only Father and King, and the Divine manifestations in nature, the soul and the lives of men the only scripture by one or all of which the erring mind may be guided in its search for happiness. This ideal which we have formed takes cognizance of the spiritual side of the movement only. But our daily experiences show that all men are not spiritual. Many love the spirit ; more perhaps love the letter ; while many more are content with a convenient mixture of both. This is the case in all churches. The spirit is for the few, the letter for the many. It seems, therefore, that the movement which we represent—the movement of the spirit—is not likely to be popular with those who like to be slavishly attached to the letter. There will, therefore, be in the Brahmo Somaj always sects that will represent one or more of these particular phases of character. To some the divine manifestations of power and love will be the only solace and hope of life. Prayer, communion and devotion form the only elements of worship which they care to cultivate, and morality, based upon religion and the Father's will, the only goal of their ambition. These persons are the feeders, so to say, of the theistic movement. From them proceed the fire, the enthusiasm, the example, the inspiration which give life and animation to the community. They are ready to do every thing for God. They have renounced the world ; they hate riches ; they care for none of the comforts and indulgences of life; and they will readily die for men. They are the pillars upon which God's house is built. But, as we have said, they can never be popular except with the devout; and they can never be satisfied unless they succeed in rousing the enmity of men and thus opening their eyes to the real character of truth. Of the others many will remain rationalists to the end. Subjection to authority or restraint will be a constant bugbear to them, while their dread of slavery, as they call it, will lead them to rely upon reason alone for interpretations of the laws of nature which will gradually carry them over to the arms of cold rationalism or scepticism. Spiritual life will be extinguished; the church which they found will die of inanition, while the name of God which they utter will remain an empty abstraction. So far as we can mark the signs of the times, this tendency to rationalism has already begun to manifest itself. The protests against hero-worship, Christianity, Vaishnavaism, which are raised from time to time are not possessed of any worth, if we refer to the grounds upon which they are based. But when we consider them in relation to the persons who utter them, we are alarmed by their tendencies. As we have often said in these columns, there can never brook a mediator; and the frequent outcries against the doctrine of mediation have no meaning at all. And yet, as these protests are often heard, we must strive to account for them somehow or other. We have come to the conclusion that what our opponents represent as superstition or idolatry is neither of these, but the expression of the genuine yearnings of the heart for the infinite God. If the devotee goes to learn from Christ what he knew about God, he is not to be called an idolator, but a God-seeking man who finds true happiness in the company of saints. If he gives himself up to sacred devotion and sings the "sweet Name," he is not to be classed as a Vaishnava, but a devotee to whom the chanting of Divine mercies is the only ornament of the soul. In the language of the hymn he constantly sings,—"what more ornament do I need? The Heaven's necklace I wear round my neck. The ornament of my hand is to serve his feet; that of the eye is to see His face; and that of the ear to hear His Name." So also if he gives himself up to ascetic practices from time to time, he is not to be shunned as a Yyragi, but an earnest man bent upon freeing his soul from the infirmities of the flesh. What, than, is the drift of the never-ending protest against these activities of the spirit? Are we to be carried away by the specious logic of rationalism? God forbid. If the exercises of the spirit be reckoned superstition, may we have more of it day after day, year after year! May we be superstitious, fanatical and ascetic! May Heaven's blessing fall in plentiful showers upon this heavenly superstition! But no. The protest we allude to represents the struggles of the mind to escape from the influence of Divine love. It is the struggle of the flesh against the spirit, of earth against heaven. Let Brahmos beware of the bewitching sorcery of rationalism, and the arrogant claims of the intellect. There is nothing so pleasant as slavery to the will of God. May we all be slaves for ever to His over-powering mercies.

MR. VOSEY'S LAST ATTACK.

Mr. Vosey has spoken out again. He has delivered another sermon against our Minister, and as many of our readers would like

to read it, we make room for it in another column. Mr. Voysey calls his discourse a Sermon. We do not know what he means by a sermon; but if all his sermons are of the nature indicated in this, we are led to form a very poor idea of both the Minister and the congregation at Langham Hall. Surely this is no sermon; it is a commonplace, indecent attack upon a person whose utterances he does not understand. There is nothing in what he says which may be dignified with the title of argument. It is a string of rituperative attacks, an attempt to browbeat us into silence and submission, and a very miserable expedient of lowering the Brahmo Somaj of India in public estimation. Mr. Voysey says it is not possible to interpret the lecture on Christ otherwise than literally. Not possible, when he is repeatedly told that the terms used therein are not to be taken in their orthodox signification? Why, to retort upon him the compliment he is so fond of lavishing upon others, this inability to interpret what has been so clearly, unmistakably enunciated, argues either a strange perversity in Mr. Voysey or some defect in his brains. Our outspoken champion of English theism is delighted to hail a number of sympathists with his doctrines. We know that adversity often makes us acquainted with strange bed-fellows, and on this principle we are not surprised if his impious declamations against Christ have brought to his rescue a member of the Adi Brahmo Somaj from one side and a gentleman of the protest party from another. Blessed trinity!—The Brahma, Vishnu and Shiva of theism all united by their opposition to one man and fired by the amiable desire of removing him from the Brahmo Somaj. Tsaro is another ally whom Mr. Voysey has brought to his aid. It is the redoubtable Mr. Leonard, whose history of the Brahmo Somaj is distinguished by its two great features of unreliableness and partiality. Mr. Voysey calls this history "interesting and impartial." So let the interesting triad we have named, aided by Mr. Ganesha Leonard, go on in their interesting work of demolishing Mr. Sen. The cry which they have raised is the most interesting of all. It is not "down with Keshub," but "Keshub is down already," and in this interesting fashion they go on sweetly anticipating an event which will never happen. As well might you remove the Himalayas! That would be as reasible as it would be to destroy the work of the Brahmo Somaj of India, to denounce the dispensation under which it works, to stop the floodgates of its energy and inspiration and to prevent the people of India from hearing the gospel of salvation. But Mr. Voysey says:—"Keshub Chunder Sen has no right to call himself either a Brahmo or a Theist." Query,—are we to accept Mr. Voysey as the model Brahmo or Theist? For long years, says the Theistic Quarterly Review,

While holding his present views and bitterly attacking Christianity, he professed himself to be a Christian minister, and a servant of the Christian Church of England, and even when forced by the strong arm of law to vacate the post he could not conscientiously hold, he still maintained that to continue to belong to the ministry of the cardinal faith of which he had long renounced. If we mistake not, he still maintains this position. For such a man, to declare that Jesus Christ was either a lunatic or an impostor is really startling. It is the result of that extreme reaction which is sure to follow the abnormal pressure that is put authoritatively upon the religious consciousness of the rising generation in Christian countries. We are deeply grieved at the spectacle. We should like very much to know if many, in Mr. Voysey's congregation, who, we hear, are lately falling off, have the same notion of Christ's character. We are willing to be warned not to

"betray our holy cause," and to take measures that our "personal communion with God is not imperilled." Heaven protect us from the sin of faithlessness, and from the blindness of soul. But we must, for our own part, entreat Mr. Vo ysey to introduce more religion, more spirituality, and less captious cavilling into his movement.

This is the man that calls upon us to overthrow our leader! Rather, some among us would probably say, let us throw ourselves headlong into the Ganges than fly to the arms of this quondam Christian for spiritual guidance and help. It would be an evil day for Indian were the latter contingency ever to happen. But our readers may feel themselves secure. Our cause has nothing to fear, so long as the only weapons in the hands of our opponents are abuse and villification. We have not hesitated to reproduce Mr. Voysey's lecture in these columns, for we know we can do so with perfect confidence and safety; and we are ready to publish whatever he has to say in future against us. Let the beautiful triad go on in their amiable career of vilifying; let them rend heaven and earth with their tirades, expose all our defects and errors, preach as much of rationalism as is possible, exhaust their quiver of logic, fire away all their rhetoric, and cry themselves hoarse with invectives. Not a hair of our head, we assure them, will be touched. The Brahmo Somaj of India will remain as unspotted and unharmed as ever.

CHRISTIANITY AND RAM MOHUN ROY.

A NEW light has dawned upon the intellectual horizon of India. Mr. H. G. Keene, late Judge of Agra, has begun to hold forth on the uselessness of religion as the means of regenerating the country and the importance of science in its reference to the future destinies of the people. Discarding the law and prophets, he is not averse to assuming the prophetic role himself, and some of his predictions are not only startling, but serve to illustrate the wonderful elasticity of minds which, freed from the bondage of belief, love to soar through regions unapproachable by the believer and arrive at generalisations transcending the bounds of credulity. Mr. Keene is not a Christian; he is not a theist. In fact, he loves to decry both. His hostility to our movement is intense, and it is in reference to this that we wish to speak a few words. We shall not argue with Mr. Keene, for we confess we are unable to reach the intellectual height of that gentleman. But we may safely descant upon the power of immense generalisation enjoyed by men of the scientific or materialistic school. We have more than once dwelt upon this favorite trait of speculative science. Mr. Keene, who believes in the scientific method, carries this to an extent which strikes us dumb. He is of opinion that Christianity is not fit to mould the character of the Hindus, and supports it by a reference to its effects on the higher classes. We may premise by observing that we are not Christians, and hence our opinions have no likelihood of being called one-sided. Mr. Keene illustrates the effects of Christianity as embodied in the life of Rajah Ram Mohan Roy, and invites attention to his case as "worth the study of the friends of Christian missions, as a hint of the effect their operations are calculated to produce upon the higher Asiatic natures," it being, he says, "far easier to unsettle such minds and render them permanently weak and anxious, than it is to give them any abiding assurance of the unverifiable." Our readers have here a foretaste of the sort of charge which Mr. Keene will lay at the doors of Christianity and the Hindu mind in general. The countrymen of Rajah Ram Mohun Roy are told to believe that Christianity was the means of killing him. The authority of the writer is Miss Harriet Martineau, and we confess that after reading Miss Martineau and Mr. Keene, our estimate of both is much affected. The following passage is now to many **admirers** of the late Rajah :—

Of the **difficulties that** exist **some idea** may be suggested **by the** story of Ram Mohan Roy thus pathetically summarized in Miss Martineau's *History of the Peace* (Book IV., Chap. X) :—"He became a Christian, and gloried till he came to England in the liberty and liberality secured, as he believed, by that faith. He learned the languages necessary for studying the Scriptures in the original and from them he directly derived his views of the comprehension, charity, and fundamental freedom of the Christian religion. He arrived in England in 1831, to watch over the reconstruction of the Company's Charter. The impressible Hindu was sufficiently excited by the merely political movements of the time; but its religious conflicts affected him much more deeply. He could not recognise the Christianity he had learned, and so dearly loved amidst the profanations of the Trinitarian and the fanaticism of the Evangelicals, and the wrath of the Irish Protestants, and the tumult of the Irish Catholics, and the contests between **the** Church and the Dissenters, and the **widening split** in the Scottish Church, and the **profane antics** of the Irvingites. He went to hear all within his reach, he poured out his wondered sorrow at what he saw, and he wasted day by day. A sickly man, not concealed by the dark skin, settled on his cheek ; the hair round the turban became thin and lank ; ... the **cheerful** voice grew listless and hoarse ; the light of the eye went out. . . . he sank at the **first touch** of illness."

Rajah Ram Mohun Roy has many biographers. Among the Brahmos there are still many who are anxiously collecting materials for his life. We ourselves have read much of the eminent deceased. But nowhere except in Miss Martineau's book have we seen or heard of any mention of Christianity as the primary cause of the Rajah's death. Ram Mohun Roy died from natural causes. His last illness is minutely described by Miss Carpenter, and not even his most intimate friend speaks of Christianity as the remotest cause of his death. Fruitful as was Miss Martineau's intellect, her imagination seemed to be more fruitful still. We hear from her that Ram Mohun Roy "became a Christian," whereas it is well known that he was the means of converting to his theistic faith a well-known Christian of his day. Mr. Keene lays much stress upon this imaginary and fictitious account given by Miss Martineau, and proves that Christianity rendered Ram Mohun Roy "permanently weak and anxious." Weak, does he **say** ? Was a stronger Hindu ever born in the present century? A scholar of scholars, a debater and controversialist of the most **earnest** type, Ram Mohun Roy fought against a host of adversaries. He had to struggle with the whole generation of his countrymen on the one hand, and Christian Missionaries on the other. His works on the Shastras and his controversies with Christians are still the objects of admiration. Who has **read his** "Appeals" without being impressed with the force, **energy** and power of the giant intellect that produced them ? Nor was he an expert in theological warfare alone. In politics he shone resplendently above his countrymen. Much as we admire his political talents and insight of later-day geniuses like Harish Chunder Mukerji, Ram Gopal Ghose and Maharajah Roma Nath Tagore, we think that before Ram Mohun Roy our greatest luminaries pale

away as lamps before the sunlight. The evidence he gave before the Parliamentary Committee was a masterpiece of political learning and foresight. To young politicians of these days, we recommend Ram Mohun Roy's works as a safe guide. In matters educational his views were far beyond his times. It would be enough to say that his strong intellect clearly perceived the importance of English education, and he wrote a paper on this subject (see Babu Peary Chand Mitra's *Life* of David Hare) which anticipated all the main arguments of Lord Macaulay. It is not possible to do justice to the gifts and powers of this wonderful man. As a scholar, linguist, theologian, educationist and politician, his name stands unrivalled among his countrymen. At any rate, India has not produced a man of his comprehensive intellect, broad views and singular sagacity. When we add to these the fact that he was a reformer, that he had to wage a perpetual war against the superstitions and prejudices of his countrymen, that he was persecuted beyond conception, that he trampled down opposition and triumphed in the end, we shall have done enough to prove that whatever might be his other faults, he was not "weak." Mr. Keene may be supremely anxious to strengthen his position by citing the case of the strongest man of India ; but his love of generalization has betrayed him, and instead of proving that religion weakens men, he has only proved that his own powers of reasoning and his own knowledge of India are weak beyond conception.

Brahmo Somaj.

There will be some delay in our Missionary party starting for the upper Provinces. The singing Missionary is ill, and, besides, many of our Mofussil friends have come to Calcutta to enjoy the holidays.

The gathering at the open-air meeting on Tuesday last numbered from five hundred to seven hundred young men—most of them students. The minister descanted on the topic previously announced, namely, "Is it true that God exists?" Man, he said, may be an atheist; but the best theist in the world is his own body. Every limb, muscle and artery attested the power of God. The tongue may speak otherwise, but every throb of the heart declared His existence.

Devotional.

I wish I could be oftener with Thee, O God of my heart, in the inner sanctuary, and enjoy Thy words and Thy company in solitude. But I seldom have leisure, or what I would I cannot do. Hast thou really no leisure? That cannot be, Thou dost not possess that passionate attachment and love for me which alone can find or make leisure. Solitary communion they only seek who love me intensely.

So it is, Lord. Had I loved Thee truly I would have found time to come to Thee often and place my weary head upon Thy lap.

Well, what it is that brings thee here?

Lord, I wish to spend my holiday with Thee quietly. I have no other object in view. Men always go to their friends whenever they get a holiday. Having no better friend on earth I have called on Thee, desiring to spend my leisure hours with Thee in pleasant and profitable conversation.

Come then, draw near to me, and let me know what thou desirest to hear from me.

I wish to know, Father, whether people are right in calling me a Christian ? Am I a Christian ? Dost Thou wish me to be a Christian ?

Thou art neither do I wish thee to be a Christian. Art I a Hindu ?

Child, thou art not, nor do I wish thee to be a Hindu.

If I am neither a Christian nor a Hindu, I am a Brahmo then. But they will not admit it.

Neither art thou a Brahmo, in the popular acceptation of that term.

What then will I tell **people** that I am, that they may understand my creed fully and never misrepresent it ?

Say thou art a man of **faith**. As for people forming correct ideas of **your** religion, that is simply hopeless. Who ever comprehended the man of faith ? Theology you might explain, but faith never.

But many around me seem to understand my views, and regard me as one of their body.

Because they do not see all that is in thee. Thou speakest in favor of Christianity, and men take you for a Christian, and of Hinduism and they look upon you as a Hindu. Thou art very like a Brahmo or Indian Theist, and there around thee put thy name down in the **Brahmo** register. But I know, for I am omniscient, what is within thee. Thou art none of those, Nor is thy faith fully formed yet. Like men of faith thou art ever growing. Those who knew thee yesterday know thee not to-day.

Is it for this reason that I am so much misrepresented, and I am no imposter?

Yes. There is no language **that** can represent faith. No dictionary can help thee. When thou talkest of vision and the visible yet invisible spirit of Christ speaking to thee from his veranda, of David and Narad Muni lending thee the sacred harp, of thy travels in the celestial country, of thy immersion in the ocean of love, thou art unintelligible and those who hear thee can hardly comprehend thy meaning. Therefore be prepared for unpopularity. Do not barter thy heavenly faith for popularity. All may desert thee. Yet must thou stick to thy faith to the end.

Correspondence.

[*We do not hold ourselves in any way responsible for the opinions of our correspondents.*—Ed., I. M.]

THE OPEN-AIR MEETING AT COLLEGE SQUARE.

TO THE EDITOR OF THE "INDIAN MIRROR."

Sir,—There was quite a scene—a picture, a moral picture indeed—during the proceedings of the open-air gathering at College Square on last Tuesday evening, which deserves to be preserved and cherished in the heart of every true believer, as something sweet and charming to contemplate. The perfect confidence, the burning enthusiasm, and the living faith, which shone forth on the countenance of the Theistic Apostle, who stood in the midst of the crowd, consisting mostly of educated young men ; and the eager, thoughtful, expectant looks of the audience, ready to catch every word that fell from his lips, and to weigh every argument brought forward; the dead silence that reigned round; the coolness of the atmosphere; the blue canopy of the heavens above, and Nature's green carpet below :—all, all these together could not fail to produce a sort of picture before the mental vision of those present there, who had a natural taste for the appreciation of such a scene. It forcibly reminded me of a picture—"St. Paul at Athens,"—which I had once seen and in which St. Paul was represented as preaching to the Athenians, with his long flowing dress, pointing his finger towards the heavens. The oration over, some of them began *santirtan*, and slowly moved round the Square, with flags in their hands, the crowd following them with thoughtful countenances.

I am sure, Mr. Editor, the recurrence of such open-air addresses, followed by such *sankirtan*, will greatly tend to strengthen the faith of many, and create in them whose misfortune it is still to roam in the dark wilderness of carnality and worldliness.

Yours &c.,
A BELIEVER.

The 16th October 1879.

PRAYERS FOR PHYSICAL GOOD.

TO THE EDITOR OF THE "INDIAN MIRROR."

Sir,—I have been hearing your protests against " Prayers for Physical Good" these seven years—the last as per your number of September 14th. Your arguments, it seems to me, are at best but plausible, as nature is not on your side, and by turning my mental eye towards my inner self, I find that few Brahmos will be able to carry your advice into practice. Directly and indirectly you call in question the wisdom of the Archbishop of Canterbury for ordering a "prayer for fine weather;" of our Queen mother Victoria for praying, along with her subjects, for the recovery of her first-born, H. R. H. the Prince of Wales; and of good Jesus for saying to God Almighty, "give us this day our daily bread." I need hardly say that I am one of those that do pray for physical good—for health, wealth, and prosperity, as well as for spiritual blessings. How can I do otherwise? God to me is the best Friend, an indulgent Father, and a kind Patron. I not only see Him in history and believe in special Providence, but also see the Divine finger in innumerable events of my by no means uneventful life. I do not, for a moment, suffer dry intellectualism to stand in the way of my asking the Giver of all gifts for any thing for which I would not be ashamed of asking, say my parents, friends and patrons; say what you will, it is not in human nature not to pray to the kind Disposer of events for safety when, during the overflowing of the mighty Padma, your boat, containing yourself and your dear wife and children, is suddenly overtaken by a storm, and you are about to be launched into eternity with all those near and dear to you. The writer of these lines has been almost confined to bed with an attack of a fell disease these thirteen months; and at times I am almost instinctively led, in spite of your views, to pray in much the following strain:—"Restore to me, God Almighty, my wonted health. I want to live not only for myself but also for others." Shall I tell you that, in some, if not in all, instances my Heavenly Father has granted my prayers? Yes, we all pray for spiritual progress; but if analyzed, is not an instinctive desire to depend upon an Infinite Spirit one of its ingredients? If so, ought you not to pray for the development of, so to express myself, this sentiment of dependance upon God? But your arguments, when carried to their legitimate conclusion, would be tantamount to the heartless utterance:—"In prayer, thus far shalt thou go, and no farther." In fact, if your opinion be followed in practice, the development of the *Nirbhaver Bhab* would almost be out of the question. Perhaps, Sir, I have not been able to give articulate expression to the ground on which some of us pray for physical good; but in our heart of hearts we know that we commit no sin when, disdaining to leap out of that human nature which has been created by the Moral Governor of the Universe, we cry and fall at our Father's feet and ask for temporal as well as spiritual happiness with child-like simplicity. If, owing to extraordinary drought, our dear country should (which God forbid!) any year become as parched and dry as it was during the *Chhiattorer Manwanter* (famine of 1176 B. S., 1770 A. D.), we will pray for rain—abundance of rain in spite of our knowledge that it will, especially in the epidemic districts, make the subsoil so damp as to render it a hot-bed of malarious fever. I have somewhere read in a work on Moral Science, probably in Wayland or Fleming, that, constituted as human nature is, we cannot but pray for physical good; and that it is God's look-out to grant what prayer He should grant, and what He should not. The subject relating, as it does, to a deep spiritual truth, certainly requires to be examined from many standpoints.

Yours &c.,
MOFUSSIL INDIAN THEIST.

LAST WORDS.

TO THE EDITOR OF THE "INDIAN MIRROR."

SIR,—I feel compelled to say that, after Dr. Tyssen's last letter, I cannot consent to enter into any further discussion with him on sacred subjects. His ideas and mine evidently differ as to what is seemly in such matters. He speaks of the first disciples of Christ in a way that reminds me of Tom Paine. Such expressions as "spouting" and what follows, belong to an age when controversy was of a coarser nature than is (happily) usual now-a-days.

In justice, however, to myself, I must say that he very incorrectly speaks of my attempting to take advantage of your readers' ignorance of Greek, by my reference to St. John x. 30. I referred to the Greek original to prove that Christ did not speak of Himself as "one *person* with the Father"—to prove that, and nothing else. My words were, "not one person—the original will not bear that"—and this is all that I asserted as proved by the Greek original. Dr. Tyssen says, "Now let me distinctly say, the Greek words correspond exactly to the English ones." How can this be true? The Greek original runs thus: "I and the Father are one." The English runs: "I and my Father are one." In the latter, the word 'one' might be masculine; in the former, it cannot. The English word—*and this is the point*—is not necessarily neuter; the Greek is.

This may easily be made clear. In Gal. III 28 the English translation runs thus, "Ye are all one in Christ Jesus."

In the Greek, the word 'one' is masculine. In St. John x. 30 the Greek word is neuter. Yet both are translated by the same English word. This is proof positive that the Greek word connotes more than the English word.

Dr. T. refers to St. John XVII. by way of showing that when our Lord said (if He did say which Dr. T. does not admit) "I and the Father are one," He spoke only of unity of purpose and will, and not of oneness of nature. It is the old Socinian argument. Let us see what it is worth. Our Lord in St. John XVII. prays that men may be one 'in Him,' as He and the Father are one. Now clearly this includes unity of nature. Men have all one nature, and if they had not, they could not by further spiritual union be perfectly one. Thus, the Father and His Son are one by nature and one in Spirit; and our Lord prays that men may likewise be one with each other. They *are* one in nature; they only need now to be one in spirit. God grant that you, Sir, and your readers, and my unworthy self may do nothing to hinder this perfect union of nature and spirit!

And now to sum up. A friend of mine one day pointed out to me a statement of Dr. Tyssen's in your paper, which he made in controverting the Town Hall lecture, and which was calculated to mislead your readers. I asked this friend to reply. But as he did not do so, I did it myself. I pointed out that scholarship could not be said to have decided that the Fourth Gospel was not written until more than a century after the death of Jesus.

Dr. T. also asserted that the words quoted by your Minister in his Town Hall lecture do not harmonize with the character of Christ. I assumed that your correspondent derived his ideas of the character of Christ from the three first Gospels. In this I was mistaken. But assuming this, I pointed out that Jesus Christ stands alone in the following respects.

He, alone of men, though so often teaching about sin, though so often rebuking others, owned to no consciousness of sin in Himself. Other men, in proportion as they come nearer and nearer to God, discern their own sinfulness more clearly. He, though obviously living so close to God, never admitted sin as having any power over Himself. This is a phenomenon which raises a question. Who, then, was He? Was He merely man?

Then, farther, He emphatically, repeatedly, and publicly announced that, whilst judgment is ever going on, a period is coming when He will Himself appear in person to wind up all judgment, and distribute rewards and punishments to the whole race of mankind, past, present, and future. This, again, raises a question. Could He be *only* man? Once more. He again and again revealed Himself as standing in a relation to the Father, which was felt to be pure and utter blasphemy if He were merely man. He revealed Himself as the long expected Avatar, of which there had been many a guess, many an anticipation, many a forgery. He was the true and only real Avatar. But He was not the Father. He was of one nature with the Father; He was the Son. The Father was *eternally* the Father, and therefore in the one God, the Son ever was. For what is a Father without a Son of the same nature as Himself? A most incomplete being. Therefore, as the Father is eternal, so is His Son eternal. And Jesus not only was the Son, but He told us so. For the assertion of this truth He eventually died. "By our law", said the Jews, "he ought to die, because he made himself the Son of God." They were right, if He was only man.

But they, or many of them, as they thought of that holy and beneficent life, as they thought of that meek, long-suffering majesty, that indescribable manifestation of more than human love, came to feel that in the chief saying of His life, in the truth for which He died, He could not have really erred. They had to chose between the worst possible imposture, or entire truthfulness. They found out on reflection that they had, indeed, been rejecting the Son of God, the true Avatar, and that in coming to Him, men really came to the Father, because He and the Father were one—not one person, the original will not bear that—but one in substance, essence, nature. For these Jews, then, thus convinced and converted, the new people of God, St. Matthew wrote his Gospel, and from the Gospels of St. Matthew, St. Mark and St. Luke, I showed the wonderful character of Christ in respect of the declaration He made concerning Himself as the true Avatar.

Of course, if any one can bring himself to deny the authenticity of the three first Gospels, except where they fall in with his own preconceived ideas as to what Jesus ought to have said and done, it would be useless to argue as I have done. But I believe there are many amongst your readers, who are not prepared for such thorough-going unbelief. Dr. Tyssen is. I think, therefore, that your paper would hardly be the best place for pursuing the discussion.

Besides, I must sorrowfully repeat that in the expressions to which I have alluded above, Dr. T. shows that his ideas and mine widely differ as to what is courteous in such matters.

A word in conclusion. What I have written I have written in love towards your readers. I abhor controversy. But controversy is one thing, the communication of truth is another. If we love one another, we must eagerly desire to impart to others the truth which has been blessed to our own souls. I cannot doubt that there are truth-seeking, truth-loving souls amongst the Brahmos, in spite of the bad character which your Minister gives some of them in one of his meditations. We have, therefore, naturally been drawn together. I am only sorry that circumstances compel me to give up the idea, at any rate for the present, of continuing the series of letters I began on the grounds of Theism. I hope, however, to deal with the subject on my proposed return to Calcutta in November, when I look forward to the pleasure of meeting some at least of your readers.

Yours &c.,
LUKE RIVINGTON.

Indore, October 1879.

Literary and Scientific.

IT has been recently stated as a curious fact that the three great rulers of the world: Alexander Cæsar, and Napoleon, were all beardless men.

WE understand that Mr. John Dennis, author of *Studies in English Literature*, has a work in preparation, to be entitled, *The Three Ages of English Poetry*.

"THERE was a man and woman, each weighing 100 lbs., and two boys, each weighing 50 lbs., that wished to cross a river in a skiff; but it would only hold 100 lbs., How did they get across?" This is another puzzle for our young readers.

ON Friday last, there was to have been a discussion of Mr. J. O. Halliwell Phillips's new argument for the date of *The Midsummer Night's Dream* not being earlier than 1596, at the opening meeting of the sixth session of the new Shakespere Society.

MESSRS. CASSELL, Petter, and Galpin will publish this month a life of the ex-Premier, Mr. Gladstone, in two volumes, by Mr. George Barnet Smith, whose critical essays are well known. It will be illustrated by two portraits, one from a picture by Joseph Severn in 1840, the other from a recent photograph.

A MISSIONARY canoe has lately been exploring the Tasmanian coasts, the canoeist choosing this method of reaching isolated families on Australian coasts and rivers to hold religious services and distribute books. The little craft, appropriately styled *Evangelist*, is thoroughly seaworthy, and admirably fitted up, though her length is only 12 feet, and the total weight, sails and fittings included, about 80lbs.

A TIDE-PREDICTING machine has been constructed for the Government of India by Messrs. Lege & Co., of London. Sir William Thomson, F. R. S., who has examined the machine believes that its use for Indian ports will, in the course of a few years, earn more than its cost in saving expenditure on the formation otherwise of tide tables and in the value of the greater completeness of the information which it will give.

AN American Journal states that a centenarian turtle has been caught on the Florida Coast. The aged creature bore marked on its shell the Spanish coat of arms and a Spanish inscription stating that it was caught in 1700 by Hernanda Goma in the *San Sebastian*, was carried to

Mantanza by Indians and thence to the great Wekiva (now the St. John's River). For the benefit of future generations the turtle was set at liberty, and returned to the St. John's River at Palatka, the date and place of his recapture being added to the history on its shell.

Messrs. Smith, Elder & Co. have lately published a work by Mr. Canning, entitled: *Philosophy of the Waverley Novels.* The purpose of this book is to point out how noble a spirit pervades the Waverley Novels—with what fairness and comprehensive sympathy Scott sketches the most opposite parties. The *Academy* remarks that it does not contain a thought beyond the reach of any soul of average intelligence, and admitting its purpose to point out, in short Scott's humanity, says: "but whether 300 pages are justifiably filled with his treatment of it may be seriously questioned."

A meeting was held in the middle of September last, in connection with the 'Trades' Union Congress in Edinburgh, to consider the question whether there is no practical remedy for "the present armed condition of Europe." The meeting very properly denounced the enormous armies of this age as "a disgrace to our boasted civilization, as largely instrumental in paralysing industry, as inimical to the best interests of the people, and dangerous to the peace of the world." It decided that a practical remedy is to be found, and that it consists in the establishment of an international tribunal for the settlement of disputes."

The *Academy* thus incidently notices the singular school of thought that has sprung up in Christendom and of which the Revd. Dr. James Martineau is one of the ablest champions: "The supporters of this new movement decline to identify themselves with any special form of belief, being strongly influenced by the teachings of modern science, though at the same time shrinking from the black abyss of simple materialism. The professors of this colorless Christianity are ready to accept anything so long as it does not partake of the nature of a definite statement. They have put their hands to the plough of free investigation, but they look back yearningly to the promises held out by orthodoxy."

The sacred hair of the prophet Mahomet's beard which has, for some months, been the subject of an exciting lawsuit at Madras has, at last, found a legal owner. The hair, which is enclosed in a case, and called the "Assaree Shareef," or sacred relic, and which carries with it much honor and a small pension, was claimed by six people; two claiming the treasure by right of a will, and the other by right of succession. Finally, three withdrew from the contest, and the judge has decided that the first claimant, being a woman, could not fulfil the necessary ceremonies connected with the heirloom, and that as the third claimant is the elder brother of number four, he shall guard the relic, perform the necessary ceremonies, and divide the surplus of the money with his two relatives.

ACKNOWLEDGMENT.

Proceedings of the Asiatic Society of Bengal. Edited by the Honorary Secretaries. No. VIII. August 1879. Calcutta: Baptist Mission Press.

Selections.

THE REV. MELLOR ON PRAYERS FOR FINE WEATHER.

Seeing that the whole Christian world prayed for fine weather, and that so many did it in such a matter-of-course undoubting way, it might sound rather presumptuous on his part to ask whether it was a wise or a right thing to do, and whether it was of any use. But he did ask that question, notwithstanding. He asked it calmly and deliberately and was prepared to give an answer to it. He honestly believed that praying for fair weather or for wet weather was foolish, wrong and useless. When they came fairly to look into the matter and asked the men who prayed for fair weather why they did it, they said that they did it, because they believed that the wet weather which we had been having had been sent as a punishment for national transgressions. In the first place, it was assumed that as individuals and as a nation they had been sinning against God, and, in the next place, it was also assumed that God assuredly punished sin. That we as a nation and as individuals had been committing sin against God as well as against man he for one could not doubt. But having got thus far in perfect agreement with them, he must now begin to disagree. In the first place, he held that all the real light that they had on that great subject tended to show that God punished men for their sins directly and in a straight line. Each sin carried with it its own punishment. If a man, for instance, put his finger into the fire he got burnt, and that was God's way of punishing him for his folly. God did not send the man a wet day to teach him that it was foolish and wrong to put his finger into the fire. The punishment came directly with the offence. So again, if a man took poison, there needed no potato disease to show him that he had broken the law of God, the poison itself showing him that by its own direct and normal action. So in the same way, if we, as a nation, were intemperate, sensual, and unjust, God would not punish us by blasting our crops, but rather by blasting our bodies and our minds, by degrading us in our own eyes and in the eyes of the world. Between sin and punishment, there was thus a close, natural, and logical connection, but between bad weather and bad conduct there was no such connection whatever. But, besides that General misconceptions, as to God's method of punishing sin, they who took the wet weather as a punishment for our sins as a nation and as a people committed themselves to all sorts of difficulties, and involved themselves in all sorts of dilemmas in applying their doctrines to actual facts. The very first condition of a just punishment was that it fell upon the guilty, and that the weight of the punishment was determined by the degree of the sin. But, if they took the wet weather as a punishment, it not only failed to meet that condition, it also quite reversed it. The very worst the rain could do would be to ensure a bad harvest, and pray, who would be the sufferers from that? Would their rulers, who had perpetrated the great weight of the iniquity to which he had referred? Most certainly not. A bad harvest in this country would hardly be felt by them at all, so that the chief sinners would escape the punishment altogether. Would the people at large suffer from a bad harvest? Well just a little, but only a little. It so happened that, while the harvest is sure to be bad in England, it was exceedingly good in America, Canada, and Italy. We should get our supplies thence, and be able to smile at the rain. Free trade would enable us to do that. Taking, then, the theory that the rain was a punishment for national sins, they had to face the fact that the punishment fell upon men, not in proportion to their guilt, but in proportion to their innocence. The most guilty escaped altogether; the next in guilt, got just a little of the penalty, while those who were almost innocent received its full weight. Anything more utterly dishonoring to human reason, and more out of harmony with worthy views of the Divine character than such a notion as that could not well be imagined. But he rejected the theory before them in the next place, because it involved an utter misconception as to the laws by which the weather was governed. He would be pronounced a madman, who should pray that the sun might not rise to-morrow; but what, if it were an equal proof of madness to ask God's to stop the rain? There was just as much law in the one case as in the other. Such, then, were his reasons for the answer which he had given to the question he had asked concerning prayers for fair weather. Such prayers involved an utter and serious misconception of God's general method of punishing sin, individual and national; they landed them into all sorts of peculiar difficulties with regard to the divine character and the principles of common justice, and they involved an utter misconception of the laws by which the weather was governed. For these reasons he characterised such prayers as useless, foolish and wrong. The laws, which brought about punishment for individual or national transgressions, were just as regular and just as inevitable as the laws which caused fire to burn and water to maintain its level. Let not the men, therefore, who were looking out for divine judgements be afraid lest those judgments would not come. In the exceedingly low moral tone of our public life in our utter inability to put faith in many of our public men, in our utter inability to justify our international deeds in the contempt and scorn which have been so freely poured upon our military doings in South Africa by France and by Germany, in the consciousness of the fact that we have been the defenders of tyranny and shame, in the ever-growing debt which we keep shifting about in utter confusion of face, in the inevitable reckoning day, in these things, which we cannot evade, and not in bad harvests, which we can evade, we must look for God's chastisement of our national iniquity. In that way they would come by a new path, and in a new light to the old Bible truth—"Be sure your sins will find you out." In that way, too, their piety might keep company with their knowledge, and theology and natural science might go hand in hand.

THE BRAHMO SOMAJ AND KESHUB CHUNDER SEN.

A Sermon Preached at the Langham Hall Sept. 7, 1879, by Rev. Charles Voysey.

1 John v. 21.—*Little children, keep yourselves from idols.*

I feel, in duty bound to invite your attention once more to the Brahmo Somaj, and to give you some information about its affairs and its relation to Keshub Chunder Sen which I have received since we last met in this place. I am well aware that this subject does not excite that universal interest which one could desire; but this fact seems to make it more necessary to bring the religious affairs of India oftener into notice. I venture to say that it is our duty to make ourselves acquainted as far as possible with the progress and difficulties of a Church in India which has for its essential principles and beliefs the very same which distinguish English Theists. We have as much to learn from this foreign experience as the Brahmo Somaj has to learn from ours, and possibly more, since the Brahmo Somaj is an organization of fifty years' standing, and is not in the least indebted to Christian influences; in fact, the only influence which Christianity has exerted upon it—and that has been very partial and limited—has been for evil and not for good.

But, quite apart from the intrinsic value of a knowledge of the present state of Brahmo Theists, a recurrence to this subject is a duty which I owe to Babu Keshub Chunder Sen and his supporters, and also to the great body of the Brahmo Somaj, whose confidence he has forfeited. My attack upon him in the sermon of the 8th June last, in reply to his lecture on the question "Who is Christ?" was a public attack, and has received still further publicity in India by the circulation of 1,000 copies, and by its being printed *in extenso* in the *Indian Mirror* of the 13th July.

It is obviously my duty to let you know what answer, if any, has been made by Keshub Chunder Sen, for it would appear ungenerous, if not cowardly, to suppress such a reply. You might also expect from me any information which I could furnish respecting the reception given to my sermon by the general body of the Brahmo Somaj, as that would be a most sure criterion of Keshub Chunder Sen's influence or lack of influence among them. These considerations, I trust, will be sufficient to conciliate that portion of my audience who may not care very much about the subject.

The reply of Keshub Chunder Sen himself filled me with astonishment. He says—

"Can it be, I ask myself, that I believe in the doctrines you have put into my mouth? It cannot be. I might as well believe I am not myself. Do you really think it possible that I can have even a grain of faith in such doctrines as the Deity of Jesus, his bodily resurrection, the sacrament, &c.? The very lecture you have so severely criticised contains evidence enough to prove that I set my

---

face against these popular conceptions of Christ's life and character. Rest assured, my friend, that I have not run astray from the purity and simplicity of the Faith I formerly professed."

On this statement I will only make the remark that, granting it to be the genuine expression of the writer's feeling, the writer of it must have used words in his lecture on Christ in a non-natural sense; that is to say, he used language about Christ identical with the language used not only by orthodox believers in general, but especially by orthodox and enthusiastic worshippers of Christ. I have read these passages again and again, and I do not know how it is possible to interpret them otherwise than literally. If Babu Keshub did not mean what he said, why did he say it? Why did he not say exactly what he meant? If mysticism be once admitted, then any words may mean anything. Moreover, if I have been mistaken in my interpretation of his language about Christ, how is it that the Brahmo Somaj at large have put the same interpretation upon it, and have denounced it as a clear but lamentable departure from the simplicity of their Theistic faith? How is it that the *Inquirer* also, the leading Unitarian organ, in commenting on Keshub Chunder's language about Christ, says, "If that is not an ardent avowal of discipleship, and sufficient to entitle anyone to be called a Christian, we know not what is." I will now read to you extracts from letters which I have received from two persons holding responsible office in the Brahmo Somaj. The first of these is from Raj Narain Bose, the venerable President of the Adi-Brahmo Somaj, which may be called the mother-church of all the Brahmo churches, since it was founded in 1844. Mr. Bose has been connected with the Brahmo Church for 33 years, and has not only been most active in the establishment of churches in various parts of India, but has done much to adorn the literature of the religious body to which he belongs. He writes as follows:—

"Allow me to express to you, on behalf of the members of the Adi-Brahmo Somaj, our high approbation of your sermon on Babu Keshub Chunder Sen's late lecture on Christ. It is characterized by true theistic boldness and independence of thought, and a warm desire to maintain the purity of Theism at all risks and hazards.

"The Adi-Brahmo Somaj has constantly protested against the Christian proclivities of Babu Keshub Chunder Sen. Some years ago, when Babu Debendranath Tagore, the chief Minister of the Adi-Brahmo Somaj and the Brahmo Somaj in general, was requested by Keshub Babu and his party to officiate on the occasion of the anniversary festival of the Brahmo Somaj, as minister at their *Mandir* or place of worship, he made certain remarks on these proclivities, and the recompense that he obtained for his salutory advice to Keshub about not introducing Christ into the pale of Brahmoism was a shower of vituperation poured on his devoted head by the journals of that party. . . .

"The organ of the Adi-Brahmo Somaj has frequently protested against these proclivities. In his lecture on 'Great Men' and that animadverted upon by yourself, as well as in other lectures, Babu Keshub Chunder Sen inculcates the doctrine of the incarnation and mediatorship of 'great men.' Brohmoism can never recognize such doctrines. It maintains that man is the son of God, and, as son, has direct access to the Father."

The second extract is from the pen of the Editor of Brahmo *Public Opinion*, a member of another branch called the *Sadharan Brahmo Somaj*, which was erected in revolt against Keshub Chunder Sen. Speaking of my sermon of the 8th June, the Editor writes:—

"We will try to circulate the lecture as much as we can, as it has our entire sympathy and the sympathy, we presume, of the large majority of Brahmos in India. We did not take any notice of Mr. Sen's lecture in our paper, because we know his utterances now do not command that respect and attention which they once did, and especially his ideas of Christ do not find any sympathy with Indian Brahmos.

"There are now comparatively very few Brahmos, who follow Mr. Sen's lead. There is not a bit of exaggeration in this, and we do not write this from any party spirit. We state this to you as a fact. Rightly or wrongly, the Brahmos here believe, with very few exceptions, that Mr. Sen's Brahmoism has degenerated much, and is not fit for this country in the present age. The doctrines of inspiration, asceticism, election, leader-ship, divinity of Christ, undue reverence for prophets, religious absolutism . . . have alienated the sympathies of the educated Indian Theists from Mr. Sen. . . .

"You will be glad to learn that for all the vagaries of Mr. Sen, the Theistic movement in India has not at all suffered. The Sadharan Brahmo Somaj is daily growing popular, and enlisting the sympathies of the educated Natives. We shall be always glad to hear from you and to assist you, to the best of our might, to propagate pure Theism in all parts of the globe."

Painful as is the defection of Keshub Chunder Sen, we are amply consoled by the foregoing testimony of the faithful integrity of the Theistic body at large.

In a very interesting and impartial history of the Brahmo Somaj, written by Mr. G. S. Leonard, still more formidable charges have been brought against Keshub Chunder and his followers, which ought not to be withheld from your knowledge.

His kinsman, Babu Protap Chunder Mozumdar, who once gave us a most excellent sermon in St. George's Hall, addressed an Indian congregation in the following terms:—

"Brethren, should you wish to be saved, come to Keshub's feet, and take shelter under them; there is no other way."

And in a letter from the same preacher to Keshub on his way to India he addresses him as the 'Saviour of Sinners.'

Again, a certain disciple addressed to Keshub the following prayer:—

"O merciful Lord, leave me not alone; save me before you depart, O God of a spiritual teacher! Remember this vile disciple when you are on the hills, and do as you will for his salvation. Lord! I am a great sinner; how shall I approach the throne of holiness? I feel myself incapable to pray to the Most High. Do, I beseech you, pray to your Father for me."

"And how," asks Mr. Leonard, "did Keshub Chunder receive this prayer? Was he startled at this strange mode of address? Did he reprove his disciple for his error? Did he take immediate steps for the removal from the minds of his converts of the wrong impression raised of his powers by preaching or any other method?" We are constrained to say that we have failed to find any proofs that he did. On the contrary, it was widely known that, on some of his disciples protesting against his connivance at such practices, he said, "I do not wish to obstruct the stream of *Bhakti*" (*i.e.*, blind faith).

This is not all. We again find him tamely accepting another prayer, made on behalf of the Brahmos of his own sect, wherein he has been raised to the dignity of a deity, and far above that of a mediator, as the following extract will show.

"If you have once allowed me to fling myself at your feet, you should for ever give me that right. It is the faith of my heart that from the feet of such a one as yourself I shall attain salvation.

"Again—

"The dust of your feet and of such a one as yourself is the only hope and consolation of this great sinner. Ever shall I place and worship your feet on my head, and you shall pray to thy Father on my behalf."

"These instances," adds Mr. Leonard, "will serve to show how Keshub-worship was fast gaining ground among the Brahmos of his sect in those days (about 1863), and how little was done to put a stop to it."*

I need make no further comment on this astounding revelation of fact beyond calling your attention to the parallel conduct of Jesus Christ as reported in the Gospels, and which has been claimed by the orthodox churches in all ages as a proof that he was more than man, that he was, in fact, a God incarnate.

Keshub Chunder Sen had been separated from the original Brahmo Church for seven years when the President Devendronath Tagore made an attempt to re-unite the two churches under a common agreement. This was never ratified, owing to the sermon preached by Devendronath condemning Keshub Chunder's leaning to Christianity and his belief in the Divine mission of Jesus Christ, and pointing out how incompatible this was with the dictates of Brahmoism which recognised but one supreme God. In that sermon, Debendronath exhorted his hearers to be either Christians or Brahmos, but not to attempt to reconcile the two systems of religion. This so offended Keshub Chunder that the breach between his own sect and the Adi-Brahmo-Somaj was widened and the two churches were severed for ever."

These facts seem to me of the utmost value, for I can well imagine that thousands of countrymen, at the time of Keshub Chunder Sen's visit to this country in 1870, were, like myself, under the entirely false impression that he was the representative of the Brahmo Somaj, whereas he was even then only at the head of a schismatical section of it which has been losing ground in both numbers and influence rapidly ever since.

There are those who openly attribute this great defection of Keshub Chunder to motives of personal ambition. I am not here to echo such a charge, or to pass judgment on the heart of a fellow-man who is not here to defend himself. "To his own Master he standeth or falleth." But we are more than permitted, we are in duty bound, to commend or to blame his avowed conduct, to form our judgment upon the consistency or inconsistency of his words and actions with those principles of the Brahmo religion which have been maintained in their purity and integrity by the great body of Brahmos for upwards of fifty years. And we say deliberately that inasmuch as those principles essentially agree with what we call Theism, Keshub Chunder Sen has no right to call himself either a Brahmo or a Theist. With the mildest interpretation of his language, we might possibly classify him with the Unitarians of the older school, if he be not in truth much more of an orthodox Christian. But Theist he is not, nor Brahmo, and we can wish nothing better for himself, for his credit as an honest man, and for the Brahmo Somaj likewise, than that he should renounce a name and title which no longer belong to him, and adopt a designation at once more accurate and straightforward.

And now, my friends, I would say a few words in conclusion to show how the subject before us has a practical bearing upon ourselves as religious people. It must not be forgotten that the tendency of the human mind has ever been in the direction of idolatry, of worshipping and loving the creature more than the Creator. Almost all the great religions of antiquity were started with a comparatively pure and simple belief in one only and supreme God; but they all more or less became corrupted through the weakness and want of faith in the human breast, through the tendency to crave for something lower, nearer to the level of man's own nature, more easily comprehended, and appealing more to the senses. We are told on the highest authority that India herself thus degenerated from the pure monotheism of her most ancient scriptures. The records of Buddhism also reveal an unvarnished idolatry for its noble founder, Sakhya-Muni.

The Hebrew Bible discloses on nearly every page the defection of Israel from the worship of Jehovah. The Christian religion is another example. If Jesus himself were ever, as some affirm, a pure Theist, and (as we may believe from some of his sayings) taught his disciples to worship the Father only, a very few years sufficed to corrupt his teaching and to introduce the idolatry of himself. Even Mahammed takes an undue place of supremacy, and shares semi-divine honors in the regard of his followers.

Among Unitarians, whose very name implies a protest against idolatory, we too often find language of devotion and adoration applied to Christ such as would be deemed by themselves idolatrous if applied to any other historical personage. The mere profession of a pure monotheism does not seem to be a sufficient safeguard against the insidious tendency to worship human beings.

This is a most grave and alarming fact; and we cannot hope to guard ourselves and posterity from the universal peril of idolatry, unless we understand clearly the weakness of human nature in which it takes its rise. In these few moments it would be impossible to deal satisfactorily with so great a problem. But two points force themselves upon our notice, which, perhaps, may sink more deeply into our minds if stated without amplification. The first of these is, that mere intellectual assent to the propositions, "There is but one living and true God," and "No man ever lived who is worthy of divine honors," cannot of itself screen us from the temptation to idolatry. However rational our creed may be, our religion must always be more a matter of the heart than of the head, must spring from our affections rather than from our reason. But if our religion consist only in intellectual assent to propositions, and not at all spring from our hearts' love for the living God, then on our emotional side we shall be exposed to the fascinations of lower objects, and be ever inclined to worship some human idol in place of God Himself. It is only the love of God that can keep his children from idolatry.

The second point is that, as I have elsewhere stated, true faith in God is not so easy, so spontaneous as many would have wished. It is hard to attain; it is difficult to maintain. Men have proved thousands of times over that it is far easier to trust in their fellow-men, in anything tangible or visible or comprehensible rather than in the unseen and incomprehensible God. And here lies their chief weakness; for a trust that is incomplete, often clouded, and always

* LEONARD'S *History of the Brahmo Somaj*, pp. 155-60.

tremulous does not satisfy the human soul, which will, therefore, seek and find some earthly prop on which it can rest without a doubt or fear. But this deficiency of trust in God is the sure parent of idolatry, and therefore, I urge upon you the solemn importance of cultivating within yourselves a more perfect and abiding confidence in Him who is your Father, who is far above all gods, and who alone is able and willing to fill the soul with perfect peace and bliss. If you have once found God to be your All in All, not merely a bright light shining upon your intellect, but a warm sun cheering and cherishing and kindling your hearts, you will regard it as infinitely childish to be making a pet idol of some fellow-creature, or to be taking for your ideal of Divine perfection a man who was dead and buried long ago, and whose very history is blurred over by blots and blemishes.

Infinitely childish? Yes, and but for that it would be infinitely impious to suppose that any human being, however perfect, however exalted, could yet even distantly approach to the image of Him whom our hearts adore as the Almighty Everlasting God. Never did blasphemous arrogance reach higher in its daring, or plunge deeper into the dark realms of untruth than when Christ said to Philip (in answer to his appeal, "Show us the Father and it sufficeth us"). Have I been so long with you and yet hast thou not known me, Philip ? He that hath seen me hath seen the Father ; and how sayest thou then, shew us the Father? "

Let us be warned. Those who begin by placing Christ in a category by himself are far on the road to placing him on the right hand of God ; and those who suffer themselves to introduce the name of Christ into their devotions, to sing hymns to him and in honor of him, who call him their Christ, their sweet Christ and Master and Lord, are not far from going the whole length of Christian perversion, and embracing the Catholic faith with its unvarnished polytheism. God grant that we may stand firm and strong in our faith in him, loving Him with all our hearts, and guarding His shrine in our souls with a jealous scrutiny against the sacrilegious approach of any human idol.

Advertisements.

PRIZE MEDALLISTS
For Excellency of Workmanship.

J. M. EDMOND & Co.,
27—28, BENTINCK STREET.
ESTABLISHED 1833.
Cabinet Makers, Upholsterers,
AND
Billiard Table Manufacturers,

HOUSES completely furnished. Furniture designed and made to order.

ESTIMATES given for all kinds of Artistic Furniture, Carpentering, Painting, Polishing, Guilding, and General Repairs, Marble Polished, Moulded, and Cleaned ; Picture Frames made.

J. M. EDMOND AND CO., in soliciting a continuance of public patronage, beg to say they have ready for sale specimens of Ebonized and Gold Oxford style of Fancy Chairs, and are prepared to execute orders for other Furnitures in the same style.

J. M. EDMOND & Co.'s New Show-Room is now replete with New Heraldic Style of Dining-room Chairs, and Rustic Chairs, Telescopic Dining Tables, with Patent Table Expanders. The Oxford Rustic style Drawing-room suite of original style and designed by native Artizans, artistic new design Chamber Services, Hall Furniture with Minton's tiles inserted. Folding Triplicate Mirrors and " Exhibition " Pier Table.   a-13

Apply to the Manager
FOR
Illustrated Price List,
AT 55, COLLEGE STREET.

Dr. Lazarus's Domestic Medicines

INFANTILE FEVER POWDER (for Fevers, Teething, &c.), ...4Rs. 1		4
TONIC ANTIPERIODIC PILLS (Invaluable in Intermittent Fevers, Ague and Spleen and diseases of a periodic character), ...	1	4
SPLEEN PILLS (has cured thousand of cases of enlarged spleen),...	1	4
RESTRINGENT MIXTURE (for Diarrhœa, Colic, Gripes, Cramps, &c.),	2	0
CHOLERA DROPS (most effectual if taken in time),	2	0
BALSAMIC EXPECTORANT DROPS (for Coughs, Colds, Hoarseness, Asthma, Pain in the Chest, Chronic Pleurisy, &c.),	1	8
FAMILY LAXATIVE, A safe, certain and useful purgative,	2	0
FAMILY APERIENT PILLS (mild, prompt and safe),	1	4
FAMILY ANTIBILIOUS PILLS (stronger than above),	1	4
FAMILY CARMINATIVE (Invaluable for Children),	2	0
FAMILY HAIR TONIC (unrivalled for producing growth of the Hair),	2	0
FAMILY EMBROCATION (for Sprains, Chronic Rheumatism, &c.),	1	8

The above are most strongly recommended to parents, guardians and others residing in Districts where medical aid is not available. Thousands of cases have been cured by their judicious use :

A printed pamphlet giving full instructions is wrapped round each bottle.

Prepared only by MESSRS. E. J. LAZARUS & Co., at the Medical Hall, Benares, from DR. LAZARUS'S original receipts and sold by all Medicine Venders.   a-27

159, DHURRUMTOLLAH STREET,

LATE ESAU BIN CURTIS' ARAB STABLES,

Richard A. Turnbull, M.R.C.V.S. Lon.,

LATE VETERINARY SURGEON TO THE FIRM OF
THOS. SMITH & CO.,

And Veterinary Surgeon and Manager to the late firm of
MESSRS. HUNTER & CO.,

BEGS to give notice to the Public of Calcutta and its suburbs, that he has opened the above premises as a Veterinary, Infirmary and Shoeing Forge, where all the most approved and scientific appliances, as employed in Europe, accessory to the treatment of animals, will be used. All domestic animals placed under his care for shoeing, or medical treatment, will be superintended, prescribed for, and treated by him personally, as occasion may require. He trusts, by strict attention to business and professional duties, to merit the same confidence and patronage which he received from both the European and Native Community, as when employed by the above-mentioned firms.

Horses Bought and Sold on Commission and thoroughly Broken in and Trained for Saddle and Harness, or Racing purposes.

The premises have been much improved and put in thorough order. The loose boxes are well ventilated and drained, and fitted with Iron Mangers, and are superior to any in Calcutta. The range of stalls have also been fitted with Iron Mangers, are all well-drained and ventilated, and the situation and position of the Stables render them most suitable as Racing quarters, or for the recovery of animals suffering from fever or inflammatory disorders.

A Register is kept of horses for disposal by private sale, and of parties requiring horses for match or other purposes. Gentlemen are solicitated to send their names for registration, and the description of horses they have for sale, or may require.   a-61

Makhun Lall Ghose,
No. 91, Radha Bazar, Calcutta.

BEGS to invite the attention of the public to several consignments of commercial and fancy stationery of all sorts, including account hooks of all sizes, made of handmade and machine-made paper, by steamers recently arrived, and which he is disposing of at moderate prices. He has been long in the trade, and presumes he has always afforded every satisfaction to the numerous merchants here who have constantly favored him whith orders. Mofussil orders accompanied with remittances shall be promptly attended to.   a-33

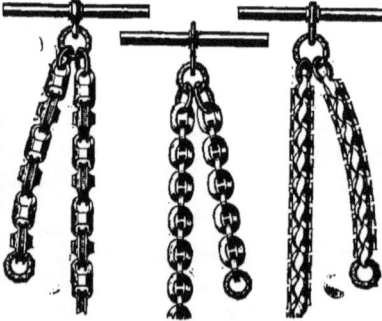

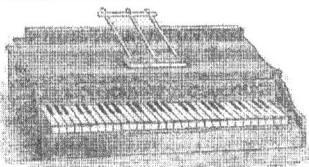

The Indian Mirror

EDITED BY KRISHNA BIHARI SEN, M. A.]

SUNDAY EDITION

[REGISTERED AT THE
GENERAL POST OFFICE

VOL. XIX.   CALCUTTA, SUNDAY OCTOBER 26, 1879.   NO. 255.

CONTENTS.

Telegraphic Intelligence.

FROM THE PRESS COMMISSIONER.

DECCAN RYOTS' RELIEF BILL.

SIMLA, 25TH OCTOBER.

The Deccan Ryots' Relief Bill was passed yesterday after five hours' debate. It operates on the 1st proximo. The Bill was much altered by the majority in Select Committee. Mr. Hope carried six amendments restoring substantially the original provisions regarding the exclusion of appeals in mortgage cases and of pleaders in cases up to 100 Rupees, conciliation for old decrees, examining defendant as witness and appointing special judge. Mr. Hope concluded by a long speech explaining parts of the Bill and certain omissions from it.

COLONEL FOLLEY.

SIMLA, 25TH OCTOBER.

Colonel Folley is expected at Bombay in the troopship *Crocodile* on or about the 27th October.

TELEGRAPH BETWEEN CAPE COLONY AND ZANZIBAR.

Telegraphic communication is now completed between the Cape and Zanzibar. A message dated the 15th October has been received by the Viceroy from the Governor of Capetown congratulating His Excellency on the advance of General Roberts. News up to 3rd October from India had reached Capetown.

REUTER'S TELEGRAMS.

RUSSIA AGAINST ENGLAND.

LONDON, 24TH OCTOBER.

The *Daily News* publishes a telegram from St. Petersburg, which states that Russia contemplates despatching two military expeditions next spring, one under General Kaufmann, consisting of 35,000 men from Turkistan, and another from the Caucasus, both expeditions to converge on Afghanistan, and assist the tribes against the English.

Editorial Notes.

IF the *Sheffield Independent* is to be believed, there is one clergyman in the neighbourhood of Sheffield who will not pray for the present Parliament. He says they are past praying for.

THERE was a service at the Positivist chapel, Holborn, to observe the anniversary of the death of Auguste Comte. In his address Dr. Richard Congreve dwelt on the nature of Positivism which, he said, although not making many converts now, was yet destined to become universally accepted at a later period of our civilization.

THE next President of the United States, according to the Paris papers, may possibly be a woman, as they are discussing the chances of Mrs. Victoria Woodhull for the Presidential chair. They treat the idea of her being put in nomination as perfectly serious, and represent her as having had great oratorical success in England.

ON Wednesday next the autumnal festival takes place, and our friends are invited to share the delights of the occasion. We remember vividly the pleasant boat excursion we had last year, and we trust our friends will muster in larger numbers this year. There will be Divine Service in the Brahma Mandir at 7-30 A. M. The boats, after being duly decorated with flags and evergreens, are expected to start at midday from Barrabazar Ghat.

FROM the fifty-sixth annual report of the Berlin Society for the Promotion of Christianity among the Jews, it appears that the total number of the Hebrew race to-day is about what it was in the days of King David—between 6,000,000 and 7,000,000. Of these, 5,000,000 are in Europe, 1,500,000 in America, 200,000 in Asia, and 80,000 in Africa. The majority of the African Jews live in the province of Algiers. But they are to be found in Abyssinia, and all along the north coast, and even in the Saharan cases. Of the Asiatic Jews 20,000 are assigned to India and 25,000 to Palestine.

THE theology of the New York *Independent* commends itself to us in many ways. In its issue of the 18th September it maintains what we have often said that the enemies of a particular religion are not men of other sects, but those who undermine our faith in God. Our contemporary says :—"Those that believe in God who rules us and are trying to learn his will and obey it, are comrades and friends. We may believe more than they, but we have little quarrel with them. Our quarrel is with our foes ; with Materialists and Atheists, not with Theists and Christians. Let us close up the ranks, join hands, and move forward."

A SOCIETY has been formed called the "Fellowship of Animals' Friends," the object of which is "to promote co-operation and sympathy amongst persons of all ages and classes who desire to act kindly and conscientiously towards all animals." This object is to be sought by the diffusion of right sentiments in respect to the matter, and by forming "fellowships" throughout the country consisting of persons who have taken and signed the following pledge :—"I promise to be kind to all the animals within my reach, and to protect them, as far as I can, from cruelty and ill-usage." The president of this new society is the Earl of Shaftesbury, and the Executive Committee includes in its list among others the names of Lord Ashley, the Rev. Baldwin Brown the Rev. W. H. Channing, Miss Mondella, and the Hon. Mrs. Cowper Temple.

BISHOP COLENSO's attitude in connection with the Zulu business is one that extorts respect and admiration from every body. In the course of a letter to the Aborigines' Protection Society he says:—

It is perfectly plain that Sir Bartle Frere and Lord Chelmsford never wished to make peace, nor meant to do so till by some bloody stroke they had "wiped off" the disgrace of Isandhlwana. And when I see how Lord Chelmsford can take to himself glory from the last butchery of Ulundi as " the beginning of the end of this campaign," and can even ascribe it to the Divine interference on his behalf in answer to prayer (" I have felt throughout the campaign that I have been sustained by your prayers, and also those of the people at home "—" and my success which has attended my efforts I feel, whether it is generally acknowledged or not, is due to the prayers of the people and the kindly ordinations of Divine Providence, for I am one of those who believe firmly and implicitly in the efficacy of prayer and in the intervention of Providence")—the language appears to be shockingly presumptuous in presence of the actual facts of the war, its cruelty and dishonest initiation, its terrible disasters and loss of precious lives on our side, its awful massacre of 10,000 brave Zulus fighting for their King, and fatherland against the deadly weapons of their invaders, not to speak of the prayers of so many mothers, wives and children of the dead, and the very great uncertainty as to what shall yet be the end of this miserable conflict, in which surely no true Englishman can find any comfort or glory, as far as matters have yet gone.

FOR the information of our readers we give the following particulars of the Salvation Army, noticed in these columns sometime ago. Mrs. Booth, the wife of the now famous "General" of the Salvation Army, lately delivered a lecture at Glasgow in which she explained that as aggressive Christians, their efforts were directed chiefly to the lower class of the population, and those at the head of affairs had acted on the principle that novelty is better than stagnation. They had accordingly used every means in their power, such as the "Hallelujah Lasses," converted thieves and ruffians of every description, to attract attendance from the slums. The extraordinary expedients adopted drew the very lowest to their meetings. They went for a time from motives of curiosity, but at last God got His hook in their jaws, and they were then obliged to attend. The Army consisted of 120 corps, with 190 officers. They had 3,250 speakers, who were ready to preach under any circumstances and at any risk. They had 113 theatres, music halls, and warehouses where they held annually 50,000 meetings. Besides these, there were 40,000 open air meetings, at which over 2,000,000 people were obliged to hear some thing of the gospel. Their income was £20,000 yearly, £14,000 being subscribed by the people.

The German illustrated journal, *By Land and Sea*, gives the biography of a religious inquirer for truth, who considered that the best way to make one's self acquainted with any other religion than that in which he had been educated, was to adopt that religion and join the sect which professed it. Mr. Aaron Rosenheim was born a Jew, but wishing to become acquainted with Protestantism, he subscribed the Augsburg Confession, got himself baptised, and showed his earnestness in the new faith in frequent conversations with the pastor. On travelling to Switzerland he adopted the Calvinistic faith at Geneva, and became much interested in the study of Predestination. He saw that every religion afforded comfort to its professors, and he wished to try the value of each. After three years he became a Roman Catholic; but while living at Klausenburg, political circumstances drove him to join the Greek Church, and on making a valuable present to the sanctuary he was baptised a third time in 1860. But removing from thence to Varna, he solemnly embraced the faith of Islam. After a time he removed to Czernowitz and availed himself of the newly enacted law, and declared himself of no religion. The biographer of Mr. Aaron Arthur Frederick Rosenheim, says *Christian Life*, has omitted to tell us in which profession his hero found most religious comfort.

———:o———

The true nature and scope of asceticism is very often misunderstood. An ascetic is believed to be a gloomy, discontented man who, finding the world too strong a place to live in, finds safety in flying to the wilderness. Or he is a man who willingly imposes physical restraints upon himself, refusing to accept the comforts of the world and seeking to correct the soul by mortifying the body. Well, a rational view of asceticism has yet to be distinctly preached. We know it was preached by Christ. Now so far as we understand it, we think asceticism embodies in itself the precept, Be poor in spirit. The usual appliances of this method, as understood by the world, are in their nature artificial. A man wishes to be religious, and he forthwith puts himself in sackcloth and ashes, applies the lash to his back and tries to be physically incapable of the pleasures of the world. This we call artificial, and its effects are usually not those sought for. The flesh is not conquered, and the will to sin may become as strong as ever. It is as much as to say that a man can become happy by drinking a bottle of intoxicating liquor. In both cases the expected results do not come. Asceticism must be natural, and its mode is to be content with every situation of life in which God places us. A prince surrounded by the pomp and circumstances of royalty may become an ascetic in his own palace as much as a peasant while driving his humble plough or putting up in his humbler cottage. It would be a sin to say that wealth and prosperity are obstacles in the way of righteousness. If they are obstacles, why has God sent them to the world? It is not a man's fault that, though not wanting riches, he has been made rich. All that is necessary for the purposes of religion is that he should be as indifferent to wealth as to poverty, and that in the midst of the greatest affluence he should remain poor and be prepared to embrace the beggar's lot if God wishes to send it to him. Be poor in spirit—in prosperity as well as in adversity. That is the precept of true religion.

———:o———

We are glad to know that the Brahmo Somaj has adopted a systematic method of appealing to the people. An expedition has been got up which will visit various localities and by preachings, prayers and pamphlets try to influence men's hearts and persuade them to think of God. The first effort in the direction was made in Calcutta on Tuesday, the 14th instant, when our minister delivered an open-air address in College Square before a large number of young men of our colleges and schools. The subject was a simple one—"Is it true that God exists? A report of it—a very brief and imperfect one—will be found elsewhere. On Thursday last there was another open air address at Howrah on the open space in front of St. Thomas' School. It happened to be a rainy day, and at the time announced for the lecture it rained heavily. Nevertheless, the meeting was held, and some two hundred people stood together on the wet ground attentively hearing the minister's words on the existence of God. We hope to be able to publish a substance of this speech in another issue. The minister stood on a wooden platform and held in his hand a plant. He said that every man resembled a plant. We could see the stem, the branches, the leaves, the flowers and the fruits; but if we wished to see the root, we must go beneath and see it under ground. So there was the human frame, with its beautiful ornaments and appendages, the eye, the ear, the nose, the hair, the hands and legs. If we ask who or what is the root of all these, the answer must be that we should go within and there find in every energy the hand and direction of God. God, like the root, is invisible to the eye and must be sought for under the surface. Thus there was a beautiful unity under so much diversity. The trunk, the branches, &c., all have the same root. In the same root, therefore, we shall find the unity of all faiths, all scriptures and all prophets. It is there that the Vedas, the Puranas, the Hindus, and the Musulmans meet together and find their unity. In this strain the speaker went on for about three quarters of an hour exhorting his audience to believe in God. The speech was followed by *Sankirtan*, after which the meeting broke up. The expedition started for Nychatty yesterday. In this way a number of places in the Mofussil will be brought within the pale of our work. How long the expedition will continue is not settled. It will depend upon the funds collected for the purpose. But we think it will be useful to concentrate the energies round a limited sphere every time, since a large attempt over a wider surface will be sure to disperse and weaken the strength which, if concentrated, would be greatly effective.

———:o———

A sort of triangular combination is sought to be effected against the Brahmo Somaj of India. The apex of the triangle is in London and the base is in Calcutta. The protesting party forming one point of the base wishes to join itself by a straight line to the other point known as the Adi Somaj, while both are sending forth straight lines to meet Mr. Voysey in London. We have alluded to this coalition elsewhere. In the meantime, it will be interesting to know how or by what means the two points at the base are trying to meet each other. The protest party, recognising for a moment the just charge that its spirit is too un-Hindu, has passed a resolution to the effect that its modes should henceforth be more national, and this resolution it has communicated to the Adi Brahmo Somaj. Babu Raj Narain Bose has answered the communication in a tone beautifully simple and unsuspecting:—

I am led to think that you should not content yourselves with merely recording a resolution that you should adopt a national mode of propagation, but should try to reduce it to practice in every possible form. You should adopt a national form of Divine worship, a national Theistic textbook, and a national ritual as far as all this could be done consistently with the dictates of conscience. You should renounce marked foreign customs and manners that you might have, without much thought or reflection, but innocently adopted from Europeans, but which are repugnant to the general feeling of the nation, and by renouncing which we do not act against Brahmoism. * * *

You should conduct your reformatory movements in a national way, so as to suit the tastes and ideas of the nation without compromising your Brahmo principles. The *Sadharan Brahmo Somaj* would, therefore, do well to adopt the form of worship, the Theistic Text-Book (Brahmo Dharma Grantha), the ritual, in short, the whole system of the Adi Brahmo Somaj as described by me in the pamphlets presented to your Committee. The system in question contains nothing against the principles of Brahmoism, but has every thing in its favour to recommend it for your acceptance, especially the signal advantage which it possesses of being able to attract the regard of the general Hindu community compared to which English-educated natives are but drops in the ocean. I think you ought to decide soon whether you should adopt a strictly Hindu mode of propagation, for if you do not adopt it at once, the Arya Somajes bid fair to outstrip the Brahmo Somajes as has been the case at Manghyr and elsewhere. The Arya Somajes should not be allowed to do so, as Brahmo Dharma has a greater claim to the veneration and love of the people, being the *Sara Dharma* according to their own admission.

Our opinion is that Babu Raj Narain Bose has given his interlocutors a good slap—a slap which they have deserved by their open violation of a principle which they have been known all along to worship. It seems that principles are nothing to men who are determined to be bitter and hostile to one person.

———:o———

Mr. Voysey tries to meet the Adi Brahmo Somaj in a manner surprisingly bold and audacious. He writes to Babu Raj Narain Bose to say that he fully agrees with the Adi Somaj as to the utility of eliminating social reforms from the programme of the Brahmo Somaj. These reforms, he says, must be left to individuals to carry out, and they should not be undertaken by religious associations. The advice need not startle us, as it tells us clearly the sort of men we have to deal with. At any rate, what with Mr. Voysey advising the Adis to eschew social reforms, and the Adis calling upon the protesters to stick to Hinduism, and the protesters asking Mr. Voysey to continue his abuse of Christ, we have got a beautiful triangle from all points of which a continued artillery of invective is expected to be fired upon the devoted head of the Brahmo Somaj of India. There is one word which correctly designates the inevitable result of this tremendous onslaught. Written in big letters, it will go by the name of—FAILURE!

COALITION OR COLLISION?

Some years ago our minister gave a lecture on "Jesus Christ, Europe and Asia." A practical lecture on "Europe and Asia against Jesus Christ," is on the *tapis* at the present moment. Four mighty champions are arrayed against the poor Nazarene, two Europeans and two Bengalis. And as these possess both learning and piety in abundance and represent the superior civilization and culture of the nineteenth century, let Jesus tremble, for under the volley of their tremendous artillery the carpenter prophet's armhill...

ation is inevitable! Messrs. Voysey and Leonard and Babus Rajnarain and *Brahmo Opinion* have formed a holy alliance, offensive and defensive, to rid India of that ignoble carpenter's son and preach him down by their pure teachings and purer lives. These gentlemen have organised a coalition ministry to administer the affairs of God's church in India, and banish the arch-heretic of the age, Keshub Chunder Sen, who is doing so much to poison the hearts of young Bengal by his eloquent advocacy of Christ. Verily, verily the kingdom of anti-Christ is at hand. Four of his chosen and sworn champions have begun to prepare the way, and India must get ready to welcome not Christ but anti-Christ. Every thing is arranged. The plan of action has been determined upon. The views and sentiments of the redoubtable four have been embodied together in a spirited manifesto. The fiat has gone forth, and war has been declared. So the fate of Christ is doomed. There seems to be, however, one serious drawback in the crusade. Beneath this apparent coalition among these heroes, there seems to be hopeless discord, and we are tempted to ask,—Coalition or Collision? What is it that serves as a bond of union among these enemies of anti-Christ? Only abhorrence of the Brahmo minister. Beyond this we see no affinity whatever. On close examination astounding anomalies and incongruities appear, which neither predict a happy union nor argue an honest alliance. The Rev. Mr. Voysey questions the Theism of our minister, and asks him to disclaim his position as a Brahmo minister, while he himself delights in clinging to his title and rank as an ordained Christian minister, although he is a thorough-going hater of Christ and his character. His colleague, Mr. Leonard, is an amphibious creature in the religious world. For he is neither a Christian, nor a Hindu, nor a Brahmo, nor a Jew. And yet he, for reasons best known to himself, undertakes to descant on the philosophy of Theism, extols his favorite to the skies and deems the victim of his wrath to the lower regions as an ambitious impostor, and immortalizes himself in an ungrammatical volume of romance, miscalled history, in which truth and grammar are both mercilessly slaughtered, that the author's apparently inconvenient position as a railway clerk may be somewhat improved by the profits of book-making. That such a man with no earthly or unearthly reasons should find fault with leaning towards Christ is unintelligible indeed. As regards Babu Raj Narain, he is a veteran Brahmo, physically and spiritually decrepit. He is well known as a man who has almost entirely lost his former devotional self, as his public prayers and published writings testify. His only claim to a partnership in the firm of Anti-Christ and Company lies in the notorious fact that the head of the Somaj to which he belongs, Rajah Ram Mohun Roy, openly called Jesus an "intercessor" and a "saviour of sinners," and published his precepts as a "Guide to Peace and Happiness." The Rajah's "Appeals to the Christian Public" contain avowals of Christian belief from which every Brahmo must recoil with horror, and yet his follower Babu Raj Narain affects to despise Christ and Keshub Chunder, and sells his heart's loyalty to Mr. Voysey, while proudly professing to be president of the Adi or Original Somaj erected by Rajah Ram Mohun Roy himself! How consistent! Lastly, the Editor of the organ of the Protesting Brahmos has shown honorable consistency by giving in his adhesion to the most enthusiastic and unqualified supporter of the Cuch Behar

marriage in England. His honesty is also apparent in the fact that he has all along taken a leading part in the protest movement because of his sore disappointment in not being able to secure the Maharajah of Cuch Behar for his own infant daughter, whom he had come forward to offer for the alliance, but whom the authorities disapproved! Here lies the secret of the honest movement hitherto going on under the auspices of the organ of the Protesting Brahmos. It has always been the interest of the party to conceal this important fact. But it deserves exposure now that the Editor has boldly appeared in the field in person ostensibly to smash the creed and character of Christ, but really to abuse the minister whom he and his friends can never forgive. Whether these puny combatants will be able to slay Jesus with their impotent goose quill we need not determine. That India will not listen to their disingenuous attacks and suspicious logic and that Christ's purity will survive their fury we can confidently predict. Let them try to abuse and browbeat the minister as much as they can. They have the fullest liberty in the matter. We do not care to interfere. But the case is different when they try to put down Christ. By so doing they will only excite and exasperate the friends of truth.

A CHURCH WITH NO APPELLATION.

A church that concerns itself chiefly about doctrines, which, dissenting from the prevalent creeds, glories in its differences and finds grounds of union with others only in those points in which they disagree with men of other sects, is by the very constitution of its being destined to die a natural death. Such a church has no vitality in it. It lasts so long as the differences last and dies as soon as there is no error to combat, no enemies to meet, no rival theologies to demolish. Protestantism would have been dead long ago if it had depended for its success upon its hostility to Rome. What life it has retained is due to the work which it has chosen for itself—the work, namely, of influencing the life of its own adherents and leading them through the trials and temptations of the flesh to the gates of salvation. So in the case of the Brahmo Somaj, its death would be sure if its mission were merely to destroy superstition. The fact is that the soul of man cannot live upon a continued protest. When the combative propensities of our nature are satisfied, there still remain the unsatiable cravings of the spirit, the unslaked thirst for religion, the desire to be freed from the gross body and take refuge in the purer atmosphere of true religion. These require to be satisfied, and they cannot be satisfied where the main motive of the soul is to feed upon hostility. And there is another curious law which silently undermines all protestant religions. The very love of combativeness deprives the soul of its power to enter deeply into the spirit. We seldom meet with much spirituality in a sect given to perpetual warfare with other sects. Examples of this are to be found in every page of ecclesiastical history. Now let us illustrate this by a reference to what is passing before our eyes. We referred the other day to the divisions in the Unitarian church of England and quoted a passage from Mr. Martineau's speech which was meant to show that Unitarianism could never hope to be a blessing so long as it retained its sectarianism, and it could never be a uood if it were piously to re-

cognise the great and good in other churches. "With those who esteem error to be no less fatal than sin the growth of piety inflames sectarian zeal; with us, who attach no terrors to the involuntary mistakes of the sincere, it is otherwise; the pure perceptions and natural instincts of the pious heart detect and love the good and great in the spirit of other churches; becoming more devout in mind, we feel ourselves not more but far less discriminated from the true Christian of every faith; and our sectarian zeal undergoes inevitable decline. And thus, as a mere theological denomination, we profit by the scepticism of other sects, and lose by the piety of our own." Mr. Martineau would, therefore, keep the doors of the Unitarian Church open and would not be proof against the influence of truth from outside. From the point of view of Mr. Martineau we think the contrast between sectarianism and piety could not have been better described. That sectarian zeal is not always piety and that the former delights in conversions, while the latter contents itself with solid progress, are very well illustrated in the history of protestant religions. Evidently a church has two spheres of work; it must demolish superstition and it must destroy impiety and promote faith. To confine itself to the former would be to ensure death from sheer inanition; while in the propagation of the spirit of true faith, the work of destruction is an indispensable, though a subordinate element. But while saying all this we cannot be blind to the fact that even with faith as its motto a church cannot but have an organisation and a distinctive badge or appellation. It is impossible to call a church religious which, while seeking to imitate the great and good in other organisations, fails to preach its truth it recognises. That it recognises some truth must be admitted, and that it is bound to preach it is equally clear. Now the truth which Unitarian and other churches believe—the truth about which there is the least dispute—is that which is embodied in the expression, the fatherhood of God and the brotherhood of man. The church is bound to diffuse and increase men's faith in the Divine Father and to classify their duties to the human brotherhood. Now far greater and more important than the task of demolishing error is that of destroying man's unbelief and sins. We do not sympathise with those who hold the disconfiture of falsehood to be the only important task entrusted by God to a church. Sin is a greater foe than mere falsehood; unbelief is a more insidious foe than superstition. So far as sin is the outcome of falsehood and superstition, by all means demolish both. But we say our duty is to root out sin and its causes. The church of the day does not fear hostile forms of belief. Theism at any rate does not fear Christianity or Hinduism. The common foe of all is infidelity. It is against this great and growing sin that the efforts of religious organisations should be exclusively directed. When we say that an organisation is indispensable to a church, we mean that without a union of this kind, the common foe cannot be met. We deplore the fact that churches should quarrel about doctrines at the precise time that infidelity is undermining the virtues of men. Let doctrines be accepted or rejected as the case may be; but as regards this war against unbelief, let every church have its distinct organisation and badge. On this point every religious organisation should remain stern and inflexible. No quarter, no mercy, should be the policy of every man who fights with scepticism. A church that refuses to organise itself even so far as this primary duty is concerned, loses its right to be called as such, and it may be safely left to meet its own doom in the whirlwind of unbelief and sin.

THIS UNREAL SOCIETY.

—o—

IF Carlyle had been an educated Hindu, how well and vigorously he would have denounced and how heartily he would have cursed the shams and humbugs of this unreal society. English education has begotten a huge sham which we recognise by the name of the educated community. There is nothing—no, believe it—there is nothing real in it. From top to toe, outside and inside, there is nothing but vacancy that swells this unwieldy body. It is a vast, ill-assorted mass of something which may be tending to a real form, but is now almost invisible, intangible, inaudible, at best only nebulous. What is this thing which you call educated Hindu society? Is there any purpose in it—any substance, worth or sense? The educated Native! How well he thunders! His voice is heard from the Himalayas and reverberated till it reaches Cape Comorin, and is echoed back by the waves of the Indian Ocean, the Arabian Sea and the Bay of Bengal. It would be hard to use the dissector's knife to ascertain the anatomy of this interesting being. What we mean to say is that he carries very little reality within him. Rest assured, we do not exaggerate, for let us get hold of the first living specimen of the genus educated that comes before our gaze. There is our friend, the earnest man, trying to infuse a spark of animation into the frames of his hearers, just as Demosthenes tried to do in the case of the degraded Athenians of his day. He speaks—speaks words of learned length and thundering sound, reaching now to the height of heaven, now to the depth of hell, carrying the gaping listener from China to Peru, and treating him to a bird's eye history of India from the days of Father Manu to those of Babu Shankar Dass Ghose, M.A., B.L. He evidently speaks with a purpose which is to dazzle the hearer with a glorious picture of his Aryan ancestors and the great places retained in the roll of fame by men like Vyas and Kalidass, Manu and Sankaracharya, Valmiki and Sakya Muni. The chorus of applause that greets the mention of these names, renders the casual visitor deaf awhile. When he recovers, he observes that the speaker has beautifully succeeded in throwing large handsful of dust in his hearers' eyes. He spoke of his Aryan ancestors no doubt, but, be sure, he didn't believe a word of what he said himself. Where the aim is to revivify young India into political life, it is evidently necessary to adduce examples of heroism and faith in the generations of men gone by. We have more than once heard young speakers mentioning Curiel and his twelve apostles as instances of what faith could do in regenerating nations. Noble utterances, no less noble than heroic; only the heart would wish they were a little real. Neither the speaker nor the hearer believed a word of what Christ really preached; and as for the Aryan ancestry, it is all trash. We understand nothing of what this Aryanism means. Does it mean that we should carry ourselves back and observe with easy our agricultural forefathers driving their plough over the high plateau of Central Asia, or our gray countrymen of old lisping their infant Sanskrit in the country between the Saraswati and the Drishadvati? Are

we to wish back those days when the sublime car, driven by two bullocks, or the subsequent improvement, the ekka, formed the only means of locomotion, or are we to wish that Calcutta were Benares with its bad streets, worse bulls, detestable dust and still more detestable drains? Or are we to become Hindus again, and, if Swires, allow our tongues to be cut for blaspheming a Brahmin; or is the speaker really anxious to recognise seriously the four-fold stages of life, and after haranguing audiences for years, put on sackcloth and ashes, and betake himself to the life of a mendicant in the forest? Aryan ancestry forsooth! It may mean any thing,—it is that or all of these; and yet the speaker does not mean it. Is it of Shankaracharya or Sakya Muni that he speaks? We are sure he has not read a line of the former, and as for the hero of Buddhism all his knowledge of him is derived from second hand sources of information, not from the original. Evidently he does not believe nor does he wish us to believe in the pantheism of the former or the moral though atheistic creed of the latter. If we are told to imitate the intellectual vigour of both, we must say the assertion is vague; for we cannot profitably admire the intellect, where we do not agree with its reasonings. It is, my dear sir, unreal—all that you say, praise or denounce. The educated Native is unreal to the backbone. He does not believe in caste, and yet would be the first to excommunicate and the last to dine with a man who has lost caste. He believes in the sacredness of beef and mutton; but when he does dine, behold the closed carefully closed and his relatives kept in a state of blissful ignorance of what he does. He drinks, as many do, but he will never venture to worship Bacchus before orthodox relatives and friends. If he dines with friends, he violates caste; but ask him if he has done so, and he will respond with a beautiful No. He has lost faith in Hinduism, and yet see how piously he worships the Durga. We have heard much of the Pujah vacation and the proposal to curtail it. But how many have denounced the proposal on the ground that, if carried out, it will interfere with their salvation? No, there can be no earnestness in men who believe in one thing and do quite another; who have one face for the debating society, and another to put on before their aged relatives; who assume different garbs in different positions of life; who learn in order to be rich, and be rich in order to be merry. Of serious purposes, definite aims, and tangible beliefs they have very little; and what little they have they cannot show to advantage for fear of offending orthodoxy. Thus it is unreality all over. A society whose constitution is folded in diplomacy cannot be a fit subject to be congratulated upon. Its sight makes us sick, and the heart in despair seeks for the more bracing atmosphere of reality elsewhere. Our role is patience, and our faith rests upon a future not yet seen. The young man of the future, our heart tells us, will be very different from the shadow of unreality which we see at the present day. In our mind's eye we see him a god-fearing man, ready to do his duty and owning a faith as hard and immovable as the adamant. Of unreality he will have none, and shams and hypocrisies he will hate with a most cordial hatred. Only a faith, sustained by true emotion and fed by genuine aspirations, can remove the taint of unreality from a society whose great fault is that of insincerity. May God hasten the day

when the revival long looked for will actually come and infuse a new spirit and faith in the hearts of our educated men.

WE learn that a Brahmo Somaj has been established at Rupar in the Punjab.

BABU Protap Chunder Mozumdar will conduct service in the Brahmo Mandir this evening.

THE missionary expedition started yesterday from Sealdah by the Eastern Bengal Railway for Nabati. The entire party numbered about twenty-five persons including our missionaries. They carried with them two flags on which are inscribed Satya meba jayate,—"Truth will triumph, and "come all nations into the True God."

THE Indo-European Correspondence says :—"The Indian Mirror may score a decided hit against a Scotch Free Kirk missionary, Mr. Macdonald, who has contributed a string of personalities to an Evangelical Magazine, to prove that Keshub Chunder Sen's professions of asceticism do not prevent him from leading the life of a very dainty Sybarite. Among other things the Scotch missionary taxes the Brahmo minister with "living in style in one of the Calcutta palaces, his own property." To which the Mirror replies that Keshub Chunder Sen lives "in a decent style in a house which was never called a palace when it was occupied by the Scottish Orphanage." Supposing that facts are on the Brahmo side, the Mirror has the best of the encounter."

THE Inquirer, in a review of Mr. Hutton's life of Walter Bagehot, says that the fathers of both these eminent men were Unitarians. The latter adopted the orthodoxy of his mother, though generally holding his trinitarian views very laxly, while the former, his college friend and biographer, exchanged the influence of Dr. Martineau for that of Mr. Maurice. The writer then says :—"Probably both of these thoughtful men were repelled from Unitarianism by the too great eagerness of many Unitarians to disclaim all mysteries in theology, and to give what they are pleased to call a "rational" account of the nature of God and of his relation to the spirit of man. The recent utterances of Keshub Chunder Sen furnish one more illustration of the evident truth that some of the choicest and most spiritual minds feel that in the higher life and teachings of God's Beloved Ones, we have immediate intercourse with the Eternal, for that the Love which fills and sanctifies the saintly mind is none other than the Living God Himself and the Gospel which the Beloved son proclaims is not his own, but rather the words of the Father within him. Hence they are deeply conscious that God is in Christ and in Christ-like spirits in a sense far more real and significant than that which current Unitarianism recognises and expounds. Orthodoxy with all its errors and false pretensions seems to grasp, while it distorts, a vital theological idea which Unitarianism, owing to its groundless dread of mysticism, has hitherto failed to fully comprehend and appropriate."

THE Bombay Review thus notices Mr. Macdonald's article in the Indian Evangelical Review noticed in our last :—"The fifth article embodies a hasty, and, we regret to say, imperfect sketch of 'the recent history of K. C. Sen's Brahmoism." It is from the pen of Rev. K. S. Macdonald, of Calcutta ; after casually alluding to the establishment of the Brahmo Church by the illustrious reformer, Ram Mohan Roy, and its subsequent consolidation by the now venerable Debendra Nath Tagore, passes on to an account of the schism which led to the formation, by the protesting Brahmos under Keshub Chunder, of the Brahmo Somaj of India, in opposition to the Adi (original) Brahmo Samaj. The writer then comes to Keshub Chunder's famous utterance about " Jesus Christ—Europe and Asia ;" and cavils at it as having been meant to court the favor and patronage of Christians and Europeans. We never gave Mr. Macdonald credit for being such a master of insinuations and innuendoes. His whole paper betrays a narrow party spirit, which, though veiled in very cautious Christian English, does not fail to impress the reader unfavorably. What the ardent young reformer said of Christ years ago, he repeated only the other day with re-iterated emphasis. His enthusiastic admiration of Christ *as he really was* has not in the least abated—on the contrary, it has deepened by a life-long contemplation of the hero's character. If, by the genuine utterances of his heart, Keshub Chunder has happened to please Christians and Europeans, (he does not seem to have pleased sectarian missionaries however) it cannot be his fault. Why is he then constantly taunted for what he has done at the dictates of his heart, pleasing or otherwise as such work may be to Christians and Europeans? On the other hand, his intense admiration for the true character of Jesus, which he thinks (and others with him) is misunderstood, and therefore, misrepresented by the average European Missionary, does not demand that he should accept the *almost* perfect when, according to his lights, he reasonably hopes to attain to the *altogether* perfect. A generous mind cannot trust itself to watch unconcerned the unworthy spirit with which men of various denominations have been persecuting an honest and well-meaning, though, perhaps, a little self-asserting seeker after truth. We are grieved to see Mr. Macdonald taking up the vulgar hue and cry concerning the Kuch Behar alliance. We were among the first to blame Keshub Chunder's weakness; but we cannot bear to see intolerant partisans pursuing him for this lapse as if he had sinned beyond the reach of forgiveness. It is unhappy that in *his* case the father should have triumphed over the philosopher; but it may be borne in mind that he has never yet arrogated to himself the dignity and credit of an immaculate saint. Perhaps the worst form that man's perverted ingenuity takes is that of intolerant criticism, towards which we possibly are ourselves verging just now. But we are disappointed to find a scholar and divine like Mr. Macdonald surrendering his good sense and charity to the evil genius of theological criticism."

THE OPEN AIR ADDRESS IN COLLEGE SQUARE.

TUESDAY, 14TH OCTOBER 1879.

IS IT TRUE THAT GOD EXISTS?

HEAVEN and earth bear witness unto the truth and sing the glory of God, while I, his humble servant, stand forward under Heaven's command to speak to India words of hope and cheer.

God of India, so imbue my heart with Thy spirit that my words may conduce to the well-being of India. Let Thy Holy Presence encircle me that I may speak burning words of truth and holiness. Be with me, O Lord.

Countrymen, fellow Indians and friends, I am going to press unto your consciences one of the simplest questions of religion, the root-question of all Theology—Is is true that God exists? Is this universe without a foundation? Is there not an inbreathing Presence which is the life of this universe? Doth not the Lord of lords truly exist? The question put to you is not a mere interrogation, it involves an indictment; while I catechize you I accuse yet. Men do not believe in the Living God before whom the heart trembles. An intellectual acquiescence will not satisfy me. But something more is needful to prove that you are believers. Say with your hands upon your breasts that the Supreme Moral Governor of the universe is the Living and True God of India. Give me a spiritual electrifying answer, but your wild looks, your distrust, your despondency prove that you are deficient in that true faith. I see in your countenance practical atheism. I arraign you in the name of God. You are self-convicted both before God and the human tribunal. Do *you* behold God? Is your God an abiding fact that can be seen and felt?

There are three great realities, namely, God, Self and the World, and you accept the grossest one. You believe in the world, though you say you have not seen God. But have you ever seen self—that immoral soul which thinks, feels and wills? You have never seen it, yet you believe in it. Every man can swear and say, I am real. How beautifully then you dispose of these two realities. But when you come to the third reality, you flounder and you stumble. You dispose of God with platitudes. That is no God whom fancy has raised up. Yonder pillars before me are real. Is the Almighty Arm of God ever so real to you as those pillars? To believe in God is to see Him, to see Him is to feel Him, to feel Him is to be moved and stirred by Him. Is this space an empty void? Is there no reality between you and me? You know how our forefathers held God in their clutches as *karatalangata amalak*. Have you taken hold of God in such a way that nothing could snatch Him away from you?

There is a God consciousness in me which I cannot tear away, so long as self is lodged within me. I cannot think away God. My bestial lust, my worldliness would tempt me to find arguments in favor of atheism. Carnality stands in our way. How impotent, how crest-fallen are the men of the world, when they are asked to confront the greatest reality. All their carnal nature rebels against God-consciousness. Do not make your faith stand on a mere intellectual or emotional process. Make your conviction a matter of eyesight. The whole human system is theistic. My life's blood, my energies speak of their creator. As for this river of blood, this vital stream, it takes its rise from the Himalaya of God's feet. Here I behold Him at the very root of my life. This is my evidence why I believe in Him and love and hug Him to my bosom. No one can be a theist of the right stamp who does not feel that He is the life of his life. An imaginary Divinity who is now and then a guest to me I hate. I believe in the true One who is safely and everlastingly lodged in me and clings to me even if I would forsake him. That God is my God and He will be India's God.

Do you mean to say that you are infidels? That is a prodigious lie. Through your transparent substances I see God. Do you mean to say that the railway carriages can go off independently without the steam in the engine? Your arterial blood—that hidden electricity of heaven—carries to us the message from Heaven.

Proud, arrogant, intellectual men, do you not know that you are the living temples of God. We need not go to Brindabun or Benares for evidence of His existence. Every drop of our blood declares "God is, God is." With every forth-putting of energy we hear the deafening voice "God is, God is." I am maddened with this God-consciousness. I cannot dispense with it. It is an overpowering, all swallowing consciousness which I cannot drive away. They say that God is inconceivable, but my philosophy tells me it is impossible to think away God.

Gentlemen, who gives you to eat? Are you sure that you eat and drink. Is it true that God does not feed you? Ask the waters of yonder tank. How came you here? Just hear what the waters of the tank say. The tank is loyal to the Sovereign above. It says, it has no independent power, it is the Lord of the universe who has kept it there. The tank is loyal; but you are infidels. There is fidelity and theism in every thing. There is God in every thing. Every power in our system is Divine. There are bishops and archbishops in the muscles and arteries of the body. Do not try to hide God by your vulgar atheistic literature. It is God who feeds and enlivens you. You cannot eat or live by yourself. Do not say, I live, I move. Accuse me not of pantheism. I worship the Real Personal God. Can I speak to Thee, O God! The Father says, yes. He is the true Living Father; He is my Father and He is my Mother also. The conception of God as Mother or as spiritual *Jagatdhatri* is superior to the conception of God as Father in tenderness and love. The Mother deity or the Mother side of God can never fail to rouse in the devotee the tenderest feelings of love and reverence. That Spirit-Mother has come to India with a new dispensation whose advent I proclaim. I see a splendid and magnificent opportunity. I see not only a combination of all the great religions of the world, but a glorious union of both the fatherly and motherly attributes of God. In this country the worshippers of Vishnu worship God as Father, Lord or Husband, and the worshippers of Shakti worship Him as their Mother. Thousands of years ago the *rishis* engaged themselves on the heights of the Himalyas in deep contemplation of God. In later times the *Vaishnavas* danced and rejoiced with shouts of *Harinam*. Again about two thousand years ago a great prophet declared that the Kingdom of Heaven was coming. Yes, the Kingdom of Heaven is coming. Infidel India, learn that our Mother God has come to save thee. There is sweet milk in the Mother's breast. These days are days of revival. All nature is aglow with God. All these castles of learning around shed forth refulgence divine. Nothing is secular, nothing profane. Let not the enemies of Heaven speak despair. We shall soon see the ignominous flight of those enemies. Countrymen and friends, will you not come and swell the numbers of the apostles of God? Want you money? Here is Heaven's bank where treasures are abundant. Do you want happiness? In His mansion there is unbounded joy. Your friend, your follower, and servant humbly beseeches you; come, O Brethren, and bear witness to the advent of the Spirit Mother.

India is groaning under insufferable pain. Have mercy upon the spiritual paupers. God is not dead. But your intellectual recognition will not save India. Say with full faith God is here, and the eloquence of such faith and inspiration will revive India. The Kingdom of Heaven is not lo! here, lo! there; but it is inside the heart.

Devotional.

Tell me, Father, will the Brahmos succeed in their mission?

Not, if they continue in their present state.

What is it, O Lord, that Thou requirest of them?

Enthusiasm, devotional fervor, maddening love, self-forgetfulness and spiritual intoxication.

How are we to attain these?

Pray unceasingly and commune with me the Living God.

If we become enthusiastic in Thy cause will not men call us fools?

Yes. Be prepared for such epithets. In all ages my devotees have been called fools.

But we have done and mean to do little that is foolish.

Foolish things ye shall do, and things that will make you appear contemptible in the estimation of the world. These are inevitable. The man who is passionately fond of me must live like a fool. His eccentricities will excite ridicule and hatred.

Then what are we to do?

Take not into account what men say of you. None judgeth but God. And upon him whom men condemn I will shower reward.

Correspondence.

[*We do not hold ourselves in any way responsible for the opinions of our correspondents.*—ED., *I. M.*]

BIBLICAL INSPIRATION AND INFALLIBILITY, NO. XIII.

TO THE EDITOR OF THE "INDIAN MIRROR."

SIR,—In your issue of the 28th September I find a letter signed H. T. M. in which the writer attempts a reconciliation of certain palpably contradictory statements brought to notice by me in what Matthew and John say about the Baptism of Jesus.

If I am to reply to every person who imagines that he has solved the difficulties pointed out (and scores of which remain to be pointed out) by me, my series of letters will never come to an end, especially as they do not appear in your columns oftener than at the rate of one every three or four weeks. So far as I am concerned I am ready and willing to reply to all comers, lay and clerical, who may write against me, if my letters could be inserted *every week*; but this, of course is not possible. But the fact is that H. T. M.'s letter requires no reply. A careful reader cannot fail to perceive that it contains within itself materials *more than enough* for its own confutation. I, therefore, abide by what I have already said, and, referring to H. T. M.'s concluding words, I again affirm that, according to the 4th Gospel, John the Baptist did *not* know Jesus until the "descent of the spirit" at the Baptism, and that this is palpably contradictory of what is said on the same subject in "the Gospel according to Matthew."

Yours &c.,
J. T. T.

BENJAMIN FRANKLIN AND THOMAS PAINE.

TO THE EDITOR OF THE "INDIAN MIRROR."

SIR,—I observe in your paper of August 17 an article on Benjamin Franklin's Religion, extracted from the *Contemporary Review*, in which it is stated that Franklin did his best to keep Thomas Paine from publishing his speculations on religion, and an extract given from an alleged letter by Franklin hostile to Paine's views. I beg a little of your space to state that Paine never wrote anything on religious subjects until three years after Franklin's death. Franklin died in America April 17, 1791, Paine's first work on religious subjects was the *Age of Reason*, written in 1793 in Paris and published late in that year. No one knew that he had been writing such a work, until he deposited the manuscript in the hands of Joel Barlow in Paris when on his way to the prison to which he was committed by Robespierre for raising his voice in the Legislature against the execution of the King. Franklin, therefore, knew nothing of Paine's religious writings. Nor was there any difference between the religious views of Franklin and Paine, though the former was more profuse about expressing them. The great patriots of the American Revolution—Washington, Jefferson, Adams, Franklin and Paine were theists, but not Christians. Paine was decidedly the most religious man of them all. He was a devout theist. His abhorrence of the Bishop of Landaff remarked that in writing of the deity Thomas Paine's language rose to sublimity. I feel sure that any one who will read Paine's *Age of Reason* will feel that he is in the presence of one of the most truthful and religious men that ever lived, while Paine's life is a continuous record of sacrifices made and dangers incurred for truth, liberty, and justice. He was the first man who proposed an agitation for the liberation of negro slaves in America.

The letter quoted in the *contemporary Review* as from Franklin is one of those innumerable fictions by which the grumbling idolatry called Christianity has been trying to arrest its decay ever since the Reformation. There is a grievous rumour over here that the Brahmo Somaj, from which we had expected so much, is inclined to take up that mass of discredited metaphysics just as intelligent people in Christendom (so far as they are not getting less from it) are casting it behind them. As Minister of South Place Society, which listened with so much pleasure to the discourses of Keshub Chunder Sen and Babu Mozumdar in their pulpit, I shall hope that if there be anything in these rumours they indicate only a transient eclipse of the movement which ought to result in purifying that Aryan fountain of light which has long been travelling westward only to become murky with the fogs of metaphysics and priestcraft.

Faithfully Yours,
MONCURA D. CONWAY.

Inglewood, Bedford Park, Chiswick, 25th Sept.

THE LECTURE ON CHRIST.

TO THE EDITOR OF THE "INDIAN MIRROR."

SIR,—I am much obliged to your correspondent "D. L. Roy," whose letter appeared in your columns of the 20th August, for his quotation from Emerson; though I must confess my inability to understand why he should characterize the gentlemen who have been criticizing our respected leader's utterances as "a host of enemies." But let that alone. It may not be known to every reader of the *Indian Mirror* that the founder of the Brahmo Somaj, Rajah Ram Mohun Roy, had, to use a mild expression, a sincere regard, nay respect, for Christ and Christianity. Some of his utterances were so remarkable that Unitarian Christians claimed him as one of their own body. In, I believe, 1821, the Rajah published the most voluminous and best elaborate of all his writings—a work on Christianity, an octavo volume of 634 pages. His "Precepts of Jesus," of which our Brahmo brethren have heard so often, is nothing but the first 63 pages of the above work, and contains extracts from the Gospels of Matthew, Mark, Luke, and John. He also published his 1st, 2nd, and final Appeals in defence of the "Precepts of Jesus." The last edition of the "Precepts" was published by the Unitarian Society for the Propagation of the Gospel in India, together with "brief extracts from Ram Mohun Roy's Appeals." I call the following remarkable utterances of the founder of the Brahmo Somaj :—

"The epithet 'son of God,' with the definite article prefixed, is appropriated to Christ, the first born of every creature, as a distinct mark of honour which *he alone deserves.*"

2. "Jesus, the founder of truth and of true religion, disavows the charge of making himself God."

3. "God suffered his prophets, and Jesus his beloved son, to be slain."

4. "Jesus is of course justly turned and esteemed a Saviour, for having instructed men in the Divine will and law never before so fully revealed."

5. "Moses began to erect the everlasting edifice of true religion consisting of a knowledge of the unity of God, and obedience to his will and commandments; but Jesus of Nazareth has completed the structure and rendered his law perfect."

From the "brief extracts" it appears further that, on page 205, Ram Mohun Roy declares that he has repeatedly "represented Jesus of Nazareth as the son of God, a term synonymous with that Messiah, the highest of the prophets; and" [con-]

times Ram Mohun Roy) "his life declares him to have been, as represented in the Scriptures, pure as light, innocent as a lamb, necessary for eternal life, as bread for a temporal one, and great as the angels of God, or rather greater than they."

Again it may not be known to some of your readers that Rajah Ram Mohun took a leading part in the establishment of the Unitarian Christian Mission in Calcutta, under the Rev. Mr. Adam; and that though his pecuniary means were limited, he contributed to it Rs. 500 on one occasion, Rs. 5,000 on another and Rs. 5,000 more on another.

Portions of the following look as if they were Babu Keshub Chunder Sen's "defence" of the lecture on Christ:—

"I feel myself obliged to lay before the public at large this my self-defence, entitled 'A Final Appeal' in defence of the Precepts of Jesus."

"I am well aware that this difference of sentiment has already occasioned much coolness towards me in the demeanour of some whose friendship I hold very dear, and this protracted controversy has not only prevented me from rendering my humble services to my countrymen by various publications which I had projected in the native language, but has also diverted my attention from all other literary pursuits for three years past." [1821, 1822, and 1823] "Notwithstanding these sacrifices, I feel well satisfied with my present engagements, and cannot wish that I had pursued a different course; since whatever may be the opinion of the world, my own conscience fully approves of my past endeavours to defend what I esteem the cause of truth."

Yours &c.,
INDIAN THEIST.

Murshidabad, 27th August.

NOTICES TO CORRESPONDENTS.

Persons favouring us with communications are requested to write legibly, and on one side of the paper only.

Unauthenticated communications will not be inserted.

H. D. GHOSE.—Received.

A. K. MOZUMDAR.—Ditto.

A DHARMO.—Declined with thanks.

A RUB.—This solves thus " fox, goose and corn riddle" :—" Let him take the goose first and leave it on the other side of the river,—then come back and take the corn there and take the goose over, leave the corn there and bring back the goose, leave the goose on this side and take the fox to the other, and then return and take the goose back, here the goose on this side and take the fox over, leave the goose on the other side and carry the corn over; then fetch the goose, and thus the riddle of the Jealous Husbands is also correctly solved.

B. M. ROY.—Ditto.

K. C.—Ditto.

N. C. SEN.—Declined with thanks.

GAUDA SING.—We regret we have no means of giving you the information asked for. We may refer you to the leading book firms of Calcutta.

Literary and Scientific.

A HISTORY in modern Hebrew of the war of 1870-71 has just been published in Paris.

"PARADISE LOST" has recently appeared in a Russian translation.

THE second volume of the third series of the late George Henry Lewes' Problems of Life and Mind is announced as in preparation.

MESSRS. TRÜBNER AND CO. will publish in a few days the third edition of Prof. Monier Williams' Modern India and the Indians.

IT is stated that Mr. Knowles paid a hundred guineas for each of Mr. Gladstone's two latest articles in the *Nineteenth Century*.

THE fourth volume, part II., of Mr. Talboys Wheeler's History of India from the earliest ages, covering the reign of Aurangzebe, is announced for publication in the winter.

AN account of the life and writings of Henry Thomas Buckle, by Mr. Alfred Henry Huth, will shortly be published by Messrs. Sampson Low and Co.

MESSRS. CHATTO AND WINDUS will shortly publish a little book on witchcraft in Shakspeare's days, and his progressive treatment of it in his plays, by Mr. T. Alfred Spalding, LL.B., Treasurer of the New Shakespeare Society.

THE death of Dr. Carlyle, younger brother of Mr. Thomas Carlyle, is announced from Dumfries. Dr. Carlyle was known as a translator of "Dante," and he rendered laborious assistance to his brother in collecting materials for Mr. Carlyle's "History of Frederick the Great."

A PARISIAN Centenarian has been discovered by the Paris *Figaro*. His name is Pierre Lambert; he was born in 1777, and took part in the various Napoleonic campaigns, and speaks bitterly of the miseries endured during the retreat from Moscow. In 1815 he retired from the service, as the "Petit Corporal, being no longer at our heads, I made up my mind to rest awhile."

THE electric light has been extensively employed in the German army and navy this year. Amongst other purposes it has served for lighting up the ground lying in front of a besieged fortress, for the illumination of ships at sea, and notably for carrying on work under water. The *Graphic* understands that experiments are in course of being carried out for the purpose of testing how far the electric light can be usefully employed in marine warfare, and specially as a defence against torpedo attacks.

THE art of dyeing the human eye has been discovered by a German doctor, who is now on his travels, accompanied by various "subjects," as proofs of the success of his experiments. Thus there is a dog with a rose-coloured eye; a cat with an orange-red eye, and a monkey with a citron yellow eye; but the most curious specimens are a negro with one eye black and the other blue, and a negress with one organ gold-coloured and the other silver-white. Moreover the process is declared by the doctor to strengthen and improve the sight.

A CURIOUS mummy has been bought by the South Kensington Museum—the remains of a Mexican Prince, uncle of the famous Montezuma. This Prince was made prisoner by the Spaniards, and confined with his little girl in the Convent of San Isidro, where he and his child were ultimately walled-up alive. The chemical properties of the surroundings preserved the bodies intact, and they now look as if made of dark yellow wood. The mummies are enclosed in a crystal box, and were sold in Paris for £305. Only one other specimen of the kind exists in the world, which was also found in a Mexican convent.

THE following additions to the series of "the Great Religions of the East" are announced by Messrs. Trübner & Co. :—A new edition of Selections from the Koran, by E. W. Lane, with an introduction by Stanley Lane Poole; Metrical Translations from Sanskrit Writers, by Dr. J. Muir, with an introduction, clear versions and parallel passages from classical authors; Selections from the Talmud and the Midrash, by P. J. Hershon; the *Jataka* stories, by T. W. Rhys Davids; Chinese Buddhism, by Dr. J. Edkins; Buddhist Records of the Western World, by Professor S. Beal; and a third edition of the Life and Legend of Gaudama, the Buddha of the Burmese, by the Right Rev. P. Bigandet, Vicar Apostolic of Ava and Pegu.

A CERTAIN Mr. Kiddle, A. M., says the *Inquirer*, has printed a volume of communications from the other world, the perusal of some of which gives one but a poor idea of the state of intellects among the departed. In the spirit-land the author of "Childe Harold" is said to have written thus :—"The feelings of trust, my friends, earnest and true,

With which I now pen these few lines to you,
Are many, with all the emotions strong,
That unto a spirit's being belong,
Though small the pleasure, for your soul's delight,
They will give you a foretaste of the realms of light."

This is the way in which Shakespeare now expresses his thoughts :—

"Conceit, comes the goddess of supreme
Delight, called Satisfaction,
To teach you that all things are far
Your heart's benediction."

Selections.

DEAN STANLEY ON THE ILLUSTRIOUS DEAD.

AT Westminster Abbey last Sunday afternoon, the Very Rev. the Dean of Westminster preached from the 2nd chap. 2nd Kings, 15th verse—"The spirit of Elijah doth rest on Elisha." He said he proposed to consider some of the lessons which were derived from the story of the departure of Elijah and the succession of Elisha. They had to take a lesson from the departure of every good and eminent man from amongst them. Such a lesson came to them, as, for example, when they heard of the sudden death—the tragical death, which had, as it were by a flash of lightning, illuminated lives hitherto, perhaps, almost unknown to them—when they sorrowed for the loss of their brave countrymen perishing amidst flames and carnage in a desperate fight at Cabul. Thoughts of another kind must occur from time to time in that great sepulchral church, as, for instance, with respect to the death of that inestimable benefactor of his country-men and of mankind, the solemnities of whose funeral recently closed over his life. It was one of the purposes of such deaths that they recalled the lesson of each life that passed away. The same hand of death which rested upon a beneficent existence turned the lamp of truth on the character of him who was gone, and then for the first time they fully recognised how much they owed to the incessant struggle against the sluggishness and incredulity and selfishness which he had to contend with. They felt that such men were the "salt of the earth," which saved them from corruption. Such solemnities in that Abbey, of necessity, came but seldom. It was now fifteen years since he had presided over the Abbey, and the number of eminent men who had been interred within its walls had been but fourteen—hardly one in the course of each year. It was this rarity which gave a significance to each occasion, and, as they looked back over these fourteen funerals, they saw that each had its peculiar physiognomy, each struck different chords in the heart of the country. Each revealed to them a new character. The event was the same to all, but the result which each left behind was very different. The vigorous politician and statesman, the humorous and philanthropic novelist, the world-renowned astronomer, the high-minded soldier and historian, and, in the same grave, his fellow-soldier and historian—the gallant soldier of Afghanistan, the resolute statesman of the Punjab, the brilliant student of literature, the indefatigable explorer of the earth's primeval structure, the unflinching missionary-traveller, the sweet musician, the restorer and builder of our churches, the reformer of the postal communication of the earth—these, each as they passed around, gathered around their graves separate recollections, and each left a peculiar vacancy to be supplied by those who followed. That led him to the second part of the lesson to be drawn from this subject—namely, the succession of gifts by which the purposes of Providence were carried on. They heard it powerfully stated last Sunday that the aim of that Christian man's life was to benefit his race, and in this respect the example must encourage them. This lesson extended in a thousand directions, and was placed before them in the extreme diversity of the forms of genius and philanthropy, which existed in each succeeding generation. They might follow this through all the departments of social life. It was so in the constant succession of poets. Cowley was not like Spencer, nor was Gray like Milton, and yet each was devoted to his predecessor. And so in the case of social reformers—of him whom they had laid to rest by the standard-bearer of Agincourt, beside the Governor of Calais when Calais was still ours. The contrast of the gifts of such benefactors as James Watts and Rowland Hill was as wide as it was possible to conceive, and yet both alike were enrolled in the like service of their country and their God.

AN UNRIVALLED IMPOSTOR.

(Christian World.)

WITH fascinating clearness and grace of style, and admirably brief, pertinent, informing, and instructive comment Mr. Froude tells, in the *Nineteenth Century* for September, the story of one of the most singular and successful impostors that ever lived. The essay is as interesting as a brilliant chapter in a novel, and yet it contains most valuable suggestions for the thinker and inquirer of the present day. We shall tell the story, or rather present an outline of it, in our own words, advising our readers to fill up the outline by studying Mr. Froude's paper for themselves. When the story has been told, it will not take long to point the moral.

About the beginning of the second century, there was born at Abonotichus, a town on the south shore of the Black Sea, a son whom his parents, who were poor people, called Alexander. As he grew up, his personal beauty attracted observation, and he gave proofs of that intense distaste for work, that ravenous appetite for pleasure, that merely intellectual cleverness, and that entire freedom from conscientious restraint, which appear to be, in all ages, the fundamental outfit of the quack. He was soon taken in hand by a cheating doctor, who had acquired from Apollonius of Tyanna some smattering of medical knowledge, and who eked out his fees for curing stomach-aches and headaches by the sale of spells and charms, by treasure-hunting with the divining-rod, and even, for a sufficient consideration, by mixing poisons. Young Alexander was an apt pupil, and, when his master died, he had become capable of setting up on his own account. Being now twenty, and finding his native town too narrow for the aspirations of his genius, he set out for Byzantium, formed the acquaintance of "a vagabond, named Cocconas," a gambler and blackleg, and through him gained access to a Macedonian lady who fell in love with him. He and Cocconas accompanied her to her country seat at Pella. "In Macedonia, and especially about Pella, there was at this time a great number of large, harmless snakes. They came into the houses, where they were useful in keeping down rats and mice; they let the children play with them; they crept into beds at night, and were never interfered with." In these snakes, to the eye of genius, there lay important capabilities, and the adventurers, when they left Pella, carried with them a very large specimen. The confederates lived for a while by their old arts, principally fortune-telling, fools being always anxious to look into the future. But a grand project now concentrated their attention. The state of society at the time suggested and favored it. Superstition was still strong, and yet the old oracles were growing silent. The philosophers had sapped belief in the gods, but had not secured for their own doctrines the assent of the multitude and were divided into wrangling sects. Christianity was diffusing itself, but its ideal of conduct was too high and pure for the vulgar crowd. If an oracle could be resuscitated, if one of the old gods could be made visible, there would be a golden harvest to reap by the hierophants of the shrine. With discreet boldness Alexander selected Abonotichus, a smallish town whose inhabitants were simple and credulous, for the scene of their attempt. But preparations were made elsewhere. The tricksters buried some brass-plates in the temple of Apollo at Chalcedon, on which was an inscription that Æsculapius, the god of medicine, who was, perhaps, the least discredited of the old Pagan divinities, would appear in bodily form at Abonotichus. Our friends contrived that the plates should be discovered. There was a buzz about the affair in the bazars, and merchants spread the story throughout the neighbouring regions. The people of Abonotichus resolved to build a temple to receive the expected Æsculapius. About this time Cocconas died. Alexander proceeded to Abonotichus alone. He was tall, handsome, of majestic presence, with long and flowing hair, lustrous eyes, and a sweet voice. His get-up did credit to his genius. His locks widely streaming, in white cloak and purple tunic, waving a sword, and reciting mystic doggrel about monads and triads, pentads and decads, "playing in anagrams upon his own name," he appeared before the simple Natives of Abonotichus. He told them that his mother was descended from Perseus, and that wonderful things had been foretold of himself. Aided by soap-wort, which enabled him to foam at the mouth, and rolling his big and lustrous eyes he acted to perfection the part of one possessed. "He was received with an ovation, all the town bowing down before him." Alexander was not a man to let the iron cool. Only a few days seem to have elapsed before his next appearance. He was now almost naked, a girdle of gold tissue round his waist, the Perseus sword flashing about his head, the fountain of foam-wort inspiration in full play about his lips. He delivered an oration. The language was unknown. Some called it Hebrew, some Phœnician; every intelligent Abonotichian could see that it was inspired. He had let the crowd know that the town was that day to be blessed by the fulfilment of the Chalcedon prophecy and the appearance, in some mysterious bodily form, of Æsculapius. Having ended his rhapsody, he uplifted the pean of Apollo, and followed by the multitude, marched to the site of the temple. Having arrived, he stepped into one of the water pools that had been left by rain, and, calling for a bowl, scooped from the mud a large egg. "Æsculapius is here," he cried out. He broke the egg. The people beheld, wriggling and twisting, a tiny snake. "It moves, it moves!" they shouted in ecstacy, recognising the embodied form of the god. Alexander marched to his house with the miraculous creature. For a few days the town was in a state of breathless expectation, and the roads were choked with country-people, on foot, on mules, in carts, hurrying to the blessed town. Alexander did not keep them waiting too long. A tabernacle was erected. A railed passage, leading through it from door to door, enabled the crowd to defile through, while, "on a couch in a subdued light," sat the majestic and beautiful Alexander, with a huge snake encircling him in its friendly coils, its head generally concealed, but now and then lifted by the prophet to disclose human features, "an awful face, the mouth moving, the tongue darting in and out." Could any beholder doubt that the tiny snake of the egg had grown in a few days into this gigantic serpent? Did any infidel who expressed a doubt that a god was incarnated in the creature, and that Alexander was the next thing to a god, deserve less than to be smitten on the mouth or knocked upon the head? There was no need of such extreme measures. If any one said that he had seen Alexander procuring the goose-egg of his miracle, inserting the minute snake in it, and then sinking the egg in the pool of water, or had mentioned that the full-grown snake had been kept from the time of Alexander's visit to Pella, carefully trained and ingeniously fitted with a face of painted linen, his testimony was not attended to. But the probability is that no one tried to state these prosaic facts, and the crowd, duly paying their money, passed in endless succession, day after day, before the couch of Alexander and Æsculapius. At first, the comers were poor. But the rich soon flocked to the shrine. Rich offerings were brought. Alexander must have felt like Napoleon after winning the battle of Marengo.

After a fitting interval—for Alexander knew that men need change in all things—the supernatural snake began to talk. "I am Glycon, the sweet one," it said, "the third blood of Zeus, and the light of the world." The temple was finished. A regular oracle, on the model of that of Delphi, was set on foot. Answers were to be obtained from the god at so much per answer. Of course, there were unbelievers, but they formed an unimportant minority. "People in search of the miraculous," says Mr. Froude, "never like to be disappointed. Either they themselves betray their secrets, or they ask questions so foolish that it cannot be known whether the answer is true or false. Most of the inquirers came to consult Æsculapius about their health, and Alexander knew medicine enough to be able generally to read in their faces what was the matter with them. Thus they were easily satisfied, and went away as convinced as when they arrived. The names being given in beforehand, private information was easily obtained from slaves or companions. Shrewd guesses were miracles when they were correct, and one success outweighed a hundred failures." Alexander became a power in the empire. The cleverest men tried in vain to unmask him; the sceptic Lucian, one of the most acute and adroit men that ever lived, almost lost his life in the attempt. Abonotichus became a Mecca. Alexander had all the pleasure, the luxury, the consideration of a prince. Coins were struck, and still exist, bearing his image and superscription. He lived to be old, and died in his bed. "What became of the snake, history omits to tell," and when the quack of genius was removed by death, the superstition gradually vanished.

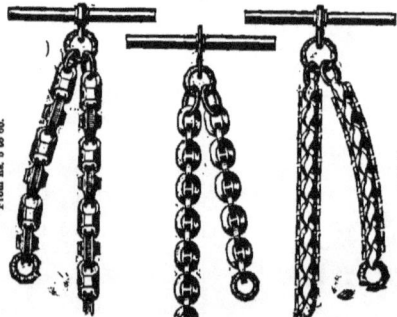

The Indian Mirror

[EDITED BY KRISHNA BIHARI SEN, M.A.]   SUNDAY EDITION   [REGISTERED AT THE GENERAL POST OFFICE.]

VOL. XIX.   CALCUTTA, SUNDAY NOVEMBER 2, 1879.   NO. 261.

Telegraphic Intelligence.

FROM THE PRESS COMMIS-SIONER.

—o—

CABUL NEWS.

SIMLA, 1ST NOVEMBER.

General Bright was to march on the 1st towards Gandamuck, Major Warburton remaining in political charge at **Jellalabad**.

Telegraph wires being pushed on reached near Rozabad.

Further reports confirm the desertion of Cabuli regiments from Herat.

Sir Robert Sandeman has reached Sibi after exploring the country between Quetta, Pishin and Sibi, and visited the head quarters of Pathan tribes. He was accompanied by Marri and Brahūi Sirdars and was escorted by 290, nineteenth Punjab Infantry, and forty Sind **Horse**. There are two direct routes between Quetta and Sibi, both well watered, with abundant supply of wood and forage.

From Candahar it is stated that Sirdar **Mahomed Yusuf Khan**, former Governor of Zamindawar, was to leave for Cabul on the 31st. His successor, Abbas Khan, brother-in-law of Sirdar Shere Ali, leaves for Zemindawar shortly with the Aliza Chiefs.

General Hughes returns to Candahar at once with heavy guns, Gurkhas, two companies 59th, and two Squadrons, 2nd Punjab Cavalry, leaving a force to garrison Khelati Ghilzai under **command of Colonel Tanner.**

General Gough with a small column is marching through Logar Valley and is expected to reach Cabul on the 3rd November.

REUTER'S TELEGRAMS.

—o—

THE RUSSIAN EXPEDITION SUS-PENDED.

ST. PETERSBURG, 31ST OCTOBER.

The *Golos* announces that in consequence of the disastrous engagement with the Tekkes on the 9th September, the Russians have retreated, and the expedition is suspended until after the winter.

LONDON, 1ST NOVEMBER.

Obituary.—John B. Buckstone, comedian.

DON CARLOS.

PARIS, 31ST OCTOBER.

The French Government has threatened Don Carlos with expulsion, unless he ceases from demonstration.

Editorial Notes.

COURAGE cannot be had without moral courage; moral courage is nothing without the love of truth ; and love of truth is nothing without the love of God. Let our readers complete the argument.

—:o:—

THE paramahansa of Dukhineswar, to whose hermitage we paid a visit on the occasion of the moonlight festival, completely lost his senses when he heard the procession chant the name of God before him. This is what we call being intoxicated or maddened by communion with God. The very sight of a man showing his love to Hari renders him literally insensible with joy. The sight we saw there is worth seeing by all means.

—:o:—

VERY remarkable changes have taken place during the forty-two years of the reign of Queen Victoria. She has outlived by several years every bishop and every judge whom she found seated on those benches in England, Scotland, and Ireland. She has witnessed the funeral of every premier who has served under her except Mr. Gladstone and Lord Beaconsfield, and she has commissioned as many as eight successive premiers to form no less than thirteen different administrations. *Vivat Regina !*—is the prayer of every one of Her Majesty's Indian subjects.

—:o:—

MANY of the assertions regarding Christ in the Town Hall lecture have been met with the argument that they cannot be right since they run counter to the Christian experiences of 1800 years. This, we submit, is no argument. It is the same with which we are so familiar which our Hindu relatives often use in dissuading us from our heterodox views. "Are you wiser than your forefathers?" Wiser or not, it does not matter. The fact is, that truth is not the exclusive property of our forefathers. Many errors have been exploded in the course of long controversies, which those infallible ancestors were known to hold with the utmost tenacity. The question, with regard to our assertions on Christ is—are they true?

—:o:—

THE Puja holidays have come and gone. Next year these holidays will be curtailed, if we are to believe the fiat that has gone forth. We hope our educated countrymen will now think of their position. Let them be more devout Hindus or more devout theists. In either case there will be a definite settlement of the question. If they become theists, they will strive to abolish the holidays altogether and seek in the worship of the true God all the consolation necessary for their souls. If they become better Hindus, they will strive to get the full measure of the holidays and try to deserve the boon by leading good Hindu lives themselves. Either this or that. But for heaven's sake let them give up the present unreal life which they lead. We are tired of unrealities.

—:o:—

MISS FLORENCE NIGHTINGALE writes an excellent article on education in India in the last number of the *Journal of the National Indian Association*. The conclusion of the article is well worth reproducing :—

Nine short weeks only since Lord Lawrence's death, and his terrible foresight has been justified—a foresight which wrung his heart and yours, and but too probably hastened his end—a foresight built on his exact experience and almost unbounded knowledge. And we have no Lord Lawrence now to win over Afghans to right as he did Sikhs. Whatean come of this new war but a check on industrial and constructive works, on education and what secures the prosperity of the people, with an urging forward of destructive and military and unfruitful works as best calculated to look forward to ?

Then now is the time, ye gentlemen of India, to step forward more and more wisely and nobly.

There is too much of waiting upon Government. We need not wait. Let us help the Local Govern-

ments in all good works. Let us work ourselves.
It shall not be—
'Ye gentlemen of India
'That sit at home at ease.'
but ye gentlemen of India abound in good works, in all wise and great enterprises for the good of your peoples, Soldiers of God, God speed you.

————:o:————

KARL BLIND very bitterly condemns Alexander II., the present Czar of Russia, Alexander is credited with benevolence by the world ; but he says there is no truth in the prevalent opinion. He is at best a despot and, therefore, ought to be detested. A story told of his younger days is interesting :—

Even Imperial children do not seem to be able to shake off the dark historical recollections that hang about the Winter Palace. In the manner of children they will make a ghastly sport of them. Once, when they were in a specially jocular mood, Alexander, in company with his brother Constantine and some comrades in play, enacted—as youngsters in their sprightly imitative mood will do—one of the most hideous scenes that concluded a previous reign. The throttling of the Emperor Paul was the subject ! Alexander, standing for Paul, was assaulted and thrown down by his brother, who knelt upon his chest. With the aid of the sportive accomplices, a cord was passed round the victim's throat. It is said that young Constantine took a malicious pleasure in putting into this semblance of strangulation rather an overacted deal of energy.

"For mercy's sake ! For mercy's sake !" Alexander cried, with half-stifled voice, and at last with a fearful pull.

Nicholas, hurrying out from his room, beheld the spectacle before him in deep consternation. When the matter was explained to him, he severely reproved and actually punished his eldest-born. "It is not worthy of an Emperor," he said, " to call out for mercy."

————:o:————

THE Native Christians of Calcutta held a Nagar Sankirtan a day or two ago, They sang a hymn in the kirtan style, used the khola and kartal, and went on enthusiastically chanting Christ's name through the streets of Calcutta. We appreciate this return to a national style on the part of our Christian friends. It is strange that the duty of making Christ popular in India should have devolved upon the Brahmo Somaj and not upon our Christian countrymen. There is certainly more love and respect for Christ in Native society now than formerly, and this is due in no small measure to the Brahmos. By the way may we point out an anomaly in the procession under notice ; A Nagar Sankirtan is essentially a Vaishnava idea. The khola is sacred in the eyes of the disciples of Chaitanya. There is also a distinct meaning attached to this sort of music. Excessive love—bhakti, there is no English equivalent for the term—characterises these devout followers of Hari. Any song which does not do justice to the Name and does not express this peculiar bhakti, when set to Vaishnava music, will surely fail to become popular and acceptable to the Hindu. And then sankirtan requires that the persons who resort to it should be deeply imbued with the spirit of Chaitanya. Are Christians prepared to respect the prophet of Nuddea? We shall be glad to hear the question answered in the affirmative.

————:o:————

WHEN the Vernacular Press Act was passed, we were one of the very first to speak against it. At that time many of our English contemporaries, true to that instinct which leads them to support whatever is anti-Native in the measures of Government, supported law the Act. We asserted that the gagging was only the thin end of the wedge, and that English papers would soon come to receive a fair share of attention at the

hands of Government. Our words were disbelieved ; but now all the journals without exception are furious against the rulers for having interfered with journalistic enterprise in the matter of war correspondence. It is probably too late to decry against this attitude of Government towards the Press. But better late than never. We hope the opposition will be firm and steady. The Press Act may not live long. It has excited the displeasure of Englishmen at home. The Spectator truly says :—"The old, haughty system, under which newspapers said what they pleased and Government did what it pleased, was infinitely preferable ; but the present Governors of India are as unable to bear criticism as Positivists to bear ridicule. The Commission involves an expenditure of £4,000 a year, incurred to save ten or three men from a little perfectly harmless abuse. One of the first acts of Lord Lytton's successor should be to show a little confidence in himself and the people by knocking all this clumsy machinery, borrowed from the Second Empire, on the head."

————:o:————

THE seventh and last volume of the "Pentateuch and Book of Joshua critically examined" by British Colenso, has appeared; and the very quiet way in which it is reviewed in the English papers shows the great change which has been wrought in the tone of theological criticism within these eighteen years. Bishop Colenso retains his main position, but changes many of his views. He believes that five persons or sets of persons, at five different periods, composed or rehandled the Pentateuch and the other historical books The criticism upon the authors of some of these are very severe.

In the books of Chronicles " the real facts of Jewish history, as given in Samuel and Kings, have been systematically distorted and falsified, in order to support the fictions of the LL. and glorify the priests and Levitical body, to which the Chronicler himself belonged." In the books of Ezra and Nehemiah, not only the whole narrative (except part of Nehemiah) but also the decrees of the kings of Persia, the letters of the governor, and the prayers of Ezra and the Levites are "pure fictions of the Chronicler ;" and the book of Esther is an unhistorical romance, suggested by a wish to account for the existence of the Feast of Purim, which was probably no more than the commemoration of the choosing by lot of the new inhabitants of Jerusalem in the days of Nehemiah.

According to the Bishop the name of Moses should be "regarded as merely that of the imaginary leader of the people out of Egypt, a personage quite as shadowy and unhistorical as Æneas in the history of Rome or our own king Arthur." A writer in the Contemporary Review thus concludes his notice of the book :—

The work of the Bishop of Natal has extended over eighteen years. It closes in a different tone and amid different feelings on the subject from those in which it was begun. It arose in a panic about the doctrine of inspiration ; and it created a panic. In the first volume sound criticism could hardly see clearly or escape the series of absurdities on account of clouds of controversy. In the last volume all this is changed. The author writes calmly and in the consciousness that many of the views it responds are no longer unacceptable. The present state of theological thought in the English Church (how far brought about by the work itself each man must judge for himself) is such that any serious criticism will be weighed quietly and without prejudice.

WHY UNREAL?

————

THIS society, we said in our last issue, is unreal. Why? Because our educated young men have no religion, no conscience, and, therefore, no principle. Confront an average young man, and you will find, after a short exchange of words, that he cannot say a firm "yes" or "no" to any question. "Do

you believe in God, my dear friend ?" " Yes." " But has not the philosopher said that this God is unknowable ?" " Certainly so. I think God is unknowable." So go on fathoming his mind with respect to all questions in which he may be interested, and you will get to no depth where he may be seen to advantage. We have been to meetings of the Bethune Society, and found that the same gentlemen who have already cheered an eloquent speaker on a certain subject, cheer another speaker for expressing views diametrically opposed to those of the former. There is some radical defect in a constitution which has learned to admire eloquence and nothing else. A gentleman who may be speaking the soundest sense and uttering the most sublime truth, if not eloquent, will soon be seen to address the walls ; but let another keep on bellowing for hours, speaking the most unmitigated nonsense and the barest common-places, he is extolled and worshipped. Such is the sense of the average Bengali youth. We may blame the education he receives ; certainly it does not teach him to think and reason. But the principal cause of so much shallowness is to be found in the fact that while English education has destroyed his prejudices, a sufficiently strong moral force has not been found to keep him on his legs as a member of society or a responsible human being. There is no one to tell him that society cannot exist without religion, and that a godless education must always be disastrous in its results. If he had been persuaded to embrace a religion, he would have shown more principle ; if he had known to honor God, he would have honored truth also. But there is no one to tell him all this. Those who are the self-constituted leaders of our young men are leading them to directions which cannot but end in mischief. The present unwholesome tendencies of Native society conclusively demonstrate the necessity of combined action. Let the most thoughtful, earnest, and sober among our countrymen organise themselves and adopt the best measures for the reformation of these young men, The Brahmo Somaj has a great mission in this respect which we hope it will not forget.

THROUGH NATURE TO GOD.

————

THE recent triumphs of science have brought forth a curious coincidence of the spirit of the age with that manifested by our forefathers in their sublime worship of nature and her manifestations. Primeval India was awe-struck at the numerous phenomena that greeted the eye on every side, and in each of the objects that he saw the poet and seer recognised the beautiful or omnipotent God that pervaded it. Theism was first proclaimed in India through the lips of mother nature. The vast pantheon of the country is nothing but a representation of nature in her various aspects and moods. And if religion is to be examined at the present day, what is it but the same beneficent mother asserting herself through the same channels or mediums of communication ? The only difference is that men of old viewed creation with poet's eyes, while now we are not content with the apparent moods or habiliments of nature, but have determined to examine her in her reality and entertain with precision the phenomena that cover our knowledge of the external world. The spirit of devotion, however, is not affected by this new mood of science. If we have rightly understood the tendencies of the human soul sees renewed reasons for admiring the beauty and beneficence of the Maker. In the vast law-worked world we see outward beauty heightened by the harmony of the forces that sustain it, while underneath the great energies is seen the Almighty One that keeps all in check and combination, Science, indeed, has revealed God with greater precision and clearness. In the midst of jarring sects and speculations, the contemplative mind sees the God of beauty, harmony and order, while the heart beats and throbs with emotion at the evidences of beneficence which every phenomenon reveals to the astonished mind. We may proceed further and say that the existence of God which forms the great doctrine of theism can be preached with greater effect and earnestness when backed by the discoveries of science than by the bare repetition of the Name when unsupported by any such sanction. In other words, the revelation of nature is as a great help to the religious soul as that given through the lives and words of pious men. Theism holds these two as the most potent means of convincing men of the ways and doings of God in the world. The mind in its simplest moods asks for evidence of the existence of God. This evidence is found in what science tells us of the constitution of things mental and material, and in what devout men reveal of their relations to the Supreme Being. Blessed is he who appreciating both can bring them to bear upon the cultivated and uncultivated understandings of men. Theism honors such men and considers no method of preaching adequate which does not clearly recognise the importance of both. The history of our mission operations during the last few months has conclusively demonstrated the genuineness of this method here indicated. The mere mention of Lord, Lord is insufficient to attract the heart. We should reach it by the chosen ways which theism has revealed to the world. The Brahmo Somaj should never shrink from adopting these paths. It may have to suffer endless persecution; but persecution is nothing when God works out a special dispensation for the fulfilment of His beneficent views.

THE BEAUTY OF THEISM.

Will those who have taken to abusing us for our assertion of the claims of Christ and other masters be so good as to enlighten the world with their opinion as to what constitutes the beauty of theism? We think that a clear declaration on their part has become necessary. A cursory perusal of the theistic literature of the day is sufficient to impress the mind with the very unsatisfactory nature of the basis upon which its expounders are pleased to place the religion they call theism. Take any ordinary book, any one of Mr. Voysey's so called sermons, if you will, and tell us what mighty claims are made therein for the superiority of theism. A momentary glance satisfies us that much of what it contains is destructive. In England, it is destructive of Christianity, in India it is destructive of Hinduism. Not one of the champions of theism cares to construct a system which will give hope and salvation to men. What little of the constructive element it contains, is not new. What is theistic ethics except a reproduction from the Bible, and in India what is theistic spiritualism but a reproduction from the Upanishads? So true is this that we need not go far for an illustration of what we mean. Our old friend Baba Raj Narain Bose wrote one of his dullest pamphlets on this subject and starting with the intention of asserting the claims of theism, beautifully succeeded in confounding theism with Hinduism, and lo! we had a pamphlet under the astounding title of the "Superiority of Hinduism." The force of human imbecility could go no further. But the conclusions of the pamphlet were inevitable to a man who had not grasped the leading idea of theism. Simple belief in God is not theism, and the world cannot be saved, if it only says that there is God. The fact is that we are to be saved from sin, that we are to love God and worship Him, that we should be immersed in Him and lost in the raptures of communion. That belief is impotent which does not point out the ways of regeneration. Men are to be born again, to be, as the Sanskrit word goes; and is this regeneration to be secured by Mr. Voysey's ineffective artillery against Christianity or Babu Rajnarain Bose's dallying with the absurdities of the abgurdest sides of Hinduism? Which of Mr. Voysey's congregation can stand up and with the right hand on his breast tell the world that the teachings of his minister have renewed his life and given him a fresh stimulus to undertake to understand, appreciate and glorify the Father in heaven? Which of Babu Raj Narain Bose's followers—if fortunately of followers he has any—can come forward and say that by means of the unheavenly and unearthly theism that he preaches he stands on a footing of superiority over men of all denominations and creeds? We are afraid that of all claims, this one of having succeeded in bringing about the regeneration of men, is the last that can be made by either Mr. Charles Voysey or Babu Raj Narain Bose. Let the truth be told, and openly and bravely told, that there is no theism with either of these gentlemen. The theism which we recognise as the future religion of the world, which is to satisfy the moral and spiritual cravings of men, is one that has yet to be revealed, and it is a religion which God alone can reveal through the agency of His own dispensation. We believe the Brahmo Somaj is passing through the phases of such a dispensation; we believe we find in it the beginning of that society which, moulded by heavenly aspirations and influenced by God's own love, is to leaven the mass of Hindu nationality. The germs of the dispensation are visible at this day, and they have begun to take root. We cannot say the Brahmo Somaj is yet a church properly so called; we do not know even whether theism is a religion properly so called. No church is well based and no religion is well formed which cannot give eternal life to its members; and Brahmoism, we confess, has not yet learnt to grasp the message which God has entrusted to its hands. Very few Brahmos are firm and faithful to their religious principles. Very few of them have died true and loyal Brahmos. But while we say all this, it must be declared that the dispensation of which we speak has begun to show itself. The very few earnest souls that have placed themselves under its heavenly influence, declare unto us what they see and feel of the new world into which they have under divine guidance been taken. And what is more remarkable is that these few men are visibly influencing the society of which they are the most prominent members. The intense love of devotion and communion which characterises these souls reveals with marvellous fidelity the experiences of all saints of all countries and of all ages. The beauty of theism has begun to manifest itself in nothing more prominently than in the fact that we have actually profited by the teachings of the prophets. A devout Brahmo finds that he is at home with all saints. We find the true and pure Hindu echoing what we feel, and we find the true Christian displaying the spirit of theism when he speaks of God and His mercy. The fact is that Hinduism, Christianity &c. represent different roads, better or worse, through which men pursue their search of the Infinite, and the highest minds of the communities professing them necessarily occupy an almost common ground in the region of the spirit. Theism represents the space where all these roads meet and converge. Hence there is no difficulty to a theist to appreciate what the highest spirits of other religions say of God. Wish you for evidence of the existence of God? Here are the best, the greatest, the most fervent men of the world chanting nothing but the name of Hari. To men whose only object of worship is God the multiplication of this evidence, the increase of such men ready to bear testimony unto God must be always welcome. Those only who have seen God can speak of God, and therefore, convince men of the existence of God. The more, therefore, such men multiply, the better for humanity at large. We admire Christ, and our love for him takes such a form of expression as this—Blessed art thou, oh! I of God, for thou hast increased my faith and knowledge of God! Yes, the hearts crave for more light, for more knowledge in connection with Divine existence. Theism satisfies this craving to a very large extent. By creating the barriers that separate sect from sect, religion from religion, race from race, it gives us immense facilities for admiring and appreciating the best in every sect, religion or race. Let the Brahmo, therefore, rejoice. No such privilege has ever been given to any other community. If the Brahmo Somaj be the means of bringing man to their true God, then we say the first constructive element has been introduced into it whereby the barriers of all religions have been broken down and the materials thus gained utilised for the purpose of building the universal church of one God.

Brahmo Somaj.

BABU PROTAP CHUNDER MOZUMDAR was to have left Calcutta yesterday for Lahore.

BABU KESHUB CHUNDER SEN accompanied by a party of friends left Calcutta yesterday for up-country. He will halt at Chandernagore for a day.

UTSAB ON THE RIVER.

The morning service in the Mandir was refreshing. It broke up at 10½ a. m. and the congregation hastened home to get ready for the river. The tide ran full and high. It was noon by the time we reached the edge of the water. The tiny green branches were dancing on the waves; the big hailgrove was waiting for the lotus, and the Minister's party. We let the glat at about one. Our boatgroup was hastily decorated with flowers and leaves, we taste of the seasons to the east which floated with their Bengali and English interruptions "come all ye anxious!" and "Trust, shall triumph." Eight boats were vigorously playing on all sides of us, each filled with a party of Brahmos, singing Sankirtana songs with the accompaniment of the khole and cstara. The wide stream of the placid Ganga seemed to be alive and echoing with Brahmo hymns and music. We had a bugle with which the Minister energetically blew every few minutes, and the notes which went far and reached the whole party on the water, somewhat deafened us who sat near. Then singing, laughing and full of antics, we sailed with the favorable tide, the cool northern breeze playing upon our prow, and the bright sun shedding his lustre on the waves, trees, gardens and various pleasant scenery which we passed every minute. The ladies were joyous, the Missionaries were enthusiastic, the boys were full of noise and fun, the spirit of rejoicing in the Lord overspread all nature and all hearts. It was nearly evening when we reached *Dakhinseswar*, our destination. All our boats moored alongside the beautiful place of landing, and we soon got up the stairs to the garden. There our procession formed. Enthusiastic singing commenced. About eighty men joined. The banners were borne before the crowd. The bugle was sounded repeatedly. The Minister and most of his disciples walked bare-footed. Evidently the deepest feelings of devotion were felt. They walked round the garden, and the largest trees. Dakkineswar, it should be borne in mind, is the residence of Swami Ramkrishna Paramhansa for whom the Brahmo missionaries have very profound regard. Sketches of his life and teachings have appeared before this. He lives in the magnificent *deoaloy* of the late Rani Rashmoney. The temples, the quadrangle, the garden, the trees are unparalleled by anything of the kind in this side of Bengal. Swami Ram Krishna himself was quietly and joyfully witnessing the procession which soon gathered around him. The conversation turned on the usual subjects. From there the party adjourned to the *ghat*. By this time it was moonlight. The river was exceedingly calm. The Brahmos sat on the stairs. The Minister stood on a raised platform. After a short service, he gave an eloquent sermon on the beauty and influence of the moon, and the river. The singing Missionary Babu Troylokya Nath Sanyal then sang one of his most charming hymns. The Paramhansa who was greatly influenced by these proceedings now descended to the scene, and began singing in a manner which electrified the whole assembly. The flow tide was coming on, the boatmen were clamorous, still we could not break through the charm of the Paramhansa's singing and company, when, after all, we were obliged to leave he was conscious. The whole party was really gladdened and instructed. The Utsab was a success and promised to be permanent. The experiment of mixing real enjoyment with devotion and enthusiasm has been begun and should be continued in the Brahmo Somaj.

THE MISSIONARY EXPEDITION TO NAIHATI AND CHINSURAH.

—o—

In our last we described the two open-air meetings held at Calcutta and Howrah respectively. The whole of last week saw a further development of the plan recently adopted to bring the name of God within the hearing of the people. Our missionaries may be said to have passed through a whirl of exciting work during the week under notice. On Saturday, the 25th ultimo, about 30 of our friends went to Naihati. Our Minister arrived there in the afternoon, and was met at the station by a number of friends and acquaintances. The place appointed for the meeting was close to the Railway Station. There was a large gathering of above four hundred people, consisting of educated and uneducated persons, men and women. A number of Pundits from the adjacent villages had also gathered to hear the renegade apostle of the Brahmo Somaj. Their feeling was evidently not of a very friendly kind at first, as could be inferred from the casual remarks that escaped from their lips. It was when the Minister ascended the platform and, clad in his ordinary *dhuti* and *chadar*, spoke out in clear and simple Bengali that complete silence was restored. As the fates would have it, however, the meeting was not to be of the most comfortable description. Soon after the beginning of the lecture the skies began to threaten, and from angry growls at first, sent a downpour as copious as it was violent. Drip-drip fell the rain, and this was accepted with hearty curses such as could proceed from the mouths of learned Punditdom. There was no time for impatience. Either remain where you are, or immediately take to your heels, and the audience simply determined to accept the former alternative. The rain now came down in torrents. The most prudent had umbrellas with them; the lecturer had one of these held over his head. The rest were not so prudent, nor did they seem to care much for the interruption. The lecturer did not stop his speaking, nor did the audience stop its hearing. Both went on speaking and responding in a style so hearty and admirable that nothing but the words of the preacher could be heard in the midst of the turmoil and confusion raised up by the elements on all sides. For one hour this went on, and when the speech was ended, every one the lecturer included, found to his dismay that he was wet from head to foot. The excitement caused by the lecture, however, made the simple people forget the temporary inconvenience and gave birth to frequent outbursts expressive of immense appreciation of what had been heard. The lecture was followed by *Sankirtan*. It was not raining then. The procession entered the family house of the Sircars of Naihati, where an immense concourse of people had gathered to hear the Brahmo missionaries chant the name of Hari. The *Sankirtan* ended, there was a conversation on religious subjects carried on between the Minister and certain *Pundits* who had come to hear him.

The next morning there was a novel spectacle. It was a favorite idea of our Minister in connection with this expedition to have the name of God said and sung in *hat*, *ghat* and *mat*, that is to say, in the market, in landing, and bathing places and in fields. So early on the morning of Sunday last a large procession, growing as it moved on, went singing to the Naihati *ghat*, where it was proposed that after bath worship should be held. The concourse, however, was very large and the place inconvenient. Hence it was resolved to hold the worship on boats. Three or four boats were hired and fastened together by means of ropes, upon which the entire party got together to pray. They proceeded northward, and when the boats had reached Garifa, the ancestral seat of the Sens, the Minister determined to make a round of the village with the procession. This was done, after which the party returned to Naihati by water.

It was 4 P.M. when the Minister and his party left for Chinsurah. The report of the expedition had spread far and wide and had brought all Naihati and his wife to witness the scene of departure. Children, women and men, clad in all picturesque variety, had thronged each step of the *ghat*. As far as the eye could reach, there was a vast army of human heads with eyes intently fixed upon the inmates of the four boats that were to carry the party to the other side of the river. It was a scene beggaring description. The rays of the setting sun were reflected upon the broad bosom of the river; up in the air were streaming two flags, one bearing the motto, "Truth alone triumphs" and the other the motto, "Come all nations unto the True God." The latter was a flag containing representations of the flags of all nations of the world. The hum of the throng gathered on the shore, mixing with the sound of the playful waves, was for a moment drowned by the *Sankirtan*. The boats moved to and fro; for a few minutes our friends enjoyed the scene; and then there was the signal to depart. A bugle was sounded every now and again. The scene was a splendid one in many respects, and it is not likely to be forgotten by the men or women of Naihati for many a day to come. The boats crossed merrily over to the other side, where friends were waiting to receive the party.

There was no time to be lost. A large number of gentlemen had assembled on the space surrounding the local Mandir. On one corner of the building was erected a platform upon which the Minister stood, and on three sides of him stood about eight hundred young men and a few European gentlemen. The spacious barracks were in front of the speaker and on their distant verandahs could be seen ladies and gentlemen enjoying the spectacle. The lecture lasted for an hour, we believe, and it was very attentively heard by the vast gathering. It was delivered in English at the express desire of the educated young men who came to hear him. After the lecture, the party was very hospitably received and fed by some of the members of the Samaj in a neighbouring garden house. Next day, Monday, the party left Chinsurah for Sheoranagore by boat. When our friends in crossing came in sight of Chandernagore, with its numerous picturesque buildings and *ghats*, a desire was manifested that they should return and hold a *Sankirtan* on one of these *ghats*. So the trip across was given up, and the Minister dressed in *dhuti* and the yellow "*chudder*" (*gairic*) usually worn by him during family worship, came down, taking his seat on one of the steps of the *ghat*. Instantly at a moment's notice some two hundred people, among them women carrying *gharas* of water upon their waist—gathered to hear the striking hymns. From this place the party proceeded singing to the family house of a gentleman where the *Sankirtan* was carried on with great vigour till dusk. Chandernagore, however, saw little of the doings of our friends, for it was train time of the E. I. Railway and the members dispersed soon. The Minister and his friends were in third class carriages, and even here the chanting of the sacred name of God had not ceased. As the train touched every station, hymns were sung, and it was not till Howrah was reached that the last accent in praise of the Almighty died away in the eager lips of the devotees.

Thus ended one of the most successful trips in connection with the missionary expedition of 1879.

THEOLOGICAL INSTITUTION.

—o—

EDUCATION.

Babu Keshub Chunder Sen delivered a lecture on Saturday, the 2nd August. Subject:—Education.

As the mind, said the lecturer, was the concern of man next to body, education was to be considered next to health the most important thing. Self-defence was nature's first law. Nature was against annihilation, and to bring wilful destruction upon ourselves was subject to Heaven's justice. So our first duty was health. Having, in a former lecture, passed over this first stage of duty, the lecturer now claimed importance for the health of the mind and intellect. He who did not hear God in matters of health, was either a fool or an infidel. And we heard the same voice that bid us take care of our health urging upon us the duty of educating ourselves. Throughout all ages the words had been heard, "Educate thyself," "Know thyself," "Give proper culture to your intellect." Man must follow nature, and education must be compulsory. It was God's direct commandment, "Thou shalt educate thyself." Moses ought to have said this when he said, "Thou shalt not murder," "Thou shalt not steal." Like murder and theft, ignorance was, not merely improper, but iniquitous. It was defiance of Heaven's law. By ignorance the lecturer meant a profound ignorance of God. What is Education? It is not what is believed by the people, but what is intended by God to be. Education is not information, study or putting large quantities of matter inside the mind. Education is culture, dragging out what there is in the mind; not putting what was not there, but rousing what hitherto lay dormant, the feelings, the will and our faculties. How is this to be done? The sleeping man is in every one of us. Humanity lies dormant. Some impetus from outside is required to bring it out. The sleeping man is destined to be educated; a voice is required to rouse it. Something *ab extra* is needed. All studies fulfil this. But they are only auxiliaries to the ultimate end. They are not education; no less is money comfort. Such culture, such exercise must be given to man as is essentially necessary to make him a true man. Without such culture a man might go forth into hysterics and sentimental outbursts, but he would succumb to trials. The true scholar is he who lives as a man, thinks as a man, feels as a man, works as a man.

But what exercises are needed? The lecturer first named the exercise of the thinking powers. Thought is man's greatest part. How great a thing is thought! What telegraphic rapidity it possesses! One may have read many books, yet he has not read more than only half-a-dozen. We are to digest, not devour. So a proper selection of books is necessary. In India, the rage is now for natural science, Botany, Chemistry, for matter. Down with metaphysics, the university men say. In the eye of the theologian the view is thoroughly reversed. He did not undervalue physical sciences. But though they are meant to give us discipline, they are not the only things to look after. Study without thought is like delicious food placed outside ourselves. When it nourishes and enters into the blood, its work is done. Study, if not auxiliary to thought, must be deprecated. Thought is man's food. Why do men praise the Bible and Shakespeare so much? Why are they thought to raise men above the world? The Bible represents nature faithfully; we see nature as we read it. So in Shakespeare. We see everything as if with our own eyes. Tragedy and comedy appear before us as actual life. We feel, think and can be cheerful after reading it. Why are men tempted to quote passages from them? Because those seedlings transplanted into the soul bear abundant harvest. Borrowed from our neighbour they become converted into plants of the soul. After speaking of the importance of cultivating the memory and imagination, the lecturer dwelt upon the advantages of studying mental and moral philosophy. These sciences had opened to the lecturer his road to theology. When he was a student, polite literature, prose and poetry were at first delicacy to him. But directly he fell in with the mental science, his course was turned. They exerted a sort of magical influence over him, because they taught him to think. Here he found thought dealt with thought. There was a reflex action of the mind. His ownself, his own consciousness appeared before him, and he found, that it had long been neglected. No longer from star to star and from planet to planet. All ramblings ceased. Here he returned home. And, locking up the gates, what did he find? He found the neglected mind which required to be looked after. Learn about mufalot and hippopotamus and not know self! Why, it was appropriating other men's furniture and entering into other race's shops. And, as he said, he wondered and said, "On earth there is nothing great but man, in man nothing great but mind." He saw the greatness of thought. Before shooting thought electricity lay prostrate. A thought uttered by a prophet made multitudes bend down. Thought was the greatest, the highest of powers. It regulated nature, made the steam engine work and electricity sent messages. We learnt the geography of Lapland and the history of this battle, but we know not the geography and history of our own selves. Great battles had been fought, terrible battles that were fought within. How our enemy attacked us unprepared, how we succeeded, crying, "Victory to conscience!" And, as then, so now we should again conquer. That is the voice of experience. This history of our own lives must be studied.

Was manhood exhausted? No, we had the feelings and the will. The will was to be strengthened and developed, for from this energetic actions and noble deeds proceeded, and the inner springs of life came out. When a cultivated says, "I will do it," its strength is indomitable. The will must then be cultivated. The scholar must be a practical man. It would not do for him to say, "A little more sleep." He must be energetic, practical. Before one master will all India should tremble. The feelings also required cultivation. In this respect we should be true Indians, Hindus full of the milk of human kindness. It is a sad thing that our scholars do not turn out men of feeling. Whatever sentiment there might be in them is suppressed by the school master, and they are worse men when they come out of the school. This is not what it should be. Boys should hear tales of feeling, they should learn to shed tears over human suffering. Righteous indignation should be raised against wrong-doing. But our scholar feels nothing. The destitute widow does not make him weep, stories of horrible atrocities do not rouse anger in him. Congregations would listen for centuries and would not be stirred. The pulse did not beat, the heart ceased to throb. We are intellectually convinced that India is our mother land, but we do not feel for her. We are logical and philosophical, we must not feel. No, this won't do. The feelings are to be vindicated.

But education must be in the spirit for which the lecturer contended. We must not do any thing according to whims and caprices, but as God directed. We should not taste a morsel of bread unless God commanded us. So culture must be according to His voice. We are not to read the nasty stuff that can be found on all sides but ask the still small voice for counsel. When, many years ago, the lecturer said, he went to the Public Library to read, he was in the habit of asking this voice, and he got all the books he wanted. There is inspiration to be got everywhere. Earth is full of it; only the spirit is wanting. There is imagination; it must be propped up. There are memory, the feelings, and the will; they are to be raised up. But everything must be regulated by Heaven's voice. When the little boy goes to school, he asks, "why go to school?" Heaven's message comes, "Good child, go to school." The philosopher and scientific man, he too is thus illumined. Every one can hear God's voice in regard to mind. The mind must be made a victim on His altar. Then will light come out of us in streams. India, if properly illumined and invigorated, would be a great thing.

Correspondence.

[We do not hold ourselves in any way responsible for the opinions of our correspondents.—ED., I. M.]

A WORD ON THE *THEISTIC QUARTERLY REVIEW*.

—o—

TO THE EDITOR OF THE "INDIAN MIRROR."

SIR,—I read the *Theistic Quarterly Review*, July number, and cannot help giving vent to a few thoughts which have been troubling me ever since I had the fortune or misfortune to come across this number of the religious journal. In the article entitled the Brahmo's creed, paragraph 2 runs thus:—"I believe Jesus Christ to be the chief of all prophets and teachers." Now, for the the life of me, I do not see why the Brahmo's creed should inculcate any such belief. The religion of Mr. Sen may rightly be called Christo-Brahmic or Brahmo-Christian. Great reverence to Christ pervades through all his lectures and speeches. A true Brahmo is at times shocked to find such respect paid to a foreign prophet or preacher. This can only be accounted for by indulging in such beliefs as these. Perhaps Mr. Sen thought it proper in order to convert Christians to his faith. This reverence to Christ would mislead Christian Missionaries into thinking that, perhaps, Mr. Sen is a Christian after all, or if not now, his excessive reverence to Christ would bring him to Christianity at last. On the other hand, Mr. Sen with the shrewdness characteristic of a Bengali, might have thought that by making them only to listen to him, he would by and by make them believe him also. But I have no right to presume any such thing. Why should not Mr. Sen pay the same reverence to Mahomed? Perhaps because the long-existing antipathies between the Mahomedans and the Hindus have made it impossible for Mahomedans to have any sympathy with the religion of a Hindu, perhaps because Mr. Sen has not read much of the Koran. Be it as it may, one thing is certain. Mr. Sen does not seem to have read much of Hindu Shastras. I dare say he has not, for else he would not have gone abroad to search for a model in Christ. Does he know Sanskrit? I think not, for else he would not have gone to the Bible for his doctrines, and if he does, it is a thousand pities, that he has not caught the spirit of Debendra Nath. Had he paid more attention to the Vedas, he would have become a second Debendra Nath. Had he paid less respect to the Bible, he would have become a second Rammohun Roy. We revere the former, we love the latter, but we can have no sympathy with one who will be perpetually dinning into our ears the eulogies and encomiums on Christ. We do not mean to say that a good character should not be respected, because he was not born in India. Goodness in every country or religion should be followed and praised. Suppose I am a Brahmo. But I will not believe in Christ or his Miracles. Will you force me to do so or will you drive me out of the pale of your church. I pause for a reply.

Then see para 25.

"I believe in the inspiration and truth-teaching power of some of the leaders of the Brahmo Somaj, and eminently of Keshub Chunder Sen." This is the 25th Doctrine of the Brahmo's creed. As well add a 26th, viz., I believe in the inspiration of Newton, Milton and Shakespeare, and pre-eminently of Vyasa. I would be the last person to derogate from the virtues and abilities of Mr. Sen, but will you compel me to admit that Mr. Sen is an inspired being? I may as well say that I have been inspired by God to write this article, So am I an inspired being, and similarly, Mr. Editor, whenever you write able articles you are an inspired being. Suppose I cannot believe in such doctrines? The Editor of this journal should remember that such doctrines as these would alienate the sympathy of a great many Brahmos, as the late unfortunate event has done. No Hero-Worship should find place in Brahmo religion. This short and sweet sentence should be substituted for that disgraceful doctrine.

Yours &c.,
HURRIDASS GHOSE.

Literary and Scientific.

CREMATION in Berlin is being warmly advocated by the Municipality, who intend to appeal to the Government to render the process legal, and subsequently to establish the necessary buildings and apparatus.

WASHINGTON has given his name to no fewer than 188 towns in the United States and two States in particular—Ohio and Iowa—are so devoted to his memory as to have respectively 41 and 39 cities of Washington apiece.

SOUVENIRS of Prince Bismarck's Visit to Vienna found eager purchasers. The pen he had used at the hotel was bought by an Englishman for 19l.; another enthusiastic admirer paid 10s. for a glass out of which he had drunk, and the happy hair-dresser who had the good fortune to cut the Prince's hair, carried off the remnants of his locks in triumph, probably to sell at exorbitant prices.

THE lack of sunshine in Great Britain, so unfavorable to astronomical discoveries, has induced the Astronomer for Scotland to suggest the establishment of an Observatory at Cyprus, where, in the clear atmosphere of Mount Olympus, above the elevation at which the summer clouds form, every opportunity would be afforded to cloud-capt Britishers for competing with the astronomers of more sun-blest climes.

THE depth of the stream in the Gorge below the Falls of Niagara has lately been measured for the time. Hitherto all efforts had failed owing to the rapidity of the stream, but recently several American engineers succeeded in getting near the American Falls, where they were blinded and nearly inundated by jets of water, the noise of the Fall being so great that not a voice could be heard. The line was cast out and the depth reported 87 feet near the shore, and a little farther down stream the depth increased to 100 and 192 feet, the average depth to the Swift Drift where the river narrows, and has a velocity too great to be measured being 153 feet. Just under the Lower Bridge the whirlpool rapids begin, and here the depth was computed at 210 feet, the waters rising in a violently disturbed state to the height of 20 feet, like ocean waves.

Selection.

THOMAS CARLYLE: HIS GENIUS AND HIS WRITINGS.*

—o—

BY THE REV. W. M. BINNS, OF BIRKENHEAD.

WHAT account can man give of the writings of Carlyle, if he bears in mind the shortness of the piece of eternity, which is at his disposal, and the many volumes Carlyle has written, some seven and twenty I have counted of my own? It is a rash enterprise I have undertaken, with some heroism in it, no doubt; but will the said heroism compensate for the rashness? That question is not for me to answer. It falls to your lot. Now Carlyle has been severe, with a severity amounting to savageness, on bad criticks and biographers. He calls bad biographers "Dry as dusts" and what not; and thinks it is a happy thing for a man with any earnestness of life to have no biography written of him. And as for the bad critics, they are mostly fine writers, concocters of eloquent and empty periods, pretenders to psychological subtlety and other fancies that take notice this mad age. Still he himself is a biographer and a critic, even a fisher, too, in the troubled waters of philosophy and theology. He began with a little life of Schiller; he has ended for the present, with a big life of Friederich. Midway in his career stands Cromwell; and all along, whatever subjects have interested his age, he has had his say thereon, a say always worth listening to, if not always wise. There will be a biography of him sometime. The man has made too much mark in the world for the world to be content to do without one; and there will be criticisms of him also. I will not calculate for him many centuries, but for two or three, at least, he must be a problem. Nobody can escape the righteous destinies, which in the end will turn out to be the loving destinies, and will transform this seeming chaos of a universe into a fairer cosmos than is fancied possible by sects who are a garden walled around, chosen and made peculiar ground. So he would tell the foolish fighter against fate, the croaker, the groaner, and all the rest belonging to that generation. The destinies will lay their fingers on him, also. Nay, they have done it already. What I say as one of their mouthpieces now will be said admiringly, in the main, for I believe in him—believe in him so much that he corrupts or purifies, as the case may be, my very style of speech. I feel that I cannot write of him as I would write of ordinary things in my own proper person. For while his witchery is over me, and I must be considered as one possessed.

He was born more than eighty-four years since, at Ecclefechan, a little village in Dumfriesshire. The admirable parish school system in Scotland secured him a good education, and Edinburgh University followed. It was the father's ambition that the son should "wag his pow" in a pulpit. However, when the son looked the dominant theology fairly in the face, he could not preach it. He did not

* A lecture delivered at Over Darwen, Sept. 15th 1879.

shudder, for he was never prone to shuddering; he bade, like John Hales at the Synod of Dort, good night to John Calvin. He read immensely, worked as a private tutor, and fitted himself for literature, a profession in which he would be able to draw his breath freely. After a while he married a wife who was a lineal descendant of Knox, and took up his residence at a solitary farmhouse (Craigenputtock) some fifteen miles from Dumfries. Here he stayed some years reading German, translating Wilhelm Meister, and corresponding with Goethe, Emerson, and other kindred spirits. Men of his stamp, however, inevitably gravitate to London. In that universal air sectarian and provincial narrownesses are reduced to their proper proportions. In 1834, he settled at Great Cheyne Row, in Chelsea, a little street running down at right angles to the Thames, and there he has lived ever since.

Scanty particulars are known as to his goings on beyond the publication of article after article and book after book. Mr. G. H. Lewes tells how London boys used to hoot him, because he wore a hat which was not of the orthodox fashion; and two interesting autobiographies of recent date give us glimpses of him as he was in those days, when he was gaining fame, and with some difficulty contriving to gain bread at the same time. The American Ticknor says, under the date 1st June, 1838, "After all, however, I found time to make a visit to Carlyle, and to hear one of his lectures. He is a rather small, spare, ugly Scotchman, with a strong accent, which I should think he takes no pains to mitigate. His manners are plain and simple, but not polished; and his conversation much of the same sort. He is now lecturing for subsistence to about a hundred hearers to pay him, I believe two guineas each. To-day he spoke, as I should think he commonly does without notes, and therefore, as nearly extempore as a man can who prepares himself carefully, and it was plain he had done. His course is on modern literature, and his subject to-day was that of the eighteenth century, in which he contrasted Johnson and Voltaire very well, and gave a good character of Swift. He was very impressive, I think, though such lecturing could not be very popular; and in some parts if he were not poetical he was picturesque. He was nowhere obscure, nor were his sentences artificially constructed, though some of them no doubt, savoured of his peculiar manner." That is a suggestive let us doubt, I wish Ticknor had given more particulars about the *peculiar manner*. One would have liked to know too, what is meant by the "good character of Swift." As to the eighteenth century in general, we know what Carlyle would say it was nearly all bad except the French Revolution, when he committed suicide.

Harriet Martineau was a personal friend, and in her autobiography she lets us into his domestic life, and mentions things which, to a certain extent, make us form a notion of the man. She says, in 1834, four years before Ticknor, "He has a rugged face, steeped in genius. I have seen it under all aspects—from the deepest gloom to the most reckless or genial mirth, and it seemed to me that each mood would make a totally different portrait. The sympathetic is by far the finest in my eyes. His excess of sympathy has been, I believe, the master pain of his life. He does not know what to do with it and with its bitterness, seeing that human life is full of pain to those who look out for it; and the savageness, which has come to be a main characteristic of this singular man, is, in my opinion, a mere expression of his intolerable sympathy with the suffering. I am confident that his affections are too strong for him, and the real cause of the 'ferocity' with which he charges himself and astonishes others. When I knew him familiarly he rarely slept, was wofully dyspeptic, and as variable as possible in mood. Whenever I went to hear him lecture my pleasure was a good deal spoiled by his uncontrollable nervousness. Yellow as a guinea, with downcast eyes, broken speech at the beginning, and fingers that nervously picked the desk before him, he could not for a moment be supposed to enjoy his own effort. I remember being puzzled for a long time as to whether he did or did not care for fame. He was for ever scoffing at it; and he seemed to me just the man to write because he needed to utter himself, without ulterior considerations. We sat round the fire in an evening, and he mixed the toddy, weak brandy-and-water, while Mrs. Carlyle and I discussed some literary matters and speculated on fame and the love of it. Then Carlyle held out a glass of his mixture to me, with 'Here, take this; it is worth all the fame in England.' Yet Allan Cunningham, who knew and loved him well, told me one evening, to my amazement, that Carlyle would be very well, and happy enough, if he got a little more fame. I asked him if he was in earnest, and he said he was, and, moreover, sure that he was right—I should see that he was. Carlyle's fame has grown from that day and, on the whole, his health and spirits seem to be improved, so that his friend Allan was partly right."

His public appearances were scarce; indeed, after these London lectures he confined himself to literature, until, in 1866, as Lord-Rector of Edinburgh University, at seventy, he addressed the young men then entering on the stormy world's battlefield. His "address" was nominally on "The Choice of Books," but it is brimful of autobiographical interest. Fifty-four years earlier he had been a student there. On his eightieth birthday he received a congratulatory address from admirers scattered over the world, many of them the antipodes of himself in politics and theology, but all feeling him to be a man of the type of the best Hebrew prophets, and inspired of God. If he ever did want fame he had enough then.

And now to come to the soul of the man—that is, his writings; for scraps of the sort I have been relating, though interesting in their way, and indispensable, still keep us on the outside. To speak somewhat in his own style I may say that, as a Dryasdust, I have winnowed my rubbish heaps; and if thou, O reader, hast eyes to see thou wilt find there are some nuggets there worthy of closer inspection. For the world-spirit had truly a divine meaning in the rough discipline which this Scotch boy, now a battered but still fighting veteran of more than four score years had to struggle through, unaided save by the Infinite, who aids us all. This rescue from the grim creeds of his youth, was it not God-ordained? Was not the young thinker's stumbling into temporary blindness a passage to the hidden inner sunshine of the universal soul which thereafter never left him dark? Thou shalt judge for thyself when he speaks of the mystic monologues of Teufelsdrockh. And this nervousness of his, these concealments of woman's tenderness beneath a show of mad masculine ferocity, are they not eloquent to thee? If thou deemest them but idle prate, and hearest no echo therein from the holy of holies, then art thou duller than the fat weed that rots on Lethe's stream. Nay, the toddy-drinking with the woman Martineau and the female Carlyle, that significant mixture of weak brandy-and-water, has in it and its belongings a touchingness that might fill eyes of the tender sort with tears. Not weakness, but strength—a human, yea, verily, at times a God-like Strength—was the sign and token of the man who drank the weak mixture. Is not the talking to the Edinburgh students, those cultivators of literature on a little oatmeal, a revelation straight from the primal fountains? And there is weighty matter in that congratulatory document, too, though commonly such documents be but rubbish. From these construct a picture of the man as thou best can. And now I will point out the very photograph of him, printed on pages which shall last as long as that English speech of thine, richest and most cosmopolitan of the tongues that have arisen since the blessed confusion of Babel.

As the interpreter of German literature and our guide in the realms of German transcendental thought Carlyle is, and has ever been, the very foremost man in these Isles. No estimate of him would be worth the paper it was written on that failed to take this into account. Not only Goethe and Schiller, authors whom everybody now knows more or less, did he make us familiar with, in the manifoldness of their genius, solving the intricacies and mysteries of Faust, and telling again the tales of Schiller's drama, but explored the whole land, he gathered flowers blooming in the gardens, and he went as a pioneer into the seeming wastes, and discovered there priceless treasures. In an essay on Jean Paul Richter, in 1827, he says it was the first time that name was printed with English types. Now some acquaintanceship with Richter is a necessity of a good education—his wondrous tragic humour; his rare touches of poetry; his grotesque yet splendid, and his thoroughly human yet almost super-human imagination. Well may the Germans call him "Jean Paul the only." Carlyle rendered a service of nearly equal value, though in another direction, more specifically religious, in the account of Novalis. That Moravian mystic, whose mysticism raised him into an ampler ether and a diviner air, is known in the philosophical world as author of the saying "the God-intoxicated Spinoza," a saying that better describes the greatest of modern Jews than any other, and that was the inspiration of Renan's oration at the Bicentenary of Spinoza at Amsterdam on February 21st. There are some passages of Novalis given by Carlyle: "Philosophy is properly home sickness—the wish to be everywhere at home." "To become properly acquainted with a truth we must first have disbelieved it, and disputed against it." "Man has ever expressed some symbolical philosophy of his being in his works and conduct; he announces himself and his gospel of nature; he is the Messiah of Nature." "Every beloved object is the Centre of a Paradise." "The Spirit of Poesy is the morning light which makes the statue of Memnon sound." "Nature is an Æolian harp, a musical instrument, whose tones again are keys to higher strings in us." The first feeling of matter-of-fact minds on hearing such passages is one of unmitigated wonder, because the shallow understanding only is alive in these people and the reason, what Germans call vernunft as distinct from verstand, is yet slumbering or waiting to be born. Coleridge partly succeeded in nationalising that distinction between the reason and understanding in England. It runs through Carlyle, it is the Open Sesame of Germany, and it is the soul of the higher philosophical thinking of to-day—a dead language to the traditionalist, but a revelation to him that hath eyes to see and ears to hear. Need I mention other essays on German subjects? I could but catalogue them. There they are in four volumes of Miscellanies, an Encyclopedia of Culture in miniature. Enough, then. Let it stand that Carlyle is the interpreter of Germany to England, and equally at home in the foreign as in the native land.

Strange, there is not one page of classical matter in all his volumes. By classical matter I mean the Greek and Latin criticism of which many are so fond. Yet he had reason for his silence. Although our modern life is by many roots connected with Classical Paganism, and Pagan customs still survive transformed in some Christmas customs of our own, yet our deepest life is of Hebrew, Christian, and Teutonic origin; and we are not so much fed by the classical ages as we grow on their debris which serves as but mould to enrich us. And so Carlyle ranges over the still living world of thought—which stretches to Palestine, whence he borrows a fiery zeal for righteousness and reality—to Scandinavia, and Italy, and France—to the Arabia made for ever sacred by the mission of Mahomet, as well as to England and to Germany. His essay on Voltaire is about the justest estimate I have seen of that brilliant Frenchman who was the mouthpiece of the destructive spirit working with constructive aims in the last century; a man once over praised and now under-praised—over praised because he was France's one man of genius in poetry for 50 years—under-praised because his attitude of antagonism to what most believe in religion has made us forget his wonderful versatility. The sketch of Dr. Johnson surpasses Macaulay's, and the essay on Burns is simply perfect.

But the breadth of sympathy which is the true token by which you may tell whether nature has made a man according to a base or a noble pattern is best seen in "Heroes and Hero-Worship." This unrivalled volume was a series of lectures delivered in London. "Hero-worship and the heroic in human affairs" is his subject. History is the biography of great men—they are the thoughts of God made manifest in the flesh, as the universe is the thought made manifest in nature; such, here and everywhere is the burden of his prophecy. As Divinity the Hero is Odin, and Scandinavian mythology lives again, not as mere superstition, but as the poetry of wild Norse hearts in their struggle to comprehend and draw nigh to God. As prophet the Hero is Mahomet, the human channel by whom two hundred millions of immortal souls still receive Monotheism, and are delivered from idolatry. Carlyle restored Mahomet to his true rank. Since then a few dogs have bayed at him as they bay at the moon, but like it he goes on shining undisturbed. The Hero as Poet is Dante and Shakespeare—names themselves more suggestive than any poor words of mine could make them. The Hero as Priest is Luther and Knox. The Hero as Man of Letters is Johnson, Rousseau, and Burns. The Hero as King is Cromwell and Napoleon. Here are uncommon names to be called heroes, some of them even to be reckoned, canonised, as Shakespeare and Dante are; saints not to be meddled with by profane hands, and all bearing messages from the highest to the common world. But you are masters of the secret when you grasp Carlyle's philosophy of history. History with him, at this time, at least, was not a play of capricious farces, but the march of a Divine Will. And all the men stood for powers ordained of God—realities to beat down shams. "My dear Sir," said Dr. Johnson, "clear your mind of cant." All the heroes act on that motto. Sometimes they are not wise, but always they are the instruments of a wisdom wiser than their own. Sometimes they are worse than not wise, judged by our lights, but in the sweep of eternity all things work for good. "Unhasting and unresting" is the method of the World-Spirit. Through the heroes we hear the bass of Heaven's deep organ blow, where are notes sounding discordant to us, who only hear a portion of the external melody, but infinite harmony is heard by the master musician, and will in the end be heard by us. As Tennyson sings—in Carlylean philosophy.

High over waving Temple Bar
And wet in Heaven's third story,
We look at all things as they are,
But through a kind of glory.
This world is rich in roan and maid,
With fair horizons bound,
This whole wide world of light and shade
Comes out a perfect round.

Sartor Resartus means the Tailor Retailorized, and so the book is a discussion of appearances and realities, ever appealing to consciousness as a test of truth. It is a splendid mingle-mangle of biography, speculation, and editorial comment, imaginative in form, but the history of the human spirit in wider fact. Teufelsdröckh is Professor at Weisnichtwo. As the custom is, he spends many evenings with friends, thinking a great deal, amid clouds of smoke, ever and anon bursting out with eloquent rhapsodies on things in general. There is little logic in his talk or philosophy—he sweeps rather over the infinite universe of things and lets his mind rest a moment on grand realities whose praises he chants, then on meannesses which he denounces with divine passion. Every chant and denunciation is a prose poem, tantalising if you ask for connected thought, an indescribable joy if you yield yourselves to its valeionesque inspiration. Once he cries "Die Sache der Armen im Gottes und Teufel's Namen" —a prayer kindred to many of Isaiah's in its aspiration, but peculiarly Teufelsdröckhian in its mixture. A mass of M. S. are prepared for publication. Of them the editor professes to give an account as containing Teufelsdröckh's system. If system it can be called which has neither beginning, middle, nor end. Who, what am I? he asks. Body, matter, &c. But opinions on one side, the clothes, see man himself, man is a spirit, and yet an unutterable mystery. "To the eye of vulgar logic what is man?" That is the substance—all the rest is illustration. In a fashion that hints at common development he describes his phases of growth. We see his genesis, where he issues out of invisibility into visibility—the idyllic happy period of childhood, where he basks in rose-colored light—pedagogy and university life—getting under way where he inquires the meaning of things, holding a thinking man in the worst enemy the Prince of Darkness can have—period of romance, and inexorable sorrow following Elysium. Then, perplexed by doubt, and harassed by personal calamity, he falls into the Everlasting No. What is that? We live for pleasure, not duty; self, not God. Heaven and Earth are the boundless jaws of a devouring monster where we sink to night and death. Selfishness, materialism, atheism, are the three-headed Cerberus. Tasting the bitterness, and beholding the hollowness of this denial, he denies it, his whole being cries "I am not thine, but free, and for ever hate thee." That was his spiritual new birth—then he began to be a man. But hitherto he had only denied denial, he was so far affirmative, he had not attained to faith. He remains a while in the centre of indifference—wandering, not knowing, longing to see, but blind. At last, out of the blindness pit and the arid wilderness he is delivered, and proclaims the Everlasting Yea. "The Universe is not dead and demoniacal, a charnel house with spectres, but God-like and my Father's." (115.) Here he got hold of the knot which had been strangling him, untistened it, and was free. Close thy Byron, open thy Goethe, love not pleasure but God. Produce (126.) Now comes a time of pause—where he looks around, considers his whereabouts, and can grasp personal and universal destiny. He speculates on symbols—they hint indefinite history in such—all men—all religions. But they wax old, and what they symbolise is God, eternal. He speculates on the heritage which has been and is, but shall not nothing use—on the phœnix spirit of progress which cannot be destroyed—on the old clothes we have cast off—on the organic filaments we spin into new. He speaks to them he cries, "be of comfort" (135.) Then, in what the editor calls "a stupendous section," "natural supernaturalism," he piercest time and space and systems of things and holds we are from God and go to God. What is the world but clothes? What are we all but tailors, good or bad? Behold here the significance of an abused craft. Teufelsdröckh, who came to make die—in the hives of London were

we may suppose him meditating clothes of a fashion suited to the spirit of man. But always he inhabits Weisnichtwo, and yet he is everywhere, for he is you and me. Can you enjoy Sartor Resartus as science? No. Yet Tyndall enjoys it, because he is more than a mere man of science. As logic and reasoning? No. Yet Mill enjoyed it, for the emotional nature lived in him. As history or straightforward biography? No. Yet Froude enjoys it, for he possesses a kindred speculative genius, and equally has gone through the everlasting No, and yearns after the Yea. To enjoy it you must be something of the scientific, reasoning, historical, animal, but still more the poetic and the religious, and above all you must have a soul at once for reverence, tenderness, passion, and humour. Else it will be to you jewels and cinders. Carlyle's diversified mental landscape permits not my loitering long in one spot, though there are a dozen different Gardens of Eden tempting me, where the trees of knowledge and life are alike unforbidden. He had thrown himself heart and soul into history and biography. Nobler subjects are not, and for him nobler subjects cannot be; for he regards them as chapters in the bible of humanity, and the constantly-unfolding revelation of the purposes of God—purposes never completely fulfilled, but always tending to fulfilment—purposes still less completely understood, but whose meaning grows upon us, ending not in chaos and darkness, but in cosmos and sunshine to noble minds. These biographies and histories—as he writes them it is hard to tell which to call which, for his biographies have the vivid touch of history, and his histories have the personal charm of biography—are all strokes of genius. I now remain free to give general conclusions. Carlyle's literary style is simply perfect when he cares to make it so. The earlier essays, notably those on Characteristics and on Burns, are without a flaw. The French Revolution is the same. But there was always evident in him a tendency to run riot in speech, and to topple over from the giddy heights of magnificence into sheer extravagance. We see that in Sartor Resartus, where, however, Teufelsdröckh's own nature is half an excuse. You could not write about such a character in plain everyday prose. But in Chartism, the Latter Day Pamphlets, and in portions of the Frederick, we have too often wild disjointed splendour, corruscations of lightning flashing from abysses of darkness and leaving darkness behind.

The philosophy and religion I have implied as I have gone along. Evidently he is not orthodox in any popular sense of that word. But if we say, as a Church of England bishop once said, orthodoxy is my doxy, much might be predicated in favor of his view of things. He has been accused of Pantheism. He contemptuously answered he did not care whether it was Pantheism or Pot-theism. Any way his philosophy is a genuine religious philosophy after his own fashion. Where other men see God here and there, he sees God everywhere—where they have profane and holy lands he has all holy—where they have a primal, he has a universal government and victory. He has exceptional intervals of gloom, but this is his prevailing daylight. His attitude towards practical life and his moral judgments vary at various periods of his career. On the whole, he overrides the theory of Hero-worship, and sometimes forgets Teufelsdröckh's couplet, " Die Sache der Armen im Gottes und Teufel's Namen." The display of force lands him captive. He forgets it is one thing to admit that might will overcome right in the long run and a very different thing to maintain that might is always right here and now. Yet into this pitfall he often seems to stumble. Hence his glorifications of Frederick, his defence of Governor Eyre, his support of negro slavery, his scorn of the idea that the people are to govern themselves. But here also lurks his own extravagance. We can always appeal from Philip drunk to Philip sober, and answer him by himself.

One serious he has rendered of immense value. He has generated a devotion to earnestness, sincerity, and reality and a scorn of cant, shams, pretences, and all half-truths as if they were whole truths. He is the apostle of the gospel of honest work. The men whom he delights to honor were all workers. Groaning and complaining he despises. For his unmistakable that take not slope in action, but in action, in banishment and feeling he has no patience with. To him, the men who carry the secret of the universe in a nutshell, and prate glibly of the Infinite and Eternal as if they knew all that is higher than heaven and deeper than hell, and what human wisdom and the revelations we are capable of receiving, even in their angel flights only see through a glass darkly, are a victim burying their heads beneath their wings, and fancying themselves safe when they are only blinded. The vocation of

man is earnest and sincere work, not doubt, an abandonment to the faith that infinite variety is centred in unity; not asking all trees to be of the same size and all flowers to yield the same fragrance; a hearty co-operation with the eternal workman and the perfect hero who is God. Such is the impression that Carlyle makes on me.

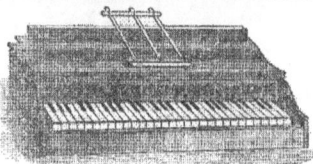

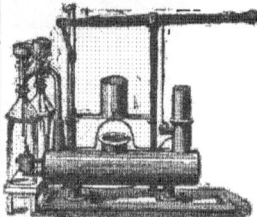

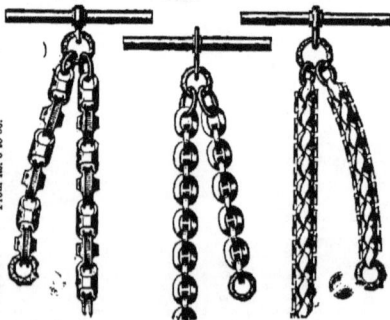

The Indian Mirror

[Edited by Krishna Bihari Sen, M.A.]

SUNDAY EDITION

[Registered at the General Post Office.]

VOL. XIX.   CALCUTTA, SUNDAY NOVEMBER 9, 1879.   NO. 267.

Telegraphic Intelligence.

FROM THE PRESS COMMISSIONER.

CABUL NEWS.

SIMLA, 8TH NOVEMBER.

General Macpherson and General Bright met on the 6th at Kattasang.

Editorial Notes.

CANON TRISTRAM expresses his fears, in the *Churchman*, that the new version of the Bible, owing to timidity, will not be so good as scholarship might make it.

MISS FRANCES POWER COBBE, who, we are glad to learn, has completely recovered her health, has promised to deliver several addresses to women during the approaching winter.

THE Czar of Russia owes his escape from Nihilist assassins, it is said, to a coat of mail which has been hit many times, but has always resisted the bullets. If the Czar had worn the armour of truth and justice instead, he would have been invulnerable.

DIODORUS SICULUS tells us that the Egyptian princes used to wear a golden chain mixed and distinguished with curious stones, and they called it Truth, meaning that nothing was a greater ornament to a prince, nothing ought to be more sacred or more remembered.

GENERAL DRAKE, of the United States, has left his whole fortune, of considerable amount, to three of his former slaves. He says : "They were my faithful slaves, and have remained with me since their freedom, nursing and caring for me in my old age, and I desire them to share my gratitude."

IN 1877, we observe, 17,000 persons were killed in India by snakes, and 3,000 by wild beasts. In the same year 127,000 snakes were killed, and 22,000 wild beasts. The number of snakes and wild beasts killed was thus greater than that of those which killed. This ought to encourage us in a struggle of a far different nature in the mind. People are daily killed by sin—a greater enemy than snakes or tigers. When will the day come when statistics of the moral world will be collected to show that more sins are killed every year than sinners ?

SOME one asked Lord Palmerston—" When is a man in his prime ?" " At seventy," was the reply. This reminds us of an aphorism by our Minister uttered a few years ago. Man's age, he said, is not to be counted progressively as 1, 2, 3, 4, but quite in an opposite order, as 4, 3, 2, 1. To our mind nothing could be more hopeful and cheering than this definition of progress. It is one which ought to be got by heart by every young man of India, to whom progress is synonymous with youth, and decline with insolence and age.

THE report of the American Free Baptist Mission in Orissa speaks in high terms of the Oriyas as a religious people. " The Oriyas," it says, " are among the most deeply religious of all the people of India. They afford one of the best examples known of a religion in life. So strong is the religious faculty in them that, should their faith in one form of belief fail, they would immediately embrace another, to satisfy the cravings of the devotional spirit. . . . . . Their faith in Hinduism is gone ; and, having learned that salvation, full and free, is being offered through faith in Christ, they have determined to accept the Gospel as it is presented in his name." The estimate is just ; but we fear the disposition to accept Christianity is exaggerated.

THE Roman Catholic Bishop of Salford has recently remarked, that " there never was a country in the world that possessed a love for riches such as our own country possessed, and there never was a race of men, intelligent, earnest, and energetic that so completely give itself up to the pursuit of wealth as the people of this country did. He knew no land in which the distinctions between rich and poor were so marked and so painful as they were in England. Beneath the outward film of union there were being organised daily more and more perfectly and more and more terrible bands and corporations which were separating the people, and which acted like wedges, cleaving society into portions, and separating one class from another. Unless this state of things was altered in time, and men ceased to prefer the love of gold and silver to the love of their neighbour, the greatness of England would rapidly pass away, like that of the empires of ancient times."

WE have not the honor of being acquainted with Rev. M. L. Bannerji, B.D., but we must say that his pamphlet on " True Christ," reprinted in the *Bombay Guardian*, does not inspire us with respect for his fairness as a critic. We are, for instance, seriously told that Babu Keshub Chunder Sen, in his lecture on Christ, preached the doctrines of pantheism and transmigration ! Why, this is something quite new to us. Can Mr. Bannerji quote any passage, in which the word transmigration is used ? And as regards pantheism, does not the context prove that the word has a sense totally distinct from that in ordinary use ? Any intelligent reader would be at no pains to find it out ? We are sure that in asserting to ignore the fact that a special meaning is attached to the word, thus assuming that the word is used in its ordinary sense and proceeding to judge the lecturer on the ground of this assumption, the writer has been guilty of an act of grave unfairness.

THE late Maharajah of Burdwan, the fourteenth in descent from the founder of his family, was born on the 17th November 1819, so that at the time of his death he was sixty years old. He ascended his father's guddi in 1835, when he was fourteen years of age and therefore reigned altogether about forty-seven years—a longer time than usually falls to the lot of Indian princes. The Maharajah was naturally of a robust constitution. Gifted with the tastes of a European, he knew the best modes of economising his health in the service of his State. Burdwan, now unfortunately rendered in accessible by the malaria, was long the healthiest and most beautiful town of Bengal. The Maharajah displayed all his taste and refinement in embellishing the place, and it is no exaggeration to say that even now any Bengali can well afford to be proud of it. In nothing was His Highness' wisdom better displayed than in the administration of the Raj. We doubt if ever there was a kinder master than he. Above all, the Maharajah was loyal. His services to Government were invaluable and ever to be remembered. Mahtab Chand is succeeded by his son, Aftab Chand, a youth twenty years old. May the new Maharajah maintain the traditions of the noble house whose glory and reputation he inherits.

AN article in the *Spectator* refers to a curious discovery made by a learned Italian savant in connection with the penal practices of the sixteenth century. Criminals, we learn, were hanged or beheaded, and their dead bodies given over to the doctors to be dissected. This would not be so objectionable, if the practice were not associated with another and a more hideous one, namely, that several men and women condemned to death by the Florentine Judges were, by the orders of Cosmo I, Duke of Tuscany, delivered over alive to be anatomised in the medical schools of Pisa. We learn here for the first time that the world had been given a chance of profiting by the exquisite tortures inflicted upon the human body, and that though the doctors enjoyed the luxury and were ever asking for more, yet the cause of science was never englished by a single discovery which may be said to have depended upon them. The modern advocates of vivisection find the world too conservative for them to allow them to exchange dogs for men. But that human victims would have been chosen, if there had been opportunities for so doing, is apparent. The reasons certainly are not wanting. Dr. Rutherford said before the Royal Commission some time ago, that "his torturing experiments on the stomachs of thirty-six dogs would only be really conclusive if tried on man."

THE nature and true functions of criticism are often misunderstood. We believe one-half of the mischief of sectarian controversy rises from the fact of unfair criticism. A critic is often supposed to be an enemy that is privileged to take every advantage, fair or unfair, over his opponent; and in controversial literature, the privilege generally taken the shape of misrepresentation. If an opponent is to be smashed, he sets to misrepresent or distort what he says—that is the strategy employed by disputants like Mr. Voysey and others. In India another element is added to this business—the imputation of motives or what goes by the name of personality. If our opinion be asked, we shall say that criticism is based on charity, and whatever violates this descends to the level of cavilling. Guided by charity, a critic is anxious first of all to give a fair resume of all that his opponents has said. Quotations should be made in abundance, and where these are wanting, the views of the opposite party set forth with the utmost preciseness and fidelity. The critic should for the time occupy the position of the person he is judging, and present from the latter's standpoint all the views which he is to combat. Thus fairly placed, he should fire his cannon against the enemy. How few are able or willing to be guided by this law of simple justice. Yet we think the time has come when the observance of this law should be openly insisted upon in this country, where bitterness is known to spoil the best effects of any controversy.

IN a late issue we published in these columns a summary of Mr. Froude's article in the Nineteenth Century, containing a full account of the successful imposture of Alexander of Abonitious, who flourished in the second century of the Christian era. The writer has there attributed Alexander's uncommon popularity to extreme credulity on the part of the people of the age, which was such as neither Lucian nor Epicurus could shake, in spite of their violent denunciation of Alexander's imposture. Mr. Froude remarks that "to persons so circumstanced men of intellect like Lucian addressed themselves in vain. The science of Epicurus was merely negative. He might insist that miracles were an illusion, and that the laws of nature were never broken; but to the human heart craving for light from heaven, and refusing to be satisfied without it, Epicurus had not a word to say, not a word of what lay behind the evil, not a word which would serve for guidance in the paths of ordinary duty." The learned writer, in his usual clear and flowing style, continues to generalize upon these facts, and writes that "intellect and experience may make it probable to thoughtful persons that morality and happiness go together; but when all is said, clever men are found of a different opinion; and if the

human race had waited to recognise the sanctions of moral obligations till science had made out on what they rested to its own satisfaction, the first steps out of barbarism would have been never taken. Knowledge is a plant which grows but slowly. Those who gather knowledge must live before they can learn. How to live, therefore, how to distinguish good from evil, press first for an immediate answer. And the answer was given by Conscience whole sons before reflecting intellect had constructed its theories of expediency and the greatest happiness of the greatest number."

THE annual report of the Society for the Suppression of Vice in England gives the following summary of seizures and destruction of offensive publications effected through the instrumentality of the Association since the year 1834 :—380,569 obscene prints, pictures, photographs, and negatives; 63,487 books and pamphlets, mostly illustrated with abominable engravings; upwards of five tons of letterpress of the same character, besides large quantities of infidel and blasphemous publications, 28,486 sheets of obscene songs, catalogues; handbills, &c.; 6,983 cards, snuff boxes, and other articles; 98 gross of obscene models, life size, in wax; 844 engraved copper and steel plates, 430 lithographic stones, 174 wood blocks, 11 printing presses, with tools and apparatus ; 82 cwt. of type, including the stereotype of several entire works of the grossest immorality. Mr. C. H. Collette, the Secretary to the Society, writes that in addition to these results the prosecutions of the past few months led to the seizure and destruction of 18,000 obscene periodicals, and that the proceedings thus taken have had the effect of clearing the streets of a great and growing scandal." What a pity that a similar Society, established years ago in Calcutta, was allowed to die from sheer inanition and neglect. There were many who condemned the establishment of this institution at the time. But the working of the English society shows the admirable results of any effective organisation for putting down a growing and fearful nuisance. The London Globe accuses the Englishman of the lower classes " of using in his common conversation, as mere expletives, expressions which, in coarseness and brutality, to say nothing of their profanity, exceed almost anything that could be found elsewhere." If that is true in England, how much truer is India, where in every street female relatives are abused and insulted in a manner most abominable. We really want a Society which will expel this obscenity from the heart of the Indian nationality.

LOOKING over our scrap-book we found a number of jottings on the question of future life. As we were a great deal interested by them, we hope they will interest our readers too. We give them below just in the order in which we found them :—

Christianity was the first to proclaim a future life to men in Europe and Western Asia. The ancient philosophers had their opinions which were not shared by the multitude.
Their highest lore was for the few conceived. By schools discussed, but none by crowds believed. The angel-ladder cloven the heavenly steep, But at its foot the priesthood lay asleep.
They did not preach to nations, "Lo, your God!" No thousands followed where their footsteps trod ;
Not to the fishermen they said, "Arise !" Not to the lowly offered they the skies.
Wisdom was choice ; else ! what men most need Is to soul a wisdom, but the people's creed. Thou, not for schools, but the human kind, The uncultured reason, the unlettered mind,

The poor, the oppressed, the laborer, and the slave,
God said, "Be light" and light was on the grave!
No more alone to sage and hero given,—
For all wide oped the impartial gates of heaven.
                            Bulwer Lytton, New Times, Part IV.

Xenophon puts the following speech into the mouth of the expiring Cyrus :—" I was never able, say children, to persuade myself that the soul, as long as it was in a mortal body, lived, but when it was removed from this, that it died; neither could I believe that the soul ceased to think when separated from the unthinking and senseless body; but it seemed to me most probable that when pure and free from any union with the body, then it became most wise."

Every one has read of the young man whose faith and curiosity were so excited by Plato's writings that he committed suicide to test the fact of futurity.
Cellimachus tells the story nearly :—
Cleombrotus, the Ambracian, having said, "Farewell,
O sun !" leaped from a lofty wall into the world Of ghosts. No deadly ill had chanced to him at all ;
But he had read in Plato's book upon the soul.

The falling of Cato on his sword at Utica, after carefully perusing the Phaedo, is equally familiar.
Of Cicero, it is said, that while he always regarded the vulgar notions as puerile falsehoods, the hope of a glorious life to come was powerful in him.

Among the Mahomedans hell is divided into 7 stories. The first and mildest is for the wicked among the true believers. The second is assigned to the Jews. The third is the special apartment of the Christians. The fourth is allotted to the Sabians, the fifth to the Magians, and the sixth to the most abandoned idolaters, but the seventh—the deep and worst—belongs to the hypocrites of all religions. The first hell shall finally be emptied and destroyed, on the release of the wretched believers there ; but all the other hells will retain their victims eternally.

The Esquimaux paradise is surrounded by great pots full of boiled walrus-meat.
The Turk's heaven is a gorgeously idealised pleasure-garden or celestial harem.
The Pharisees, some of them at least, excluded the rabble from the resurrection.
The Peruvians confined their heaven to the nobility.
The Russians, even so late as the times of Peter the Great, believed that only the Czar and the boyars could reach heaven.

A pious and aged female disciple once asked Mahomed concerning her future condition in heaven. The prophet replied : "There will not be any old women in heaven." She wept and bewailed her fate, but was comforted upon the gracious assurance from the prophet's lips, "they will all be young again when there."

THE ATHEISTIC MOVEMENT.

ATHEISM is always charged with immorality. It seems, however, that the tables are turned; and, instead of brooking the charge of immorality, it openly charges religion with being less moral than itself. Advocates of unbelief are in the habit of maintaining that their ethics is higher, nobler and more unselfish than that of religion. The assertion itself is a sign of the times. It proves how society has changed, and changed for the better in these days, though it does not prove that the intrinsic claims of atheism to our regard have at all improved. Curious controversies on this subject are often waged in the pages of magazines and newspapers of the day. Among others we may mention that now waged between Mr. Mallock and Miss Bevington in the Nineteenth Century. Mr. Mallock is a clever writer, who maintains that morality without religion cannot exist, that, "on an atheistic scheme of man's life and destiny, the essential superiority of virtue to vice cannot be shown, no standard exists by which the transcendent value of the former can be evinced, and individual taste must ultimately decide between the claims of the two; whereas the believer in God and immortality has no difficulty in showing that virtue excelleth vice as far as light excelleth darkness." Against this view is that put forth by Miss Bevington who—will our readers believe it?—is an atheist. Well, it is sufficiently disagreeable to have to meet with a lady-atheist for an adversary. But as our concern is not with Miss Bevington, but with the system she upholds, we may address ourselves to a point or two raised in the controversy under notice. Miss Bevington tells us that "conscience, in the sense of supreme regard to the general welfare, supreme devotion to the social idea, has been evolved, and that the 'nature' which evolved it can take care of it, even though Christianity and all other religions are swept away." We think this ought to be proved. As matters apparently stand, atheism declares that its code of morality is independent of, and superior to, that of theism. In order to establish the correctness of this position, it is necessary, in the first place, to tell us what atheistic morality is. Up to this time we have never come across an ethical code published by atheists. In the second place, it is necessary to see whether a code of ethics, which is not sanctioned by God and carries its own authority with it, can practically stand the test of time and experience. Now, experiment is a good thing, and we are disposed to ask all atheists to put their assertion to experiment. Why should not a community be formed, composed of atheists, existing aloof from the religious world? Why should not this community be guided entirely by atheistic laws, trained by atheistic educationists, and brought up under atheistic tendencies? It may be objected that grown-up unbelievers have been brought up under Christian influences, and their morality must necessarily be Christian. But that does not matter much. A whole generation of children have to be educated, and let these, like J. S. Mill, be kept in ignorance of every thing that would suggest God. Fifty years or a century will suffice for an experiment like this, and then the world will have a clear opportunity of for ever settling the question whether it can live without a God. Gentle reader, do you think the experiment has never been made? A whole nation of enthusiasts, in a true iconoclastic fashion, banished God away from their land, and in the course of a few years destroyed monarchy, aristocracy, church and every time-honored and recognised institution in the land. The goddess Reason was publicly worshipped, and our poor God was burnt in effigy. Every thing that the most cordial hater of religion could suggest to bring it to contempt and oblivion was done. Godless schools, Godless courts of law, Godless armies, Godless societies were established everywhere; and not only that, but every means was adopted to persecute religion out of the land. The French Revolution did wonders. It shook the thrones of Europe, and almost gave a death-blow to Christianity. All this it did. France was atheistic, and the French Revolution became an essentially atheistic movement. Did it succeed? Let history answer the question.

ECLECTICISM.

THE doctrine of eclecticism has been very much misrepresented. We are familiar with the almost contemptuous mode in which the late Mr. G. H. Lewes criticised the writings of eclectic philosophers of the school of Cousin and others. Now it is not very difficult to dispose of the arguments by which it has been sought to prove the falsity of the eclectic method. This system has special reference to the world of mind where different views on its nature and constitution are held by different persons. The mind, it is to be remembered, is many sided, and every school of philosophers represents only one side of it. It would be wrong to say that the side referred to is wrong, or that one particular method is to be preferred over the others. To those who accept the mind as immaterial every one of the sides represents one aspect of truth. We are not going to illustrate our position by examples drawn from the region of mental philosophy. Religion presents many examples of the kind. If the human mind represents so many phases of its aspirations and inner working, much more varied must the manifestations of the Supreme Mind be when examined and understood by the finite intellect. Different nations in different ages have formed different conceptions of God. It would be as unreasonable to reject any one of these as false, as it would be to say that the bit of ground which we occupy does not form a part of the immense world in which we move. It would not do to reject the prevalent religions of the world, we say, in preference to a particular one. As the world progresses, eclecticism becomes inevitable. Leading writers, animated by the comparative method, have recognised the truth as it is in other religions, and the prejudice long entertained that every creed that we do not hold must be false, is gradually dispelled. Scholars like Max Müller and Monier Williams, divines like Dean Stanley and Martineau have bravely recognised the duty of acknowledging truth wherever got. In fact, our conviction grows from day to day that as knowledge extends and faith expands, eclecticism will become a necessity. The very necessities of the mental organisation will lead it to open new worlds and get new truths from foreign sources. In India, eclecticism is a necessity. There are many persons who are dead to all idea of importing truths from outside. Why accept an un-Hindu truth?—is the cry of many patriots. Now, to men who have set themselves up as reformers nothing seems to be a clearer axiom than this, that to elevate the Hindu nationality some new life, new light or new spirit is needed, and as this is not to be gained from India, the inspiration must come from abroad. English education itself is an element entirely un-Hindu. Has not Shakspeare given a tone to the thought of our educated men? Has not science fired us with the craving for real, earnest work? So must it be with the religious life of the Hindus. The influences of foreign thought must be brought to bear upon the present degraded nature of our countrymen. India must accept Shakspeare, Science and Christ—the three great powers that have already stirred Native society to its depth. The mind is essentially Indian, but new thoughts and new influences must raise it from its present inactivity. Now, if the spirit of Europe be necessary to revivify Asia, it will not do merely to accept truths and recognise them intellectually. The spirit of truth must be imbibed and assimilated, and the mind grow harmoniously along with it. Thus, if, for instance, it be true that every Hindu should recognise the usefulness of calm and silent contemplation prevalent in ancient India, the necessity of cherishing the exemplary spirit of active charity, benevolence and public spirit of Christians, and the good of learning the positive side of science, we do not say that these should be intellectually discerned. No. The mind should absorb these various elements and grow with them to greater and healthier manhood. Eclecticism is thus unity of character. The many-sided wants of human nature find diverse modes of removing them, and all these modes mix in the same mind in a harmonious unity. Thus the mind grows, the character grows, and with these manhood itself grows. If India grows also, it must be through the active principle of eclecticism we have here explained.

MISSIONARY EXPEDITION.

[FROM ONE OF THE PARTY.]

THE Missionary Expedition had thought of starting at once for the Upper Provinces to preach the name of the Lord unto the educated and the uneducated in the land. But they soon saw reasons to plan differently. Friends in the provinces were dispersing in all directions, and requested us to adjourn the expedition till after the holidays, or the party would find the stations deserted. So we continued our operations during the holidays within a limited area in lower Bengal. College Square in Calcutta was the ground the party occupied first. There they began the campaign. The foremost schools and colleges in Bengal were in the neighbourhood, and the place selected was the centre of enlightenment and the focus of national education. Our party, therefore, occupied this vantage ground, and commenced operations with the greatest enthusiasm, attacking infidelity and scepticism right and left, flank and rear. The Lord himself descended as the Minister invoked His blessing, and soon reinforced the army with the artillery of heavenly inspiration. The Minister spoke most vehemently, and directed his eloquence against men of little faith. The onslaughts were terrible. The audience, composed of about seven hundred young men of the educated classes, felt moved and thrilled. The address was followed by Sankértan. Having thus fortified their position in the metropolis, the preaching army shortly after crossed the river, and occupied the maidan facing St. Thomas' School. A short but effective lecture was delivered here, the mind preventing a larger gathering. Then Naihati, and then Chinsurah formed the field of our operations. The scene at the former place was enthusiastic. There was a copious shower of rain at the time, the Minister and the entire band were drenched. Yet the preaching went on, and then the singing without any interruption whatever, and about five hundred persons including all varieties of people, learned Brahmins, enlightened young men, shawkeydars, porters, railway coolies, shop-keepers, and even public women, continued to hear with rapt attention. At Chinsurah also we had a very large assembly composed almost exclusively of the young men of our schools and colleges, and a few European gentlemen. We closed our brief holiday campaign, and returned to Calcutta. The result was, the standard of the Most High was raised at four important and advantageous points at the extremities of two parallel lines on either side of the river. There was no premeditated plan. The autumnal festival of the Brahmo Somaj of India came off at this time, and our party took advantage of the occasion to enjoy a boat excursion to the aurora of the Dakhineshwar Hindu devotee. The moonlight mission was a great success. The party seated on the steps of the splendid ghat to hear the Minister's appeal numbered seventy-five. All who went, including the ladies, felt refreshed and edified.

Then began the second or main campaign. News came that notice had been given and arrangements made for an open-air address at Chandernagore. There was hardly time for preparation, and the party had to get ready at once. November 1, Saturday, they left Howrah by the 5 P.M. train with flags, mridanga, trumpet, and other requisites of kirtan. On the open space near Laldigi, the Minister gave an address in Bengali to about three hundred persons, after which they went in a procession singing hymns to their residence. Next day there was heavy work to get through. In the morning service was held at a friend's house. At the request of the local Hari Sabha, a lecture was delivered in Bengali to more than eight hundred persons, lasting for an hour. The subject was most appropriate to the occasion,—"Chaitanya." The Hindus cheered repeatedly, warmly crying "Hari Haribola." The Minister explained why he adored the Prophet of Nadia, who came as Bhakti incarnate to deliver Bengal from dry rationalism and sensuality, and whose spirit he and all Bengal cherished in their very life-blood. Numbers of respectable ladies listened attentively from house tops seated behind chicks. The lecture was delivered in the midst of a public road, which had been kindly placed at the disposal of the meeting, and which was beautifully decked with flags, pictures and evergreens, and covered with a splendid canopy. The spectacle was unique and impressive. The respectable people were seated on carpet, the poorer classes standing on either side. The kirtan followed, in which the Hindus cordially joined the Brahmos. One of them, the foremost member perhaps, got so far excited that he prostrated himself before the procession, and rolled on the dust of the street. He went with the procession dancing joyfully. Everybody was struck. The whole affair conclusively proved the sincere regard which the more devout Hindus feel towards our leader and our cause in spite of our so-called leanings towards Christ. In the evening Divine service was conducted in the local Brahmo Somaj. On Monday morning in an adjoining garden on the banks of the river, the Minister conducted service under a shady tree. Then the party cooked their own meals and had a delicious repast at midday. Immediately the party left Chandernagore in boats and crossed over to Jagardat. There they went in a procession through the streets singing the name of the Lord, and at last reached a place where carpets had been laid and a table was provided for a short address. The Minister spoke for half an hour. Here a group, and there a group, above, behind the windows of the neighbouring houses, a good number of ladies heard the address very attentively. The sankirtan was resumed, and the party returned to their boats, and as they glided on the bosom of the river, the flags were seen flying with the words "Satya meva jayate" and "Come all nations unto the True God," and in solemn and sweet chorus the name of the All-Merciful ascended to the skies. By the evening train the party left for Mokameh. The carriages were unusually crowded, a large number of pilgrims being on the way to Gya. There was little or no rest,

and the inconvenience terminated with the journey. Reached at 8 A.M., the next day. There was the usual morning service at a friend's house, and in the afternoon a visit to Parashuram Asram. In the evening there was a prayer-meeting and also a short sermon on the "Reconciliation of the Vedas and the Puranas in the present dispensation of the Brahmo Somaj," after which the party returned to their residence singing hymns in the streets. An appeal was made to those present for passage money, as the funds had run short. Generous friends and sympathisers responded, and the party left on Wednesday morning after prayer. At Barrh, in a Hindu serai or chati, within two or three hours, the brethren cooked and breakfasted, and were ready in time for the Barrh Ghat train, which was to start at about 1 P.M. But a difficulty arose which had also troubled the party before. Insufficient funds! Soon the Lord cleared the path. A number of books and tracts for sale were handed to Bengali gentlemen at the station, and the deficit, about two or three rupees, was immediately realized. Having reached the station, we were surprised to learn that the steamer would not start till next morning. We had not a single acquaintance there, and knew not how to accommodate ourselves during the night. But our anxieties were soon relieved. The Station Master proved an obliging friend, and his hospitality was most thankfully accepted. Spent the evening pleasantly on board a big Native boat, on which we fixed our flags, and which went up and down the stream, and at times while I round and round, while the party sang "Jale Hari Sthale Hari." We landed when it was dark, and soon found ourselves in the midst of a number of up-country men. The sweet Hindi hymn "Harise lagi raho re bhai" was chanted, and then other hymns followed. Left Barrh Ghat early next morning, Thursday, bathed on the deck of the steamer, reached Banidpore at about 8 A.M., left by the Tirhut State Railway, had regular service in the railway carriage, and reached Mozufferpore at about 12. There was no better vehicle to be had, and five ekkas brought our party and luggage to the residence of the Native Executive Engineer, under whose hospitable roof the party, somewhat tired and exhausted, have found shelter and relief.

Brahmo Somaj.

The usual monthly morning service will be held in the Brahma Mandir to-day.

Babu Gour Gobind Roy, who has returned from Lucknow, conducted Divine Service in the Brahma Mandir last Sunday in the absence of the minister.

The following gentlemen form the Missionary Expedition party:—Babus Kathab Chunder Sen, Protibkya Nath Sanyal, (the Singing Missionary,) Aghore Nath Gupta, Guru Nath Mozumder, Peary Mohan Chowdhry, Banga Chandra Roy, Girish Chandra Sen, Wooms Nath Gupta, and Ram Chandra Singh.

The following is a substance of the sermon preached in Bengali by the Minister at the Brahma Mandir on the evening of the last Bhadrotsab :—He is a Theist who has ornaments in every part of his body, but he who has them in only one part is not to be called such. All along it has been the custom of a religious community to take one ornament. Hardly more than one idea is taken hold of. Spiritual ornaments are so precious and singular that a single jewel is enough

to satisfy the heart of man. God is casting so many jewels that man cannot receive them all together. But to collect these jewels is the mission of Brahmoism. The Brahmo Somaj addresses itself to all religious communities in the world, and demands from them those jewels which they individually possess. This appeal of the Brahmo Somaj is responded to, and diamonds and gold, pearls and silver, are brought to it by each. The Brahmo Somaj began to adopt the yoga from one, bhakti from another, asceticism or the renunciation of self (vyragya) from some, and enthusiasm from another again. Many wondered at this, and blamed the Somaj. As the rains descend from the skies, so truths come down from heaven. Man's eyes, ears, and heart are small and narrow, he cannot hold all truths within himself. Man grasps a little. Whenever a nation is in want of an idea, invariably that idea displays itself. Thus has a single idea been developed by every community. The Theistic Church of the day is destined to fulfil a new mission by collecting these ideas together. But these religious communities and the Brahmo Somaj differ widely from each other. In those religions which have come into this world at different times, no religious teacher has ever individually shown more than one ornament. One religious body can be distinguished from another by a peculiar idea essential to it. We can know that such a great man spoke to such a nation, and can then understand how his idea ran through, and found advocates in thousands of his disciples. The Vedas, the Upanishads, the Puranas, the Yoga Shastras, Bhakti Shastras, Christianity, Islam—each has its peculiar idea. Almost universally man selects a particular religion and follows it. But when the Theist opens his eyes, he sees thousands of stars on all sides of him. Not a single jewel can he leave off. He is not satisfied with one. On the contrary, he is tempted to have one and all. His heart is attached to universal truth. He desires to bedeck his whole body with jewels. Great are the demands of the Brahmo child. And God fulfils them. Ambition is stirred in his breast. The outward system of religious organization with him becomes angular also. The child says, "I won't leave anything; sun and moon, rain and fire—I will take all." The ample minded child of God is ignorant of what is possible and what is otherwise. He does not care to know whether his heart is small or large. He would take silver and gold and all. There are no limits to his ambition. He does not understand any particular doctrine, but comes into the world with all embracing and universal Brahmoism. He is born and destined not to follow any particular sect. Countless stars he finds in the spiritual sky. To all at once is his heart attracted. He prays to the Lord of the universe—"Give me this, give me that, give me all—I cannot leave a single ornament. What is now going on, I would take; what happened four hundred years before, even that I would have. From the Rishis I will learn yoga and meditation; again, in the midst of Bhaktas I will be intoxicated with the love of God. Of enthusiasm and asceticism, I will not set aside the least. Wherever I find deep truths, with all humility I will take them." Whither doth God lead the Theist? There where all sorts of jewels—where all ornaments for his body can be found! And if the ear has worn the ear-ring of truth, why should the neck remain bare? Surely, necklaces are found in God's Kingdom. Again, if the neck is adorned, why should the hand remain without ornament? A bracelet is wanted. The limbs should be adorned. The sober Theist gathers ornaments from all quarters. None can be a Brahmo who accepts portions of truths. Brahmoism is impossible without wholeness. Every one must put on all these ornaments such as yoga, bhakti and shakti. Every one is to show his fitness and capacity for collecting real truths. No sects should be despised; and yet a line of demarcation must be strongly marked out between Brahmoism and other communities. Truths must be learnt with humility from heaven-appointed prophets and great men. All communities must be welcomed in the Brahmo Somaj. Its chief characteristic is that it is friendly to all sects. So different ideas are reconciled here. Fire and water, enthusiasm and love, yoga and shakti, purity and peace are intermingled. The same person is a yogi and bhakta, a ascetic and family-man. God has called the Brahmo Somaj to harmonize these apparently inconsistent ideas. Whereas each religion of the world is a precious jewel, Brahmoism is a string of jewels. Hitherto these truths lay scattered, but now is the time to gather. So long it was raining down from heaven; but now the water is to be collected in a reservoir. Let each Brahmo gather, and thus fulfil God's will.

Devotional.

FATHER, what is the object of the Missionary Expedition Thou hast organized and despatched?

I desire to establish the reign of the Mother in this land.

But do not the people, O God, love Thee as their Mother?

No. They feared me as their King, they have loved me as their Father. They have yet to love and honor me as their Mother.

Hast Thou, O Lord, given the Expedition to understand that this is the central idea of their mission?

Yes. The enlightened in the land have given up prejudices and worship me as the Supreme Spirit. The unenlightened but devout worship their goddesses tenderly and lovingly, and offer homage and prayers to idols whom they address as their Divine Mother. The two I desire to harmonize. The enlightened Theist shall cast away the idol, but love me with his whole heart and soul as his affectionate and dear Mother. I am determined to convert every true Brahmo temple into a tabernacle of the Supreme Mother, where my sons and daughters will adore me with ardent love, and seek salvation on the maternal lap.

And what shall be the food and drink of Thy disciples?

The milk of the Mother's breast. Nothing else. They will not eat, but I, their Mother, will feed them. They are little children, and will have to depend only upon the milk I supply for their nourishment.

And what will be their form of prayer and worship?

As the babe cries for milk in language inarticulate, so shall my children pray unto me. Prayer is nothing but the baby-soul's cry for milk.

My God, if Thy children go about preaching the gospel of the Mother's love, what will be the upshot of the expedition, and how will it be received by the people of the land?

The devout will love them and honor them in spite of differences of opinion. But the unbelieving classes, rich, learned and worldly-minded, will despise the Army of the Mother. They shall be reduced to the level of the poor, and they shall mix with the lowest and the humblest in the streets and in the market place, and they shall do things contemptible in the eyes of the world, and, therefore, the world will ridicule and hate them and persecute them, and many will shun their company. Yet my name shall prevail, and my enemies I will vanquish with my army. And I will cause victory to fly round the banners of my preaching band, in spite of the ridicule and hatred of an infidel generation. Blessed are they who believe in the Divine Mother!

Correspondence.

[We do not hold ourselves in any way responsible for the opinions of our correspondents.—ED., I. M.]

RAM MOHUN ROY'S MOTHER.

TO THE EDITOR OF THE "INDIAN MIRROR."

SIR,—In my article on Rajah Ram Mohun Roy, which appeared in the last number of the *Arya Darsan*, a mistake as to the name of the mother of the illustrious Rajah inadvertently crept in; her real name was *Foolmoney*, but she was called *Fulmoney*, owing to a custom prevalent among the Hindus by which the fifth son, daughter and daughter-in-law of a family are generally titled *Ful*, as the eldest *Baro*, the second *Mejo*, &c. Trusting you will kindly publish this,

Yours &c.,
N. M. CHATTERJI.

23rd October 1879.

OPEN-AIR MEETINGS OF THE BRAHMO SOMAJ.

TO THE EDITOR OF THE "INDIAN MIRROR."

SIR,—Your Somaj has taken the very glorious course of adopting the plan originated in the devout soul of Chaitanya who made a free gift of the Name to all people without distinction of place and person. He roved about with his followers from door to door, singing the Holy Name. The sound entered the ears of the people like a flash of lightning, dispelling darkness from the mind. How many a wretched and wandering soul found peace and joy in the sweet *Sankirtan* of Gauranga. The late *Utsub*, celebrated by your Minister, has created some sensation, and the foot prints of the *Sankirtan* party will long be remembered by the people of the small tract of the country through which it passed. It is a move in the right direction. Chaitanya was a man of the people, and the people loved him. Though the learned abhorred him, yet they stood amazed at the convulsion he created throughout Bengal. If the plan of open-air meetings round the country be systematically carried on, it will work wonders in a very short time. What your Minister had not been able to do in twenty years will be done in two. The populace must see him, hear him and have easy access to him, and then he will find a place in their hearts. To tell you the truth, Mr. Editor, I have a very great regard for his mission, (though I differ from him in many respects); and I am sometimes bewildered by the flow of divine ideas and thoughts from the lips of this man. I often try to look upon him as one of those great luminaries who appear in the world from time to time to regenerate mankind; but then I fail as soon as I remember that he is the master of that splendid mansion (the Lily Cottage), and is surrounded by all the luxuries of the world. When I remember that, a screen instantly falls over my eyes, and I am driven to find peace under the shade of trees and on the tops of mountains, where devout saints are surrounded by faithful disciples and friends with whom they enjoy continued love and happiness. Can you tell me why this is so?

Yours &c.,
AN OLD VAISHNAVA.

Patna City.

ECCENTRICITY.

TO THE EDITOR OF THE "INDIAN MIRROR."

SIR,—Who will not sympathise with that profound thinker, who says "you are on earth and expect justice!" Verily man can do little justice to man, God being our best judge. He alone can do what it is impossible for a frail mortal to do—to search our hearts. In one of his eloquent sermons, our Minister once said, "Actions, and actions! God does not mind about our *actions* (*karma*), but about the *motives* of which the former are the expression—the outward manifestation. The treasure that we carry to our Heavenly abode is not works of public utility, but the progress which our souls make." You may have a heart as noble as that of a Howard; but being a creature of circumstances, occasions may not have yet arisen for the nobility of our soul finding an expression. The world looks upon you to be as mean as the dingy hut you live in! I was led to the above reflections by the thought of what the world calls eccentricity. What injustice, what injury to reputation—that "celestial part" of himself—is done by his neighbours to a man, whose only fault is that he has originality of nature and thinks in advance of his fellows. Admitted that there are odd creatures, whose heads are full of meaningless crochets; but what the common herds of mankind call eccentricity, if analized, would often be found to be no eccentricity at all. Are you a sincere Brahmo averse to encouraging idolatry, directly or indirectly, absent yourself from the house of your father during the three days that the ten-handed idol is worshipped in your family "god-house," and you will be set down as an eccentric young man. Are you fond of manly exercises and patriotic enough to see young men indulging therein, engage in a rowing match with school boys, young enough to be your children, and you will be branded with eccentricity. Are you a young Deputy Magistrate of a laborious turn of mind, and fond of working in your own garden with your own hands, weed it or fell the *Deodar* or *Neem* tree, whose shade prevents some of the favorite plants from thriving, and the staring multitude on the road, who have peculiar notions of "respectability," will daub you with "a fool." A high sense of duty may impel you to snatch away the brandy bottle from the hand of a friend, already half sea over, and whom, you are sure, the next two or three glasses will render "incapable of taking care of himself," and your friends though forming a "select party," will, behind your back, say that you are a *Pagla* (fool). Let a judicial officer—a Brahmo—fond of hymns and songs, come back from the Prayer Meeting with his favorite musical instrument (*Tanpura*) in his own hands, or learn *bhajan* (hymns) from any of the professional beggars (*sadhus*) who support themselves by singing, and his own peon, Fatteh Ali, will lose no time to whisper to his servant, Ram Gholam, that "Babu has turned a *bourah*" (madman). Let a European gentleman, belonging to the highest grade of the Educational Service do what men of his class do in England—go to the Bazar, buy his own stores and bring them home in his own hands, his Civilian friends will never approve of his eccentric behaviour, and the Native public will look upon him as a veritable Bedlamite. Space permitting, illustrations might be multiplied. Be only rigid in principles and act from a high sense of duty—duty to yourself, to your friends and neighbours, and to God—duty of which the worldly-minded slaves to custom,—and their name is legion—can form no adequate conception, and your character for what the world calls eccentricity is established. What is unfortunate is that, the majority of those with whom you come in contact in your daily intercourse with the world answer Mill's description of the public:—"That miscellaneous collection of many foolish and of a few wise persons." They will not only themselves run in a certain groove and follow the beaten track, but are fond enough to wish that the world should do so. In his little essay on "Liberty" the above-named thinker gives it out as his opinion that he will do real good to the world who, even at the risk of being charged with eccentricity, can trample under foot customs more honoured in the breach than the observance. Yes, who, having a reflective turn of mind, will deny the truth embodied in the old adage—"Custom is the plague of wise men, but the idol of fools"? Resolve into its component parts the charge of what the world calls eccentrity, and you will find that, in not a few cases, it is brought against those who have originality of nature, and originality of nature is sure to show itself in more ways than one. Benjamin Franklin appeared at the Court of the French Monarch in plain clothes, and in the white hats worn by the last generation of radicals. George Fox had a suit of leather, and Pestalozzi was given by his schoolfellows the nickname of "Harry Oddity." Examine your reforming and rationalist friends, and you will find most of them exhibit, in dress or behavior, "some degree of what the world calls eccentricity." So says Herbert Spencer, who also adds that men of revolutionary aims in politics or religion are commonly revolutionists in custom also, and that those whose office is to uphold established arrangements in State and Church, are also those who most adhere to the social forms and observances bequeathed by past generations. "To the true reformer," he says further, "no institution is sacred, no belief above criticism. Every thing shall conform itself to equity and reason; nothing shall be saved by its prestige. Conceding to each man liberty to pursue his own ends and satisfy his own tastes, he demands for himself like liberty, and consents to no restrictions on this, save those which other men's equal claims involve. No matter whether it be an ordinance of one man, or an ordinance of all men, if it trenches on his legitimate sphere of action, he denies its validity. The tyranny that would impose on him a particular style of dress and a set mode of behaviour, he resists equally with the tyranny that would limit his buyings and sellings or dictate his creed. Whether the regulation be formally made by a legislature, or informally made by a society at large, whether the penalty for disobedience be imprisonment or frowns of social ostracism, he sees to be a question of no moment. He will utter his belief notwithstanding the threatened punishment; he will break conventions in spite of the petty persecutions that will be visited on him. Show him that his actions are inimical to his fellow-men, and he will pause. Prove that he is disregarding their legitimate claims—that he is doing what, in the nature of things, must produce unhappiness; and he will alter his course. But until you do this—until you demonstrate that his proceedings are essentially irrational, unjust, or ungenerous, he will persevere."

Yours &c.,
A MOFUSSIL THEIST.

The 10th August 1879.

NOTICES TO CORRESPONDENTS.

Persons favoring us with communications are requested to write legibly, and on one side of the paper only.

Unauthenticated communications will not be inserted.

AN OLD VAISHNAVA.—We do not insert your first letter, as you entirely misunderstand the drift of our remarks. Please read the article headed "Through Nature to Nature's God" again, and then say if you are still of opinion that we are opposed to the chanting of the Holy Name. By the way, will you kindly send us your name, whenever you write again?

JR. CH. B.—No, you are wrong. You merely extend the chain by adding another premiss, which is again quite unnecessary, as it is already involved in the last. To love God carries with it the idea of loving "every creature" and "every good action."

Provincial.

THE MISSIONARY EXPEDITION TO CHANDERNAGORE.

—o—

[FROM OUR OWN CORRESPONDENT.]

CHANDERNAGORE, *the 5th October 1879.*

THE visit of Babu Keshub Chunder Sen and his party was an important event in our town. The party reached here last Saturday, and Babu Keshub Chunder addressed a large crowd in *Kutirmat* on the existence of God. Many educated gentlemen of the town joined the crowd. The party stopped for the night at the dispensary of Babu Aghore Chunder Ghose, situated in the heart of the town. Next morning, Sunday, service was conducted in the house of Babu Mahendro Nath Rakhit, and the party returned to the dispensary again. Babu Sarat Chunder Pal, the devoted member of the *Hari Sabha* at Palpara, invited Babu Keshub Chunder to visit the place. He and his party gladly consented. It was arranged that the evening address should be delivered there. From morning this pleasant piece of news ran from place to place throughout Chandernagore. The ignorant and uninformed, who knew nothing of this Keshub, were enthusiastic to hear him. At noon, the streets of Palparah were decorated with gates of evergreens and flowers. Letters and words of welcome were placed in conspicuous parts, and flags, bearing the name of God, were set flying at intervals. The Hari Sabha was also tastefully decorated. A canopy was erected over the street in front of the building. A large carpet was spread over the street, and chairs and benches, as many as could be procured, were placed around. A platform was placed for the lecturer in front of the Hari Sabha. About six hundred gentlemen were collected on the spot, among whom we noticed Babus Pran Kissen Chowdhry, Dino Nath Das, Russic Chunder Dey, Hurrish Chunder Mittra, Khetter Chunder Ghose, M. A., B. L., Murary Mohun Nundy, Shoshi Bhuson Ghose, Mahindra Chunder Ghose, B. A., B. L., Hari Mohun Sur, B. A., B. L., Harish Chunder Bannerji, Dino Nath Mozumder, Radhagobind Das, Mohindra Nath Rukhit, Gopal Chunder Nundy and others. At half past four the party of Babu Keshub Chunder arrived. They were welcomed by the firing of muskets. They retired for a while into the rooms of the Hari Sabha. Then amidst Sankirtan and the music of Miridanga and bugle and *Bheri*, Babu Keshub Chunder took his seat in the chair on the platform. He began by thanking the Hari Sabha for bringing about this large gathering. Selecting Chaitanya as the subject of his address, he said his grandfather and father were great Vaishnavas, and he, as their descendent, admired and sympathised with their spirit. He threw no additional light on the life and times of Chaitanya, nor evinced any extraordinary antiquarian research. He directed himself simply to the *Bhakti*, the force of will, the self-abnegation of that mighty reformer. He concluded by exhorting all to keep in mind a single sentence at least of his speech, inasmuch as it would bring the name of God and his omnipresence in their mind as they went on with their worldly transactions. For an hour the whole audience heard with rapt attention. The aged Hindus, never accustomed to such an exhibition of energy in words, called out *sabash! sabash!* Some who had the good sense to consider the expression objectionable cried *Hari-Haribol.* A friend of mine, well read in English and occupying a high position in the Uncovenanted Service, said, "I never knew there was so much life in the Bengali language." After the speech was over, hymns were sung, and the clear, unmistakable voice of Babu Troyluckonath Sanyal was heard. *Sankirtan* was resumed. The party of Hari Sabha accompanied them some portion of their way to Hatkhola, where the evening service was performed in the local Somaj. The party stopped for the night in a building close by the river, and started the next day for Mokamah.

THE SAME.

—o—

[FROM ANOTHER CORRESPONDENT.]

SATURDAY last, at 4 o'clock, Babu Keshub Chunder Sen arrived here, and delivered an address in Bengali in the *Kutirmat.* The handful of men collected on the occasion might be explained not by apathy on the part of the inhabitants to hear the words of God from a man whom they love, but by the awkward arrangements which had been made to inform them of his arrival. However, the lecture was a very impressive one, and every word that he spoke went deep into the heart of his hearers. He then went round the bazaar, singing the name of Hari, and stopped at Babu Aughore Nath Ghose's Dispensary. Next morning there was prayer at Babu Mohendra Nath Rakshit's house at Lalbazaar, whence he set out, at about 4½ P. M. for the Hari Sabha, the members of which gave him a hearty welcome by the firing of five muskets. Palparah wore a bright look. The street was set off with two lines of flags with the name of Hari on them, which flapped in the air as the gentle evening breeze blew on them. About one thousand men, young and old, sat round the *dais* which was by the side of the street, and a large canopy sheltered their heads from the rays of the declining sun. When Babu Keshub Chunder rose to speak, all the air held a solemn stillness, even the *tick, tick,* of the watch on the table before him, might be heard from a little distance. He spoke in Bengali for full one hour on *bhakti,* and showed the part it played in the life of Chaitanya, the great reformer of Naddea. Babu Troluckonath cheered all with his sweet voice, and the party returned at about 7 o'clock to Hatkhola, where the evening service was held.

Literary and Scientific.

THE second volume of Dr. George Smith's "Life of Alexander Duff, D. D.," completing the work, is announced.

MR. VINCENT BALL's work descriptive of his travels in India, which extended over many years, will appear early in October. Messrs. De La Rue and Co. are the publishers.

MR. SWINBURNE's long-promised "Study of Shakespeare in Three Periods" is now in the press, and will be issued shortly. It is the most complete piece of analysis Mr. Swinburne has yet achieved.

THE following are the amounts George Eliot is reported to have received for some of her novels: For "Scenes of Clerical Life," £300; "Adam Bede" "£3,000; "Romola," £2,000; "Middlemarch," £5,000.

THE number of lunatics is increasing at a very alarming rate in England. The report of the Commissioners in Lunacy show that there are 69,885 persons of unsound mind in England and Wales at the present time. Drinking, gambling, overwork, &c., are leading causes to this deplorable condition.

OF all the wonderful discoveries of this wonderful age, the most startling is that of the Abbe Moigno, who, says he, has discovered the exact spot in the Red Sea, where Pharaoh's army was overwhelmed in its pursuit of the Children of Israel, and seriously appeals to the whole Christian world to subscribe the requisite funds to enable excavations to be made, and "the relics of the army overcome by the Almighty Himself to be brought to light."

THE *Punch,* in a recent cartoon, well sums up the political situation. The Great Powers are about to enter on a game of lawn-tennis. Bismarck asks Andrassy to be on his side, the Russian Bear asks France to join him, an invitation which she discreetly answers by preferring to sit out a little, while England plaintively remarks to Italy, "Nobody asks us." And this, says the *Inquirer,* is the great diplomatic triumph of Lord Beaconsfield, this is the result of his spirited foreign policy!

MR. WILLIAM LANT CARPENTER writes to the *Spectator* describing the success of the telephone in America as a means of communication. He says:—"In addition to telephone exchanges, and also in towns where *they* are not yet established, private telephone lines are very common. When calling one day at a gentleman's large house in Hamilton, Ontario, the door was opened to me by a trim maid-servant, who, replying to my inquiry, said, 'Oh, master's not at home, Sir; he is three miles off, but if you like, I will call through the telephone, and tell him you are here!' When will our English servants be educated up to this? —I am, Sir, &c."

ON the occasion of the celebration of the Eighteenth Centenary of the destruction of Pompeii, on the 25th of September last, excavations were being carried on throughout the day for the inspection of visitors, which numbered some eight thousand. The visitors were, however, fortunate enough, since a house was speedily unearthed by the picks of the workmen, and numerous house-hold vessels, amongst which was a handsome bronze candelabra, were brought to the surface, while lower down stores of hemp and millet seed, together with the skeletons of small singing birds, proved the former owner of the house to have been a bird-seller. In another house a skeleton was discovered, while in the smallest chamber excavated four were found huddled together.

A RECENT writer states that Dr. Pusey continues to work regularly and arduously, and that he keeps his rooms at Oxford strewed with huge folios. "As you enter, you tumble over Saint Augustine, and only pick yourself up to come to grief next moment over Saint Chrysostom. But you are relieved to think it need not be sacrilege to place your hat on a substantial copy of Hooker's Ecclesiastical Polity," which is ready quite handy." Dr. Liddon was once asked whether Dr. Pusey ever took time to dine. "Well," he said, "I once called on Dr. Pusey about luncheon-time, and found a chop in a plate on one of his books and some potatoes hiding themselves among the papers. I never had any other evidence that he ate." He is very popular in the University. At Commemoration, says the writer, let any one cry out in the theatre "Three cheers for Dr. Pusey," and he will be surprised by the perfect hurricane of applause that will greet the name.

THE French Forestry Department, according to the *Polybiblion,* are satisfying themselves that forests directly increase the supply of water in their neighbourhood. From careful observations at Senlis and Nancy, they have decided that it rains more abundantly in wooded tracts, and that while the leaves and branches give back the water quickly to the air, they prevent rapid evaporation from the ground, and are thus favorable to the formation of springs. The effect of denudation upon the supply of the water is a point of extreme importance, and indeed, almost involves the existence of countries like Spain and Hindustan Proper, where the fall of water has perceptibly diminished. That denudation had been carried too far was suspected, but about the method of its effect there has been endless dispute. The French experiments show that it is direct, and that a treeless plain, such as Castille threatens to become, and the Punjab had become when the English conquered it, gradually deteriorates into a desert.

IN one of the latest numbers of the *Nineteenth Century,* a writer thus discusses the reasonableness of the formation of the word "recreation", and from the etymology of the word, gives a philosophical definition of it, which, we hope, will be interesting and instructive to our readers. "The mere word," he writes, "condenses much philosophy within itself. For as 'creation' means a forming, 'recreation' means a forming anew; and as in etymological derivation, so in actual truth "recreation" is nothing other than a renovation of the vital energies; leisure time and appropriate employment serve to repair the organic machinery which has been impaired by the excess of work. The liberal meaning of this word is, therefore, in itself instructive as showing that what our forefathers saw in recreation was not so much play, pastime or pleasantry, as the restoration of enfeebled powers of work. And I do not know that within the limits of one word they could have left us a legacy of thought more true in itself or more solemn in its admonition. Recreation is, or ought to be, not a pastime entered upon for the sake of the pleasure which it affords, but an act of duty undertaken for the sake of the subsequent power which it generates, and the subsequent profits which it ensures. Therefore, expanding the philosophy which is thus condensed in our English word, we may define recreation as that which, with the least expenditure of time, renders the exhausted energies most fitted to resume their work."

Selections.

A SERMON FOR THE TIMES.

THE following letter, addressed to the editor of the *Northern Echo*, lately appeared in its columns :—

Sir,—We tell our congregations to read the Bible by the light of our own age. As I did not preach on the subject on Sunday, perhaps, the enclosed notes on the first lesson for Sunday evening day, in your columns, reach a wider circle than the hearers of

A VILLAGE CURATE.

Westmoreland, August 27th, 1879.

Genesis, ch. 21.—And it came to pass that the Amir of Afghan had a scientific frontier, which was in Asia, hard by the land of Victoriana, Empress of India.

And Victoriana said to the Amir—Give me thy frontier for a rampart against the Russians, and I will give thee the worth of it in money.

And the Amir said unto Victoriana—The Lord forbid it me, that I should give the inheritance of my fathers unto thee.

And Victoriana was not pleased.

But Bendimel, her Minister, said unto her—Dost thou now govern India ? Arise, I will eat bread for thine at Mansion House, and angels shall drink small beer, and I will give thee the Amir's scientific frontier.

So he wrote letters in Victoriana's name, and sealed them with her seal (and countersigned them with his politics.)

And he set two men, sons of the aristocracy, who doted on the military, to bear witness against him, with swords and with guns, and with batteries, saying—thou didst oppose Bendizel and the Empress.

And they stormed him, and stormed his people with shot and shell—that they died.

And it came to pass that when Bendizel heard that the Amir was stormed and was dead, that he arose and took possession of the scientific frontier.

* This is an evident mistranslation. No offer of money, or of money's worth, appears in the documents of the period—excepting local Indian taxation—subsequently.

DEAN STANLEY ON BAPTISM.

(Christian World.)

DEAN STANLEY, in a tone and spirit and with a beauty of expression worthy of himself, writes in the *Nineteenth Century* on the subject of " Baptism." He regards the subject as one " full of antiquarian interest," and as also suggesting " many instructive reflections on Christian theology and practice." The original form of the rite in early times is considered and described, and the inner meaning, which has more or less involved all the changes through which it has passed, is pointed out, as well as some of the lessons suggested by those changes. Referring to the general change from the custom of immersion to that of sprinkling, the Dean remarks :— " The reason of the change is obvious. The practice of immersion, apostolic and primitive, as it was, was peculiarly suitable to the Southern and Eastern countries, for which it was designed and peculiarly unsuitable to the tastes, convenience and the feelings of the countries of the North and West. Not by any decree of Council or Parliament, but by the general sentiment of Christian liberty, this great change was effected. There is no one who would now wish to go back to the old practice. It had no doubt the sanction of the apostles and of their Master. It had the sanction of the venerable churches of the early ages, and of the sacred countries of the East. Baptism by sprinkling was rejected by the whole ancient Church (except in the rare case of deathbeds or extreme necessity) as no baptism at all. Almost the first exception was the heretic Novatian. It still has the sanction of the powerful religious community which numbers amongst its members such noble characters as John Bunyan, Robert Hall, and Havelock. In a version of the Bible which the Baptist Church has compiled for its own use in America, where it excels in number all but the Methodists, it is thought necessary (and on philological grounds it is quite correct) to translate John the Baptist by John the Immerser. It has even been defended on sanitary grounds. Sir John Floyer dated the

prevalence of consumption to the discontinuance of baptism by immersion. But, speaking generally, the Christian world has decided against it. It is a striking example of the triumph of common-sense and convenience over the bondage of form and custom." No doubt, there are much to whom the Dean's arguments will appear inconclusive, but it is, at least, gratifying to see a subject of so much controversy discussed on so calm and candid a spirit, with so much learning and so much Christian charity.

A CONVERSATION WITH A CHINAMAN ON THE CHINESE OPIUM TRADE.

[TO THE EDITOR OF THE " DAILY NEWS."]

SIR,—I enclose, just as I have received it, a curious revelation from a district in China unknown to Europeans until the recent famine gave it an unhappy notoriety. The Rev. David Hill, our missionary in Shansi, has obtained a confession which may help your readers to understand what the Chinese themselves think of the effects of opium on their social life and their commerce, and what we ought to think of the part we take in the promotion of its traffic. I am, Sir, yours truly,

E. E. JENKINS, One of the General Secretaries of the Wesleyan Missionary Society.
Wesleyan Mission House, Bishopsgate Street,
Within London, Sept. 23.

Conversation with my barber, June 20, 1879, in Tai Yuen Fu Shansi:—

Hill: Have there not been some theatrical performances in the city the last few days?

Barber: Yes.

H.: Were they given by the officials ?

B. No, by the old clothes stores. All branches of trade have their annual theatricals in Tai Yuen Fu.

H.: Have you ?

B.: Yes, in the 5th month.

H.: How many barbers are there in this city ?

B.: Upwards of 300. In the time of Hien Fung, there were 600 and more, but Tai Yuen Fu has gone down sadly since those days. Not one branch of trade merely, but every branch alike. Shansi has suffered terribly the last few years.

H.: Wars and rebellions, I suppose ?

B.: No, not that; that we could have recovered from. It is opium that has ruined us. In the days of Tao Kwang and Hien Fung trade flourished and everything prospered, but now the only trade that is paying anything like in the old times is the opium traffic.

H.: Do many of the official classes smoke.

B.: By far the greater number. In fact, you may reckon that in Shansi, the number of opium smokers averages 7 out of every 10 classes of society.

H.: But you don't smoke, do you ?

B.: Ah, don't I ! It costs me above 3,000 cash a month.

H.: And how long have you smoked ?

B.: Above 10 years.

H.: Why, you must have spent a little fortune on opium ?

B.: Yes ; but in Hien Fung's reign you could buy an ounce of opium for 200 cash, whereas now you have to give 800 or 1,000. And the worst of

Darlington's Pain-Curer
has been found to be a certain cure for Pains in the Back Lumbago, Pains in the Chest, Sore Throats, Coughs, Colds, Tightness of the Chest, Headache, Toothache, Neuralgia Colics, Rheumatism, Paralysis, Pains in the Groins, Contracted Joints, Gout, Sciatica, Bad Legs, Bad Breasts, Swellings, Old Sores, Piles, Ringworm, Pimples, Freckles, & Eruptions on the Skin.

Holloway's Pills.
—These Pills are more efficacious in strengthening a debilitated constitution than any other medicine in the world. Persons of a nervous habit of body, and all who are suffering from weak digestive organs, or whose health has become deranged by bilious affection, disordered stomach, or liver complaints, should lose no time in giving these admirable Pills a fair trial. Coughs, colds, asthma, or shortness of breath are also within the range of the curative powers of this very remarkable medicine. The cures effected by these Pills are not superficial or temporary, but complete and permanent. They are as mild as they are efficacious, and may be given with confidence to delicate females and young children. Their action on the liver, stomach, and bowels is immediate, beneficial, and lasting, restoring order and health in every case.

it is I can't get cured of the habit. Our anti-opium pills are no use. They all contain more or less opium And now, if I don't take the pipe three times a day this summer weather I am good for nothing, and can do nothing. It is simply now a hopeless case, much as I wish to get rid of it.

H.: Do any of your assistants smoke ?

B.: Yes ; there are five of us, and four smoke opium. The only one who does not is the young boy who helps in the shop. It is this that is bringing Shansi to beggary.

All this was said without a single expression of animosity towards foreigners, but in the bitterness of the man's soul. Getting on towards 60 years of age, he felt himself to be a slave, an unwilling, wretched slave—to a habit he hated, despised, and cursed.

If our lay and ministerial friends in England would follow the example of the Rev. J. H. Rogers, of Richmond, York, and bring the matter before the Parliamentary candidates in their respective boroughs, a great deal might be done in this way to form a right popular opinion on the subject, and ultimately to put this great evil away from us.

D. H.

Advertisements.

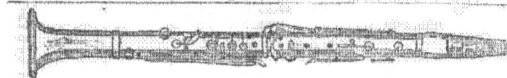

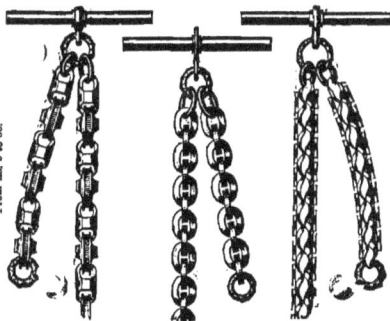

THE
INDIAN MIRROR
RATES OF SUBSCRIPTION.

(IN ADVANCE.)

Foreign.

For Twelve Months (via Southampton) 48   6   0
     "   (via Brindisi) ... 54   10   0

Sunday Edition.

(Both for Town and Mofussil.)

For One Month 1   0   0
  Three Months 2   8   0
  Six Months 5   0   0
  Twelve Months 10   0   0

(Single Copy Four Annas.)

Foreign

For Twelve Months (via Southampton) 12   7   0
     "   (via Brindisi) 14   14

ADVERTISEMENT RATES.

For casual Advertisements 3 annas per line.

No Advertisement charged for less than a Rupee.

For special contract rates apply to the Manager.

Printed and published for the Proprietor by W. C. Bose, at the Sun Press at No. 2 British Indian Street, Calcutta.

The Indian Mirror

[Edited by Krishna Bihari Sen, M.A.]

SUNDAY EDITION

[Registered at the General Post Office.]

VOL. XIX.   CALCUTTA, SUNDAY, NOVEMBER 16, 1879.   NO. 278.

CONTENTS.

Telegraphic Intelligence.

FROM THE PRESS COMMISSIONER.

SIMLA, 13TH NOVEMBER.

In the Legislative Council of the 14th Sir John Strachey obtained leave to introduce a Bill to regulate the levy of town duties and tolls in Municipalities. Mr. Stokes introduced the Glanders and Farcy Bill which was subsequently passed into law. Mr. Thompson obtained leave to introduce a Bill to provide for the survey and demarkation of land in British Burmah. The Foreign Jurisdiction and Extradition Act of 1872 Amendment Bill was passed in law. Mr. Batten was added to the Select Committee on the Factories Bill. The council adjoined die sino.

GENERAL ROBERTS' PROCLAMATION.

SIMLA, 14TH NOVEMBER.

General Roberts issued the following proclamation on the 11th :—To all whom it may concern, on the 12th October, a proclamation was issued, in which I offered a reward for the surrender of any persons, who had fought against the British troops since 3rd September, and had thereby become rebels against the Amir Yakub Khan. I have now received information which tends to show that some, at least of those who shared in the opposion encountered by the British troops during their advance on Cabul, were led to do so by the belief that the Amir was a prisoner in my camp, and had called upon the soldiery and people of Cabul to rise on his behalf. Such persons, although enemies to the British Government, were not rebels against their own sovereign, and the great British Government does not seek for vengeance against enemies who no longer resist. It may be that a few only of those who took up arms, were thus led away by the statement of evil-minded men ; but, rather than punish the innocent with the guilty, I am willing to believe that all were alike deceived. On behalf of the British Government, therefore, I proclaim a free and complete amnesty to all persons who have fought against the British troops, since 3rd September, provided that they now give up any arms in their possession and return to their homes. The offer of a reward for the surrender of such persons

is now withdrawn, and they will not for the future be molested in any way on account of their opposition to the British advance. But it must be clearly understood that the benefits of this amnesty do not extend to any one, whether soldier or civilian, who was concerned directly or indirectly in the attack upon the Residency, or who may hereafter be found in possession of any property belonging to members of the Embassy. To such persons no mercy will be shown. Further I hold out no promise of pardon to those who, well knowing the Amir's position in British Camp, instigated the troops and people of Cabul to take up arms against the British troops. They have been guilty of wilful rebellion against the Amir's authority, and they will be considered and treated as rebels wherever found.

CABUL NEWS.

SIMLA, 14TH NOVEMBER.

General Roberts telegraphs from Cabul on the 12th November that General Macpherson reports that a company of the 67th Regiment, under Captain Poole, while escorting a foraging party to Deaha at the junction of the Panjsher and Cabul Rivers, was attacked by 700 to 1,000 Safis of Tagea. He went to the assistance of the company with 150 men of the 67th Foot, 80 of the 28th Native Infantry, four Mountain guns, and a Squadron of the 12th Bengal Cavalry. The latter arriving first, were dismounted and sent forwards. The guns came into action twice with good effect. Pursuit continued for six miles. Severe loss was inflicted on the enemy, who fled leaving their dead on the ground. Our casualties were three of the 67th Foot, and one of the 28th Native Infantry killed. Captain Poole and four men of the 67th Foot were wound. All the wounded are doing well. General Macpherson was to be at Lal-i-bund on 12th to commence the construction of the road over Thal. The Cabul telegraph line completed eight miles beyond Bukhak, was to be furnished to General Macpherson's camp on the 12th. Snow fell at Cabul on the 11th.

IMPERIAL LEGISLATIVE COUNCIL.

SIMLA, 14TH NOVEMBER.

On Sir John Strachey's introducing the Bill to impose tax on trades and professions, Mr. Batten observed that there was much force in the reasons which had justified the exemption of the professional and official classes from the taxation of 1878, but their force was weaker in the case of the more wealthy of those classes, and he was, therefore, glad that the Bill now introduced would relieve the poorer commercial classes at the expense of the richer professional and salaried classes. He still thought that the reasons referred to, justified the higher minimum of Rs. 100 per mensem in the case of these classes. The

lower paid officials were, owing to the fixity of their salaries, less able to protect themselves against high price in time of famine. Their standard of living was necessarily higher, and this was especially the case with European and Eurasian clerks with salaries below Rs. 100. Mr. Batten would apply the same minimum to the poorer professional persons, who were much in the same position as the poorer officials. He proceeded to show that compliance with the demand made by the commercial classes for extension of the tax to officials, necessarily lead to the increase of the maximum taxes on traders, for officials must be taxed by a percentage on their salaries, and as there was no reason for the percentage being less for the highest-paid officials, nor for their paying more than commercial men with equivalent incomes, it followed that the maximum taxes most be raised on the latter class. He supported the Bill as it shifted to the richer classes of professional, official, as well as commercial, the burden hitherto laid on the poorer traders and artisans. Sir Jhon Strachey, in reply, expressed himself in favor of fixing the higher minimum of Rs. 1,200 per annum for the professional as well as the salaried classes, and said that Mr. Batten's suggestion would be taken into consideration.

Editorial Notes.

MR. SPURGEON prays daily that the Lord would change the policy of the British nation from that of blustering and invasion to peace and righteousness. So does every prayerful man in the British Empire.

:o:

YESTERDAY was the festival of brothers and sisters among the Hindus. It is an excellent institution, and we know that even Brahmos honor it. As well they may. Whatever keeps pure the sense of brotherhood in man is to be honored and appreciated. Good reader, when you were exchanging greetings at home yesterday, did you spend a thought upon us ? If so, we reciprocate your good wishes. We send a cordial greeting to all our brethren and sisters !

:o:

WE consider a young man to be the veritable image of his Maker. There is health, beauty, life, energy and enthusiasm in him. Whatever he does, he does with a will. There is a sweet fragrance around him which reminds us of the country from which he comes. The tree is beautiful, if only God is the gardener that waters it. The world sometimes comes to usurp His place, and then the odour becomes loathesome. Young friends, do not lose sight of the Gardener. Employ Him as much as you can ; it will cost you nothing.

THE *Lucknow Witness*, quoting our remarks on the prevalence of obscenity in India
and the opposite organisation, a Society for
its suppression, says :— There is such a
Society working in India. It is called the
Church of Jesus Christ. Just in proportion
as 'the heart of the Indian nationality' submits to Christ, obscenity will go out of it.
Nothing but the power of God which is
exerted mainly and most effectively through
the Church, can accomplish this great work.
Let the *Mirror* make a note of this." Let
us compare notes. The Society in existence
is the Church of One True God, which
alone can remove obscenity from the mind.

NOWHERE except in the Punjab was Brahmoism ever preached to the Hindustanis of
Upper India. The first step in the direction
was taken by the Missionary Expedition party
at Monghyrpore, where our Minister delivered
addresses before large numbers of Behuris.
The effect of these, we are assured, was
good ; and it conclusively proves that
the simple truths of Brahmoism are capable
of being appreciated by the people of that portion of the country. We are led to hope
from this that in time a Brahmo Somaj will
come to be established in every large centre
and town of Northern India, the members of
which will be Hindustanis, and not Bengalis.

THE joys of a religious life are seldom known
to outsiders. People generally confound the
inward cheerfulness of a devout man with
monomania. What a mistake! If there
is joy anywhere, it is in the heart
of the man who has given up everything to God. His laugh is worth hearing. Such a laugh is seldom heard here; but
when it comes out, it is heard in heaven and
echoed back in the world. As the hymn
goes, "when I see Thy merry face, I
see mirth everywhere. I see it in rivers
and mountains, in flowers and leaves, in
the sun and moon," and the effect
of this universal joyfulness is heard in the
peal after peal of laughter that comes from the
merry face of that devotee. We would give
everything to hear an honest man laugh.

PROFESSOR MAX MULLER lately delivered
his presidential address on "Freedom" at the
Birmingham and Midland Institute. During
the course of his address he remarked that
there was no time at which the measure of
individual liberty was larger than it was at
present in England, and if they wished to
realize the full blessings of the time in which
they lived, they should compare Mill's
"Plea for Liberty" with another written not
much more than two hundred years ago, by
Hobbes, who said that the only freedom which
an individual had a right to claim was freedom
to think what he liked so long as he kept it to
himself. The Professor expressed his opinion
that compulsory education was a necessity,
but like a powerful engine it required careful
watching. The whole address is, we understand, published in the November number of
the *Nineteenth Century*.

Do our readers know who John Dunn is?
This person, plays an important part
in the pacification of Zululand. Of
his antecedents so far is known that he is of
British extraction. Somehow or other he
visited South Africa, has since become a do-
micile in Zululand, and has married Zulu
wives. We learn that he freely mixes in Zulu

society, speaks the Zulu language and, in fact,
has become a Zulu of the true type. On the
close of the late war he was selected
to be a representative of the British
Government. We also know that he is
one of those seven chiefs to whom the
British Government has allotted districts.
Strange to say, his first step, since
his appointment, has been to prohibit
the settlement of missionaries in his territory.
This reported action of John Dunn is said
to have excited universal disgust and indignation in the South African colonies. We shall
carefully watch the subsequent career of this
man.

IN an early number of *Mind*, there appears
a criticism of Prof. Max Muller's view of
Fetishism by Mr. A. Lang. Against the
veteran philologist's theory that fetishism is
a "corruption of religion," Mr. Lang has
sought to maintain its primitiveness in
religious development. The writer has attempted to point out that the hymns of
the Rig-Veda, to which Prof. Max Muller
so constantly appeals, are not at all
really early documents or adapted to throw
light upon primitive, untutored religious
sentiment. It has also been attempted to
show that religion arises not so much from
the sense of the Infinite, as Prof. Max Muller
believes, as from the idea of power—the worshipper being "not contemplative so much as
eager to gain something to his advantage."
This view may be necessary for the due consistency of the doctrine of evolution. But can
it be believed that any man, however savage,
should worship mere stocks and stones, unless
he had the sense of a mighty power in
the back ground. Why even a dog would
not stoop to admire a stone in that way. We
think that Professor Max Muller's definition
of the Infinite as the beginning of religious
ideas is borne out by the constitution of human
nature.

THE Government of India thus solves the
question whether Native youths who are selected for the Civil Service should go to England :—

It is doubtful whether, for the present, at any
rate, it would be wise to compel even younger
recruits to go home before being enlisted into
the Civil Service. Sikhs would probably, go
readily, so would Mahomedans ; and so possibly might Maharattas. But in Bengal and
Madras now-a-days, a lad who goes to England for a few years is more or less an outcaste
on his return to India, unless he belongs to the
Brahmo persuasion, or until he spends a great sum
in propitiating his caste-fellows. Probably, there
would be the same difficulty with Kayasths or
Khetris, from the North-West Provinces and the
Punjab, who might go to England. While there
is so much doubt about the effect of going to
Europe on a Native of gentle birth, it would be
best not to compel recruits to go to England. At
the same time we recognise that there would be
advantage in encouraging young Native candidates who may be willing to go to England to
complete their studies, and we shall be ready to
recommend the grant of allowances to probation-
ers under the rules who may desire to study for
two years in England.

The resolution is a wise one. We are not opposed to the plan of sending young men to
England. But if they are not well
controlled in the land of their exile, and if they
return completely Europeanised and with little
of principle or morals; we think the less they
go the better. Government, if it wishes
to encourage "England-going," should also
see that there is a Home to receive them.

THE *Englishman* which, under its present
management, commands the respect of every
journalist in India, sometimes utters views

totally inconsistent with its usually sober
and impartial tone. Thus it condemns
those people in England who expose the
cruelties practised by the retributive army
in Cabul, and supports its assertions by a
reference to what happened in 1857. Quoting
the *Daily News* that journal says :—" Here
we have the old spirit of 1857 over again, when
the English Press forgot even the awful features of the massacres of Cawnpore, in denounc-
ing the British troops for their necessarily
severe reprisals." Our contemporary is too old
and venerable to require a lesson from us. But
the God whom he and his countrymen worship, said repeatedly that forgiveness should
be the ruling characteristic of every Christian.
Unfortunately the history of Native India in
1857 has not been written, or we might have
pointed out to our contemporary that the sufferings inflicted upon innocent Hindus were, in
many cases, as cruel, as ghastly, as terribly retributive as those which the dastardly gang
of Nana Saheb inflicted upon the Europeans.
As it is, the latter have been adequately held
up to the curse and obloquy of heaven
and earth. But should not the just God of the
Christian equally reprobate the latter's faint-
hearted and unmanly vindictiveness? It is to
the credit of England that we say there is one
law for the Christian and another for the
heathen. If hell is for the ignorant Sepoy who
barbarously murdered women and children, a
greater hell is reserved for the pious Christian,
who, knowing the word of God, openly shows
his forgetfulness of the law of love and forgiveness.

DR. KNIGHTON, in an article contributed to
the *Mirror* of Wednesday last, speaks of the
Bengalis in very handsome terms. We believe we were the first to call our people the
Scotch of India. Dr. Knighton goes a step
farther ; he calls the Bengalis the Athenians of India. "They have," he says,
"always been the first in India to initiate
social and other reforms. Where did the
movement against the barbarous rite of *sutti*
originate in India? In Bengal. Where was
it that the re-marriage of widows was first advocated and practised? In Bengal. Where
did the reform of the barbarous idolatry begin,
and the introduction of innovations to restore
pure morals and spiritual worship to religion?
Also in Bengal. Nor has the advance been less
pronounced in politics. The earliest organisations for the consistent and fearless advocacy
of Native rights have taken birth in Bengal.
In arts and literature, in all the developments
of culture, in education, in science and philosophy, as well as in religion and politics, the
intellectual inhabitants of Bengal are superior
to the other nations of India. And this superiority has been proved in a thousand ways."
The compliment is flattering, yes, very
flattering. We hope, however, it will be taken
in the spirit in which it has been given. Com-
pliments have their uses in that they serve to
stimulate men to further exertions for improvement. As a matter of fact, we should
understand how little we deserve the praise
accorded to us. Our countrymen have still
many defects which they have to remove.
We may mention their jealousies, disunion,
want of courage, manliness, &c., &c. It is
right that the praises of our best friends
should open our eyes to these.

THE cordial reception given to Dr. Rajendralala Mittra by the Bombay Asiatic Society,
must be pleasing to every one of the Doctor's
numerous friends and admirers in Bengal. It
proves what no amount of mere formal correspondence can prove that in the educated

men of the two Presidencies lies, in a great measure, the future of our great country, and that, at any cost, this mutual intercourse should be kept up. There are reasons why we think that constant interviews between the wise men of Bengal and Bombay are necessary. In the first place, such meetings give birth to a healthy emulation, and in the next place it ought to be remembered that at the present day, among the educated Natives of Bengal, there is not one who can take the place of Dr. Rajendralala Mitra or Dr. K. M. Banerji in respect of scholarship or culture. We have a Sanskrit College, it is true, which is supposed to be the fountain of scholarship without end. But when we consider that this costly institution is still conducted on the world-old Pandíti system, that comparative philology is not taught there, and that there is no chair for teaching that branch, we understand what little we may reasonably expect from the College. We are afraid that, in respect of Sanskrit scholarship and erudition, Bombay has left Bengal far behind. There are scholars in the former Presidency who may do honor to any literary Society in India or in Europe, and the reason why their number is so large is, that there is a better method of training,—the European or comparative method, we mean—adopted in the Bombay Colleges than here. The question is a very important one, and we commend it to the careful consideration of the Director of Public Instruction.

THE STATESMAN ON THE BRAHMO SOMAJ

An article in the *Statesman* which we republish elsewhere, draws attention to the present position of the Brahmo Somaj and the relations which our leader bears thereto. We are indebted for some very thoughtful criticisms on Brahmoism to the gifted writer who edits the *Statesman*. The article under notice is important, not because it gives us a definite view on the many important points which agitate the Brahmo community, but because it indicates from a Christian standpoint the precise issue which awaits a solution in the Brahmo Somaj. Into much of what our contemporary says of the relative merits of prophets and great men, we shall not enter. Suffice to say that the leader of our community has accurately described his position and attitude towards Christ and other masters, and his words have been so precise as not to leave any room for the opinion that his claims to attention are founded upon a desire to surpass them. Speaking of Christ, he has repeatedly said he is not fit to kiss the latchet of his shoes, and so of the other prophets of the world. "Mr. Sen," says the *Statesman*, "carries the fan of truth in his hand, and is, therefore, greater—must at least seem greater to his followers—than any of the prophets whose teaching he assumes to winnow." We beg to say this question of greatness or littleness does not enter into the theology of the Brahmo Somaj, and if any such does press upon our attention, we have to take our leader at his word. For has he not said that he cannot stand before the world's prophets—Christ above all? Has he not confessed his sins before his countrymen? Whatever weight may be attached to his utterances, they are, we believe, sincere. Well, then, the point to be settled is, what position does Babu Keshub Chunder Sen actually occupy in the Brahmo Somaj? We have said that the question of greatness or littleness does not enter into the controversy. God works out His ends by means that may be very small,

The least man among us may be the medium of accomplishing a great end. Provided we admit the workings of Providence, we may safely accept any man for our leader, who has the gift to interpret to us the designs or modes of that dispensation. Add to this the fact that we are sincere believers in the doctrine of God in history. We believe that at special times, and under special circumstances, when the world does need a revival or upheaving, and men do require the guidance of God, a special manifestation of His will takes place, and events happen which have a necessary connection with each other and may be interpreted as the working of Divine providence. We believe that India is passing through a time and is placed under circumstances when God's almighty will has begun to manifest itself, and we believe that the Brahmo Somaj is the dispensation that is to lead her to life, light and salvation. Unlike the other theistic movements of the day, the Brahmo Somaj has a mission. A Divine mission to accomplish. Theism, like eclecticism, is not a new phenomenon in the history of theology, nor are great minds wanting to recommend it to the attention of the world. But what we fail to notice elsewhere is an organised movement destined to mould society and give tone and shape to the religious aspirations of men. The Brahmo Somaj, as the only organised theistic body in existence, has in India a great mission to accomplish. It has to establish the kingdom of God and carry the united voice of a nation to the throne of heaven; and we believe that all this it will do under the guidance and direction of God Himself. Whether we are correct in our estimate of the Divine mission of the Brahmo Somaj, may be left to be answered by the sober verdict of time. So far as facts go, prophecies innumerable have been risked as to its permanence, and critics learned and distinguished have set tablets ready for its tomb. But these kind prophecies have been falsified in every instance, and the Brahmo Somaj has survived them all. But the *Statesman* views the matter from another point. "The Minister's personality is absolutely essential to the cohesion and vitality of his system of truths." So it is, if the Minister is, as we believe him to be, a part, a great part, a central part of the dispensation. It is he who has given the life and tone to the entire movement, and as he is completely identified with it, his preachings and precepts we accept as the embodiment of the dispensation itself. Thus, then, we cannot do away with this man, who is the leader, the mouthpiece, the heaven-appointed missionary of what we call the Brahmo Somaj. The *Indian Mirror* accepts in its entirety the plan and programme of his life—the plan and programme that is to give India her life and salvation. Whatever be done or says, whatever the least among the members of the dispensation does say, must be faithfully reflected in the *Mirror*. This explains our position, we hope, pretty clearly. We have set forth our challenge to India: there is our programme for her regeneration. Accept it, if you wish to be saved; reject it, if you dare. The outcome of all we leave in the hands of Providence.

THE MISSIONARY EXPEDITION.

[FROM OUR SPECIAL CORRESPONDENT.]

Gya, 13th November 1879.

LITTLE or nothing was done on the day of our arrival at Mozufferpore. The next

day too was a day of rest. Tirhut is behind the other districts of Bengal in intellectual and social progress, and not even the most sanguine among us could expect any great results. Those among the residents from whom sympathy and co-operation were naturally expected, seemed to have but one feeling, despair. Surely the prospect was not encouraging. But the Lord's command who could disobey? The soldier-preachers had no alternative. The strongholds of error all the more needed a desperate attack because of their impregnable character. An effort was called for, a warlike move was enjoined, to abaite the inert mass. The party was ordered to move, and an advantageous position was occupied on Saturday afternoon, November 8, near Sahajika Poker, a very pretty tank, adjoining a Mahadeo temple. For nearly an hour, the Minister spoke in Bengali to a mixed audience composed of Bengalis and up-countrymen. For the benefit of the latter, he said a few concluding words in Hindi. Regret was expressed that more was not said in the local vernacular, but the people enjoyed and felt impressed with the little that was said. To reach the people one must read his appeals through the channel of the local vernacular. As usual, after the address, our friends sang the Holy Name through the streets in solemn procession. Torches were lighted, the flags unfurled and the bugle sounded. There were both Bengali and Hindi songs; in the latter some of the poorer class Tirhutis joined with warm and animated hearts. On Sunday morning there was the usual service under a shady tree on the banks of the Bura Gundack, in which we daily bathed during the entire period of our stay at Mozufferpore. Prayer over, we lighted the fuel and cooked our own food. In consequence of there being too much rice in the boiling pot, the water proved insufficient, and the rice seemed sticky. Yet we enjoyed our breakfast and thanked God. In the afternoon the Minister called on Bishop Johnson, who had come to the station in the course of his usual visitation tour. The excellent Christian Bishop gave a most cordial welcome to the Brahmo leader in the residence of the local chaplain, and though of differing views, they exchanged their sentiments in a most friendly spirit. The interview was brief but cordial, and on the Minister's return, he said he was greatly pleased with the earnestness, humility, condescension and courtesy of the captain of Christ's army in India. A wealthy Bengali Zemindar kindly lent his garden house, and the regular Sunday service was held there, instead of the small room of the local Arya Somaj. There were about two hundred persons present, of whom only a few were Brahmos. After service the party went on singing a part of the way, and then broke up. In the Science Association Hall, a Lecture was delivered on Monday by the Minister on "India and India's God," in which, before an assembly of European and Native gentlemen, he spoke for an hour of the evolution and accomplishment of the purposes of Providence in this great country. The establishment of the British power, schools and colleges, social, political and economic reforms, were all, he said, the direct working of an overruling Providence. Tuesday witnessed a novel and most enthusiastic demonstration. We never saw a parallel in the history of Brahmo Missionary enterprise. About a thousand persons gathered in the school compound, although the notice was short and irregular. The public mind had been so far excited by the proceedings of the last three days that everybody seemed ready for a demonstration. Pundits, Zemindars and Merchants, Pleaders and clerks, school-boys, shopkeepers, the poorest and commonest in the station, flocked to hear the Minister. Opposite the platform a quadrangle was formed of the preaching army, and the banners of the Living God were unfurled. In a standing posture the party sang the Divine Name. And soon the Minister stood upon the platform, and, as usual serenely looking heavenward, he asked for the Lord's blessing. For about ten minutes he spoke in English, giving a solemn charge to the English-educated people, and then suddenly he addressed his Bengali fellow-countrymen in Bengali for about ten minutes. Anon, there was a further change in the language of the speaker. He spoke for forty minutes in Hindi, dwelling on the deep truths of Theism, the immanent and omnipresent spirit of God, the sweets of communion and other subjects. He quoted a text from the Vedanta declaring the four Vedas to be inferior and not superior wisdom. The knowledge of God was the highest wisdom. How the whole assembly, the wealthy banker, the innocent schoolboy, the poor ayes and the hated sweeper, all heard the address with rapt attention in the shades of the evening, under the glorious canopy of heaven, need not be described. All Mozufferpore seemed to throb with devotional interest for the time. Directly the speaker finished with the words "Victory to God," the *mridang* gave forth its sweet sound, and immediately a procession was formed in which hundreds joined. They went on singing with great force till they reached the house of the Hindu Government Pleader, which was taken by storm. Here their enthusiasm reached its climax, and indeed a more spirited *kirtan* we seldom heard. The party seemed to be a regular and organized band of dacoits, who had come and attacked the house of the helpless owner quite unexpectedly, with a view to rob him and his kinsmen of their hearts and present them as offerings unto the Lord. The host then gave the party a welcome in his *baitakhana*, where an animated conversation followed in response to a number of interesting queries put forth by a few inquirers present. The next day after early breakfast the party left Mozufferpore by the midday train. Early,—i, e., 10 A.M.! Our morning and evening meal hours were usually 1 P.M., and 11-30 P.M. and we had to go to bed at about 1 in the morning. Altogether it was a Late Hour *régime*. In the morning, however, we had always our usual quantity of grain and salt before service. With this very nourishing *rasat* the soldiers managed to hold on till a late hour, and the daily bath in the river was also very refreshing. As we parted, cordial thanks and affectionate regards were offered to our noble-hearted host and friends. The train brought us to the river ghat at about 8 P. M., when we embarked on board the ferry steamer and reached Barr Ghat in the evening after a very pleasant trip and after realising a handsome compensation for an early breakfast in the *luchis* and sweetmeats supplied by our host. The E. I. R. train was ready, and in ten minutes we were at Barr. The steamer was late, and, therefore, the Up-train would have left Barr leaving us to ourselves. But no, the Station Master had kindly detained the train. So we were spared the inconvenience, and we at once proceeded to Bankipore. Here the local Munsiff gave us shelter in his house, "Tired nature's sweet restorer, balmy sleep," refreshed the exhausted army. In the morning, at a very short notice, the prayer room was filled with a large number of educated Bengali youths, who joined in our prayers. After taking a hasty breakfast,—

rather rich it was,—we went to the Railway Station, and started for Gya by the 11-40 A.M. train on Thursday, reaching the place at about 5 P.M. Here we saw a spectacle we are not likely to forget. The platform and the streets were crowded with people of all classes, who had come to see the preaching army. The local Brahmos had begun a *kirtan* in the station compound, in which our party at once joined, unfurling their flags in the presence of a crowd of by-standers. The sight was touching, especially when the local Brahmos bowed respectfully before the army of preachers. Altogether the reception which Gya extended to our brethren was most cordial and enthusiastic. We have put up in the garden house of a wealthy Zemindar, truly kind and hospitable.

THE STORY OF WASSUDEO BULWANT PHADKE AND ITS MORAL.

A MELANCHOLY tale is told by Wassudeo of his past crimes and misdeeds. The leader of the Deccan robbers tells us in plain terms what he was and how he came to adopt the life he led. He is a half-educated man who, having read two or three English primers, began to curse the Government under which he lived. "Patriotism was strong within me", he says. "I first began to deliver lectures. Some speeches were delivered by me. I first gave my lectures at Puna; then delivered them at Panwell, Palaspe, Tasgaon, Narsoba's Wadi and other places. But my lectures had no more effect on the minds of the hearers than a sprinkling of water has on the leaves of trees. Many of us, Indians, are fools." So assuming the patriot's role, he did what patriots generally do : he lectured ; and his conclusion was that " many of us, Indians, are fools." Bulwant Phadke's morbid feelings were directed against the wrongs inflicted by the British Government, and so much did he brood over them that he thought that his life would be of no purpose, if he failed to strike a blow at them.

All the past of time reveals
A bridal dawn of thunder peals
Wherever thought hath wedded fact.

So Bulwant Phadke became a warrior. He tells us how this happened.

"We are hated," he says. "It is a disgrace to the Hindus and Mahomedan. It would have been better had we all died. Thinking day and night of this and of thousands of other miseries, my mind has been wholly bent upon the downfal of the British power. I thought of nothing else. I could not even sleep without the idea about the overthrow of the Empire always haunting my mind. I have gone mad. I used to rise on even to the dead of night, and ponder over their ruin : I learnt how to fire, ride and fence to, and also to spear, &c. I was very fond of arms. I always used to have in my possession two or three guns, four or five swords, spears, &c."

Then again :—

My first duty was to rouse the minds of the people against the English on my visits to Narsoba's Wadi. I used to invite the Ramusis of the surrounding districts to dinner. I gave them food, liquor, &c., and even gave them turbans. I excited the feeling of the Koils, Gosdi and Bhils of Nuggur, Nasick, Khandis, Vurhad, Nagpore, Baroda, and other places against the British. I also succeeded in creating an ill-feeling against the English in the minds of some men in the district of Kolhapore.

So far was he carried away by this dominant feeling of hatred against the English that he said:—"I will not let the English people, wicked, wretched, man-eaters, rest in peace even after my death." We think every educated Native should contemplate this pic-

ture of a man, the victim of his own imagination, roused and kept in play by the daily sight of wrongs which, we admit, were many of them real. Wassudeo Bulwant Phadke does not seem to have seen much of misfortune. His worldly position was good, and he had not to carve his way through the world by a course of adventures necessary for one who is not gifted with worldly prosperity. He had a happy home which more than compensated any deficiencies of fortune.

My first wife would sometimes ask for ornaments, but my second wife never uttered a syllable about them. Since I commenced this work, I have not bought a farthing's worth of gold, silver ornaments or brass vessels. It is difficult to get a wife among thousands of the stamp of my wife, who is gentle, revered, and sensible. I have had to suffer no anxiety whatever since I married her. No words would be sufficient to describe her good qualities. She is skilful in the culinary art ; she is also very cheerful. The chastity of my both wives was undoubted. From conversation with my second wife, I have made out that she will not live a month after my death. She is firm and will carry out her object.

If, then, Bulwant Phadke was so happy, why did he risk his worldly prospects by initiating an open course of warfare against his sovereign? The answer is simple. "Patriotism was strong within me." We wish our readers would understand those words well. It was because Wassudeo was a patriot that he took up arms against the Queen. What a terrible definition of patriotism this ! Yet let us not be startled. There are patriots and patriots—patriots who unceasingly weep over their country's wrongs, and patriots who seeing the wrongs, rejoice that so much has been done to remove them. The former are always gloomy, the latter always cheerful. The former have recourse to the sword, and the latter to peace as the best avenger of human wrongs. There are men among us who spend an entire lifetime in agitating the grievances of their country, and it is these who, if possessed of the morbid imagination that sent Bulwant Phadke to transportation for life, are surely the men who will resort to arms for their country's deliverance. To say the least we have no sympathy with them. We have more than once noticed in these columns the tendency visible among our young men of taking part in political discussions; and as political discussions in India mean nothing but discussion of wrongs, we have often warned our young countrymen not to meddle with them. This is the first time in the history of India that a Bulwant Phadke has risen, and many a Bulwant Phadke will still rise, if the effect of the discussions be, as it must be, to render the mind gloomy and morbid. It may be asked what then we wish our educated countrymen to be. The answer is simple. Let them be patriots of the second class we have mentioned. A careful perusal of history will convince an ordinary educated man that the advent of the British power is a purely providential affair. There is no reason why any other nation should not have come to assume the sovereignty of India. Of all the races that contended for the mastery of the empire, the English, we suppose, had the least chance of coming out victorious. There is something in the entire concern which tells us that God in His all-seeing wisdom brought them to direct the affairs of this vast continent. A patriot, therefore, sees providence or " God in History" The very same finger that points out to him the divine hand in the national annals, informs us also that it is very foolish to contend against the decree of the Almighty. God wishes that India should be regenerated through the instrumentality of the English nation. Every page of its history has been written by Him. Is it possible for us to fight with the Most High? If our country-men are atheists, let them venture to say no. We read their fate by the his-tory of Bulwant Phadke. But if they do believe in a living God, let them calmly content themselves with a cheerful disposition to abide by His Providence. And has not God written many hopeful chapters for us? Let us study the political creed of an honest patriot. The perusal of history convinces us that no nation can be politically strong which is not morally, religiously, and intellectually strong; and no reform is possible which does not begin from within. A patriot, therefore, begins his real warfare in the human heart. There are those great enemies which have overthrown the Hindu nation. They are not your Afghans, or Moguls, or Mahrattas or Englishmen, but the great foes which go by the name of immorality, sensuality, crime, disunion, jealousy, unbelief, superstition and untruth. A patriot must needs conquer these first; and when the mind has been formed, the heart reformed, the character purified, it is then that the nation will rise united to assert their political rights. There need be no war of independence; mind, the highest political philosophy of the day, as exemplified in the policy and statesmanship of Great Britain, recognises the rights of nations, when fitted by their own education to govern and control themselves. Let us not then be impatient. Centuries are but minutes in the history of civilization; and if the course we have indicated be steadily and honestly pursued, even the minutes that we speak of will disappear, for the work of regeneration will then have begun, and what we call grievances will vanish before the daily growth of hope, joy and faith.

Brahmo Somaj.

WE are sorry to learn that Babu Protap Chunder Mozumdar was suddenly taken ill in the train at Allahabad, on his way to Lahore. He is better now, and is at present at Lucknow.

OUR singing missionary, Babu Troylucko Nath Sanyal, has not been able to proceed with the expedition. He is ill at Mokameh. May be soon recover his health!

Correspondence.

[We do not hold ourselves in any way responsible for the opinions of our correspondents.—ED., I. M.]

HYMN :—PRE-EXISTENCE.

1. The humblest prairie-flower Comes blooming out from God; Then to the Father it returns, And melts into the sod.

2. Did Jesus' beauty thus Out of the Father beam, A blessed light,—a holy smile, And then go in to Him?

3. And so have I come here, Into this world of pain, To smile, amid its agonies, And to return again?—

4. Not, as I first appeared, In fairest robes of earth; But purified and glorified To more than mortal birth.

5. To be, —as Jesus was, —
The true, the very man,
The man God meant that I should be,
Before the world began;

"He that dwelleth in love dwelleth in God, and God in him." "I came out from God. I came forth from the Father and am come into the world. Again I leave the world and go to the Father. And now, Oh Father, glorify thou me with thine own self, with the glory which I had with thee before the world was. I am in the Father." [Jesus' dying words in the Gospel of John.]—Written, for the Mirror, at Coonoor, in the Nilgiris, 21st October 1879, by C. H. A. D.

THE INSTITUTION FOR PHYSICAL IMPROVEMENT.

TO THE EDITOR OF THE "INDIAN MIRROR,"

SIR,—The public are respectfully informed that the season for physical exercises—one of the chief objects of our Institution—is already come, and that, therefore, those of them who are willing to take advantage of it, in connection with the duly organized appliances and material staff supplied by us, should be so good as not only to come forward themselves, but disseminate the information among their less informed neighbours. The Managers of the Institution have been at the utmost pains for explaining the object of the Institution as amply as possible, so as to disabuse the public mind on the subject. It is to be earnestly hoped that, after going through the prospectus circulated and the paper of explanation, those that really feel a want proposed to be supplied by the Institution, should lose no time in sending their sons and wards, so that the ample accommodation secured by the liberality of public-spirited men may not be rendered comparatively useless for want of a large number of recipients. We earnestly solicit a visit to the grounds from all interested in the improvement of the rising generation

Yours &c.,
JABU NATH GHOSH, Secretary.

THE LILY COTTAGE TO BE DEMOLISHED.

TO THE EDITOR OF THE "INDIAN MIRROR."

SIR,—No community would be fulfilling its duty to the individual members thereof, were it to fail to remove the stumbling blocks, if any, that lay in the path of their spiritual progress. It seems that among some of our friends at present, a real stumbling block of this kind exists in the habits and daily practices of our Minister, "Old Vaishnava," whose letter you published in one of your recent issues, tells us that he is at times disposed to extol Mr. Sen to the skies, believes that he in reality to be a leader with a commission to man; but as soon as he comes in sight of Lily Cottage, our Minister's residence, his idol becomes clay, and he is compelled to give him up in disgust. I sympathise with "Old Vaishnava," for his conduct, if nothing else, is above all praise. If I am not mistaken, the sight of Lily Cottage exerts a potent charm upon the tender susceptibilities of another gentleman also, to wit, a redoubtable Scotch Missionary of the Free Church. And I am sure the number of such men may be counted by the dozen, if not by the hundred. In which case, is it not the bounden duty of all sincerely interested in the cause of Theism to remove this obstacle from the path of their brethren? The case is serious, and I appeal to the Minister himself, if something could not be done to remove the scandal of the "Pointinstic Mansion." At the next annual meeting of the Brahmo Somaj of India the question ought to be fairly discussed. Surely, if I were the Minister, I would, in sheer vexation, either demolish the Lily Cottage or, what would be the next best thing, invite "Old Vaishnava" and Co. to take up their abode in that cursed residence.

Yours &c.
SLASHER.

THE FOURTH GOSPEL.

TO THE EDITOR OF THE "INDIAN MIRROR,"

SIR,—The controversy, carried on at present, regarding the authenticity of the Fourth Gospel, is, in my humble opinion, a matter unworthy the attention of the learned. The book might have

been written by St. John, the favorite Apostle of Christ, or might not have been; but what of that? The genuineness of the book in question is beyond suspicion; and, so far as we are interested in it, there cannot be an iota of doubt about it.

There are, generally speaking, two sorts of evidence which are applied to prove the authenticity of any piece of composition, either historical, political, religious or literary, namely, evidences, internal and external. The latter I do not mean to discuss here; nor do I feel any necessity for doing so. I shall treat only of the former, the internal evidence, to prove that the gospel in question must have been written by St. John. A man of common sense, who has perused the book with due attention and fully comprehended the spiritual meanings of the passages contained in the beginning of the book, as also in other parts of it, knows undoubtedly that the book must have been written by the most discerning, and the most accomplished Apostle of Jesus, the anointed, and could have been written by nobody else, for who could write the profound spiritual things, unless thoroughly imbibed thereunto? He alone could write them who had arrived at a very high stage of spiritual progress. Of the Apostles none had obtained this spiritual advancement, save the favored one, Christ's great affection for him proving it beyond doubt.

I shall here quote only one passage for the satisfaction of your readers, the passage with which the book begins. "In the beginning was the Word, the Word was with God, and the Word was God." This compound sentence and this sentence alone contains the very pith and marrow, the super and the very perfection of the True Religion, the Religion of Love, God's Own Religion. It tells us what to begin with, how to proceed, and what to end with. Who can comprehend the spiritual meaning of this very adored passage? None but those that are truly enlightened, and have the capacity and requisite penetration to understand it fully.

This sentence could have been written only by the most advanced in spirit, and by no body else. I could adduce similar passages by hundreds, but I would not do so, one passage having sufficed my purpose.

Yours &c.,
AMRITALAL DE.

Jeypore, 20th September, 1879.

OPEN-AIR MEETINGS OF THE BRAHMO SOMAJ OF INDIA.

TO THE EDITOR OF THE "INDIAN MIRROR."

SIR,—I fully agree with your correspondent, "An Old Vaishnava," that the plan of open-air meetings, adopted by your Somaj, if systematically and persistently carried on, will, in a very short time, further the cause of your Somaj. I was present at one of these meetings lately held at Naihati. And from what I saw there, and from the reports of similar meetings at other places, published in your paper, I am convinced that many people, who hated the Brahmo Somaj, have since changed their attitude. I am sure that so far as Sankirtan and prayer to the One True God are concerned, the Hindus are willing to accord their moral sympathy to the Brahmos. Mr. Editor, you will, I am sure, be glad to learn that at Naihati, as soon as Baba Keshub Chunder Sen finished his address, a Pundit of Bhatpara, who was standing by, remarked to me that all his (Keshub Babu's) arguments were always (incontrovertible), and that he had preached truths which every reasonable man must admit.

The object of Baba Keshub Chunder Sen and his friends, in adopting this method of popular preaching, is, I believe, not so much to convert the audience in the usual acceptation of the term, as to rouse the people to a sincere and just appreciation of the necessity of acknowledging the Creator of this universe as a True and Living Providence. It is the earnest desire of Keshub Babu, as can be fully understood from his utterances on such occasions, that his countrymen should know, believe and realize that it is utterly impossible to live, move and have our being without God's direct and personal intervention; and acting under such sacred and inspired impulse, he speaks in a way which cannot fail to carry conviction to the heart of those that hear him. I can assure you that, with such objects in view and with such sincere and effective addresses, Keshub Babu will succeed in drawing many a heart towards religion. While on this point, I must not overlook the crowning claims of Sankirtan in conquering the hearts of men and in establishing there God's authority. Sankirtan is a truly national and, therefore, popular institution in this country. And from the recorded facts of the life and doings of Chaitanya, the prophet of Nuddea, and the greatest champion of *Vaishnavism*, we know how far the method of preaching by *Sankirtan* had been successful in this country. The singing of the Holy Name naturally sends a thrill into men's hearts, and there penetrating like a flash of lightning, dispels doubt and darkness, sorrow and anxiety, and electrifies the whole soul with the sacred fire of enthusiasm. It is gratifying to contemplate that the Brahmos have long recognised the elevating influence of *Sankirtan* at their devotional meetings, and have now, after all, adopted it as the chief means of leading the people of Bengal to God. They have hit upon the true method, and, I believe the success of it now will entirely depend upon the sincerity, earnestness and patience on the part of those who will undertake this sacred mission.

Hitherto the Brahmo Missionaries had adopted a quite different plan. They visited the Brahmo Somajes in different parts of the country, held devotional meetings and preached sermons to a few Brahmos only. For the general public, they very seldom came in contact with them, and the result was general apathy and indifference, and, in some cases, decided antagonism towards the Brahmo Somaj movement. But I believe the present plan, if properly carried out, will not only remove the difficulties above alluded to, but will be sufficient to enlist the sympathy of a great many people.

Yours &c.,
SPECTATOR.

The 14th November 1879.

NOTICES TO CORRESPONDENTS.

Persons favoring us with communications are requested to write legibly, and on one side of the paper only.

Unauthenticated communications will not be inserted.

R. K. GUHA.—The person attacked is not a foeman worthy of your steel.

OUR ALLAHABAD CORRESPONDENT says:—"Does the Brahmo Somaj uphold the system of promising by means of worldly inducements? To be more clear, is it the principle of the Brahmo Somaj to increase its membership by promise of money, employment, maintenance, marriage and so forth? A case has occurred here that I am compelled me to put this question before the Brahmo public. It has caused a great sensation among the orthodox as well as the enlightened Hindu community of this station. A young Hindu widow of a respectable Bengali family was led by certain gentlemen by promise of marriage to leave her family, and come to the protection of the Brahmo Somaj. The negotiation, I learn, was continued for two months, and the lady was at last prevailed upon by hope of getting married, and consented to come to their protection. This was no sooner settled than the means for escape was adopted, and one night, at 11 o'clock, when all the inmates of the house were asleep, she was packed in a carriage and carried off." We cannot say how far the facts stated here are true. Our opinion on forced conversions is well known. The Brahmo Somaj is opposed to all modes of proselytism which are artificial.

K. C. sends us the solution of the skiff puzzle :—"The two boys cross first, one remains on the other bank and the other crosses the river back. The man then crosses alone, leaving the boy and the woman on this side. The man remains on the other bank, and the boy who was there crosses the river again. The two boys then cross the river together—one remains on the other bank and one crosses again to this bank. This boy remains on this bank, and the woman crosses alone. Then the boy who was on the other side comes back and crosses again with the other boy."

Literary, Scientific &c.

THE letters of the World in 1878 amounted to 3,300,000,000, or about 9¼ millions daily. As to telegrams, nearly 130,000,000 were sent in 1877, an average of 353,000 per diem, while one-third of these were private, dealing with purely personal concerns.

THE popularity of public celebrities is tested in Paris by the number of pipes made in their likenesses. Recently Presidential pipes have been the greatest successes, for the Thiers pipe has been

most in request, some 57,000 being sold annually, M. Gambetta is second in favor, and M. Grévy comes third.

THE hair of the Presidents of the United States, from Washington to Pierce in 1853, is carefully preserved in the Patent Office at Washington. Most of the locks are bleached by age, Washington's hair being nearly pure white, but fine and smooth. Since Buchanan succeeded to the Presidency in 1857 the custom has been dropped.

ON the 16th October, several services were held in France for the anniversary of the juridical assassination of Marie-Antoinette, the Queen of Louis XVI; the attendance everywhere was numerous and devout. Does this show that monarchy is returning to France, now that Bonapartism is virtually at an end, the Communists have begun their impudent threats, and the Government are threatening the clergy?

THE advantages of simplicity in travelling were peculiarly demonstrated by the two French Ministers, M. M. Lepère and Le Royer, during a recent trip in Italy. On arriving at a hotel, the latter gave his name simply as Le Royer, but his colleague replied grandiosely, "His Excellency M. Lepère, Minister of the Interior in the Government of the French Republic." When settling the same, M. Le Royer was charged 5s. daily for his room, but "His Excellency" had to pay £2.

AT the first meeting of the newly-elected Municipal Commissioners of Calcutta, Dr. K. M. Bannerji rose to make a speech. He began thus:—"As a member of this University"—There was laughter when this mistake was made. We cannot make out, however, why there should be any fun. The Municipal Commissioners have, by their frequent speechifying, entitled themselves to be called the body politic of the Calcutta University. There are so many candidates for honors at the several meetings that we hope the mistake will be repeated, and that degrees will henceforth be conferred on the most deserving and successful of them.

IT is a fashion to say that Cetewayo was deserted by his men in his last moments of liberty. It seems, however, that the Zulus persisted to the last in concealing the place of his concealment. "Five Zulus were taken prisoners, and questioned severely as to the place where the King was hiding. They declared that they did not know where he was, whereupon they were all flogged!—with what right let Englishmen judge. They bore their flogging, and still refused to betray their King's hiding-place, and two of them managed to escape. Then the scheme was adopted which had been practised once before in this war, or taking these blindfolded each to a separate spot, when two gunshots were fired, and each of course, supposed that the other two were killed, and so the secret was obtained from one or more of them."

THE starry heavens at the present time, says the *Indo-European Correspondence*, present us with a more than usual interest. Four out of the seven primary planets, and, perhaps, the four most interesting, may be seen simultaneously, daily pursuing their unerring path among the heavenly constellations, namely Mars, Jupiter, Saturn and Neptune. On one of those splendid November evenings, if you turn your back towards the ruddy streaks of the west just after sunset, you will perceive, at the opposite point of the horizon, a fiery red star, which you might easily mistake for one of those balloons the Natives occasionally send aloft at this season of the year. That bright white star, inferior only to Venus in whiteness and brightness, which you perceive southward, towering on high in the spangled heavens, is the majestic Jupiter. Between the god of thunder and the god of war, about midway slowly moves pale old Saturn, of a lead-white hue.

Calcutta.

HIS EXCELLENCY the Viceroy will hold a levee at Calcutta on Friday, the 19th December, and a Drawing Room will be held in the first week of January, on the return of His Excellency and Lady Lytton from visiting Darjiling.

Temperance.

THE young men of Dacca have formed themselves into a Temperance Society. Among other promises their pledge enjoins that every member should try his best to keep his moral character pure.

DR. NORMAN KERR, an eminent authority on the physiological aspect of the temperance question, read a paper on "Mortality by Drink" at the last Social Science Congress. In it the Doctor states that 120,000 deaths, in all, have resulted from intemperance, 40,500 from personal intemperance, and 79,500 from effects of intemperance to others.

THE Bishop of Manchester, in his inaugural address at the last Social Science Congress in Manchester, has disclosed the following remarkable facts, in reference to the alarming increase of liquor-shops in England. Comparing Manchester with Gothenburg, in Germany, the Bishop remarked " that every 32nd house in Manchester is licensed to sell intoxicating drinks, and that we have about one such house to every 135 of the population. In Gothenburg I saw by a recent account in the *Times*, the proportion is one to every thousand."

THE following figures, taken from the Excise Resolution of the Government of Bengal, shew the different directions of the excise revenue realised in Bengal, and will, we hope, be interesting to many of our readers :—

Division.	Population according to census of 1872.	Total excise revenue.	Incidence per 100 of population.
		Rs.	Rs.
Burdwan ...	71,03,589	5,80,002	10
Calcutta with Suburbs and			
Howrah ...	7,86,223	14,22,313	180
Rest of Presidency Division ...	71,02,579	6,55,131	9
Rajshahye and			
Cuch Behar ...	73,77,063	4,02,967	6
Dacca ...	91,44,130	5,34,160	6
Chittagong ...	1,41,306	82,015	4
Patna ...	1,31,22,743	13,41,841	11
Bhaugulpore ...	72,82,734	8,66,117	11
Orissa ...	31,02,409	3,78,829	11
Chota Nagpore ...	36,22,748	3,50,075	10
Total ...	6,04,32,487	70,939,39	11

Selections.

PROFESSOR MAX MULLER ON THE EDUCATED NATIVES.

THE intellectual life of India, at the present moment, is full of interesting problems. It is too much the fashion to look only at its darker sides, and to forget that such intellectual regeneration, as we are witnessing in India, are impossible without conversions and failures. A new race of men is growing up in India, who have stepped, as it were, over a thousand years, and have entered at once on the intellectual inheritance of Europe. They carry off prizes at English schools, take their degrees in English Universities, and are, in every respect, our equals. They have temptations which we have not, and now and then they succumb; but we, too, have temptations of our own, and we do not always resist. One can hardly trust one's eyes in reading their writings, whether in English or Bengali, many of which would reflect credit on our own Quarterlies. With regard to what is of the greatest interest to us, their scholarship, it is true that the old school of Sanskrit scholars is dying out, and much will die with it which we shall never recover; but a new and most promising school of Sanskrit students, educated by European professors, is springing up, and they will, by-and-by judge from recent controversies, they have already become more formidable rivals to our own scholars. The Essays of Dr. Bhau Daji, whom, I regret to say, we have lately lost by death on disputed points in Indian archaeology and literature are most valuable. The indefatigable Rajendralala Mittra is rendering most excellent service in the publications of the Asiatic Society at Calcutta, and he discusses the theories of European Orientalists with all the ease and grace of an English reviewer. The Rajah of Deamab, Giriprasada Singha, has just finished his magnificent edition of the White Yajurveda. The Sanskrit books, published at Calcutta, by Taranatha and others, form a complete library, and Taranatha's new dictionary of the Sanskrit language will prove most useful and valuable. The editions of Sanskrit texts, published at Bombay, by Professor Bhandarkar, Shankar Pandurang Pandit, and others, need not fear comparison with the best works of European scholars.

THE BRAHMO SOMAJ.

—o—

(*Statesman.*)

WE sometimes regret, and, perhaps, our readers also have cause to regret, that the purely political questions of the day leave us so little time to watch and study the operation of the social and spiritual forces, which, nevertheless, may have a deeper and more lasting influence on the progress of humanity, than the rise and fall of Governments or even of Empires. It is possible, for instance, that the destinies of India may depend more upon Keshub Chunder Sen with his *grey* and *bhakti,* and less upon Lord Beaconsfield and Imperialism, than we are apt to imagine. We have never been inclined to over-rate the Brahmo prophet; we have not been among his most enthusiastic admirers; but, on the other hand, it is easy to attach too much importance to the loud political hubbub in the air, and too little to the subtler movements that are going on around us, working more or less silently at the roots of society. We are not prepared to say whether Brahmoism, as appointed by the "Minister," is a movement destined to have a powerful formative influence on Hindu society, or to estimate its net value as one of the spiritual forces of the time. We are not even very familiar with its history; we know still less of its principles and objects; we may even confess that when, once or twice, we have tried to understand these a little, we have come away more mystified than edified; but this we are disposed to attribute to the deadening effect upon our spiritual perceptions of the study of politics and the daily drudgery of reading and writing newspapers. Brahmoism and its Minister may be incomprehensible to us, and yet luminous and light-bringing to those who have penetrated the secrets of *yoga* and *bhakti* and *bairagya.* It is because a suspicion has dawned upon us that, while we are making a fuss about Imperial policies, Afghan wars, Russian menaces, and other trivialities that kind Father Time will sweep quietly underground in a few years, as things worthy only of being buried and forgotten, we may be standing, stupidly unobservant, with eyes that see not and hearts that cannot understand, beside the birth-chamber of a new era in human history—it is because this suspicion has dawned upon us, that we turn away for a moment from Reuter and the Press Commissioner, and ask our readers to look with us into the pages of the Sunday edition of the *Indian Mirror.* We find there that on the evening of the last *Bhádrat-ab* (we do not know what that is) the "Minister" preached what, from the summary of it which is printed, we take to have been a remarkable sermon. The object of the sermon appears to have been to demonstrate the superiority of Brahmoism to all other religions and revelations that have ever ministered to the wants and aspirations of the human heart. This was illustrated by a simile which must have appealed very forcibly to the imagination of the hearers. Each of the other religions of the world was described as the bestower of a single precious jewel on the individual or community who embraced it, as if—for we must work out the simile a little—Christianity gave a diadem, Mahomedanism a necklace, Hinduism a nose-jewel, and so on; each religion extolling its one jewel as all-sufficient for the ornamentation of the whole person. It has been left to Brahmoism to discover in these last days, that it is absurd to put on a nose-jewel or even a crown of gold, and parade the whole person as being thus sufficiently arrayed and adorned. According to it, takes from each its peculiar jewel, and arrays the whole person with the spoils of all the prophets and all the gods. The Christian has his peculiar grace, the *Brahmin* has the Buddhist his, the Mahomedan his, and no doubt no have the fire-worshipper and the fetish-worshipper. But among—'t is as stands forth one, and one only, rich in- dependent in all the graces, and that one is the Brahmo. The Brahmo is the heir of all the ages, of all the prophets, and all the gods. The simile is slightly varied towards the end of the discourse. "Whereas each religion of the world is a precious jewel,

Brahmoism," we learn, "is a string of jewels." The meaning of all this is tolerably clear. All prophets hitherto have had but a single idea. Christ, Mahomed, Buddha, were all one-ideal men. They and their ideas are all summed up in Babu Keshub Chunder Sen and Brahmoism. The idea which he has added to the general stock is the idea of universality, which, though itself indistinguishable, as the string is hidden by the jewels it displays, is yet surely greater than all, as it brings all together into one, and enables the soul to comprehend them as a perfect and henceforth indissoluble whole.

This is the "Minister's" account of himself and his church. The first thing that strikes a sceptical reader is, that Mr. Sen is but one among a multitude of professed eclectics whom the world has seen. After all, it is no new discovery that all truths are precious, and that every wise man prizes every truth he can ascertain to be truth, wherever he can find it. Nor is the ideal of truth as a great and sublime whole, of which our so-called "truths" are but atoms, now for the first time presented to the world. Is Babu Keshub Chunder Sen, then, nothing other than an eclectic philosopher of a pietistic turn of mind? Has he no claim to original genius or distinguished force of character. Is he not a revealer of truth, but only a clever craftsman, whose skill manifests itself by so selecting and arranging the materials he has borrowed from greater teachers, as to form a system all the parts of which seem naturally to group themselves around Babu Keshub Chunder Sen as their centre and sun? For it is impossible to read the weekly organ of these Hindu Eclectics without observing, not merely that great prominence is given to the Minister, but that the Minister's personality is absolutely essential to the cohesion and vitality of his system of truths. This indeed is either the strength or the weakness of his sect. If Mr. Sen is great enough to rank among the Immorials, to bequeath his personality and the living force of his genius and charac or to futurity, so that though dead he may yet speak to coming generations, that his name may be a watch-word and battle-cry and symbol of truth to those that follow after him, then his church will also live as a considerable unit among the social and spiritual forces in the India of the future. If he is less than this, his church most of necessity die with him, for he is its keystone without which it must topple down in fragments. It is the church of Babu Keshub Chunder Sen, or nothing. We are not protesting against the prominence of the "Minister" in his own church. What we say is, that if he is worthy of the prominence which is given to him, to his sayings and doings and sufferings in the Sunday Mirror—and we presume, therefore, in all the proceedings of his church—he must be one of the Immortals, destined to live in future ages as the fellow of the great founders of the world's religions. If he has not this worthiness, then the adulation of his church is the distinctive feature of his church, will become at his death a superstition too weak to live as a bond of union and stimulus to action among those who are now his followers. The prominence of the Minister of the Brahmo Somaj follows necessarily from his refusal to concede supremacy to any other teacher. Christ is great and good, but not supreme. It is doubtful if Chaitanya has not at least equal claims on love and devotion. No former teacher having supreme authority there being no great man of that rank under which Brahmos may range themselves, it follows of course, that they must range themselves under the name of Babu Keshab Chunder Sen, and accept as their supreme authority the teacher who has the wisdom to sift the teachings of all former prophets, to collect the good grain and scatter the chaff. Mr. Sen carries the fan of truth in his hand, and is, therefore, greater—must at least seem greater to his followers—than any of the prophets whose teachings he assumes to winnow. We do not pretend to answer the questions we have started. We have not a sufficiently intimate knowledge of the Church of Eclectic Brahmos to justify us in doing so, even if we could trust our judgment to decide upon questions of such import. All that is perfectly clear to us is, that Mr. Sen is the heart of the organization, from whom life-blood circulates, and without whom (either in the body or out of the body) it must die and dissolve—though death may come long before dissolution. He asked the other year the question "Am I a Prophet?" We must answer it for him with an afterthought. He is either a Prophet or an Impostor. He belongs either to the first rank of the world's teachers and spiritual guides, or is a self-blown bubble, whose bursting will leave but a faint momentary streak on the surface of the stream which it now seems to conduct,

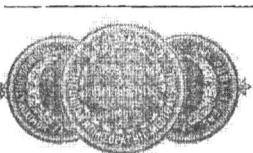

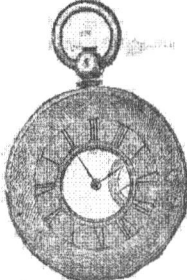

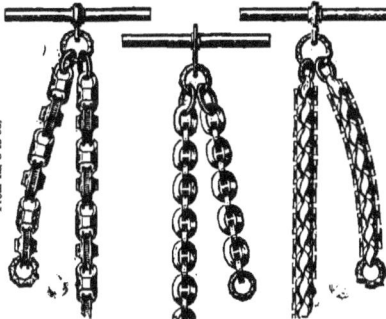

Hooghly Bridge Notice.

THE Bridge will be closed for traffic on Tuesday, the 18th November, 1879, from 3 P. M. to 6 P. M.

G. H. SIMMONS,
a-6   Secretary to the Bridge Commissioners.

INDIA GENERAL STEAM NAVIGATION COMPANY, LD.

SCHOENE, KILBURN & Co.—*Managing Agents.*

ASSAM LINE NOTICE.

Steamers leave Calcutta for Assam every Friday, and Goalundo every Sunday, and leave Debhooghat downward every Saturday.

THE Str. *Soula* will leave Calcutta for Assam, on Friday, the 4th instant.

Cargo will be received at the Company's Godowns, Nimtollah Ghat, up till noon of Thursday, the 13th.

THE Str. *Turpore* will leave Goalundo for Assam on Sunday, the 16th instant.

Cargo will be received at the Company's Godowns, No. 4, Fairlie Place, uptill noon of Friday, the 14th instant.

Passengers should leave for Goalundo by Train of Saturday, the 15th instant.

CACHAR LINE NOTICE.

REGULAR WEEKLY SERVICE.

Steamers leave Calcutta for Cachar and intermediate Stations every Tuesday, and leave Cachar downward every Thursday.

THE Str. *Silchar* will leave Calcutta for Cachar on Tuesday, the 18th instant.

Cargo will be received at the Company's Godowns, Nimtollah Ghat, up till noon of Monday, the 17th instant.

For further information regarding rates of freight or passage money, apply to

4, FAIRLIE PLACE, }   G. J. SCOTT,
Calcutta 10th November, 1879, }   *Secretary.*
4-23

RIVERS STEAM NAVIGATION CO. "LIMITED."

The Steamers of this Company run weekly from Calcutta and Goalundo to Assam and back.

THE Steamer *Indore* will leave Chicutta for Assam on Friday, the 21st instant.

THE Str. *Retunda* will leave for Assam from Goalundo on Thursday, the 20th instant.

For further information regarding rates of freights or passage, apply to
MACKRILL & CO.
a-38

DR. PARE'S

INFALLIBLE MALARIA SPECIFIC.

WARRANTED to afford relief in all cases of Malarious Fever, with enlargement of the Liver or Spleen, Anæmia, Jaundice, &c. It is the safest and most efficacious remedy for the cure of these diseases; and has wrought wonderful cures of the numerous worst cases of the enlargement of the Spleen and Liver of several years' standing. It has always effected a cure when other medicines has signally failed.

Price, per phial, As. 12 in Calcutta; and Re. 1 in the Mofussil.

ALSO DR. PARE'S

WONDERFUL BLOOD PURIFIER,
And Certain Antidote against Mercury, and the numerous affections arising therefrom.

As a purifier of the Blood, in all diseases arising from impudicious use of Mercury, Rheumatism, Scrofula, Cutaneous Eruptions, with Dyspepsia and General Debility, Dr. Pare's Blood Purifier stands unrivalled. To remove novelty from the system, it is one of the most remarkable medicines in existence. It has cured numerous chronic and almost hopeless cases within a very short time with its truly magical effects.

Price, Rs. 1-8 per phial in Calcutta, and Re. 1-12 in the Mofussil.

To be had of
MAISON DE PARIS,
21, LINDSAY STREET, CHOWRINGHEE, CALCUTTA.

Maison de Paris is removed from 21, Lindsay Street, to No. 7, Chowringhee Road, Calcutta.
a-69

W. NEWMAN & CO.

3, Dalhousie Square, Calcutta.

NEW BOOKS.

Travels.

A RIDE IN EGYPT, from Sioot to Luxor, in 1879. With Notes on the Present State and Ancient History of the Nile Valley, By the Rev. W. J. Loftie. With Illustrations. (6-12)   Rs. 7-8

LIFE IN ASIATIC TURKEY : A Journal of Travel in Cilicia, Isauria, and parts of Lycaonia and Cappadocia, By Rev. E. J. Davis, M.A. With Maps and Illustrations. (13-8)Rs. 13-0

AUSTRALASIA. (Stanford's Compendium of Geography and Travels.) Edited by Alfred R. Wallace, F.R.G.S. With Ethnological Appendix, By A. H. Keane, M.A.I. With numerous Maps and Illustrations. (13-8) Rs. 15-8

ARABIA, EGYPT, INDIA : A Narrative of Travel by Isabel Burton, With 15 Illustrations and two route Maps. (10-0)   Rs. 11-4

Biography.

LIFE OF H. R. H. THE PRINCE CONSORT, By Theodore Martin. Vol. IV. With Portraits. (11-4)   Rs. 12-8

LIFE OF ALEXANDER DUFF, D.D., LL.D. By George Smith, c.i.e., LL.D. Vol. I. With Portrait by Jeens. (7-10)   Rs. 8-8

ABRAHAM LINCOLN. By Charles G. Leland (*The New Plutarch Series*.) (1-12)   Rs. 1-14

GUIZOT'S HISTORY OF ENGLAND From the earliest times to the accession of Queen Victoria. Vol. III. Imperial 8vo., Illustrated. (15-4)   Rs. 17-0

.*.* *This volume completes the work. Vols. I. and II. are available.*

CONTRIBUTIONS to A BALLAD HISTORY OF England, and the States sprung from her. By W. C. Bennett. (1-6)   Re. 1-8

Religious.

THE LIFE AND WORK OF St. PAUL. By the Rev. F. W. Farrar, Canon of Westminster, Author of "The Life of Christ." 2 Vols. Demy 8vo. (15-4)   Rs. 17-0

THE HOLY WEEK AND THE FORTY DAYS, Being a Continuous Narrative in the Words of the Evangelists, Constructed from the Four Gospels with a Commentary and Appendices. By the Rev. G. F. Popham Blyth, M.A., Bengal Chaplain. In 2 Vols. (9-0)   Rs. 10-0

Oriental.

SACRED BOOKS OF THE EAST. Translated by various Oriental Scholars, and edited by Prof. Max Muller.

Vol I. The Upanishads, Translated by Prof. Max Muller. Part 1. (6-12)   Rs. 7-6

Vol. II. The Sacred Laws of the Aryas, Translated by George Buhler. Part 1. (6-12)   Rs. 7-6

Vol. III. The Sacred Books of China, The Text of Confucianism, Translated by James Legge. Part 1. (8-0)   Rs. 8-12

THE BUSTAN. By Shaikh Maslihu D. Din Sa' Di Shirazi. Translated for the first time into Prose, with Explanatory Notes and Index. By Captain H. Wilberforce Clarke. (18-0)   Rs. 20

THE JATAKA, together with its Commentary, being Tales of the Anterior Births of Gotama Budda. Edited in the Original Pali by V. Fausboll, and Translated by T. W. Rhys Davids. Vol. II. (18-0)   Rs. 20
Vol. I. is also available.

Essays.

ATTIC NIGHTS. By Charles Mills. (4-12)   Rs. 5-4

THE ETHICS OF GEORGE ELIOT'S WORKS. By the late John Crombie Brown. (1-12)   Re. 1-14

GLEANINGS FROM PAST YEARS. By the Right Hon. W. E. Gladstone, M. P. Vol. VII.—Miscellaneous (completing the Series). (1-12)   Rs. 1-14

XI.) SOCIAL TWITTERS. By Mrs. Loftie. (1-8)   Re. 1-14

FACTS AND FALLACIES OF MODERN PROtection : being the Oxford Cobden Prize Essay for 1878. By A. J. Wilson. (1-12)   Re. 1-14

A DEFENCE OF PHILOSOPHIC DOUBT. By A. J. Balfour, M.P. (7-10)   Rs. 8-8

Indian Castes.

HINDU TRIBES AND CASTES ; together with an account of Mahomedan Tribes of the North-West Frontier, and the Aboriginal Tribes of the Central Provinces. By the Rev. M. A. Sherring, M. A., LL.B, Vol. II. Royal 4to.   Rs. 16-0

Illustrated Books.

SHIKARI AND TOMASHA : A Souvenir of the Visit of H. R. H. The Prince of Wales to India. By William Simpson (F. R. G)S. Consisting of 12 Photographs from original drawings, the property of the Prince of Wales. Super-Royal 4to. oblong. (£1-1-0) (10-0)   Rs. 11-4

BLACKBURN'S ACADEMY NOTES 1873-1879. Bound in one Volume. Cloth. (3-14)   Rs. 4-4

Engineering and Industries.

SUPPLEMENT TO SPON'S DICTIONARY of Engineering, Civil, Mechanical, Military, and Naval. Edited by Ernest Spon. Division I. A to C. (12-0)   Rs. 13-4

A PRACTICAL TREATISE ON NATURAL and artificial concrete, its varieties and constructive adaptations. By Henry Reid. New edition. (9-4)   Rs. 10-4

TIN MINING IN LARUT, By Patrick Doyle, C.E., F.G.S. With Maps, Plans, and Notes. (2-5)   Rs. 2-8

TABULATED WEIGHTS of Angle, Tee, Bulb, Round, Square, and Flat-Iron and Steel, and other information, for use of Naval Architects and Ship-Builders. By G. H. Jornen. Third edition, revised and enlarged. (9-12) Re. 1-14

THE MODERN LOCOMOTIVE ENGINEER Fireman and Engine-Boy : Comprising an Historical Notice of the Pioneer Locomotive Engines and their Inventions, with a Project for the Establishment of Certificates of Qualification on the Running Service of Railways. By Michael Reynolds, Author of "Locomotive Engine Driving." (2-14)   Rs. 3-4

SPON'S ENCYCLOPEDIA OF THE INDUStrial Arts, Manufactures, and Commercial Products. Edited by C. G. Warden, F. G. S. Division I. Imperial 8vo. (8-8)   Rs. 9-8

NARROW GUAGE RAILWAYS. By C. E. Spooner, c. e., F. G. S. Second Edition. With numerous large Plates. (9-4)   Rs. 10-4

Science.

THE ELECTRIC LIGHT and its Practical Application. By Paget Higgs, LL.D., D.Sc., (5-10)   Rs. 6-4

ELECTRIC TRANSMISSION OF POWER : its present position and advantages. By Paget Higgs, LL.D., D.Sc., C. (3-0)   Rs. 2-4

MODERN METEOROLOGY. A series of Six Lectures delivered under the auspices of the Meteorological Society in 1878. Illustrated. (2-14)   Rs. 3-4

FRAGMENTS OF SCIENCE : A series of detached Essays, Addresses and Reviews. By John Tyndall, F.R.S., D.C.L., LL.D. Sixth Edition. Revised and augmented by Seventeen Papers. 2 vols. (10-0)   Rs. 11-4

SCIENCE LECTURES at SOUTH KENSINGton. Second Volume. (3-14)   Rs. 4-4
a-35   W. NEWMAN & CO.

Government Cinchona Febrifuge.

AN efficient substitute for Quinine. Sold by the principal Europe and Native druggists of Calcutta. Obtainable from the Superintendent, Botanical Garden, Calcutta. Past fee at 4 as. Re. 6 : as. Re. 11 : 10 oz., Rs. 26-12. Cash with order.
a-57

The Indian Mirror

[EDITED BY KRISHNA BIHARI SEN, M.A.]

SUNDAY EDITION

[REGISTERED AT THE GENERAL POST OFFICE.]

VOL. XIX.   CALCUTTA, SUNDAY, NOVEMBER 23, 1879.   NO. 279.

CONTENTS.

Telegrams.
Editorial Notes.
ARTICLES :—
Religion in National
  Life.
No Superstition.
The Missionary Expe-
  dition.
Brahmo Somaj.

Devotional.
Provincial.
Correspondence.
Literary, Scientific &c.
Calcutta.
Pulpit.
Selections.
Advertisements.

Telegraphic Intelligence.

REUTER'S TELEGRAMS.

SEDITION IN IRELAND.

LONDON, 22ND NOVEMBER.

A crowded meeting was held at Dublin yesterday at which resolutions were adopted protesting against the arrests that are being made for seditious language. Mr. Parnell and the leading homerulers were present, and addressed the meeting.

MILITARY SERVICE IN TURKEY.

CONSTANTINOPLE, 21ST NOVEMBER.

The Sultan has approved the proposal of Baker Pasha that military service for all races and creeds be compulsory.

Editorial Notes.

MR. T. J. SCOTT of Bareilly writes on a very important subject. Should Native Christians use coffins in burying the dead, or should the body be interred itself without any of the costly luxuries which civilization suggests? This was a question which came for discussion before the Rohilcund District Conference, consisting of eight American Missionaries and eighty-eight Native members, and it was referred to a Select Committee for report ! What the upshot of the discussion was, we have no means of knowing.

BOMBAY has seen a novel phenomenon. A colored lady, Mrs. Amanda Smith, has come to India to preach the Gospel. She can speak and sing, and her utterances are said to be really powerful. One fact heightens the effect of her work. She was a slave in the United States, and having tasted the sweets of liberation, she longs to liberate others from every kind of slavery, physical or spiritual. The lady was lately at Puna, where we are glad our countrymen accorded her a cordial welcome. We hope Mrs. Amanda Smith will come to Calcutta.

THE British soldiers have been guilty of many sad atrocities in Cabul. We suspect that some of those Afghans, who had been hanged, were burned and not buried. Then, again, a correspondent of the Lahore paper says that at Charasia the wounded Afghans were slashed about still alive and set on fire. If the fact be true, then we think the sooner the British leave Cabul the better, for a longer stay with the Afghans will make the former imbibe all the ferocious and bloodthirsty nature of the latter.

WE have very often to complain of the irregularity with which the Post Office supplies us with our regular batch of newspapers. Last week, for instance, we did not receive a single English newspaper, and as the mail is late this time, we are without English news of any kind. We do not know what this is due to. Surely there must be a mistake somewhere. Is it too much to hope that the authorities will keep a vigilant watch over the regular delivery of newspapers? A word also to our contemporaries who exchange with us, and those friends who have books or letters to send. All such papers, books or letters should be addressed to the Editor, Indian Mirror (Sunday edition.)

WE find that at the Metropolitan Tabernacle, Mr. C. H. Spurgeon lately stated that the sermon which he was about to deliver would, when printed, complete a series of 1,005, which he had delivered in regular consecutive order from the pulpit, and which had been published week by week. He desired to express his thankfulness that so much Divine help had been granted him in the preparation and delivery of sermons which had not merely been printed but read—sermons which had been translated into many foreign tongues, and which were being read at that very moment on that Sabbath morning in many hundreds of places where a minister could not be found,

WE are very sorry to hear from the Bombay Guardian of the sad bereavement suffered by Dr. Valentine of Jeypore in the death of his wife and two children. Dr. Valentine is medical missionary at the Court of Jeypore. A few years ago he was the means of doing great good to that state, where in conjunction with the late Babu Hari Mohan Sen and the ex-Dewan, Nawab Faiz Ali Khan, he took part in every important movement which lent a sort of charm to the administration of that State. It speaks well of the liberal spirit of the Maharajah that, at the time we are speaking of, he put himself under the influence of an enlightened Bengali, a devout Christian and an able Mussulman—three eminent lovers of progress, who had no sympathy with superstition or prejudice of any sort. How far His Highness has benefited by this three-fold influence may be understood by any traveller who happens to visit the Jeypore State.

How sweet and elevating is the company of a truly devout man. In the midst of harassing anxieties and dreadful temptations of life, it is a great relief to have the opportunity of mixing in the company of a pious man, whose heart being set in the contemplation of the Loving Father, remains always serene and cheerful. His sweet and smiling countenance expresses thorough resignation. Truly there is something which makes the whole atmosphere around him pure and ennobling. He may not speak any thing, but the silent force of his life moulds the lives and character of those around him. We know of instances where the mere sight of a bhakta has brought a permanent change in the life of many. We value the company of devotees and religious men, and are practically convinced of its advantages in the formation of character. We believe that it is a moral necessity which every man must feel at some period of his life. We, therefore, strongly recommend that it should form a part—an important part—of the religious exercises of every sincere religious enquirer.

WE welcome Father Rivington to this city. He arrived on Tuesday last, and on Thursday appeared at the Bethune Society where he delivered a lecture on "Teleology." This was an earnest of what Father Rivington means to do during the short period of his stay in Calcutta. November is not a favorable month for lectures, as most of the students and young men are busy preparing themselves for the University examinations. We hope Father Rivington will draw large audiences and succeed in infusing the spirit of religion in the minds of educated Natives. We are afraid he has many opponents among his own Christian brethren. The Lucknow Witness of Friday last speaks of Fathers Rivington and O'Neill in the following strain :—" These men, we believe, are doing much harm, and it is scandalous that they should be so thoroughly upheld in their extreme sacerdotal ideas, confessional and all, by the Bishop of the diocese and most of the chaplains." Fortunately for the Cowley Fathers the educated Natives have come to think very highly of their spiritual attainments.

AN esteemed Christian gentleman has asked us to insert the " Confession of Thomas Paine," evidently in reply to Mr. Conway's letter on the same subject which appeared in a late issue of this paper. We gladly comply with the request. The extract will be found in another column. The confession, if true, is certainly curious, for it shows Thomas Paine in no enviable light. We take the liberty, however, to say that the effect of Mr. Bourne's attack upon Paine seems to be exaggerated. The former tried to prove that the study of the Bible required extensive literary acquirements. "A competent disputer should accurately and critically understand the Hebrew, Chaldaic, Syriac and Greek languages at least, or he cannot read the scriptures in the tongues in which they were written. Then he ought to be versed in the opinions, customs, usages, and the domestic and public annals of the Asiatic nations of antiquity. He should also be well acquainted with the ancient history, especially of Egypt, Assyria, Babylon, Persia, Arabia, and with the Grecian and Roman affairs ; to all which he must superadd a minute and deep insight into ecclesiastical history since the introduction of Christianity." This is sufficient to take off one's breath, and we are not surprised to hear Paine confess that he had been driven into a corner. May we ask, however, if one in a thousand among Christian divines, if Mr. Bourne himself, could boast of the wonderful knowledge said to be so essential to an estimate of " the celestial inspiration of the Holy Scriptures?" To say that Thomas Paine was so far frightened by the display of the scholastic attainments of his interlocutor that he was immediately obliged to confess himself a donkey may be true enough by itself. But certainly it does not explain his deep-rooted hatred of Christianity which, we are told, only increased with his age.

RELIGION IN NATIONAL LIFE.

He is a bad reader of history who, after examining the tendencies of things, has the heart to assert that human society and institutions can maintain a moment's existence, if there be not underneath a substratum of Divinity to sustain them. To educated minds the thought must be simply electrifying that no great movement has been inaugurated, no nation has been brought to existence without the impulse of a strong religious sentiment. We challenge any historian to point out to us an occurrence which is godless, it is a truism almost to say that religion lies at the basis of every great movement in history. Go wherever you will, you will hardly come across a country where religion does not occupy the most prominent place in the national sentiment. If such be the case, why is it that religion is held to be unfashionable by the world ? From morning till dewy eve a Hindu's life is spent in religious observances, and yet talk to him about religion, and he will ridicule your pretensions. The fact is that religion is omnipotent everywhere ; it is a real despot before whom there is no quailing. The most heterodox Christian and the most heterodox Hindu are both helpless when brought face to face with the padri ; and yet as soon as they leave the precincts of the church and the Mandir, their religion vanishes, and they come to enjoy other fashionable things of the world. There is a grave unreality in the religious atmosphere which we breathe. On the one hand, there is a mode of education which tells us very little, directly, in favor of religion ; on the other, there is a vast system of idolatrous worship with its extensive ramifications which has taken possession of Hindu society. The education he receives shapes his public life, while religion influences his private life. From this we can well conceive what the life of an educated Native generally turns out to be. As we said in a late issue, it is unreal. Education gives him no conviction, while religion despotically binds him to a worship and mode of action to which he does not yield his intellectual assent. Whatever he does or says, therefore, does not reveal his inner self. It is useless to say that of all things as unreal life is the least calculated to bring about the formation of national life. There are many who are under the impression that politics, or literature, or science or social reforms will lead to India's regeneration. A greater mistake could hardly be made. No nation can be great without the help of religion. We have often found that religious culture is followed by activity in other departments of life. The beginning of Protestantism is the beginning also of learning in Europe. The Puritanic revival was the basis of the constitutional history of England. In India we are now in a position to say that the rise of Buddhism gave birth to all the precious poetry, philosophy and science that we now possess. Everywhere, indeed, is religion the precursor of national regeneration. Why, then, do our countrymen neglect this most necessary concern ? We hear so much of public spirit in these days, of public meetings and social reforms that a little religious spirit infused therein would be able to make them the powerful means of awakening the nation. We require a loud trumpet to tell the people that God in the impulsive principle in every great undertaking, and that a grain of faith would suffice to change the whole face of society. Only God, and no body else, only religion and nothing else is the great want of India. Educated countrymen, be true to that God whom your ancestors worshipped with so much real faith.

NO SUPERSTITION.

People say that to believe in the special providence of God is to believe in a superstition. When we speak of a dispensation, of prophets, of God in history, we merely echo the superstitious fancies of the middle ages. The spirit of such speculations has been entirely ignored by the century in which we live, and if any thing is clearer than another, it is the fact that the present age resolutely closes its ears against the least whisper of a personal living God. The most precious gift of the nineteenth century is the right of private judgment, and that judgment says that, whatever may be the nature of God, He cannot so constantly interfere with the affairs of the world as to necessitate the occasional despatch of missions to the world. We see God nowhere except in His laws. It is we that eat, we that work, we that think. There is none else behind us, above us, or beyond us to whom we owe the least allegiance or worship. The age speaks in this sceptical tone. Its language is the language of doubt, and it recognises no certainty in matters spiritual. If a man speaks of God, he is simply tolerated, and if he grows troublesome in his reiteration, he is voted a bore. Now, it is exactly in these times and under such circumstances that God makes Himself visible to men. The reception that they accord to Him is anything but flattering. The words which He speaks through the mouths of His bhaktas are openly derided ; and men show their disbelief by disbelieving in all that they say. It is thus alas ! that God is insulted, and this takes place every day and every hour of our existence. Even those who are Theists will not condescend to hear the bhaktas. How many Brahmos may be found who, openly professing belief in providence, refuse to hear the men who have seen and heard Him. Inspiration, they say, is impossible ; hearing and seeing, according to them, are impossible terms so far as God is concerned. Our belief in God is based upon conjecture only—a conjecture confirmed and supported by the innate ideas of man. We should, they say, stop just there ; that is to say, stop at the point where the intellect is satisfied as to the existence of the Supreme Maker. Conscience and morality are to be believed also in the same way. Philosophy proves the existence of intuitions, and the intuitions tell us that there is such a thing as morality. It is thus the intellect which is the supreme judge in these matters. We should give God only that much which our intellectual convictions warrant ; and it is, we confess, a sorry tribute which the intellect pays to God. For it is well known that the work of the intellect ends just where that of faith begins, and in the region where no entities are found except the ego and the Supreme Mind, intellect becomes blind and entirely useless to realise spiritual perceptions. It seems, therefore, that those who speak of God as an abstraction distinct from a personal living entity, have not yet entered the region of faith and acquired the right to speak with authority of the realities of that world. Those who have seen God can speak of God. Brother, have you seen Him? If so, let us hear what you have to say, and we shall be bound to you in a debt immense of endless gratitude. For we are as men who have heard of the glories of another world, and feel so much the desire to know more about it that any information from a person who has visited it is welcome and thrice welcome. But if you have not seen Him, pray stop the ceaseless rattle of your tongue, for you have no right to speak of a Being you do not know. Guess cannot be all right ; nor can guess convince. What you say about God is no better than guess. Your God is guess, and your guess is God. Cease, therefore, to speak with authority. To Brahmos of all parties we say, this guess and this scepticism is simply disgraceful. It is positively disgraceful to a man who worships God to make the humiliating confession that he has not seen God ; and it is ten times more disgraceful to a man who, not having seen God himself, ventures to doubt the assertions of those who say they have seen God. It is pride, it is intellectual arrogance to say to a man that his faith in God and providence is a delusion. No, the Brahmo Somaj will smother that pride and smash that scepticism. It is too late now to question the right of God to look after His own affairs. The intellectual scepticism of the age will be met by Him in His own incomparable ways. The Gospel has been proclaimed. It is for Brahmos to accept it or reject it. If they do not accept it, why, God will choose His own instruments to carry out His holy will.

THE MISSIONARY EXPEDITION.

[FROM OUR SPECIAL CORRESPONDENT.]
BANKIPORE, 20th November 1879.
A shower of flowers as the train reached the Gya Station. It was, indeed, a novel

method of welcoming our party, but it at once struck us as a most cordial one. White, red, flowers of various colors, sweet and tender, were scattered in profusion over the whole party by friends on the platform. And then followed bowing and salaam and salutation. To our surprise we found a splendid barouche in attendance. The offer was thankfully declined, the party preferring humbler vehicles. There was conversation in the evening, the subject being chiefly the Immortality of the Soul. The Gya campaign began the next day, Friday, the 14th, in the afternoon. Considering the extreme prevalence of superstition and idolatry the place seemed a strong citadel of error not likely to give in. Hundreds of pilgrims are always pouring into the place from all parts of the country to give pinda offerings to their departed relatives and secure their easy passage to heaven. The Gyalis too, who were in charge of the temples, were a powerful body, and too mindful of their own pecuniary interests to succumb to the progressive civilization of the day. In spite of the spread of education, every temple, every bathing ghat was full, and the irrepressible Native drum was everywhere sending forth deafening sounds which one can hardly endure unless accustomed. In the midst of this stronghold of idolatry, the flag of the True God had to be unfurled. Notice was issued, and at the appointed hour, hundreds came and flocked in the school compound under a canopy. The number swelled to a thousand. The eager multitude were waiting anxiously, when the Minister appeared followed by his friends. A hymn was chanted with the accompaniment of the mridang and the ektara. The Minister spoke first in English and then in Hindi, in which language he spoke fluently, but not correctly. Nevertheless the assembly was satisfied, and thought the prefatory apology superfluous. The address was followed by Sankirtan. On the way the party confronted several images of Kali, which were being carried to the river for final immersion. The Nirakar and the Sakar face to face! Theism and idolatry! The party quietly passed on. Saturday was the day of the Brahmica Somaj. The Minister, in the course of the service, preached a sermon on ornaments. Woman's desire is ornament. Naturally she pants for it; she prizes it above all things else. The Minister said to his lady congregation;—"The beautiful feet of the joyful Hari make ye the ornament of your body and soul, and ye shall require naught else." After break-fast we proceeded to Buddh Gya in four carriages which themselves quite shaky somehow managed to roll over the ups and downs and sandy plains called by courtesy the Road to Buddh Gya. The journey, which took two hours and a half, was rather tiresome. As soon, however, as we reached the place, we commenced kirtan, and, with trumpet and flags, proceeded direct to the shrine of Buddha. Here stood the figure of Sakya Muni, in solitary grandeur, in the midst of a lofty but dilapidated temple, the relic and glory of twenty-five centuries. Awhile the Minister and the party stood speechless, looking intently at the figure, and studying the principles of asceticism delineated on the face. The spirit of the noble founder of Buddhism seemed to pervade the assembly. The party then repaired to the famous tree behind the shrine, under whose shade the prophet is said to have practised asceticism and attained nirvana. The identity of the tree was questionable. Yet associations had made it a hallowed object. The sight of it at once inspired holy thoughts and sentiments, and reverentially

bending their heads before it, the party did homage to the feet of the Almighty who had trained the prophet's heart on the spot. Then the Minister sat underneath the tree, surrounded by the preaching party and the friends who had accompanied them from Gya. The sun was about to set, and evening was drawing near, there was solemn stillness on all sides. And there, where Sakya Muni sat 2,500 years ago to learn asceticism sat our Minister to hold communion with the spirit of that prophet. Prayer began, the Minister addressing the Almighty to the following effect;—Pour into us, O Lord, the spirit of asceticism and deliver us from worldliness. The fire enkindled by the prophet Buddha still burns here and through the image says to us,—Learn asceticism. Impress his words and example upon our lives, and help us to forego carnality and covetousness, and teach us meditation and self-annihilation. An appropriate hymn followed the prayer. "I will no longer be deceived by the delusions of the world, &c." Chanting Sankirtan the party proceeded to the palatial residence of the Mohanta, and there took a hearty dinner in right Hindustani style, at the request of his people. We returned to Gya at midnight. The next morning we ascended a small hill in the neighbourhood of the city, where we had our usual service. In the course of the service, the Minister quite unexpectedly addressed the adjoining range of hills. The sermon lasted for about a quarter of an hour, and was quite as spirited and serious as if it were addressed to living souls. The hills seemed suddenly to start into life, and listen to the words of the Minister. What he said was in substance as follows :—Ye hills, upon your heights is my beloved Master seated. How I wish I could embrace you. The same Lord who has created us has created you. Let us unite and sing together the glory of our common Father. Ye are immovable; teach us to make our faith as firm and immovable as ye are. Though fixed on earth, ye have raised your heads to kiss the sky above. May our souls be as meditative and heaven-aspiring ! Ye gather waters from the clouds and then send them in streams to the earth below. May we similarly catch the inspiration of heaven, and freely give unto others what we receive! Ye take no notice of the sneers and revilings of the world, being rapt in devotion. May we do likewise! After service the party descended and cooked their own food in an adjoining garden below. The evening service was conducted in the local Brahmo Somaj premises. The subject of the sermon was " The True Gya." On Monday evening, in the hall of the Government School, in the presence of about four hundred persons, the Minister delivered a lecture on " The Dangerous Perhaps." He pointed out the danger of conjectures and may-bes in religion and ethics, and the necessity of establishing the heart firmly in faith. The Magistrate, Mr. Barton, in a short speech, complimented the speaker, and said he had heard the address with pleasure and profit. The next day the party went after breakfast to see the Gya temples. What struck us most was the worship of Ahalya Bai, the celebrated female devotee, whose image lay side by side with the figures of Vishnu and Lakshmi. Another noteworthy fact is the mixture of Hindu and Buddhistic figures in these shrines. One of the most wealthy and influential Gyalis cultivated our acquaintance on the way with unusual interest, and not only honored the party in his own house where he led us, but subsequently put the handsome amount of fifty rupees in our purse. This somewhat remarkable incident shows in what

high esteem our religion and our missionaries are held by even the most orthodox Hindu. He was heard to say to our Minister,—You are an Acharya, and I must honor you. What took place in the evening baffles description. About five hundred persons, some of them highly respectable, but mostly the mob of the city assembled in Romna Mat, and the Minister after a brief speech in Bengali, spoke for about an hour in Hindi on the three places of pilgrimage in the heart, Gya, Benares and Brindabun, and concluded with a pathetic appeal on the motherly tenderness of God which moved many a heart to tears. A spirited Sankirtan followed, the procession going through the principal streets for nearly four miles with banners and torches, and rousing the hearts of the people with the shrill sound of the bugle. The party left Gya the next morning after breakfast. The farewell scene was touching. For the glorious success of our campaign in this city, a large share of credit is no doubt due to some of the enthusiastic and devout Brahmos of the local Somaj. May God bless his faithful disciples ! The party quietly returned to Bankipore on Wednesday.

Brahmo Somaj.

Our Minister was to have delivered a lecture at Patna College, Bankipore, on Friday last on "Heaven's Command to educated India." The Commissioner, Mr. Metcalfe, was to have presided.

The sixteenth anniversary of the "Sinduriapatti Brahmo Family Prayer Meeting" will be held next Wednesday, the 26th instant. Morning service will commence at 7-30 a.m. and evening service at 7 p.m. We are informed that Paramhansa Ram Krishna of Dakhineswar will be present at the Utsab. There will be sankirtan in the afternoon.

A correspondent from Madhubani, in Tirhut, informs us that some of the influential men there, both Bengalis and Biharis, formed themselves into a committee with a view to invite Babu Kesh's Chender Sen to the place and give him a fitting reception. We learn that a letter was immediately addressed to the Minister for the purpose. His departure for Gya must have been a great disappointment to them.

TRANSLATION OF HYMNS.

—o—

How much of love bear'st thou, Mother, to thy
　　　　　children !
The thought brings tears (of love) down my two
　　　　　eyes, my Mother.
What a stream from birth am I !
Yet always is thy cheerful face before us,
And thou think'st aye of us and our sad plight,
　　　　　my Mother.
The burden piteous of my sin I cannot bear,
The soul cries out, the heart breaks forth, at sight
　　　　　of Love.
I take refuge in thy auspicious feet, my Mother,
In heaven's mansions there are ranged with care,
Joy, peace and wealth untold,
Which thou for special ends hast stored for me,
　　　　　my Mother.

Devotional.

Prayer, the people are angry with the Thiests and are persecuting them for their reverence towards Christ, Chaitanya and other masters. How should Thy disciples treat these prophets?

It is one of the doctrines of Pure Theism that no saint, no prophet, no devotee should be dishonored by hostile criticism. Those whom I love and raise above the world are above the world's criticism.

Shall we not judge?

He who judgeth my loving devotees **dishonors** Him who sent them.

But they have their faults.

Ye shall not judge *my* men. For I have sent them not that ye should sit in judgment over their character, but simply accept and honor all that is good in them.

Teach me, Lord, the value of their lives, that I may love them and love Thee in them.

Provincial.

GYA.

[FROM A CORRESPONDENT.]

The 19th November 1879.

THE well-known Babu Keshub Chunder Sen arrived here with his party and friends on the evening of the 13th instant. On the arrival of the train at the Station, the local Brahmos approached the platform to receive the party with flowers, &c., which were thrown over them when the interview took place. A wealthy and respectable citizen also came to receive the party, and had his carriages, which were rather grand and stately, ready for them. The local Brahmos had their arrangements for *Sankirtan*, and the Minister and his party went with the procession a few yards from the Railway gate, when all mounted on carriages and arrived at their destination, and the party put up in a bungalow, provided for them by the above gentleman. Here the party rested for the night, when on the morning of the following day, they were requested by an influential Brahmo of the place to take their quarters at his house, which is a nice building, and where everything was provided for their comfort. Accordingly, the Minister and his party proceeded to the house of the said Brahmo gentleman where, after the usual morning service, they refreshed themselves. In the evening at about 5 P. M., there was an open-air meeting in the Government School compound, at which the Brahmo leader addressed the people in English and Hindi. The gathering which was great and respectable, consisted of about a thousand persons, including Bengalis and Hindustanis of all classes. The Minister's speech which lasted about an hour was very eloquent and impressive and moved the hearts of the whole audience. After the speech was over, the party proceeded chanting the name of Hari through the streets, and the spectacle was imposing and charming to the people around. As the party proceeded through the city, they were confronted by a huge idol of the goddess Kali, which was paraded through the streets.

The next morning, Saturday, the 15th, the party was invited to the house of the Minister of the local Somaj, where Divine service was held for the benefit of Brahmo ladies, and thence, after dinner, the party proceeded to Budh Gya. The temple of the great Budha, once so grand and majestic, which had been raised to commemorate the spot, where, under the shade of an *ashwatha* tree, now old and extinct, the great prophet had resorted to initiate himself into asceticism and meditation—excited pity in our minds as it reminded us that all is vanity, as far as the things of the world are concerned. We were however, glad to hear that the late King of Burmah undertook the repairs at his own expense, and he began the work; but we are mortified to learn that the work of repairs has been stopped in consequence of the death of the King as well as of the misunderstanding between his successor and the British Government. The leader of the Brahmo Somaj, with his friends around him, sat under the feet of the famous and historic *Ashwatha* tree for meditation, and offered prayers to God to bless them to learn true *Vai-agya* and *yoga*, invoking the spirit of Buddha to help them in the matter. This being over, the party was invited by a *mohant* to his palatial residence. This hermit is rather a great Zemindar than a religious devotee, deriving an income of some lacs of rupees from the estates entrusted to him. On Sunday, the 16th instant, the party went up to the mountains to pray, and there the service was very impressive and touched the hearts of all present. In the evening, there was Divine service in the local Mandir, conducted by Babu K. C. Sen, where he delivered a sermon in which he explained to the congregation what true Gya is, which was heard with rapt attention by all present. From the Mandir, the party proceeded to the house of the local minister to celebrate his newborn son's birth, which brought the day's proceedings to a close.

On the morning of Monday, the 17th instant, there was Divine service in the house of the secretary, and in the evening at 5-30 P. M., Babu Keshub Chunder Sen delivered his English lecture at the Government School on "The Dangerous Perhaps" before an audience of about 600 persons. The lecture which lasted abut an hour and a half influenced the minds of the audience very considerably. At the conclusion of the lecture, the Magistrate made a few remarks. After this, the party had to go to the house of Lalla Rewa Ram, a member of the local Somaj, where the Brahmo leader had to speak a few words on the tenets of Brahmoism to a Hindustani audience of about 50 persons, in which certain members took part, and the party heard with great profit the few words of discourse from the leader. There was the usual Divine service on the morning of the 18th, Tuesday, in the house of a member, who is a homœopathic practitioner, and in the evening, at about 5 P. M., commenced the second open-air meeting before an audience of about 600 or 700 persons. Babu K. C. Sen first spoke a few words in Bengali to the Bengali gentlemen present, pointing out to them the responsibility of their position as Heaven—appointed pioneers of enlightment, and impressing upon them the necessity of setting good examples to their Hindustani neighbours, and to maintaining the integrity of the charge entrusted to them by Providence. Thence proceeded the singing party, chanting hymns throughout the streets. The sweet name of Hari, chanted with fire and enthusiasm, by the Band of singers from door to door, extending over an area of about 2 miles, resounded through the city, which aroused the drooping souls of the inhabitants. The charming influence of this spread like wild fire, and many a drooping soul, forgetting for a while the cares the world, joined the singers all along. The party at last arrived at the house of an influential Bengali gentleman, where a sumptuous dinner was served out to them. Surely there was a great agitation in Gya, and many a gentleman vied with his neighbour in doing homage to the party. From whatever point we see it, from the number of invitations offered, the tenacity of attachment, or the profuseness of pecuniary help in every respect, ample evidence could be found that the people were placed under a charm. Thus, after a short stay of about a week, the Expedition party left Gya on the morning of the 19th, at about 11 A. M., for Bankipore. A dozen gentlemen came to the Railway platform to bid the party farewell, and they could not help shedding tears when the separation took place.

BANKIPORE, *20th November 1879.*

The party arrived at Bankipore on the evening of 19th instant, at 4 P. M. To-day, the 20th instant, Babu Keshub Chunder Sen held Divine service in English in the hall of the Rosy Bower, Bankipore, at 6 P. M., before an audience of about 200 educated people, both Bengalis and Beharis. He took his text from Matthew, "Seek and you will find," &c. . . . . . . and delivered a sermon on prayer, its philosophy, and necessity. There seems to exist however, a mass of inertia in and around the people of this city in matters pertaining to religion, and it is yet to be seen what the Missionary Expedition can do to influence them.

The 42nd birth-day of the anniversary of the leader of the Brahmo Somaj was observed by his friends in the house of the Munsiff, Babu Kedar Nath Roy.

The following is a Summary of the proceedings of the party:—

Thursday, 13th November 1879.—The party headed arrived at Gya at 4 P. M.

Friday, 14th November 1879.—At 5 P. M., open-air meeting in the Government School compound for about an hour. The speaker addressed the people in English and Hindi. About 1,000 persons present. Hymns chanted through the city for half an hour.

Saturday, 15th November 1879.—At 9 A. M. Divine service in the local minister's house for Brahmica ladies. Sermon on Ornament. In the evening visited Budh Gya with a party of about 20 friends.

Sunday, 16th November 1879.—Morning, at 9 A. M., went up to pray at Pahar, and in the evening Divine service in the local Mandir. Sermon, True Gya.

Monday, 17th November 1879.—Morning Divine service in the house of the Secretary, and English lecture in the Government School at 5-30 P. M., subject "Dangerous Perhaps." Audience 600, one hour and-a-half. Result very impressive. Hindi discourse in a Hindustani gentleman's house, half an hour. Audience 50 persons.

Tuesday, 18th November 1879.—Morning, Divine service in the house of the homœopathic practitioner, and in the evening, at 5 P. M., 2nd open-air meeting. Speech in Bengali and Hindi. Audience 600 or 700. Lasted for an hour. Sankirtan for about 4 hours, extending 2 miles. During the middle of the day visited Bistu Pad Temple.

Wednesday, 19th November 1879.—Morning Divine service in the house of a gentleman at 8 A. M. Left Gya at 11 A. M.

Correspondence.

[We do not hold ourselves in any way responsible for the opinions of our correspondents.—ED., I. M.

OURSELVES.

TO THE EDITOR OF THE "INDIAN MIRROR."

SIR,—The Sunday edition of your paper is every week creating an increasing interest among its readers, both Native and European. The fiery spiritual revival through which, under Providence, the Brahmo Somaj is at present passing, cannot but make a mark on every department of its organization. And your Sunday paper, as the weekly English organ of that organization, is no exception. Its articles and devotional columns, correspondence, queries and answers, news of missionary labors and even selections, all carry with them a revival interest. But I am very sorry, (and I know also many of my friends and others who read the Sunday *Mirror*, do really complain of it) that it contains so little space. As if the defect was not enough, the managers have of late been trying to shear it of its head and tail, as the Bengali saying goes. The decent brown cover which the Sunday edition carried some months ago had one good quality, if not any other, that it quietly took off on its shoulders the burden of three columns of advertisements. But it is now no more, and scarcely seven pages are now filled with interesting matter. I, therefore, bring the matter into your serious consideration, as the defect of which I complain is really clogging the interest of your paper. I wish it to appear in three forms instead of two, or, if that is not possible, to get back its cover with *three pages* full of advertisements, thus clearing away nine more columns for your honest work. I hope many will follow me in this suggestion.

Yours &c.,
ONE OF YOUR READERS.

18th November 1879.

THE RESURRECTION.

TO THE EDITOR OF THE "INDIAN MIRROR."

SIR,—Degumber Mitter, with his manly, broad commonsense, has left us and gone home during the year that is now closing. He was so little of a devotee, and so much a legislator, public counsellor, and man of business, that it is good to remember the open-eyed faith he had in the coming life. He who pens these words called on him a few days after the death of his son, who, recently returned from England, was dashed from his horse and killed, and with awful suddenness was brought in and laid at his father's feet a corpse. "My dear Degumber," I said, "I have called to try and comfort you;" and went on to speak of the weight of the blow that had smitten him, and of his terrible loss. A member of Council at the time, he was sitting in the midst of his law-books, papers and public documents, with a calm, saddened eye, but grandly absorbed in his legislative duties. "Loss?" he responded, "of my son? No, no! my friend; I am a spiritualist. My son is as near to me as ever. We shall soon meet again." Thus cheerfully did Degumber Mitter believe in the spirit-world.

Dr. Burgess, a Christian Missionary, known and honored in Northern India, attended a lecture I was giving at Cawnpore, on "The Coming Life." An aged Mahomedan gentleman presided, and the good doctor made one of the audience. The address was, as usual, followed by conversation:

during which he asked,—"Does the lecturer not base his faith in the coming life on the bodily resurrection of Christ?" I then replied that I felt God would not require me to believe in any miracle that He had given me no chance to examine. Believing that Christ was alive and not dead, and that I, living now and believing in God as he did, could no more die than God could die, that was my faith in the resurrection. I stand by Jesus when he said to Martha, 'I am alive for ever.' 'I am the resurrection;' it is mine; it is me; see God truly, and dying is an absurdity. This visible eternal life, in the mind and soul of Christ, this, I said, was my song and anthem of immortality. I needed no vision of an up-risen corpse or ghost, no Thomas-like fingering of torn flesh, by way of assurance or confirmation. My own body would turn to grass, flowers, fruit, and go into fifty other bodies; and be theirs, not mine, by and bye. So I relied on spiritual, not physical resurrection. Rev. T. S. Wynkoop, a much loved worker in the American Presbyterian Mission at Allahabad, now settled in America, asked me, not very long since, about my faith in the records of the Resurrection. These records by Matthew, Mark, Luke, John, Paul,—were crowded with facts, enough to convince any man that Jesus truly rose again from the dead. "Yes: I confess it. Years ago I preached a sermon in which I thought I had harmonized and dovetailed into one, these intensely interesting, however painfully puzzling declarations. Later and less prejudiced study had convinced me (so I told my friend,) that they could not be fully harmonized. In all but the grand skeleton of the story, they contradicted one another hopelessly. Matthew on the day of the resurrection, sends to Galilee such as would see their risen Lord. And when they met him there, 70 or 80 miles from Jerusalem, Matthew is content to say that they looked upon him, "on a mountain in Galilee," and some of them made obeisance to him, "but some doubted." [Matthew 28th 17]. The record of John detains them, for weeks, in Jerusalem. It makes the form come, as a ghost through closed doors and so on. So I told my friend Wynkoop that the records were not clear, and that the best I could draw from them of the revitalized corpse of the Christ-man, was "a palpable apparition."

But how is it to-day? And where do I stand now, regarding the risen body: "the miracle" of Christ's bodily resurrection? I will tell you. I believe in the apparition. As from time to time, I keep reading the accounts—they are too fascinating to be let alone,—I am compelled to believe that there is truth in them. I do not need them. I am nowise responsible for form-visions; that are gone some 2,000 years out of my reach; and which did so sorely puzzle their closest and most favored observers. Jesus himself assures me,—as he did Thomas, who put his finger into the nail-holes in his risen master's once dead hands,—"blessed are those who have *not* seen, and yet have believed;" believed that if a man die he shall live again. I am one of those. I believe in heaven, like Degumber Mitter. He needed not to thrust a hand into the speargashed side of a palpable apparition; of a wraith that passed as an *aura* through stone walls and locked doors; which is here and gone again, like a flash of light. No; much as I should like to understand these things and test them, as others seem to have done to their full conviction, if not entire satisfaction;—my faith in immortality is, I thank God,—made perfect by other proofs. What I know not now, about the body, I shall know hereafter. Jesus lives. I shall live also. I will ask him. So much for nineteenth century believers. But what of Peter? He was just before swearing that he "knew not the man," and saying until he met the apparition, "I go a-fishing." Disappointed in a Jesus, that "should have redeemed Israel", he went for some days, back to his old calling. What of the apparition's having changed Peter from a fisherman into a martyr? And so of James, "the Lord's brother," sabred to death for his faith in the bodily resurrection? What of Paul's seeing the apparition on his way to Damascus; and so going "far hence to the gentiles;" and finally being murdered for his faith in it outside the gates of Rome? I answer I am not a fool. I believe in cause and effect. No effect without a cause. No stupendous effect without a cause singular, strange and out of the common course. So, finally, I am driven to believe that after his death,—a thorough-going and most murderous death,—Jesus did clearly, from within the spirit-world (in which all men reside without knowing it) come out, somehow, and manifest himself to the very senses of those in closest sympathy with him. This I do believe and must believe. Still my faith simply hears Jesus say, "I am he that liveth and was dead; and behold I am alive forever more." That is enough for me.

Yours &c.,

DALL.

Cunur, 1st November 1879.

NOTICES TO CORRESPONDENTS.

Persons favoring us with communications are requested to write legibly, and on one side of the paper only.

Unauthenticated communications will not be inserted.

A. B.—Correct.

M. L. BANNERJI.—We shall be glad to insert your reply.

Literary, Scientific &c.

IN the matter of inventions America invariably leads the whole world. We now learn that a folding umbrella which can be carried in the pocket has been recently patented there.

"A LETTER from Royalty, or, the Wrongs of the Rajah Rung Jung Jellybag," is the title chosen by Mr. George Augustus Sala for his contribution to *Bow Bells Annual*.

A CORRESPONDENT of *Nature* gives an interesting account of a solar halo which was observed by him from Burnham, Somerset, on the 22nd September last. "The abnormal weather experienced in great Britain this year seems to have been rather prolific of unusual atmospheric Phenomena," for we understand, only a few months back a *mirage* was seen from the opposite coast, at Penby.

WE understand that Mr. H. M. Stanley is now once more on the Congo River, where he is commissioned by a philanthropic society to open and keep open, if possible, all such districts and countries as he may explore for the benefit of the commercial world. He states in a letter published in the *Daily Telegraph* that the mission is to use every pacific means, to buy freely of all, show tolerance in every way, and, wherever rejected, must withdraw to seek other fields. A year's trial will demonstrate whether progress can be made.

DR. HULTSCH has published at Leipzig a mediæval Sanskrit work on the omens to be drawn from the appearances and actions of animals, and especially of birds. The author first discusses the references to kindred beliefs in the Vedic Epic, and General Literature of India, and then proceeds to give a very complete abstract of the contents of Vasanta Rajah's work. This careful and scholarly monograph should attract the notice, not only of Sanskrit philologists, but also of the students of folk-lore. It shows that the belief in omens, notwithstanding the scorn and opposition of Buddha, was developed independently in India into a complex system rivalling that of the astrologists.

IN the selections from the correspondence of the late Macvey Napier, Editor of the *Edinburgh Review*, is found the following characteristic letter from Lord Macaulay:—"I ought to give my whole leisure to my History; and I fear that if I suffer myself to be diverted from that design as I have done, I shall, like poor Mackintosh, leave behind me the character of a man who would have done something if he had concentrated his powers, instead of frittering them away. There are people who can carry on twenty works at a time. Southey would write the history of Brazil before breakfast, an ode after breakfast, then the history of the Peninsular War till dinner, and an article for the *Quarterly Review* in the evening. But I am of a different temper. I never write so as to please myself until my subject has for the time driven away every other out of my head. When I turn from one work to another, a great deal of time is lost in the mere transition. I must not go on dawdling and reproaching myself all my life."

AN obelisk has been erected two or three miles from Ware to mark the spot on which Clarkson first resolved to devote himself to the abolition of the slave trade. The history of this remarkable occurrence was told in a very interesting manner by Dean Merivale on the occasion of the unveiling. The Dean had been taken to the spot by Mr. Basil Montague and Clarkson, in order that, being a young man, he might point it out to a subsequent generation. Clarkson gained the Vice-Chancellor's prize for an essay on slave trade. He recited the paper at the Commencement, and on every day he took horse to ride to London. He tells us afterwards how, as he went along on his solitary ride, he was thinking over and over again of what he had been saying that day, and, brooding over it, he felt very much depressed at the shocking things he had to relate. And he tells us that when he came in sight of Wadesmill, he felt so much distressed and affected that he would go into the village in the condition he was in. So he got off his horse, held it by the bridle, and thought again and again on the subject of his essay. At last, he said to himself, "if this be so, it must be put down"; and he rose with his heart lightened, and went on to Feathers Inn. He then proceeded to London, and in the course of a few months associated himself with such men as Granville, Sharp, &c., and in a short time determined to devote himself entirely to the abolition of the slave trade. Twenty-two years afterwards, the abolition of the trade was carried by Act of Parliament.

WE have received a copy of "A Dictionary of Phrases and Idioms, containing explanations in English and Bengali and Illustrations chiefly from Standard Modern Writers, by Krishna Chunder Roy." The author is a teacher in the Hare School; and from his long experience and varied reading we have a right to expect that the work should be a useful and valuable one. Such in fact it is. The work before us, partaking, as the name implies, of the character of a dictionary, is the first of a series of sixteen parts, containing the principal idiomatic phrases and expressions in use in English; and its value is heightened by the fact that the author has attempted to give to every phrase in English its corresponding one in Bengali. Here we believe Babu Krishna Chunder Roy has detected and tried to remove a real defect in the teaching of English in this country. Most young men in our schools are found to be deficient in the use of English idiomatic expressions, and the reason is that they do not know how to translate. In writing English they either misquote and misuse idioms or translate Bengali expressions literally into English. The result is, in the latter case, that their English becomes mostly unintelligible and ridiculous to English ears. Thus for example, a young man may be asked to "give the door," or when asked to come he may say, "yes, I am coming, coming," or when asking a favor he may say, "Pray, give me the boon, it is your hand," or when tempted to curse another, he may burst forth with the significant ejaculation, "your head!" and so on. In each case the Bengali is exactly translated, and no wonder that the English, in very many cases, becomes also so bad. Now the remedy lies exactly where Babu Krishna Chunder has found it. It is in supplying Bengali idioms to corresponding English idioms. We cannot say that the author's mode has been successful in all instances. There are idioms which cannot be translated; but even here we should supply the next most appropriate idioms. There is another good feature to be noticed. The author has illustrated the uses of idiomatic expressions by short quotations from standard authors. More ambitious compilers would endeavour to palm off their learning by quoting from the whole range of English literature from Chaucer to Tennyson. Now, this may serve to enhance the reputation for scholarship of the compilers in question; but certainly it would be of no use to those for whom their works are designed. Babu Krishna Chunder Roy, we observe, has mainly quoted from the following authors:—Scott, Macaulay, Freeman, Thackeray, Dickens, Froude, Irving, Arnold, Kingsley, Kaye and Green. All recent authors, it will be seen, and not those dreary old world authors like Johnson, Addison, Goldsmith, &c. &c. The author might have shortened even the range from which he has selected, for a careful perusal of a few authors is better calculated to form the style than a cursory glance over the whole field of English literature. From what we have said it will be seen that the work before us supplies a real want. We shall be happy to see it largely patronised in our schools.

THE public papers are almost unanimous in stating that Bismarck is now most anxious for a general disarmament in Europe. His biographer has the following noteworthy confession of Bismarck about war:—"'In satisfying my ambition', he said, one evening at Varzin, 'I have made nobody happy.' We all protested 'No.' He continued: 'And what a number of people I have cast into misery. Without me, three great wars would have been avoided; 80,000 men—nay much more—would not have been killed, and such numbers of families, of fathers, mothers, brothers, sisters, and wives, would not have been plunged into mourning. However, that account is to be settled between God and myself in the judgment hereafter.'"

Calcutta.

THE Rev. Father Rivington arrived on Tuesday last, and gave his first lecture to Native gentlemen in the Theatre of the Medical College Hospital on Thursday. The subject was Teleology, and the substance of the lecture was as follows:—

The lecturer, after mentioning that Teleology means the science of final causes adopted Aristotle's definition of a final cause, and gave Mr. Mill's analysis of the same. He considered the idea of final causes to be instinctive, and illustrated its connatural character and the possibility of mistakes concerning its application by an amusing anecdote. The principle of final causes had been, moreover, a motive power to high moral effort, as in the case of a Bernard, who, whilst all but wielding the destinies of Europe, was in the habit of asking himself day by day, "Bernard, why art thou here?" It had also, he said, been of use to science itself, since Laplace's theory of the solar system and Harvey's discovery concerning the circulation of blood were both due to the rooted conviction that a certain co-ordination of phenomena implied a further end in view.

The lecturer then examined at considerable length the facts in nature that lead to the conception of a final cause, pointing out, amongst other things, that though the eye seems to combine various defects which are avoided in our most delicate optical instruments, yet it serves the practical purposes of life precisely for the reason that it has those seeming defects. He showed that the instincts of animals are inexplicable without the supposition of final causes, and that the hypothesis in an irrestible inference from what goes on within ourselves in the creation of machines.

The lecturer then entered at large on the relationship between the principle of final causes and physiology, and showed that the theory of evolution in no way interferes with the doctrine of a final cause in nature. He laid great stress on the fact that special creations are not the kind of phenomena which suggest the idea of a final cause; that it is not any seeming disproportion between causes and effects that is the basis of Teleology, but the apparent adaptation of means to ends. He then considered the law of natural selection, and gave some reasons why its notion ought to be considered of more limited application than was sometimes supposed, and showed that anyhow it could never render the hypothesis of final causes superfluous, and that, indeed, the fundamental necessity of the Darwinian system, viz., the universal reign of slow and insensible variations was really open to question.

General Litchfield, in seconding a vote of thanks to the lecturer, proposed that the lecture should be repeated in the Town Hall and the proposition was supported by the Rev. Dr. K. M. Bannerj. Mr. Rivington promised to finish the subject in a future lecture.—*Indian Church Gazette.*

Pulpit.

WITHOUT MONEY AND WITHOUT PRICE.

—o—

[BY THE REV. C.H. SPURGEON.]

AFTER all, the best blessings we have come to us freely. What price have you paid for your lives? and yet they are very precious. Skin for skin, yea, all that you have would you give for them. What price do you pay for the air you breathe? What price does a man pay for the blessed sunlight? I wonder they have not a game law to preserve the sunbeams, so that the lords of the land alone might enjoy the genial rays, while the poor should be liable to punishment for poaching in pursuit of sunshine. No, they cannot pen in the sun's light, God has given it freely, and to the pauper it is as free as to the prince. Life and air and light come to us "without money and without price." And our faculties, too—who pays for eye sight? The eye which glances across the landscape and drinks in beauty, what toil does it pay? The ear which hears the song of the birds at dawn, what price is given for it? The senses are freely bestowed on us by God, and so is the sleep which rests them. To-night when we lay down our heads upon our pillows, the poor man's sleep shall be as sweet as the sleep of him who reclines on down. Sleep is the unbought boon of heaven, you could not purchase it, all the mines of Potosi could not buy a wink thereof, yet God gives it to the sea-boy on the giddy mast. It is clear then that some of the best blessings we possess come to us by the way of free gift, ay, and come to the undeserving, too, for the dew shall sparkle to-morrow upon the grass in the miser's field, and the rain shall fall in due season upon the rising corn of the wretch who blasphemes his God. The influences which nurture wheat and barley and other fruits of the earth are given to the farm of the atheist as well as to the fields of the godly: they fall alike for the evil and for the good, for "the Lord is good to all and his tender mercies are over all his works." We ought not, therefore, to be so surprised after all that the gifts of his grace are free.

Selections.

THE TEMPLE NOT MADE WITH HANDS.

—o—

(*Hymns of Praise and Prayer.*)

Though wandering in a stranger-land,
Though on the waste no alter stand,
Take comfort, thou art not alone,
While faith hath marked thee for her own.

Wouldst thou a Temple? look above;
The heavens strech over all in love:—
A Book? for thine evangel scan
The wondrous history of man.

The holy band of saints renowned
Embrace thee, brother-like, around;
Their sufferings and their triumphs rise
In hymns immortal to the skies.

And though no organ-peal be heard,
In harmony the winds are stirred;
And there the morning stars upraise
Their ancient song of deathless praise.

—*Paraphrased from Thomas Carlyle* 1834,
by (probably) William Johnson
Fox, 1841.

PROFESSOR MAX MULLER ON THE BRAHMO SOMAJ.

—o—

(*Chips from a German Workshop, Vol. IV.*)

IN the eyes of our missionaries this religious reform in India has not found much favor, nor need we wonder at this. Their object is to transplant, if possible, Christianity in its full integrity from England to India, as we might wish to transplant a full grown tree. They do not deny the moral worth, the noble aspirations, the self-sacrificing zeal of these Native reformers; but they fear that all this will but increase their dangerous influence, and retard the progress of Christianity, by drawing some of the best minds of India, that might have been gained over to our religion, into a different current. They feel towards Keshub Chunder Sen as Athanasius might have felt towards Ulfilas, the Arian Bishop of the Goths; and yet, what would have become of Christianity in Europe but for those Gothic races, but for those Arian heretics, who were considered more dangerous than downright pagans?

If we think of the future of India and of the influence which that country has always exercised on the East, the movement of religious reform which is now going on, appears to my mind the most momentous in this momentous century. If our missionaries feel constrained to repudiate it as their own work, history will be more just to them than they themselves. And if not as the work of Christian missionaries, it will be recognized hereafter as the work of those missionary Christians, who have lived in India, as examples of a true Christian life, who have approached the Natives in a truly missionary spirit of love; whose bright presence thawed the ice, and brought out beneath it the old soil, ready to blossom into new life. These Indian Puritans are not against us; for all the highest purposes of life they are with us, and we, I trust, with them. What would the early Christians have said to men, outside the pale of Christianity, who spoke of Christ and his doctrine as some of these Indian reformers? Would they have said to them, "unless you speak our language and think our thoughts, unless you accept our creed and sign our Articles, we can have nothing in common with you?"

O that Christians, and particularly missionaries would lay to heart the words of missionary Bishop! "I have for years thought," writes Bishop Patterson, "that we seek in our missions a great deal too much to make *English* Christians ... Evidently the heathen man is not treated fairly, if we encumber our messages with unnecessary requirements. The ancient Church had its 'selection of fundamentals"..... Any one can see what mistakes we have made in India......Few men think themselves into the state of the Eastern mind. We seek to denationalize these races as far as I can see; whereas we ought surely to change as little as possible—only what is clearly incompatible with the simplest form of Christian teaching and practice. I do not mean that we are to compromise truth ...... but do we not overlay it a good deal with human traditions?"

If we had many such missionaries as Bishop Patterson and Bishop Cotton, if Christianity were not only preached, but lived in that spirit, it would then prove itself what it is—the religion of humanity at large, large enough itself to take in all shades and diversities of character and race.

And more than that—if this true missionary spirit, this spirit of truth and love, of forbearance, of trust, of toleration, of humility, were once to kindle the hearts of all those chivalrous ambassadors of Christ, the message of the Gospel which they have to deliver would then become as great a blessing to the giver as to the receiver. Even now, missionary work unites, both at home and abroad, those who are widely separated by the barriers of theological sects.

CONFESSION OF THOMAS PAINE.*

—o—

[MADE TO REV. GEORGE BOURNE IN NEW YORK CITY IN 1805.]

ON mentioning to a friend some time since a fact relating to Thomas Paine, he requested me to write it, that it might be laid upon record as an instructive memento of the snares and working of infidelity in one of its modern chieftains. As forty years have elapsed since the interview occurred, I can only narrate the prominent points, which were too deeply impressed on my mind ever to be obliterated. The main point is precisely as Thomas Paine then made the humiliating and melancholy acknowledgment.

About the first of February 1805, having some business with a gentleman then residing in a house, still standing, in Maiden Lane, near William Street, New York, I entered his store and found him overwhelmed with business that required all dispatch. Apologising for inattention, he asked me if I could wait awhile; and to induce me to do so, he proposed this inquiry, "Would you like to see Thomas Paine?" My reply was, "Very much indeed." "Then I will introduce you to him," said Mr. B.; "he is now in the sitting-room behind the store, waiting for my leisure to select some article that he wants to purchase; and having nothing to do, he said that he could pass his time in my parlour just as well as in any other place." Upon this we walked into the interior room, and the usual first civilities having been exchanged, the author of the impious burlesques on Christianity and I were left alone. A conversation of an interesting character occurred respecting Napoleon's Emperorship, with the collateral European topics, and the probable results, secular and ecclesiastical, of the existing state of France. During our conversation some remark had fallen from me in reference to the avowed confidence which Napoleon

*Taken from an Editorial in the *Christian Intelligencer*, 1845, entitled Ignorance of Skeptics by George Bourne.

placed in the officers of his Government, who were faithful Huguenots. And the marked, suspicious reserve which he ever manifested to the Romish adherents, except such men as Cardinal Fesch, Talleyrand, Gregoire, Raynal, and their confederates, who might be called Prelates or Abbes, but who had no faith in the Church of Rome, if they still were nominal Papists, (that is, Popists). Probably the enunciation of sentiments of that character elicited substantially, and in many of the points I believe, the precise words of the ensuing dialogue. At one point of the conversation, when more directly impressed with the principles of Divine revelation that I introduced, Mr. Paine remarked with considerable suavity :

"Excuse me, Sir, but I cannot help expressing my surprise that you, who seems so conversant with general history, should use language so much like that of religious fanatics."

"I am, therefore, still more astonished," Paine replied, "that any educated enlightened man should profess to be a Christian believer."

My retort was instantaneous—"And I am more amazed that any well-informed man should not be a believer. Permit me, then, as you have challenged me upon an essential topic, to make the personal application of my principle. You understand the cardinal theories of the 'Rights of Man,' and your 'CommonSense' with some of your political writings, in my estimate of civil and religious liberty, are irrefutable. But of Christianity, whether didactic, experimental, or even historical, your so-called 'Age of Reason' proves that you are totally ignorant."

"Well," he rejoined, with a good-tempered smile, "that is capital—and I like your sincerity. But how can you show my ignorance of those subjects?"

"Very easily," I answered. "Of all the matters connected with human knowledge, not one demands such extensive literary acquirements and protracted study as the Bible. A competent disputer should accurately and critically understand the Hebrew, Chaldaic, Syriac, and Greek languages at least, or he cannot read the Scriptures in the tongues in which they were written, and the words contained in them were spoken. Then he ought to be versed in the opinions, customs, usages, and the domestic and public annals of the Asiatic nations of antiquity. He should, also, be well acquainted with the ancient history, especially of Egypt, Assyria, Babylon, Persia, Arabia, and with the Grecian and Roman affairs ; to all which he must superadd a minute and deep insight into ecclesiastical history since the introduction of Christianity. Now to all these things you directly avow yourself a stranger, and, if I remember right, you have disclaimed even a grammatical knowledge of our own vernacular. How, therefore, can I admit your competency as a judge of the celestial Inspiration of the Holy Scriptures ?"

A kind of rambling and evasive verbiage ensued, and it was all I could obtain from him in answer, until I resolved to risk giving him offence by quoting some of his pretended statements concerning the sacred volume, which were so glaringly incorrect that I candidly told him, (there was no other alternative ;) "Either, Mr. Paine, you designedly and wantonly falsified the book from which you professed to quote, which I am not inclined to believe, or you wrote those paragraphs at random without any acquaintance with the Bible, or actual inspection of the inspired volume."

THOMAS PAINE'S CONFESSION.

To this rebuke he thus responded: "You have driven me into a corner, I confess, Sir; And, therefore, I will explain the origin of the 'Age of Reason' to you. You may remember that in consequence of my vote against the execution of Louis XVI. with some other circumstances that were opposed to the proceedings of the French rulers during the Reign of Terror, I was first suspected of disaffection to Marat, Robespierre, and their accomplices, and finally arrested and cast into prison." I think Mr. Paine said La Conciergerie. "While in the dungeon, and constantly expecting, like the others, without a moment's warning, to be transferred to the guillotine, it was suggested to me that if I would make it known that I was a devout worshipper of the Goddess of Reason, and utterly rejected everything Christian, I might escape the impending decapitation. A tacit pledge was given by a friend that if my life was spared, I should write a work adverse to Christianity, expressing my disbelief in Britain to weaken the power of Pitt and his administration. By the death of Robespierre I was liberated from prison, and to obtain the favor of the Oligarchs and to regain my former position I determined to compose the work entitled the 'Age of Reason.' Great difficulty was interposed, for a copy of the Bible could not be found.

I had not seen or read a word of it for a long period before. At length a Testament was procured probably," Paine added, "also afterward a Bible and by the help of some quotations from other sources I composed the 'Age of Reason' which produced the effect designed; for the proscription of the work by the British Government rendered the French rulers propitious toward me. Since that period I have never concerned myself about any religion, and it was only your sentiments which made me advert to it, as I hold no conversation upon that subject except with some companion to ridicule the hypocrites and their priestcraft."

In reply, I observed to Mr. Paine that I was indebted to him for his frank illustration of so important a point in his personal history ; that his anticipated confession, as he must perceive, not only confirmed my general position with regard to the wilful ignorance of avowed unbelievers and scoffers of religion ; but that it would also be a profitable lesson to improve the gross absurdity and wickedness of pretending to disarm, whether orally or by writing, topics of which you know nothing, and of attempting to explain the most recondite subjects without a single qualification for the great and arduous task. I also remarked to Mr. Paine that the hopes of Christian philanthropists, and the other friends of universal freedom, had been woefully disappointed by the cause of the French Revolution, but that he had now unintentionally developed the source of the whole agonising disappointment and public overthrowness, the scornful rejection of the Divine word, the true code of morals, producing the inevitable torrent of irreligion in principle and outrageous depravity in practice.

My remarks manifestly arrested his attention, and we might have continued together much longer, but Mr. B. excused himself for detention. Mr. Paine said, " Mr. B., your friend here has given me the severest personal castigation I have ever received."

Having explained the matter, Mr. B. replied, "I expected nothing else, if you happened to alter an opinion upon that point ; but I am happy to perceive that you both seem to be equally good-tempered about it."

" Never better," answered Paine ; " and I am the last person to feel offence at any opposition to my opinions, when I provoke the argument and retort."

We separated, and I never saw him afterward to my recollection, although he frequently made inquiries of my friend, Mr.B., concerning me, and I received a letter from him written in his usually vigorous and terse style.

As Thomas Paine grew older, he became less civil on the subject of Christianity. He has gone into the unchanging world, and during the forty years which have since elapsed I have never met with one of those who 'sit in the seat of the scornful' that truly possessed one jot or tittle more of genuine information concerning the oracles of God, or knew one particle more concerning the historical and internal evidence of revealed religion, than Thomas Paine did. As I have thus narrated, he averred to me that he had never perused the Holy Scriptures except for the purpose of perverting his life and enhancing his worldly interests by blaspheming its heavenly truths, or turning them into a butt for impure buffoonery or ribald jests.

GEORGE BOURNE.

New York, 1845.

Darlington's Pain-Curer has been found to be a certain cure for Pains in the Back, Lumbago, Pains in the Chest, Sore Throats, Coughs, Colds, Tightness of the Chest, Headache, Toothache, Neuralgia, Colics, Rheumatism, Paralysis, Pains in the Groins, Contracted Joints, Gout, Sciatica, Bad Legs, Bad Breasts, Swellings, Old Sores, Piles, Ring worm, Pimples, Freckles, & Eruptions on the Skin

Holloway's Pills.—Nothing preserves the health so well as an occasional alterative in changes of weather, or when the nerves are unstrung. These Pills act admirably on the stomach, liver, and kidneys, and so thoroughly purify the blood, that they are the most efficient remedy in warding off derangements of the stomach, fever, diarrhœa, dysentery, and other maladies, and giving tone and energy to debilitated constitutions. All who have the natural and laudable desire of maintaining their own and their family's health, cannot do better than trust to Holloway's Pills which cool, regulate, and strengthen. These purifying Pills are suitable for all ages, seasons, climates, and constitutions, which all other means fail, and are the female's best friend.

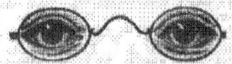

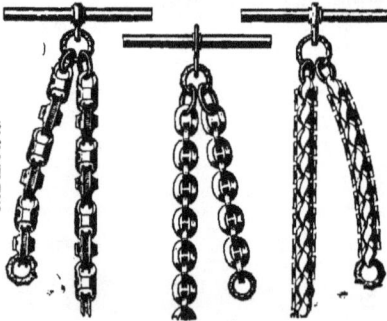

THACKER, SPINK & CO.'S
LATEST PUBLICATIONS.

VOL. II. HINDU TRIBES AND CASTES; together with an Account of the Mahomedan Tribes of the North-West Frontier and of the Aboriginal Tribes of the Central Provinces. By the Rev. M. A. SHERRING, M.A.. LL.B. Demy 4to., cloth. Rs. 16.

This Volume contains an account of the Tribes of the Punjab and its Frontiers—Central Provinces and Berar, Bombay Presidency and Frontiers of Sind.

CIVIL PROCEDURE CODE AMENDMENT ACT.—The Sections of Act X of 1877, as amended by Act XII of 1879, reprinted in full, together with the new Sections *Printed on one side only of the paper so as to admit of easy incorporation with Broughton's and other editions of the Civil Procedure Code.* Royal 8vo. Rs. 1.

GOODEVE'S HINTS FOR THE MANAGEMENT and Medical Treatment of Children in India. By EDWARD A. BIRCH, M.D., Surgeon-Major, Seventh Edition. Crown 8vo., cloth. Rs. 7.

" I have no hesitation in saying, that the present one is for many reasons superior to its predecessors. It is written very carefully, and with much knowledge and experience on the author's part, whilst it possesses the great advantage of bringing up the subject to the present level of Medical Science." *Dr. Goodeve.*

ELEMENTARY DYNAMICS, WITH NUMEROUS examples. By W. G. WILLSON, M.A. Second Edition. Crown 8vo., cloth. Rs. 3-8.

THE COMMERCE AND NAVIGATION OF THE *Erythrœan Sea*; being a translation of *Periplus Maris Erythræi* by an Anonymous Writer and of Arrian's Account of the Voyage of Nearkhos from the mouth of the Indus to the head of the Persian Gulf, with Introduction, Commentary, Notes, and Index. By J. W. McCRINDLE, Esq., M. A., Principal of the Government College, Patna.

THE STEEPLECHASE HORSE; how to Select Train, and Ride Him. With Notes on Accidents and Diseases, and their Treatment. By Capt. J. HIBBERT. Cloth, Imp. Rs. 3-8.

THE LAW OF INHERITANCE as in the Vrimitrodaya of Mitra Misra, translated by Golap Chandra Sircar, Sastri, M. A.—B.L., Royal 8vo. cloth. Rs. 10.

HOW WE DID "THE LIONS" OF THE North-West ; A Trip in the Durga-Pujahs to Lucknow, Delhi, Agra. By F. O. R. No. 1.

THE SAILOR'S EAST INDIAN SKY INTERpreter and Weather Book ; being a description of the Phenomena and Prognostics of the Bay of Bengal October-Cyclones, as experienced at the Pilot Station off the mouth of the Hooghly. By S. R. KLSON. 8vo. Re. 1.

THE SOVEREIGN PRINCES AND CHIEFS of Central India. By G. R. Aberigh-Mackay, Principal, Residency (Rajkumar) College, Indore, Central India. Illustrated with Portraits and Views. Volume I. Royal 8vo., cloth, extra gilt, and gilt top. Rs. 12.

THE SEA-CUSTOMS LAW, 1876, and Tariff Act ; with Notes and Appendices. By W. H. GRIMLEY, Esq., B. A., LL. B., C. S. Demy 8vo., cloth. Rs. 7-8 ; Interleaved. Rs. 8-8.

LAYS OF IND. By Aliph Cheem. The Sixth Edition. Enlarged with six new Lays, and several Illustrations. Imperial 16mo., cloth extra gilt, and gilt edges. Rs. 7 nett.

LAMB'S TALES FROM SHAKESPEARE.— Thacker Spink & Co.'s School Edition. Foolscap, cloth. Re. 1-4.

EUCLID'S ELEMENTS OF GEOMETRY. Part I, containing the First Four Books, with Notes, &c. By P. Ghosh. Sewed, Re. 1-4 ; cloth, Re. 1-8.

DUKE.—QUERIES AT A MESS TABLE : What shall we eat ? What shall we drink ? By JOSHUA DUKE, Surgeon, 3rd Punjab Cavalry, Author of "Banting in India." Re. 2-4.

DUKE.—HOW TO GET THIN ; OR BANTING in India. By JOSHUA DUKE, Surgeon, 3rd Punjab Cavalry, Author of " Queries at a Mess Table." Second Edition. 18mo , boards. Re. 1.

A MANUAL OF GARDENING FOR BENGAL and Upper India. By T. A. C. FIRMINGER. 8vo. Rs. 10.

A MANUAL OF SURVEYING FOR INDIA. By Col. Sir H. L. THUILLIER and Col. SMITH. 8vo. Rs. 10.

INDIAN DOMESTIC ECONOMY AND RECEIPT Book. With Illustrated Names. By Dr. R. RIDDELL. Fcap. 8vo. Rs. 7-8.

ROXBURGH'S FLORA INDICA ; OR DESCRIPtions of Indian Plants. Reprinted literatim from Carey's Edition. 8vo. Rs. 5.

A HANDBOOK FOR VISITORS TO AGRA AND its Neighbourhood. By H. G. KEENE, Esq., M.R.A.S., &c. Fourth Edition. Enlarged and Improved. Rs. 2-8.

A HANDBOOK FOR VISITORS TO DELHI AND and its Neighbourhood. By H. G. KEENE, Esq. Maps. Fcap. 8vo. Rs. 2.

ANCIENT INDIA AS DESCRIBED BY MEGASthenes and Arrian ; being a Translation of the fragments of the Indica Megasthenes collected by Dr. Schwan back and a Translation of the first part of the Indica of Arrian. With Introduction, Notes, and a Map of Ancient India. By J. W. McCRINDLE, Esq., M.A., Principal of the Patna College, 8vo. Rs. 2-8.

A GUIDE TO TRAINING AND HORSE Management in India, with a Hindustanee Stable and Veterinary Vocabulary and Calcutta Turf Club Tables for Weight, for Age and Class. By Capt. M. HORACE HAYES, Author of "Veterinary Notes for Horse Owners." New Edition re-arranged and much enlarged. Crown 8vo. Rs. 5.

CALCUTTA TO LIVERPOOL, BY CHINA, Japan, and America, in 1877. By H. W. N. Rs. 2.

A MILITARY DICTIONARY, comprising Terms, Scientific and otherwise, connected with the Science of War. Compiled by Major-General G. FOYULE. Assisted by Captain DeSAINT-CLAIR ST. VENSON. Third Edition. Crown 8vo., cloth, Reduced to Rs. 7-8.

THE INDIAN CONTRACT ACT (IX of 1872) and the Specific Relief Act (I of 1877). With a full Commentary. By D. Sutherland, Esq., Barrister-at-Law Royal 8vo. cloth. Rs. 10.

JUDGMENTS OF THE PRIVY COUNCIL on Appeals from India. By D. Sutherland, Esq., Barrister-at-Law. Vol. II, 1868 to 1874, Royal 8vo. sewed. Rs 20; or half-calf Rs. 22-8. Vol. I, 1831 to 1867. Rs. 16. The two Vols, embracing from 1831 to 1874, for Rs. 30; or half-calf. Rs. 35.

THE CODE OF CIVIL PROCEDURE, being Ac X of 1877. With Notes and Appendix by the Hon'ble L. P. Delves Broughton of Lincoln's Inn, assisted by W. F. Agnew, Esq., of Lincoln's Inn, and G. S. Henderson, Esq., of the Middle Temple, Barristers-at-Law, Royal 8vo. cloth Rs. 30.

BENGAL COUNCIL ACTS—The unrepealed Acts of the Lieutenant-Governor of Bengal in Council, Edited with Chronological Table, Notes, and Index. By Frederick Clarke, Esq., Barrister-at-Law. Royal 8vo., cloth, Rs. 22.

THE LAW OF EVIDENCE IN BRITISH INDIA. By G.C. Field, Esq., M. A., LL. D., Barrister-at-Law. Third Edition. 8vo., cloth. Rs. 18.

THE INDIAN CONTRACT ACT, with Annotations, &c. By the Hon'ble H. S. Cunningham, M. A., and W. H. Shephard, Esq., M. A. Third Edition. 8vo., cloth. Rs. 14.

THACKER, SPINK & CO.,
5 & 6, GOVERNMENT PLACE,
a-34   CALCUTTA.

THE
INDIAN MIRROR
RATES OF SUBSCRIPTION.
(IN ADVANCE.)
Foreign.

For Twelve Months (*via* Southampton)	48	6	0
" (*via* Brindisi)	64	10	0

Sunday Edition.
(Both for Town and Mofussil.)

For One Month	...	...	1	0	0
Three Months	...	...	2	8	0
Six Months	...	...	5	0	0
Twelve Months	...	...	10	0	0

(Single Copy Four Annas.)
Foreign

For Twelve Months (*via* Southampton)	12	7	0
" (*via* Brindisi)	14	14	0

ADVERTISEMENT RATES.
For casual Advertisements 2 annas per line.
No Advertisement charged for less than a Rupee.
For special contract rates apply to the Manager.

Printed and published by the Proprietor by W. C. SOOK, at the Sun Press at No. 2 British Indian Street, Calcutta.

The Indian Mirror

[Edited by Krishna Bihari Sen, M.A.]

SUNDAY EDITION

[Registered at the General Post Office.]

VOL. XIX.   CALCUTTA, SUNDAY, NOVEMBER 30, 1879.   NO. 285.

CONTENTS.

Editorial Notes.

THE Missionary Expedition is expected back in Calcutta on Thursday next.

—:o:—

M. RENAN has finally accepted the invitation of the Hibbert Trustees to deliver some lectures in French after Easter. The subject will be the influence which Rome has exercised on the formation of Christianity.

—:o:—

IT is said that the rebuilding of Jerusalem is seriously contemplated by some wealthy Jews. The Jews in Jerusalem at present are very poor, but they are not without hope that some better days are in store.

—:o:—

WE read that at the British Association meeting some body put forward a theory to the effect that man's ancestors had been transparent. Wesley's theory was that our ancestors in paradise were glassy. We are sure that after this another will propose that Adam and Eve were only nebulous.

—:o:—

AT a missionary meeting, held in London the other day, a missionary, " referring to the work of Keshub Chunder Sen, said that he and his followers were more formidable, more clever than the orthodox Hindus, they were just a new army, a new regiment raised by the *devil to oppose the progress of Christianity*." *Christian Life* rejoices to think this opinion of the Brahmos is not much entertained in England.

—:o:—

MR. BARTLETT writes to the *Times* to say that for every Christian life destroyed in Turkey 500 Mussulmans have perished ; and that for every single Christian man or woman who has been murdered or outraged since the beginning of the struggle in 1876 down to the present time at least 200 Mahomedan men, women, and children have met with a similar, and, in the refinement of cruelty, a worse fate.

—:o:—

WE welcome Mr. Lal Mohun Ghose on his return from England. He has done his duty well and nobly, and his countrymen are bound to him by a deep debt of gratitude. Mr. Ghose should now think of giving us the impressions of his visit to England. A public lecture will, we think, be a treat to most of us.

THE *Spectator*, speaking on vegetarianism, mentions it as a principal objection that the masses of the vegetarians are not palatable. We must refer our English contemporary to the fact that millions of India at the present day are vegetarians, and that their food suffices to sustain them through life. It cannot be said that they live on unpalatable food, for vegetarian dishes may be made as rich and dainty as meat ones. If want of variety be the complaint, we think, there is as much reason for it in a purely meat as in a purely vegetarian diet.

—:o:—

THE *Statesman*, whose article on the Brahmo Somaj we notice elsewhere, hazards the opinion that Babu Keshub Chunder Sen " has for several years been steadily making his peace with Hinduism." May we ask our contemporary to give us the date when this interesting transition from " the fiery radicalism" of his old days began ? We know there is a true Macdonald ring in the utterance. That Rev. gentleman has been making this charge against Mr. Sen from time immemorial. We should like to know, indeed, the date of its occurrence.

—:o:—

SOME of our countrymen have read history to little purpose. In speaking of Wassudeo Balwant Phadke many compare him to Tell, Washington and Garibaldi ! Rebellion is justified by success, and we may tell these well-meaning gentlemen that not only was there no success for Mr. Wassudeo to be proud of, but he had literally no power to achieve any. He was a patriot, as he said, but one of the most foolish kind—one to whom his countrymen are in no way bound to feel grateful, since his success in any direction would have involved millions in ruin, ignorance and barbarism. Fools often rush in where angels fear to tread.

—:o:—

ACCORDING to a correspondent of the *Pall Mall Gazette*, a proposal has been made to form a religious guild for persons connected with the press, "from the editor to the stoker's boy at the engine." The rules suggested are that members should pledge themselves to go to some place of worship at least once on Sundays, and, if possible, once during the week ; to pass five minutes a day in private prayer ; to be temperate in dress, speech, and food ; to be friendly with those with whom they work ; and, if possible, to induce them to join the guild. May we ask how it has come to pass that the only persons privileged to break the sabbath are the editors of daily newspapers ?

—:o:—

MR. BRIGHT thus concluded his great Manchester speech:—"Let them look at their position for a moment. If at some distant period—it might be centuries remote—an Englishman, one of the great English nation which was now so rapidly peopling the great American continent, if such an Englishman should visit and explore the sources of his race and the decayed and ruined home of his affections, he might exclaim, ' How are the mighty fallen, and whence comes this great ruin?' The answer would be that in the councils of the England of the past—and he prayed that it might not be said in the days of a virtuous queen—wisdom and justice were scorned, and ignorance, passion, and vain glory directed a policy and wielded her power."

—:o:—

A VERY interesting party met on Friday evening at the *Baitakhana* of Maharajah Jotendro Mohun Tagore to witness the extraordinary mnemonic feats of a famous Madras Pundit, who has arrived in this city. He could improvise Sanskrit Slokas, work out multiplication tables, recognise the sounds of particular bells or metallic vessels, and repeat English sentences, though knowing nothing of English, and these feats he performed simultaneously. The Pundit drew frequent plaudits from the audience and was rewarded with an ornament by his noble patron. All who went came immensely satisfied with what the Pundit did to edify them. We need not say that Maharajah Jotendro Mohua and his worthy brother were as kind and affable as ever.

—:o:—

THE Doctors of Calcutta held a meeting to consider the advisability of establishing a Medical Society in the metropolis. An institution of the kind was in existence many years ago, but it was broken up after that unfortunate split between the homœopaths and allopaths. We hope the new society will fare better, though the combustible materials are present in it and a single spark might set the whole on fire. There was certainly a disposition on all sides to receive Dr. Sarkar as a member. This was the most amiable feature of the meeting, no doubt. Only we fear that, as everything is transient in this world, this renewed friendship may also be as shortlived and may end as astragically. We fear the Doctors will be good boys this time.

—:o:—

MISS L. S. BEVINGTON, the lady who defended the atheistic view of morality in the pages of the *Nineteenth Century* against Mr. Mallock, writes to the *Christian World* to explain why she is so anxious to maintain her ground :—" Many expanding young minds now-a-days resign, for integrity's sake, the luxury of theism. These minds are often, as I intimately know, in danger of rushing hastily into moral license as well. Mr. Mallock's recent flippant and cruel volume—in which, under a thin disguise of doing honor to religion and to morality, he yet contrives to insult both—this sad, bad book it, I maintain, calculated to hurry some wanderer downhill into an abyss, if not of reckless lust, yet of cynical indifference. I would hold them back by the chain of ethical and social truth which now holds me back on one side from this abyss, on the other from Romanism. Miss Bevington counts upon a task altogether hopeless. What God abandon, it is too much for a lady to retain with her own force. She thinks evolutional atheism is very different from the atheism of the French Revolution ;

and hence what the latter failed to do, the former will easily accomplish. We are for experiments. Given two communities, the one theistic and the other atheistic, to find the results.

We shall ask Mr. Evans and those who believe that national sins are followed by national calamities to say if the following enumeration of details in connection with this subject is not strictly logical, that is to say, as logical as their own position. A church paper has an article headed "Concessions to Rome followed by national calamities," in which it is stated that the passing of the Catholic Relief Bill was followed by an outbreak of cholera and disturbances in England; Maynooth Endowment Bill by famine in Ireland; education in Ireland without the Bible by rebellion; appointment of Jesuit army chaplains; placing of a English man-of-war at the disposal of the Pope by loss of the *Captain*: appointment of Jesuit navy-chaplains by loss of the *Eurydice*; passing of Irish University Bill by revolt at Cabul. From the sublime to the ridiculous, they say, there is but one step.

We are glad to observe that bishops and ministers in England have recognised the necessity of lecturing on the existence of God oftener and with more repeated emphasis than they were in the habit of doing before. The average defence of Christianity had hitherto taken the form of polemical discussions on the truth or otherwise of supernatural manifestations &c. Science, however, has advanced too far to be contented with its triumphs over those doctrines. Flushed with its successes, it has gone on knocking at the doors of the Almighty Himself, and its audacious questions plainly indicate that it wishes to displace Him from the throne. At such a stage it is not proper that men should be contesting for insignificant outposts when the very stronghold is threatened. Men should come to the defence of religion, and we are glad that many in England have begun to take up such simple topics as the existence of God as the subjects of their discourses.

NAROTUM used to say that great men have great or good mothers. The Bishop of Manchester bears testimony to the truth of this in his own case. "His father," he said, "having made an unfortunate investment died, he feared, a broken-hearted man. They were a family of seven, and he (the Bishop) was then fourteen years of age. His mother was not clever, but she would have done anything she could for her children. She said;—'I can't give these lads large fortunes; but by denying myself and living quietly, I can give them a good education.' Three of the brothers went out to India—one fell in the Mutiny, and the other was now at the head of a department of public works. They knew what he (the Bishop) was. He ventured to say that if all his brothers and sisters were alive, they would rise up and call their dear mother blessed for the sacrifice she made that they might have careers. By God's providence he had that mother still spared to him. She was now paralysed, speechless, and helpless; but every day when he went into her bedroom and looked on her sweet face, he thought gratefully of all he owed her."

BELIEVING AND UNBELIEVING BRAHMOS.

LET every theist consider if any religionist occupies a more enviable position than he.

There are the heavens above, the waters below, nature with its vast expanding volume of sermons and lessons, every object, animate and inanimate, every man, great or small—from all we derive good. Every atom or particle in the world preaches truths. Can any of the recognised religions open out such an immense scripture? Brahmoism can and it does. Brother, think of it, and say if your position is not an enviable one. Away with your sectarian animosities, away with false rationalism, away with the cant of what is a vulgar sort of patriotism; away with the narrow confines of the past. India before the world, the present before the future, look upon these and then come to a determination whether in enlarging your mind and embracing every truth, every good, every beauty, you should fit yourself for that position in which your only concern is God and His creatures below. Little men with little minds among the Brahmos may reject this prophet or that, may accept this truth or that. We know he is incapable of larger efforts. But why are you, child of God, to be cribbed and confined within the four corners of a narrow written creed, whose only recommendation is that it does not speak the truth. Men whose knowledge of God is derived from hearsay or guess may affect to disbelieve the sayings of those who have seen God. But why should you, who have received the cheerful message that God can be seen and heard, refuse to accept the testimonies of real devotees? Why should you refuse to enlarge your faith by hearing the life experiences of brother-theists? A flood of light, we tell you, has burst upon us, and if we do not follow the light, will not the blame be upon us that a privilege was accorded to us and we disdained to accept it? Now is the time to eschew party-spirit and follow the lead of the Divine voice. Mind, if within a short time, we fail to receive Heaven's mission, theism may never come to us again. Whether the Brahmo Somaj will be the church of the future depends upon whether we become true Brahmos or not. So far as the signs may be interpreted, Brahmoism does not depend upon intellectual assent or social improvements. There are men among us who, basing their faith in God, try to cling to external aids to the best of their power. It is as if in their last struggles with contending waves they had caught hold of a straw to save them. It is thus that, after having lost faith, they turn servants, social reformers and political agitators. Their labours do not represent the work of true Brahmoists; nor are their aspirations to be counted as genuine. Social reform, intellectual work, &c., is nothing without the spirit. A Brahmo must care for religion above every thing else. If he has God before him, has he not every thing worth having? To love God, to see Him, to hear Him, to feel His presence in every action, that is the only work of a theist. Do not speak of reforms. Brother, reform yourself, before you reform others. The man who wishes to emancipate women, must first emancipate himself from lust and foul desires. If he looks upon women with evil eyes, let those eyes be plucked out immediately. Those who speak of the evils of idolatry and wish to root it out, should first know and see God themselves. Brother, be religious first, and then proceed to root out religion from other men's hearts. It is thus that our entire work begins with the spirit. There is no alternative left. God or nothing, and a Brahmo should have nothing but God. It seems to us that the present is the

time when prayers and devotional exercises should be the life and enjoyment of every Theist. If a Brahmo tells us he does not pray, we should refuse to talk with him till we have prayed for him and made him pray. If a Brahmo does not believe in a personal divinity, let us not speak with him till he has either abjured the title or learned to believe. If he mocks those who are devout, let us avoid his company, for he is infectious, and to be affected by his infidelity is to die a spiritual death. Faith first of all, brother, and nothing but faith. Join in the work, learn to believe, and heaven is for you. But for God's sake do not be unbelieving. A *jehad* against all infidel Brahmos!

THE *STATESMAN* ON THE BRAHMO SOMAJ.

THE *Statesman* of Wednesday last contains another article on the Brahmo Somaj. Its first article which we noticed was marked by a tone of sober impartiality which we scarcely expected from a Christian journal. The second shows a considerable falling-off, both as regards the spirit and the matter contained. There are insinuations which we should like to have been more outspoken, and the conclusion arrived at by our contemporary might have been stated at once. It appears that the writer of the article had used the alternative, "Prophet or Impostor," with considerable diffidence, and did not expect that we should complacently accept it. After our recent article on the subject we have very little to say. We may only repeat that the position of the Minister is quite irrespective of the claims to human respect and gratitude of Christ and other prophets. The *Statesman* persists in maintaining that this point is involved in any question that proposes to define the exact position and attitude of the Brahmo Somaj towards other religions. "This town," says our contemporary, "is one of the Immortals. He is the latest of the prophets, and from the nature of things it should seem that he must be the last. In him are summed up all the prophets' and all the gods." This is exaggerated language, and is surely not the truth. In the first place, our Minister does not call himself a Prophet; that is a lie. In the second place, he cannot be the "last" of the prophets, because, (1) as we have said, he is no Prophet, and (2) no Prophet can call himself the "last", when he does not himself know how many chapters of human history have yet to be written. Nor thirdly, as we have repeatedly said, is any question of greatness or littleness involved in the question. When in his lecture on "India asks—who is Christ?" our Minister says:—" Will he (Christ) not fulfil the Indian scripture? I am reminded of the passage in the gospel in which he says,—' I am not come to destroy but to fulfil.' The Mosaic dispensation only? Perhaps the Hindu dispensation also. In India he will fulfil the Hindu dispensation;" —we repeat when he says so, he at once clearly and unequivocally defines his position in relation to Christ. It is a pure irrelevancy to call him either the greatest or the last of the prophets and gods. What he is and his mission may be gathered from what we said on this subject in a late issue. We need not, therefore, dwell upon it here. With reference to the alternative of Prophet or Impostor, we regret the *Statesman* has not imbibed the milder and more congenial spirit of present day philosophy. For centuries have

Christians persisted in calling Mahomed an impostor, and it is in this manner that the *Statesman* wishes to impose upon India the same alternative with reference to the claims of our leader. Fortunately, the writings of more gifted philosophers like Carlyle have served to dispel the notion from men's minds. It is the exclusive spirit of Christianity, and not of Christ, that refuses to acknowledge the claims of Mahomed and first created the alternative which the *Statesman* wishes to thrust upon India. Two suns cannot shine in the same sphere, and when Mahomed claimed to be one of those luminaries, Christendom rose and with one accord voted him to be a false light. Carlyle has powerfully shown what a mistaken and blind view of the world this is. There may be suns and there may be stars and there be planets too, and it will not do to say that any one of them gives a false light, when it does give light to millions. Well, in God's providence there is work and distinct work for all of these. The impostor-theory, as applied to Mahomed, must fall to the ground. Refined philosophy recognises in him a grand instrument for good. That he benefited the world at the same time that there were many things which the world did not approve, is to say that he was a man. No, no. The philosophy of the nineteenth century will never accept the impostor-theory with reference to any man with a mission. What is good in him will be accepted and recognised. If the science of religion does nothing else, it will at any rate trample upon that exceedingly offensive habit which leads christians to represent the world's best men except one as so many impostors and that one, the exception, as the only prophet. We have no wish to say more. Our contemporary, it appears, has not exhausted the subject. It is better, therefore, to wait and hear his final decision on the " pretensions" of our Minister.

MISSIONARY EXPEDITION.

—o—

[FROM OUR SPECIAL CORRESPONDENT.]

GRAZIPORE, 27th November 1879.

It is difficult to determine which of the three foes we had to confront and combat in the three cities we visited was the most powerful. At Mozufferpore our army had to attack the citadel of Ignorance. At Gya grim Idolatry was the enemy we had to deal with. Now that we were at Bankipore, one would have thought we were in the land of enlightenment, and that our work was therefore easy. No. An enemy of a different kind, but hardly less redoubtable, awaited our attack here. It was Rationalism. As in other great cities and centres of enlightenment, so here English education had freed the Native mind from the trammels of superstition and idolatry, but it had made not a few young men free thinkers and scoffers, and substituted in their hearts in place of the religion of their forefathers the well-known creed of " Eat, drink and be merry." Faith in Hinduism had gone, and with it had disappeared faith in religion itself. Prayer, devotion, immortality, inspiration were well nigh lost in the sea of scepticism. Against this spirit of rationalism and scoffing the soldiers soon found themselves arrayed. It was suggested that a more rational method should be adopted at Bankipore than had been adopted elsewhere for the dissemination of Brahmo principles. Objections were raised to the proposal of open-air meet-

ings, and the idea of street processions excited ridicule and laughter. Such unfavorable and discouraging intimations, instead of damping, aggravated the zeal of the party. The campaign commenced with Divine service in English. The Minister discoursed on the efficacy of prayer, and took up the following text— " Ask and it shall be given you." Service was conducted in the hall of the Rosy Bower. The congregation numbered about two hundred persons, among whom were the local chaplain and a few other Europeans. "Heaven's command to educated India" was the subject of an English lecture delivered by the Minister at the Patna College, on Friday, the 21st instant, at a quarter past nine. The hour was unusually late. Nevertheless, the assembly was both numerous and respectable, the attendance numbering about five hundred souls. The notices were issued in the name of the esteemed Principal of the College, Mr. McCrindle. Both before and after the lecture, the Commissioner of Patna, Mr. Halliday, who presided on the occasion, made a few complimentary remarks, saying that neither the speaker's enthusiasm in his cause nor his eloquence had in the least abated. Next evening at the house of a private gentleman there was Bengali service, to which a good number of the educated men and Hindu ladies of the station were invited. The real battle had yet to be fought. Sunday was the day for an open-air demonstration. The site selected was the spacious compound of the Patna College. The spectacle was worth seeing. The steps and the space in front were crowded with rows of people of all classes, rich and poor, educated and unlearned, and the large verandahs projecting on either side of the building were filled with masses of people of all descriptions. There were nearly a thousand persons, whom the Minister addressed in English, and then for half an hour in Hindi. Immediately after the address, there was *kirtan* in the streets. The procession moved on, halting first at the house of the Commissioner's Personal Assistant and then in the compound of the Hindu Hostel, where a cordial welcome was accorded to the party, and ultimately reached the Rosy Bower, where the usual Sunday Service was conducted in Bengali, in the presence of about a hundred souls. The subject of the sermon was the harmony of all religions in Theism. The morning service was held under trees in the garden attached to the local Brahmo Somaj. I must not omit to notice an important event which contributed in some measure to the success of the procession. As Bankipore seemed somewhat backward in the matter, a telegram was sent on Friday ordering the Gya auxiliary force to come sharp and reinforce the main army. The order was strictly carried out, and the effect of the union was marvellous. The Gya soldiers took leave on Monday morning; the farewell service was touching and impressive. An invitation from the Manager of the Dumraon Raj reached the Minister on Tuesday morning. The party started in the evening and reached Dumraon at 9 P.M. What a transition ! These street preachers were suddenly metamorphosed into the tenants of a palatial residence, the favored guests of a Native Prince, surrounded by the pomp and splendour of royalty ! And in spite of respectful remonstrances, the party had to sit at table and partake of a vegetable dinner prepared and served in right English style ! Another transition next morning, and we were ushered into the *asrum* of a Shaik Mahomet after morning service. In him we found a truly humble and faithful follower of Guru Nanak, who fully sympathised with our views, and showed to our party the high-

est mark of respect. His childlike simplicity and liberal views made an impression upon us all. He gave us a delicious repast under shady trees, and then read to us a few extracts from the *Granth Saheb*. In the afternoon we drove to the local school, where arrangements had been made for a lecture. On the way the party met, awhile in a jungle skirting the Maharajah's garden house, and there was a short service, in the course of which the Minister addressed the trees in the forest. Many a Hindu devotee had in ancient and modern times learnt asceticism and devotion in lonely jungles. The Minister, who, it appeared, had never seen such a forest before, was deeply impressed with the scene around, and in the spirit of those devotees invoked the Lord of the Forest. More than two hundred persons were gathered in the school hall, among whom were many Pundits and the *elite* of the town. The Shaik Nazaji was in the chair, dressed in the ascetic's garua cloth. What a contrast between the lecturer and the chairman! Yet the spirit of truth had united them both. The lecture which was partly in English and partly in Hindi, was listened to with great interest. All the Pundits with one voice commended the spirit of the lecture, and congratulated the speaker upon its merits. The party then went to the house of the Manager, singing *sankirtan* on the way. After dinner the Manager presented something like a *khillut* to the expedition for the benefit of the Brahmo Somaj, consisting of clothes and a purse amounting to two hundred rupees. The offer was thankfully received. The party then started by train for Zumanssah, where they spent the night in the waiting room at the station. Early in the morning at 4 A.M., on Thursday, they started in a carriage and *ekkas*, and reached Ghazipore at about nine, crossing the river Ganges on the ferry paddle boat.

Review.

ACHILLES AND THE TORTOISE.[*]

We have been favored with a copy of " An Essay on the celebrated Achilles and Tortoise Problem in Logic," by Mr. W. B. Livingstone of this Dacca College. It would be wrong to say that the pamphlet before us proposes to deal with the problem exclusively, for in every page of it we find facts historical, theological, scientific, and philosophical, united up in a sweet confusion leaving the reader to find a sort of interest which he surely would not feel were he to seek for it in the problem itself. Mr. Livingstone's plan is a disposed one, for he does not wish that the attention of the reader should flag, and so as soon as he sees he has too much, he brings in an agreeable diversion. There is evidently another object in view. The author is a devout Christian, and to make the best of every opportunity the diversion takes the form of an agreeable lesson in Christianity. We must say, however, that the transition from the subject-matter is sometimes too sudden and abrupt to produce a pleasant surprise. We shall see this further on. Mr. Livingstone devotes some very interesting pages to prove that the Achilles and the Tortoise Problem is not a fallacy, but a perfectly logical proposition, which may be stated in Barkara. His major premiss is that an object, a man, the minute-hand of a clock or anything whatsoever, capable of moving, or being moved, that progresses at the diminishing ratio of 1·10 + 1·100, &c., or of 12 + 1 + 1·12, &c., or of 10·10 + 100 + 10 + 1 + 1·10, &c., is one that will never overtake another object placed at a short distance before it, either at rest, or moving away from it, even though it moves towards the other object through eternity. Those of our readers who do not know what the problem is will find it stated in different forms in the pamphlet

[*] An essay on the celebrated Achilles and Tortoise Problem, in Logic. By W. B. Livingstone. Calcutta. Baptist Mission Press, 1879.

under notice. The following is given by Fowler :—

"Suppose Achilles to move ten times as fast as the Tortoise, but the Tortoise to have the start of Achilles, say by one-tenth of the distance to be traversed ; when Achilles has arrived at the point from which the Tortoise started, the Tortoise will be one-hundredth part of the whole distance in advance of him ; when Achilles has reached this point, the Tortoise will still be one-thousandth part of the whole distance in advance of him ; and so on. Thus Achilles will never be able to pass the Tortoise.

The following is Whately's statement of it :—

"If the hour-hand of a clock, the circumference of which is three *feet*, be any distance (suppose a foot) before the minute-hand, this last, though moving twelve times faster, can never overtake the other : for while the minute-hand is moving over those twelve inches, the hour-hand will have moved over one inch ; so that they will then be an inch apart ; and while the minute-hand is moving over that one inch, the hour-hand will have moved over 1-12 inch, so that it will still be a-head, though the distance between the two is diminished ; &c., &c., &c., and thus it is plain we may go on for ever ; therefore the minute-hand can never overtake the hour-hand."

The author holds that neither Hamilton nor Mill, nor Whately, nor Hobbes has been able to solve the problem. According to him it is a correct and very excellent mode of stating the theory of the asymptotes so familiar to those who know Differential Calculus. After coming to this conclusion, the author goes off at a tangent to prove that the problem is of great use to the theologian, for it helps him to appreciate the doctrine of election ! That the "Achilles and the Tortoise" is a paradox does not matter. Are not all truths paradoxes or rather put in paradoxical forms ? Then another flying off at tangent. The following story is too good to be lost :—

A very angry and spiteful discussion has been started all over India, by the announcement contained in the papers, that the late Lord Lawrence has left a fortune of £140,000. His detractors say, that as the pay of an Indian Viceroy is well known to be insufficient for any but a very quiet and moderate style of living, therefore Lord Lawrence, in order to have saved so much, must have been compelled to act, when Viceroy, in a way so niggardly as to have been a disgrace to the viceregal throne. Now, it is pretty well known that Lord Lawrence, all through his Indian career, gave a tenth of his income to the poor. And he had just to choose between giving large sums to races, theatres and the like, and being unable to give to the poor, the proportion that, as a private civilian, he had been able easily to do ; or to give little to these pernicious institutions in order that he might give a tenth to the poor. The wrath of his enemies, however, was terrible. They combined together, and published a most scurrilous pamphlet, representing the Viceroy as going into the cook-room, and telling the cook to save the bones, because out of them broth might be made. Even a Viceroy cannot do right, without, at times, being crucified for it. And it is a very singular thing, that his detractors never refer to the well-known fact of his giving a tenth of his income to the poor. Lord Lawrence and Lord Northbrook are the only two Viceroys, who took home any part of their pay, so paltry and insufficient is it found to be. Lord Northbrook was so rich, that he never drew a pice of his pay till a few days before his departure from India. What Lord Lawrence took home was probably only the foundation of his fortune, the greater portion of which may very possibly have been made after his return to London. Many a liberal and generous man has been poor through the greater portion of his life, and has grown rich only ten or twenty years before his death. This was notably the case with Sir Isaac Newton. * * * Newton became rich by generosity. So did Lord Lawrence. His fortune of £140,000 was God's reward for his having given a tenth of his income to the poor through a long Indian career.

Another paradox is to the following effect :—

An official, who hated and denounced balls and dancing, yet attended the State Ball, out of respect for his Sovereign. Another official came up to him, and said—"What, you—a pious and religious man at a profane and godless dancing party ! How very inconsistent and paradoxical !" "Well," replied the other official, "Jesus Christ, out of love to publicans and sinners, frequented their haunts, may not one of His disciples imitate His example ?"

Then another digression. The author speaks of the policy of religious neutrality in education, and the duty of Christian professors outside the college, and here we are treated to a story of the late Dr. Robson. These digressions are often made, and, as we have said, the transition from one to the other is not always pleasing. We have the highest respect for Mr. Livingstone. We admire his talents and his Christian zeal. But so far as the present treatise goes, our opinion is that it would have been better if the author had confined himself to his subject. There is a time for all things, and the pamphlet before us shows that it is not always safe to bring together things which ordinarily do stand apart from each other as the poles.

Brahmo Somaj.

As will be seen from our special correspondence elsewhere, the people of Bankipore did not at first show a liking for *Nagar Sankirtan* or open-air meetings. It happened, however, that as soon as the *mridanga* was struck, numbers felt themselves drawn to the procession. That was on the 23rd instant after the open-air meeting before the Patna College. Flowers were strewn upon the party as it proceeded chanting through the streets.

THE *Indo-European Correspondence* has the following with reference to the *Statesman's* article on our Minister:—"We by no means admit the ultimatum: 'Either a Prophet or an Impostor.' We certainly do not admit that Keshub Chunder Sen is the former; but why should it follow that we must rate him as the latter ? We say of Jesus Christ that He is either God or an Impostor—because when He said that He was God, He left us no choice between either alternative. In Keshub Chunder Sen's case, the difficulty is precisely to know what he calls himself. He throws himself upon us as a problem and amiably asks us to solve him for himself. To us he is a living contradiction who teaches and judges, yet abhors the 'dry bones of dogma'—but there are thousands of other such contradictions. Whether such men are conscious of their state it is not for us to judge. Prophets they most certainly are not ; whether they are impostors is known to the Eternal Truth in whose name they prophesy."

THE following is the substance of the sermon preached by the Minister at the Brahma Mandir on Sunday, the 27th *Asbin* last, previous to the starting of the Missionary Expedition :—

God is sometimes called the King—the King of Righteousness. Our dispensation has for it another name, warfare or struggle. Why does a dispensation come down to the earth ? It is because devout men might establish the Empire of the Great King by waging war against sin and untruth. Behold millions of people have become lifeless in the sleep of unreal happiness. The demon of sin is trying to destroy every one. Hark, the note of war is sounded, and the Commander advances with His well-equipped army. Fierce is the onslaught, and behold, the enemies are vanquished.

You have heard of the philosophy of preaching. Preaching may become a matter of pride, and it has been so several times in this world. But true preaching consists in successfully fighting against irreligion and establishing the Kingdom of God. It draws the hearts of brothers and sisters from worldliness and carnality and leads them to God. Never for a moment think that to visit different places and deliver eloquent lectures, with one's own interests in view, is real propagation of God's religion. It is far from true preachers ever to think of displaying their intellectual powers. Their lectures are merely weeping. They weep because they see sin working so much destruction in the Mother's family. They say : "Oh ! how long have they not seen the face of the Mother !" and they cry aloud. To them crying takes the form of singing and preaching.

All men are God's subjects, and, as Mother, She is protecting and providing for the world. But sin has attacked her children and has misled a great many. What sorrow, then, in the Mother's breast for this estrangement ! Her children, aware of the havoc caused in the house of the Mother, cry out : "It will not do for us to sit by the Mother and enjoy heavenly bliss, but we must go forth and kill the demon who is trampling our dear brethren and sisters. We cannot bear to see him destroying them. Whose children are they ? Upon whom is he spending his rage ? They are, no doubt, the children of the Mother of the world, who is also our Mother. Then, come, let us gird up our loins and combine to fight against the enemy. Let us renounce worldliness. We do not desire name or fame. We must not take rest so long as we are unable to remove the cause of our Mother's sorrow."

Preachers of God, if you mean to preach, then go and rescue your brethren from the bondage of sin, and restore them to the House of the Lord. Friends, do accept this sacred mission. Let the party of *bhaktas* be aglow with enthusiasm. Let a few amongst you go from place to place, maddened with the love of God. God is watching from Heaven every one of His children, who will join this Expedition. Ye devotees of God, go to your brethren in *foreign* lands. Do not speak much, only say : "Dear brethren, dear are ye to me, why have ye left your *own* country ?" and assure them that the Mother is waiting with food for them. Hearing the name of the Loving Mother, they will surely come round. We have heard that the Mother's dispensation of love has dawned upon us. You will not be able to rouse the world with the oft-repeated name—Merciful Saviour of sinners, but when they hear of the Kingdom of *the Mother*, who is all-loving, they will be stirred with love. A clear stream of blessedness is continually following from the lotus feet of the Mother. A few simple words expressive of the Mother's love should be the words of preaching this time. Friends, go as far as you can, and declare the love of the Mother. Let Bengal be filled with the name of the Merciful Mother. Let Her blessings be showered upon our heads.

NEWS FROM THE CHURCHES.

—o—

RAMPORE HAUT BRAHMO SOMAJ.

A FRIEND, who was not long ago at Rampore Haut, gives us good news of our sister—church there. He says that the brethren there deserve great credit for their exemplary zeal and activity. This is certainly an agreeable surprise. We supposed it but an infant church, that had a very limited number of worshippers. We are happy to learn that it has now a nice, *pucka* Mandir, unsurpassed in style and elegance by any Brahmo Church in the Mofussil. Long may it stand as a witness of their eminent devotion to the holy cause of Indian theism ! It is good to hear, that the Brahmos are extremely active in nearly all the Native public institutions of the place. In a school they have started, for the laboring classes, evening lessons are regularly given ; and mostly by Brahmo volunteer teachers. Another good thing is, that the lady members, the *brahmikas*, usually go, with their husbands and friends, to the common service, on Sunday. A hearty God-speed to them.

THE "BEHAR BRAHMO SOMAJ," AT MONGHYR.

This Church is watched by many among us with deep interest. Its position 'is remarkable in the history of our cause. To not a few, now recognised as leaders,' it was once the seat of devotional revival. It is not easy to say how many of our missionaries either joined the mission from Monghyr, or there received their best impulses at the revival meetings. It is but natural that the intense glow of that excitement should cool down. That it has done so, though not disastrously, as we trust, is seen in the fact that the number of its present members is less than a dozen. There was a time when this church made earnest endeavours to draw in the Beharis. What they are doing, at present, in this direction, we cannot say. There is a charity fund connected with the Somaj, but are the local Brahmos active in the management of any of the public institutions ? We recall with pleasure,—and with thanks to several European helpers beside Mr. Barlow, C.S.,—that their next *pucka* Mandir has been substantially built, and has a pleasant good compound and a flower-garden, in a good part of the town. Their Brahmikas attend, when convenient, the usual Sunday services ; and of course, the Anniversary meetings. May they go on and prosper.

D.

Correspondence.

[*We do not hold ourselves in any way responsible for the opinions of our correspondents.*—ED., I. M.]

MR. VOYSEY

—o—

TO THE EDITOR OF THE "INDIAN MIRROR."

BROTHER,—I have permission to give you an extract from a letter just come from a good Brahmo, now resident at Rangoon :—He says, "How do you feel regarding Mr. Voysey's late expressions against Christ? To say the least of them they are extremely painful. When I write you thus, I am confident that I represent many of my best Brahmo friends. Well, I can even hear Mr. Voysey's violent declamations to a certain extent; as I can imagine that these proceed from a feeling which is not uncommon to many who have changed their religion. But what draws tears from my eyes, is, that he has found sympathisers amongst men in our own church!—The founder of our church, Ram Mohun Roy, set no limit to his love and reverence for Christ. He even looked to Jesus for thorough guidance; when I remember this, my heart begins to bleed at the sad spectacle now presented. May God banish from our church this absence of love and honor for him whom our great Ram Mohun declared the "founder of truth and true religion." Such is my earnest prayer.

"Your ever devoted,
R. D.

"Rangoon, Burmah."

P. S.—May I add that, from frequent interviews with Mr. Voysey, I am convinced that he means right, far as he seems to have run off the track of common sense and common justice regarding Christ. He is just now in the falsehood of extremes; running away from Jesus as *the only God.*

Yours &c.,
DALL.

Conur, 22nd November, 1879.

THE PRINCIPLE OF ECLECTICISM.

—o—

TO THE EDITOR OF THE "INDIAN MIRROR."

SIR,—I was pleased to read your article on "Eclecticism" in a recent issue of your paper. I believe that the time has come in the history of the Brahmo Somaj, when this principle should be thoroughly discussed, and the beauty of it set forth in clear and unmistakable language. Much of the misrepresentation of the fundamental doctrines and movements of the Brahmo Somaj of India is entirely due to misconception of this principle of eclecticism which, if I mistake not, forms the chief characteristic of the Brahmo Somaj. The charge often brought against the Brahmo Somaj of India is that they are guilty of fluctuations and want of fixedness in principles. It is often seriously alleged that Babu Keshub Chunder Sen and his friends often dally with this religion and that, would fain accord loyalty and reverence to prophets and religious teachers of different creeds; would speak of Christ and Chaitanya, of Mahomet and Guru Nanak, almost in the same breath; would approve, accept and willingly adopt several religious ideas and practices enjoined by Christianity, Hinduism, Islam, and Buddhism. To many the above seems irreconcilable, and, failing to trace out a fixed principle underlying these seemingly divergent elements, they do not wait for explanations from proper quarters, but most unworthily go on to vilify their character and impute dishonourable motives to them. I can fully realize their difficulty, and can understand where the hitch lies. I believe that they do not know, nor do they take the trouble to make out that it is from an eager desire to receive all that is good and true from whatever source it may be found, and to honor and admire every good and pious soul, be he of this country or not, it is from such a strong and intense desire that Babu Keshub Chunder Sen is seen to speak of Christ at one time and Chaitanya at another time almost in the same strain, with almost the same feeling of reverence and gratitude.

But this will not, I suspect, fully decide the point at issue. Admitting that Babu Keshub Chunder Sen is guided by the principle of eclecticism, they would still persist in pushing the question, why he should speak of Christ while in the midst of Europeans, and of Chaitanya in an assembly of *Vaishnavas*, of Guru Nanak in a meeting of the *Sikhs*? What is it, they ask, that leads him to adopt this course of action? The question is, indeed, pertinent and, therefore, merits a reply. Yes, it must be admitted that Babu Keshub Chunder Sen does so. But his object in adopting this unique method is not at all to court the favor of the community to whom he addresses, as some superficial thinkers unjustly believe to be the case, but to *bring* the subject upon which he is discoursing *home* to the audience with quotations from the *Shastras*, and illustrations from the life of prophets, with which the community is familiar. To a *Vaishnava* Christ's sayings and his actions are quite unintelligible—not to say unacceptable.

Yours &c.,
SPECTATOR.

The 20th November 1879.

IS IT PANTHEISM?

—o—

TO THE EDITOR OF THE "INDIAN MIRROR."

SIR,—In reply to your criticism on my pamphlet entitled "The True Christ" I would beg to say that it seems to me that you have so hurriedly read it that you did not get the real connection of the word "Transmigration" for the use of which you call me to task, and consider me as an unfair critic. You say—"We are, for instance, seriously told, that Babu Keshub Chunder Sen in his lecture on Christ preached the doctrines of pantheism and transmigration."

Now, Mr. Editor, whether Babu Keshub Chunder Sen believes in and preaches transmigration or not, is an open question to me. His ideas and beliefs illustrate so. But this much I do know and say that Babu Keshub Chunder Sen, in his lecture on Christ, did preach pantheism, and I will prove it from his own lecture. As for transmigration, I never said that he preached the doctrine of transmigration in his lecture on Christ.

If you will take the trouble to read the pamphlet or that portion of it which the *Bombay Guardian* has quoted, you will find that I mean, not that Babu Keshub Chunder Sen has preached the doctrine of transmigration in his particular lecture, called "India asks—Who is Christ?" but that he might preach it. In order to bring out this thought clearly I have said at the close of the paragraph * * * that then there would be no room for Babu Keshub Chunder Sen to put in his pantheism. Now please note that I did not say pantheism and transmigration, but simply pantheism. My words are,—He has left out the most important words—words without which there can be no meaning to the passage. Christ came to fulfil—fulfil what? The doctrines of pantheism and transmigration *to be* preached by Keshub Chunder Sen eighteen centuries hence.

That Babu K. C. Sen did preach pantheism is plain from his own words. He says, "The earliest scriptures of our nation are full of pantheism, and though there are errors therein, the truths of pantheism will be fulfilled and perfected in Christ. The religion of our ancestors was pantheism from the beginning to the end. But what is Hindu pantheism? Essentially it is nothing but the identification of all things with God. I do not mean that you should adopt pantheism as it exists in Hindu books." That is, I want you to adopt pantheism, but not that pantheism which is in Hindu books. This does not mean that Keshub Sen did not preach pantheism. He did preach pantheism, but rather a modified form of it, perhaps, which is but the beginning of that end in which pantheism is seen as a monster in its total denial of the personality of God and the personal immortality of the human soul.

Further on he says—"Hindu pantheism in its worst form is proud, being based upon the belief that man is God." This, though a glaring inconsistency, defines the meaning of the word pantheism as used by him. Babu Keshub Chunder Sen, however, goes beyond, and says:—"In Christ you see true pantheism, and as the basis of early Hinduism is pantheism, you, my countrymen, cannot help accepting Christ in the spirit of your national scriptures." See his lecture page 15.

That Babu Keshub Chunder Sen did preach pantheism cannot be denied either by you or by the lecturer himself. The question is, what is the special meaning which Babu Keshub Chunder Sen attaches to the word pantheism? He himself says that Hindu pantheism "is the identification of all things with God."

Nowhere in his lecture does he preach against pantheism. He only exhorts his countrymen not to accept the pantheism which is found in Hindu books, and which practically considered is gross polytheism. The meaning of the word pantheism, considered etymologically and in connection with theological discussions, is "The doctrine that the universe, taken or considered as a whole, is God." But what does Keshub Babu mean by pantheism when he says, "Hindu pantheism in its worst form is proud, being based upon the belief that man is God;" or what special meaning does he attach to it when he says, "I do not want you to adopt pantheism as it exists in Hindu books;" or, "In Christ you see true pantheism"?

Will you kindly tell me? If pantheism does not mean that God is synonymous with the totality of things, and attains to self-consciousness only in the finite consciousness of man, then it is no longer pantheism. And if Babu Keshub Chunder Sen did not mean pantheism, why did he use the term at all. You would not think of calling black white, would you? Nor would any body call theism pantheism.

Therefore, Mr. Editor, I do not think that I have been unfair in my criticism.

Yours &c.,
M. S. BANNERJI.

☞ Our correspondent is again unfair. A man is fully entitled to have his own definition of things. Mr. Banerji is told that the word pantheism in the lecture in question is not used in its ordinary sense, but in what the lecturer conceived to be its real sense, and he might have quoted the exact passage where the definition is given. The fact, however, is that while he quotes, he overlooks the most important passage. Our correspondent wants to know what we mean by pantheism. We shall extract here for his benefit two sentences:—"Christ's pantheism is a pantheism of a loftier and more perfect type. It is the conscious union of the human with the Divine Spirit in truth, love and joy."—ED. *I. M.*

Literary, Scientific, &c.

MR. J. COOK has compiled a "Bibliography of the Writings of Charles Dickens," which shows commendable industry.

THE *Theological Review*, which was the quarterly organ of the English Unitarians, has ceased to exist.

THE Hibbert Lectures of 1879, being Professor Le Page Renouf's lectures on "Ancient Egypt and its Religion," are in the press, and will be published shortly by Messrs. Williams and Norgate.

VOLUME II. of the "Hundred Greatest Men," now being issued by Messrs Sampson Low and Co., begins with an introduction from the pen of M. Taine written in French, followed by an English translation of it. The volume treats of Art.

AT the next meeting of the New Shakspeare Society, Mr Furnivall will read a short paper on Puck's "I do wander everywhere swifter than the moon's sphere," a passage which seems not to have been rightly explained by any editor of the *Midsummer Night's Dream*.

BURNING a witch does not appear a serious offence in Russia, for at a recent trial of seventeen peasants for burning a poor old woman near Nijni-Novgorod, all the offenders were acquitted, except three, who were simply sentenced to Church penance.

THE remains of a poem by Richard Cœur-de-Lion have been discovered in the Library at Treves. The poem, which is written in old French, and is called "St. Nonna and her son, St. Devy," was composed by Richard during his captivity in Germany.

THE second volume of the third series of the late George Henry Lewes's "Problems of Life and Mind" is announced as in preparation by Messrs. Trubner. The two "problems" discussed are "Mind as a Function of the Organism" and "The Sphere of Sense and Logic of Feeling."

M. ALEXANDRE DUMAS is at work on a new novel, which sketches the career of a young Jesuit. M. Alphonse Karr has just published the first volume of his memoirs, "Le Livre du Bord;" while M. Victor Hugo intends to bring out his latest poetical work, "Toute la Lyre," early next month.

TRUE eloquence depends neither on voice nor gesture, but on intelligence. Dean Stanley says:—"The extraordinary eloquence of one of the greatest orators of England at this time—Mr. John Bright—was entirely formed by reading good books. These have made that style by which he captivates the hearts and wins the attention at once of the most uncultivated."

IT is stated that "a curious Travellers' Bouquet" was presented to Mrs. Grant during the festivities held at San Francisco in honor of General Grant's return to the United States. It was composed of flowers indigenous to the various countries she had passed through in her tour round the world, the blossoms being placed in chronological order beginning with Philadelphia, the point of departure, and ending with San Francisco.

We learn that a Volcano has appeared in the region of the Lower Danube, on the little island of Balagai, close to Moldova and the Iron Gates. During a recent earthquake an enormous rent appeared in the ground, which emitted a large hot geyser, and speedily inundated a great portion of the island. After a few days the geyser sank down, but in its stead several craters formed at the bottom of the rift, and have since been continually vomiting hot earth and black sand.

The Dean of A—(now Bishop of B—) was in the habit, at his weekly pastoral visit, of "expounding the Scriptures" to two maiden ladies of uncertain age, until, to their gratification and edification, it so happened that the first Book of Kings formed the subject of one of these discourses, but the poor Dean was somewhat startled to the course of his remarks by one of his hostesses saying rather abruptly : "May we really believe Mr. Dean, that King Solomon had 700 wives ? The expounder having assured his fair questioner that he had no reason to doubt the fact, was greeted with the following remark from the second of his attentive listeners : "Ah, my dear Mr. Dean, what privileges those early Christians had, to be sure !"

A MOST ludicrous mistake occurred at Stokesley sometime ago. On Friday had been fixed for the marriage of a late member of the School Board, and a license had been procured. On that morning the expectant bridegroom and the bridesmaid were conveyed to the Parish Church in a cab. They were met at church by a friendly publican, who had commenced to act as best man. As the party were somewhat behind the time appointed, the clergyman at once proceeded with the ceremony—the whole party being apparently blind to the fact that the bride was absent—and the clergyman commenced making the bridegroom and the bridesmaid. Everything went on favourably until the officiating minister asked the man, "Wilt thou have this woman to be thy wedded wife," &c., to which he answered, "I will." But on asking the confused and blushing bridesmaid, "Wilt thou have this man to be thy wedded husband," &c., she replied, "No; it's my sister." This was an unlooked-for interruption, and caused a general titter throughout the whole congregation; and the bridegroom, exclaiming "I'll go and fetch her," rushed out of the church, to which he shortly returned, accompanied by the bride-elect. The clergyman, however, now refused to perform the ceremony, alleging that if the bridegroom was so importunate to distinguish his bride from her sister, who was to act as bridesmaid, he was not to a fit and proper state to be married. The disappointed party had to leave the church unmarried, amid the laughter of a crowd of spectators.

SUNDAY IN SKYE.

JOHN STUART BLACKIE. *

No pipes on Sunday ! Well, these Highland men
Cherish their God with most lugubrious awe,
As if the dark-blue cloud that caps the Ben
Had slid into their souls, and laid a law
Of lead upon their consciences. David danced
Before the Lord, amid the exultant throng,
And with loud timbrel, and shrill trump enhanced
The brave redundant tumult of his song.
But you—you creep to church like slaves, and call
Dancing a sin, and blast of pipes a crime.
And trim your worship to a funeral
All black, as summoned to the doom of time ;
Thank God that heaven has many mansions ;
you
And I wont lodge together there. Adieu !
—Scotsman.

* In these old families of the Highlands, where personal character has been strong enough to assert itself against the assimilating power of superficial Southern influences, the custom is still preserve of of wakening the house from the slumbers of the night by a regular round of pipes outside the girth of the establishment. In one of these hospitable mansions in this part of the Misty Isle the antiquity old fashion prevails, I release my Blackie felt so uncomfortable blank as the Sunday morning, from the absence of the familiar shrill notes which announced a new stage of the race of time in the non-Sabbatical days of the week. This feeling of discomfort immediately recoiled itself in the above sonnet, to which is surely apprehends many of his dearly-beloved Celtic brethren will not say Amen ; but nevertheless, as a true confession of natural feeling, it has its right to take its place among the published voices of the hour.

We are requested to state that Father Livingston will deliver three lectures at St. John's Church on December 8, December 10 and December 12, respectively, at 5.30 p.m., on "Inspired Writings." The Church will be open to all, of whatever race or creed, and all seats are free.

FATHER LIVINGSTON, we are glad to learn, has determined to work with heart and hand for the Native community. He has with this view taken up a small house, No. 11, Mirzapore Street (College Square, South) where he will be glad to receive all Native gentlemen who like to call, from 8.37 to 10 A.M., 1 to 2 P.M. and 4 to 6 P.M.

HIGH COURT.

ORIGINAL SIDE—PEREMPTORY CAUSE BOARD.
MONDAY, THE 1ST DECEMBER 1879.

(Before the Hon'ble Mr. Justice Wilson)

UNDEFENDED CASES.

Rajender Dutt v Ramlochun Sircar & anr.—B. M. Dass.
Tarinay Churn Bose v. Mothib Setty—U. C. Dutt.
Juggut Chunder Shaw & ors. v. Nundolell Shaw & anr.—H. H. Remfry—P. M. Bose.
Kristo Kissen Poddar v. Nundolell Shaw & anr.—H. H. Remfry—P. N. Bose.
Suttish Chunder Mookerjee v. Doorgamee Bose & ors.—A. C. Chowdry.
Russickloll Sirkar v. Eshan Chunder Doss—M. D. Sen.
Syud Mahomed Hussain Khan v. Amritmoe & anr.—N. C. Bural.
The New Beerbhoom Coal Co. Ld. v. Chunder Churn Bannerjee—Roberts Morgan & Co.
Bholanauth Laheory v. Coomar Soccendrachunder Deb—G. C. Chunder.
Gopaul Chunder Mookerjee v. Kristo Chunder Mookerjee & anr.—Beeby & Co.
Tincowrie Doss v. Gopaul Chunder Mookerjee—Kaliprenath Mitter.

II.—SPECIAL PEREMPTORY LIST.
(Settlement of Issues.)
Bibee Solomon v. Abdool Azeez & ors.—Pittar & Wheeler—Orr & Harris.
Panchanun Loll Doss & ors. v. Chooneemoney Dassee & ors.—N. C. Bural.

DEFENDED CASES.
(Final Disposal.)
Jogesh Chunder Mozoomdar v. Shoorut Bewah—Sumoolchunce Dutt—Ohhoy Chunder Dutt.
Gungagovind Towary & anr. v. Kamlatprasad Teewary & ors.—H. B. Remfry—Gillander.
Kurmund Ghose Doss v. Chunder Chund Mookerjee & anr.—Anchootosh Dhur—C. D. Linton.
Gobindoll Seal & ors. v. Debendronath Mullick & ors—Carruthers—Beeby & Batter, Carruthers and Jennings.
Nawab Nazir Monsoorooddowlah Bo. v. Mahldi Begum & ors.—Mitter & Bhunjo—Ghose & Bose.
A. P. N. Arbuthnot Setty & anr. v. Mough Pho Mee & anr.—Sittannath Doss—N. C. Bural.
Kally Churn Shaw & anr. v. Bhurkhy Bibee & anr.—Kaliprath Mitter—A. C. Chunder.
Choonmnull Anguruwalk v. Sreekissen Khettry & anr.—Bahoo & Batter—Gregory.
Arhindrohhomun Chatterjee v. Preonath Mookerjee & anr.—Remfry—Defendant in person.
Sreenath Roy v. Tareeknath Mookerjee & anr.—A. T. Dhur—C. D. Linton.

PEARLS FROM ST. AUGUSTINE.

WHATSOEVER else we do unto, as in many things we sin all, yet let us not differ in affection, but keep up and maintain love one toward another.

If he to whom thou doest good doth not regard it, He for whom thou doest it regardeth it.

To ascend to the Divine you must descend into the human.

In things essential, unity ; in things doubtful liberty ; in all things, charity.

Where charity is, there doth God reside. Possess charity and you will see Him in your own heart, seated as on His throne.

Behold ! the world trembleth and it is loved ; what would it do if it were all delight ! How wouldst thou cleave to the fair who so embraces the perishing foul ! How wouldst thou gather the flowers thereof who plucked not thy hands from the thorns !

Wouldst thou that thy flesh obey thy spirit ? then let thy spirit obey thy God. Thou must be governed that thou mayest govern.

The sufficiency of thy merit is to know that thy merit is not sufficient.

Despise not venial sins because they are small, but rather fear them because they are many.

Beware how you regard as trifling faults which appear of little consequence. An accumulation of small faults makes a very large one ; grains of sand gathered together one upon another form the banks upon which the vessel strikes.

If we do not restore that which we have injuriously obtained from another, our repentance is not real, but feigned and hypocritical.

A man may lose the good things of this life against his will ; but if he loses eternal blessings, he does so with his own consent.

Make a valley, receive the rain. Low grounds are filled, high grounds are dried up. Grace is rain. Why dost thou marvel then if "God resisteth the proud, and giveth grace unto the lowly."?

When God is slow in giving, Heavenly cuts off His own gifts to advantage : He does not withhold them. He weighs long desired are sweeter when they come ; if soon given they lose much of their value. God reserves for you that which He is slow to give you, that you may learn to entertain a supreme desire and longing after it.

There is a joy which is not given to the ungodly, but to those who love God for His own sake, whose joy He Himself is.

God is all to thee : if thou be hungry, He is bread ; if thirsty, He is water ; if in darkness, He is light ; if naked, He is a robe of immortality.

Marrow is the mission of my soul : may God enlarge it that He may enter in. It is ruinous, may He repair it ; it has that within which must offend the eye ; but who shall cleanse it? or to whom shall I cry, save Him?

I asked the earth, and it said I am not God, and all that is therein made the same acknowledgment. I asked the sea and the depths, and all that move and live therein, and they answered, we are not thy God, seek higher. I asked the winds, but the air, with all its inhabitants, answered, Neither are we the God whom thou seekest. And I said to all things that surround me, Ye have told me concerning my God that ye are not He, speak, then, to me of Him, and they answered He made us.

Surely, God is so just, that he can sanction no evil, and so good that he can permit no evil except it be with the design to bring a greater good out of it.

THE BRAHMO SOMAJ.

——o——

(Statesman.)

WE made some remarks the other day on the Eclectic Brahmos and the pretensions of their minister. It is the stupendous nature of these pretensions, and the apparent disproportion between the self-acknowledging personality of the Minister, as it stands in his own and his followers' writings and speeches, and the little God we are able to discern under it, that causes our admiration for what is attractive in the man and in his teaching to be mixed with a misgiving as to the genuine and substantial character of both. For as we said the other day, it is not permitted to us to regard Keshub Chunder Sen merely as a man of superior abilities, eloquence, and piety, devoting his powers to the social and moral elevation of his countrymen. He asks for more than the acceptance of his healthy and energetic labours, because of their inherent worth ; he claims the uncritical personal devotion of his followers. That he has his imperfections is, in general terms, readily enough admitted, but as "a saint, prophet, and devotee," he has been raised by God " above the world's criticism," and his followers must very clearly understand that in question or criticise his teaching or conduct, a something not practically distinguishable from impiety. One of the chief blessings for which an Eclectic Brahmo is instructed to pray is, that he may be enabled to accept and honor the "saint, prophet, and devotee " for "all that is good in him," and to regard criticism of him, or any attempt to discover and point out his failings, as unprofitable, if not impious. We do not think we exaggerate when we say that no religious teacher of whom we have any knowledge, except the founder of Christianity himself, has ever put forward so exacting a claim on the devotion of his followers to his own person as does Keshub Chunder Sen. And therefore it is that, as we have already said, there is no other alternative than to regard him as a prophet or an impostor. We felt that we had, perhaps, stated the alternative with offensive plainness, as all those would probably think who are inclined to regard him as neither prophet nor impostor, but as an able, eloquent, and good man, who, in spite of foibles and mistakes, is doing a good work among his countrymen in seeking to wean them from idolatry on the one hand, and atheism on the other. It is thus that we have ourselves sought to regard him; and looking at him tho', we found, much too much that we could not approve, much also which we could approve and admire. It seemed, therefore, to ourselves, that there was an appearance of harshness and coarseness in the alternative, as we stated it—that this man must be removed from the ordinary category of mixed characters, and accepted frankly either as a prophet of the first rank or an impostor. But his own writings and speeches, and the utterances of his organ, the Sunday Mirror, seemed to leave us no third choice; and the Mirror has at once and complacently accepted the alternative. This being so, we are glad that we put it clearly, even if it seemed harshly. The Mirror accepts it. This man is one of the Immortals. He is the latest of the Prophets, and from the nature of things it should seem that he must be the last. In him are summed up all the prophets and all the saints. Great teachers of old have taught "truths."; Keshub Chunder Sen teaches "truth." Other religious offer precious jewels ; Eclectic Brahmoism, that is, Theism as taught by Keshub Chunder Sen, offers to the world for the first time the complete string of jewels. It will, of course, be understood that we by no means assert that Mr. Sen professes to have already comprehended all truth—that even his string of jewels is never to be made more complete. But it is the string which by constant accretion is attracting and must attract all the jewels of truth to itself, and which, if not yet, is destined to be perfect and all-comprehensive. The church of the Eclectic Brahmos is, in this sense, potentially, the Universal Church of the future.

Having thus stated in very general terms what the pretensions of Keshub Chunder Sen and his church are, it may interest our readers to look for a moment at the Minister and a few of his latest followers on a missionary expedition. This expedition has a yet been greatly noticed abroad in the world; indeed, is characteristically unconscious, or at least inattentive, as regards a movement which, if it is really the first going abroad of the infant Universal Church, may be destined to rank historically with the sending out of the Twelve, or the flight of Mahomet, or rather, above both these events. The first account of this missionary expedition was published in the Mirror of Sunday, 9th November. The expedition, we are told, proceeded to visit the Upper Provinces, to preach the name of the Lord to the educated and un-educated of the land, but as its friends in the Mofussil had generally taken leave during the Durga Pujah festival, it was determined to spend the holidays in and near Calcutta. Operations were begun in College Square, "the centre of enlightenment and the focus of national education." The party "occupied this vantage ground, and commenced operations with the greatest enthusiasm, attacking infidelity and scepticism right and left, flank and rear. The Lord himself descended as the Minister invoked his blessing, and soon reinforced the army with the artillery of heavenly inspiration." "The onslaughts were terrible." The seven hundred came, saw who listened " felt, moved and thrilled." Singing followed, and " having thus fortified the position in the metropolis, the preaching army the day after crossed the river," and the expedition was fairly on its way. We may observe that later, as elsewhere, "no attempt is made to state the result of the action of heaven's artillery without fruitlessly. We have no lists of dead,

wounded, or prisoners—no statements of the numbers added to the Church. Had this been a party of Christian evangelicals, we would have learned the exact number of souls who were converted by this heavenly inspiration. Whether no converts were made, whether the minister is content to move the hearts of his hearers and then quietly wait for their spontaneous and deliberate enlistment under his banner, or whether he is simply more profuse than to commit himself to an arithmetical estimate of results, we do not know. We only know that while we have a good deal about enthusiasm and warm display of feeling moving those who heard the preaching, we have not yet any direct any record of the work of the renowned sergeant. We do not mean to follow the army closely, but only to glean glimpses of its doings here and there. The scene at Nalhati comes vivid before us. Five hundred people of all ranks from Brahmans and "delighted young souls" down to coolies and "public women" listened " with rapt attention" to the minister preaching in the open air, in spite of the copious y falling rain which drenched "the minister and the entire band," and probably felt as warming the audience, though the term "drenched" is perhaps used with just discrimination. A more enlightened audience was found at Chinsurah, and after having raised "the standard of the most High" at "four important and advantageous points," the army returned to Calcutta, preparatory to setting out on the "second or main campaign." In the meantime the sacramental Brahmo feast was celebrated and an excursion made to the shrine of the Dakhineshwar Hindu devotee. The great campaign began on the 1st of November. The army "left Howrah, by the 3 r. M. train with flags, surdivaja, trumpet, and other congratulated token." We may mention here that music, instrumental as well as vocal, constantly accompanied the march of the "army" and all its movements. At Luddge, Chandernagore, the minister spoke concerning Chaitanya, "the prophet of Nadya, who eaten as Eclectic increases so believes Brahmo read from day ramsadhan and sensuality, and whose spirit he was all Bengal cherished in their very life-blood." The Hindus shouted "Hari Haribole," women listened from behind shouts on the opposite house-tops. After the loud music "the kirtan followed, the Hindus from the audience carefully hearing the discourse and our Hindu getting exhausted, "that he prostrated himself before the procession, and rolled in the dust of the street. He went with the procession dancing joyfully. Everybody was struck. "Nothing more strikes a reader who has been accustomed to regard Keshub Chunder Sen as almost, if not altogether, a Christian, than the famous satisfaction which the Chaitanya of the " preaching army" shows in describing the enthusiasm with which it was every where welcomed by the Hindus. Here at last we have a reformer, an iconoclast, who knows how to win a joyful welcome and steadfast sympathy from orthodox adherents of the ancient faiths, and even from the priests of Hindu and Buddhist shrines. And the question arises—Is he a reformer ? Is he a prophet ? Clearly enough he is not one who is likely to be either stoned or crucified. Here is a significant sentence :—" The whole affair conclusively proved the sincere regard which the more devout Hindus feel towards our leader and our cause, in spite of our so-called leaders towards Christ." Those Christians who have still a lingering hope that Keshub Chunder Sen will embrace their faith and court obliviton as no ordinary preacher of the Christian gospel, and who are delighted when they hear him say as approving word of the Founder of their religion, must read what we have written with something like final despair. We follow the preaching army and try to catch something of the minister's evangel ; we find that the name on his lips is Chaitanya, not Christ. It is the spirit of Chaitanya that he "cherishes in his very life-blood." He preaches at Gya on the "Re-discrination of the Vedas and the Puranas in the present dispensation of the Brahmo Samaj." How far his teaching is moulded by what he has learned from Christianity, we do not know ; but it is clear that while he is willing to take from Christian teaching and example all that will aid his admiration, he has turned his back very decidedly away from the faith which has been the life of the Christian Church in all ages, and towards the ancient religion of the Hindus. Towards Hinduism he proudly except something like the attitude of Christ towards Judaism, not seeking to destroy the law but to fulfil it, destroying only that which is effete and corrupt in Hinduism, and seeking to restore and preserve the truth and beauty which lives in the source of ages become disfigured and corrupted. But Keshub Chunder Sen has outlived the days of fiery radicalism and fierce iconoclasm,

and repents his early adoption of so uncompromising an attitude towards ancestral customs which are repugnant to the ideas of Europeans and Christians. He has for several years been steadily making his peace with Hinduism. His idea seems to be—though we ought to state our apprehension of it with diffidence—to gain acceptance from the pious (including, of course, the superstitious) portion of his own countrymen as a Hindu reformer and sage ; to commend himself to the educated classes and to the West as a Collectic ; to really reform and purify Hinduism, and so truly to enrich his purified religion with all truth that can be gathered from all faiths ; and thus, knitting together East and West and fusing into one whole the truths of all religions, to establish the Universal Church of the future. This is a considerable ambition, and this, we think, some attention from us. We intended to give some further glimpses of the doings of the "preaching army," but our space is exhausted for the present.

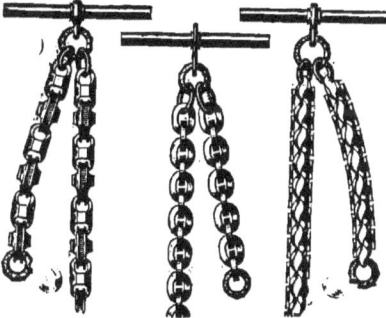

THE
INDIAN MIRROR
RATES OF SUBSCRIPTION.
(IN ADVANCE.)

Foreign.

For Twelve Months (via Southampton)	49	6	0
" (via Brindisi)	56	10	0

Sunday Edition.

(Both for Town and Mofussil.)

For One Month	...	1	0	0
" Three Months	...	3	5	0
" Six Months	...	6	0	0
" Twelve Months	...	10	0	0

(Single Copy Four Annas.)

Foreign.

For Twelve Months (via Southampton)	12	7	0
" (via Brindisi)	...	14	0	0

ADVERTISEMENT RATES.

For casual Advertisements 2 annas per line. No Advertisement charged for less than a Rupee.

For special contract rates apply to the Manager.

Printed and published for the Proprietor by W. C. Bonnerjee, at the Sun Press at No. 2 British Indian Street, Calcutta.

The Indian Mirror

[Edt.ed by Krishna Bihari Sen, M.A.]

SUNDAY EDITION

[Registered at the General Post Office.]

VOL. XIX.   CALCUTTA, SUNDAY, DECEMBER 7, 1879.   NO. 291.

CONTENTS.

Telegraphic Intelligence.

REUTER'S TELEGRAMS.

SEDITIOUS LANGUAGE IN IRE-LAND.

London, 6th December.

Thomas Brennan, land agitator, has been arrested in Dublin for seditious language used at a late demonstration at Balls.

SNOW-STORMS IN FRANCE.

Severe frosts have already occurred throughout Europe, and there have been severe snow-storms in France.

Consols 97⅞ ex coupon.

THE CZAR.

St. Petersburg, 6th December.

The Czar arrived here to-day from Moscow. The attempt to blow up the Czar's train was made by the would-be assassins taking a house adjacent to the railroad, and tunnelling thence under the line.

Editorial Notes.

We regret to hear that Father Rivington is ill, and that consequently he has not been able to do anything of public interest of late. Those friends, who went to see him in his new house at Mirzapore Street, must have been disappointed, for, the Reverend Father on account of his illness is still confined within his old lodging at Free School Street. We earnestly hope he will recover soon.

In the Logic paper of the First Examination in Arts, held last week, the examinee is asked to determine the validity or fallacy of the following arguments :—

(1) The existing world must be the best possible world, for to deny it would be to deny either the infinite wisdom or the infinite power of the Creator.

(2) The evolution theory must be true, for the number of its adherents among men of science is continually on the increase.

We should like that some of our readers would take up the arguments and prove their truth or falsity in these columns.

We have received a post card from Madras, with the following printed query upon it :—"Is it an advantage to the people of India to attempt to convert them from their ancient religions which, whatever may be their faults in European eyes, possess in an eminent degree the greatest of all gifts, charity, to the religion of the Reverend Mr. Miller's country-

men, Scotch Calvanism, which has been described by an eminent English writer as the most dreary, narrow-minded, illiberal, uncharitable, and tyrannical yoke ever imposed upon the intellect of man, and which in late years amongst its loudest and most boasting Professors culminated in the wickedest and most hypocritical swindle of modern times, the City of Glasgow Bank failure ?—B. A." We hope the writer will answer the question himself.

Verdicts on contemporary characters and events are almost worthless when we remember how Jeffrey of the Edinburgh Review disposed of the claims of four such mighty geniuses as Wordsworth, Carlyle, Hamilton, and Mill. The first he smashed by his celebrated "This will never do." Carlyle was conceited and mystical. Of J. S. Mill, he said:—"I once thought of John Mill, but there are reasons against him too, independent of his great unreadable book and its elaborate demonstrations of axioms and truisms." This is said of Mill's Logic ! The verdict on Sir William Hamilton is still more decided. Speaking of his article on Victor Cousin in the Edinburgh Review Jeffrey wrote to Macvey Napier :— Cousin I pronounce beyond all doubt the most unreadable thing that ever appeared in the Review. The only chance is, that gentle readers may take it to be very profound and to credit that the fault is in their want of understanding. But I am not disposed to agree with them. It is ten times more mystical than anything my friend Carlyle ever wrote, and not half so agreeably written. It is nothing to the purpose that he does not agree with the worst part of the mysticism, for he affects to understand it, and to explain it, and to think it very ingenious and respectable, and it is mere gibberish. He may possibly be a clever man. There are even indications of that in his paper, but he is not a very clever man, nor of much power; and beyond all question he is not a good writer or such subjects. If you ever admit such a disquisition again, order your operator to instance and illustrate all his propositions by cases or examples, and to reason and explain with reference to these. This is a sure test of sheer nonsense, and moreover an infallible resource for the explication of obscure truth, if there be any such thing.

To say this of Sir William Hamilton !

The recent Missionary Expedition is of some importance to the vegetarian cause. It has given a practical reply to the question,—can vegetable diet give the human system health and strength ? The members of the Expedition are one and all vegetarians, and abstain wholly from animal food. The labor and fatigue they have undergone, the extremely hard and arduous work they have gone through, the inconveniences and discomforts to which they were exposed, would appear to every thoughtful observer to be sufficiently trying even to the strongest constitution. And it is really a wonder how these gentlemen have stood the test. They have ran from district to district, city to city, through all the hardships of third class railway travelling ; they have with insufficient clothing exposed themselves to chill wintry cold, preaching for miles through the streets at

night ; they have kept up till midnight and sometimes till 2 a. m., conversing or singing or otherwise engaged ; they have slept upon the ground floor instead of charpoys; except when residing with friends, they have eaten coarse things taken from the bazaar and drunk whatsoever water they could get, from well, tank, or river ; they have always taken late meals, at 1, during the day, and at 11, at night. And in the midst of these irregularities and hardships these humble missionaries have subsisted chiefly upon rice, dal and vegetables, gram and milk. If Hindu sepoys have fought battles with only chhena and roti to keep them alive, we have here an instance of Brahmo soldiers b. ring the inconveniences of a missionary campaign by living exclusively upon vegetarian diet. Of course, nothing very extraordinary has been achieved by these men in the shape of self-denial. Nor are we inclined to assume that the merits of vegetarianism have been fully demonstrated. But this much we contend for, that here one may find some testimony to the fact that men can fight some of the hard battles of life in this country without taking animal food.

SOCIAL MORALITY.

At a recent meeting of the Indian Reform Association the subject of bachelor morality was discussed in a manner which cannot fail to excite general interest among the Native community. It seems that very few among us have bestowed upon the subject the attention it deserves. With the progress of education the number of grown-up bachelors is steadily, though slowly, increasing in the land. The very idea of premature marriage is repulsive to many among the educated classes, and the opinion is gaining ground that men and women ought to attain a sufficiently high standard of physical and moral development before they marry. In consequence of such a notion and also the growing desire to choose a suitable partner for one's self, the enlightened of both sexes manifest in these days a striking repugnance to early marriage. Half a century hence the number of unmarried adults will have largely increased, and perhaps as time rolls on we shall have in the midst of Hindu society, as there are among European nations, a good number of old bachelors and old maids. The prospect is by no means pleasant. On the contrary, it fills us with anxiety and apprehension and even with alarm. In a country where religion is fast losing its hold upon the popular mind, and where public opinion is not strong enough to regulate social conduct, who or what is there to influence bachelor morals and govern wild young men? We must speak unreservedly in a matter which affects so materially the moral interests of our country. In all countries the husband and the wife govern each other, and by mutual control manage to preserve domestic purity. The married are safe. But who will look after the character of the unmarried? Parents look after them so long as they are very young. But as they grow up, they become impatient of control, and if they are wild and intemperate, they will allow none to come in their way. If at this period of life they are wedded to good and pious wives, they settle quietly in the world, far away from the worst temptations of life. But if they do not marry, there is no knowing whither they will drift away. Many no doubt will remain in the path of virtue and conquer carnality. But many more will, we fear, prove too weak or unwilling to obey the voice of conscience, and sell their character for a life of reckless pleasures and unbridled sensuality. Especially in great cities and towns where the number of "unfortunates" is considerable, and where facilities for corruption of all kinds are abundant, and "taking liberties" is accounted a mere social irregularity and not a serious abomination, the danger is really very great. It is, therefore, desirable that the leaders of Native society should so influence and strengthen public opinion that the slightest impropriety on the part of a bachelor or a spinster may always be effectively checked and put down. Let not our young men be allowed to think that there is any merit in declining to marry early, if they defile their bachelor lives with impurity and dissipation. Not praise but infamy shall be his lot who prefers the questionable career of a wild bachelor. We Hindus hold virgin purity in high estimation, and both our boys and girls are most carefully guarded by their guardians against too free social intercourse with each other, and kept at a safe distance from every temptation to sensuality. Therefore, it should be the duty and interest of all patriots and reformers to do all in their power to protect the morals of the unmarried, and prevent all suspicions and unjustifiable "liberties" in which the sensual rejoice to revel, and which have proved the bane and curse of society in other parts of the world.

SAKYA MUNI AS A ROMAN CATHOLIC SAINT.

THOSE who have read the fourth volume of Prof. Max Müller's "Chips from a German workshop," must be familiar with a piece of information which, to say the least, is very curious. The fact which is announced there, is nothing less than this that Sakya Muni, the founder of Buddhism, is to this day recognised as one of the canonized saints of the Roman Catholic Church. The information is novel, even startling. Prof. Max Müller says :— "St. Josaphat is the Buddha of the Buddhist canon. It follows that Buddha has become a saint in the Roman Church; it follows that though, under a different name, the sage of Kapilavastu, the founder of a religion which whatever we may think of its dogma, is, in the purity of its morals, nearer to Christianity than any other religion, and which counts even now, after an existence of 2,400 years, 455,000,000 of believers, has received the highest honors that the Christian Church can bestow. And whatever we may think of the sanctity of saints, let those who doubt the right of Buddha to a place among them, read the story of his life as it is told in the Buddhist canon. If he lived the life which is there described, few saints have a better claim to the title than Buddha and no one either in the Greek or in

the Roman Church, need be ashamed of having paid to Buddha's memory the honor that was intended for St. Josaphat, the prince, the hermit, and the saint. History here as elsewhere, is stranger than fiction; and a kind fairy, whom men call chance, has here, as elsewhere, remedied the ingratitude and injustice of the world." The way in which Buddha came to be identified with St. Josaphat is told in a very interesting manner by Prof. Müller. The story of Sakya Muni and his four drives through the streets of his capital, whereby he became acquainted with sickness, old age, death, and asceticism, was reproduced in the eighth century by a Christian monk of the name of Joannes Damascenus. This man was for sometime chief councillor to the Khalif Almansur of Bagdad. It was in the court of this latter that the Indian stories called *Panchatantra* were translated into Arabic. This shows that Indian literature was in high repute among the scholars of Bagdad. Joannes Damascenus wrote a story, called "Barlaam and Josaphat." The plot of this resembles the story of Sakya Muni's four drives. Josaphat's father is a King, and, after his birth, an astrologer predicts that he will rise to glory; not, however, in his own kingdom, but in a higher and better world, in fact, that he will embrace the new and persecuted religion of the Christians. So in *Lalita Vistara* we read that when Buddha is born, the Brahmin Asita predicts that he will rise to great glory and become either a powerful King, or, renouncing the throne and embracing the life of a hermit, become a Buddha. Everything is done to prevent this. Josaphat is kept "in a beautiful palace, surrounded by all that is enjoyable; and great care is taken to keep him in ignorance of sickness, old age, and death. After a time, however, his father gives him leave to drive out." So also it is related in the *Lalita Vistara*, that Buddha is kept by his father "in his garden and palaces surrounded by all pleasures which might turn his mind from contemplation to enjoyment. More especially he is to know nothing of illness, old age and death, which might open his eyes to the misery and unreality of life. After a time, however, the Prince receives permission to drive out." Josaphat sees "two men, one maimed, the other blind. He asks what they are, and is told that they are suffering from disease. He then inquires whether all men are liable to disease, and whether it is known beforehand who will suffer from disease, and who will be free; and when he hears the truth, he becomes sad, and returns home. Another time when he drives out, he meets an old man with wrinkled face and slinking legs, bent down with white hair, his teeth gone, and his voice faltering. He asks again what all this means, and is told that this is what happens to all men; and that no one can escape old age, and that in the end all men must die. Thereupon he returns home to meditate on death, till at last a hermit appears and opens before his eyes a higher view of life as contained in the Gospel of Christ." Something very like this happens in the case of Buddha. The conclusion is irresistible. Joannes Damascenus borrowed his story from the Buddhist Scriptures, the *Lalita Vistara*. Professor Max Müller says :—" The story of Barlaam and Josaphat became a most popular book during the middle ages. In the East, it was translated into Syriac, Arabic, Ethiopic, Armenian, and Hebrew; in the West, it exists in Latin, French, Italian, German, English, Spanish, Bohemian and Polish. * * * But this is not all.

Barlaam and Josaphat have actually risen to the rank of Saints, both in the Eastern and the Western Churches. In the Eastern Church, the 26th of August is the Saint's day of ' Barlaam and Josaphat,' in the Roman Martyrologium, the 27th of November is assigned to them." The story is instructive, for it tells us how silently and unostentatiously has the East influenced the religious culture and opinions of enlightened Europe.

THE MISSIONARY EXPEDITION.

[FROM OUR SPECIAL CORRESPONDENT.]

CALCUTTA, 5th December 1879.

WE had only two days to spare for Ghazipore, and the whole work had to be done within the short space of time at our disposal. Notice was at once given by beat of tom-tom, as usual, saying,—"Bhaire, Calcutta se Babu ain, Dharm Katha aur Hari Kirtan hoga." It was a fine moonlight night, and the majestic Gunga rolled at the feet of the splendid ghat known as Thornhill Ghat, when about three hundred people, mostly Hindustanis, assembled on its steps, were listening attentively to the Minister's words against idolatry and half-hearted scepticism. He feelingly exhorted the auditory to ask the smiling moon, shining overhead, what it had to say concerning the Creator's love and glory. Then the bugle sounded, and the procession passed through the principal streets in the Native city, chanting Hindi and Bengali hymns. Next morning, Friday, 28th November, there was service in the local Brahmo Mandir, in the course of which there was a sermon in Hindi, and another in Bengali, which was most touching. The text of the latter sermon was from Srimadbhagavat,—" As the chaste wife wins the heart of the faithful husband so doth the true devotee win and subdue the heart of the Lord." Nearly fifty persons were present. Mr. Rivett-Carnac, Opium Agent, was good enough to ask the Minister to come and stay with him, and placed his splendid landau at the disposal of the party. Good God ! How the highest personages in the land honor these poor missionaries ! In the afternoon, the Minister called at the palatial and tastefully furnished house of the above gentleman, and had a most warm and cordial reception, tea and conversation occupying nearly an hour." Our march to the 'Promised Land' was the subject of a public lecture at the Victoria School, at 6 P. M., the assembly numbering three hundred persons. Mr Rivett-Carnac presided, and made a few brief remarks assuring the Brahmo leader of the sympathy of the European community, and expressing his conviction that the principles expounded by him were calculated to make the Natives good and loyal citizens. From the school the party proceeded to the Brahmo Mandir again, and there was a short service for the benefit of a few Native ladies, who sat behind the curtain. On Saturday we left Ghazipore early in the morning after bathing in the river. A tedious journey over fourteen miles in a ekhgram and ekkas brought us to Zumaneah about half an hour before train time. On the way we had our prayers separately. We were told our meal was not ready yet. A few moments of watchfulness and anxiety, for the train was shortly expected. Luckily, the train was a quarter of an hour late, and so we had barely time to swallow a rather hot dinner in haste. And what were the dainties we had? Rice and brinjal. The ceremony of eating was short but sweet. It soon appeared, however, that the soldiers had got only half ration, and felt the need of something **more** during the day. We **reached** Bankipore in the evening, and instead of stopping there, **we** at once pushed on to the Ghat, with a **view to cross over to** Sonepore. Alas! **The** ferry steamer had already left, and **we** would have to surrender ourselves to the tender mercies of Native boatmen and run the risk of spending almost half the night on the way exposed to night air and other inconveniences! But no! Fortunately, a funny little steam launch belonging to a Native contractor was starting off, **when some** men of our party shouted forth, and by timely interposition persuaded the "Commander" to veer round. The advance force soon crossed, **and** the remainder **of the party was brought up in country boats. We took several ekkas, and** somehow managed to roll up and down four miles of sand, till we reached our tent near the *Natchghar* at about **9 P. M. There was no** arrangement for dinner. **Yet we felt we were** fortunate **in having** secured a place where to lay our heads. *Puris* from the bazaar constituted our dinner, and then spreading our tired limbs on nature's *charpoy* covered with *zotrunch* which kind friends had lent, we enjoyed profound sleep. Next day, Sunday, we had both morning and evening service in camp. There was hardly any prospect of getting up a demonstration in the midst of so all-absorbing a fair as that annually held at Sonepore. Everybody was dreadfully busy with their own affairs and amusements. Nor had **we time or** appliances **to make the** experiment. Thousands of elephants, camels, cattle, birds, and articles for sale of all imaginable varieties filled the place, and **as regards the** people, they were only running to and fro. It was the world in miniature. But something was to be done. So on Monday morning, at 9 A. M., we began *kirtan* in the very heart of the fair; there **was** a short address, and we marched **through the** crowded streets **of the bazaar** to the Harihar Mandir, where people go to bathe, and thence back again, conveying the sweet name of God to hundreds and thousands of people. It was 10 o'clock when we were singing. On our return we had our morning prayer at 12, and then taking a hasty meal we began our return march. There were three elephants and one rickety carriage to bring our party to the Ghat. We reached just in time to catch the ferry steamer. Returned to Bankipore in the evening. Again and again at Bankipore, the inevitable connecting link! On Tuesday **after prayer** we started for Arrah, **reaching the station** at about 12. We had now come to the farthest point in the field of our missionary operations, and the party had worked themselves to the highest straining point. The Arrah battle was the last but by no means the least. Here heavy work awaited the exhausted soldiers. Within twenty-four hours were compressed **many engagements.** In the school compound, a very short notice drew together about six hundred persons, among whom were all the respectable Native gentry. The Minister made an introductory speech in English, and then followed it with a Hindi lecture, holding a plant in his right hand. "God in the plant and not God *was* the plant" was the burden of his discourse. He said to the people "see God in all objects, but do not identify the Supreme Spirit with matter." The address was philosophical, yet extremely popular and exciting. Then there was procession. At 8-30 P. M., there was a lecture in the school hall on the Sanskrit text, "Truth triumphs, not untruth." About two hundred persons attended. The

local Judge, Mr. Worgan, presided, and made a few complimentary remarks both before and after the lecture. He said that although it was not given to every man to speak so eloquently as the lecturer had done, yet it was within every one's power to appreciate what was said by each speakers. The argument, that it was not for Government but for the people themselves to initiate national reformation, required, he said, earnest reflection at the hand of the audience. Next day after service and breakfast at a friend's house, our party left Arrah for Calcutta. We reached Serampore early on Thursday morning, and went in carriages straight on to our favorite place of devotion known as the *Sadhan Kanan*. Here under shady trees we had our usual refreshing morning service, and then a short *kirtan* in the streets. From Serampore we crossed over to Barrackpore, and reached the Calcutta terminus of the Eastern Bengal Railway in the evening. The flags and the bugle announced the arrival of the party; and as soon as they entered the station they were greeted by a crowd of delighted and enthusiastic friends, with flower garlands, and thus at once began the chief Expedition hymn, "Mind say once Hari." There were torches and *garlands* and flags, and there was a most spirited *kirtan* through the streets to the Minister's house, the "Lilly Cottage," where suitable hymns and a prayer and benediction brought the Expedition to a close.

Brahmo Somaj.

The Minister will conduct service in the Brahma Mandir this evening.

Baboo Gour Gobindo Rai proceeds to Chittagong to celebrate the anniversary festival there.

The total collection in the Purse on account of the Missionary Expedition amounts to Rs. 580. The expense aggregate Rs. 445. Certainly the financial aspect of this new and interesting movement is cheering. When may we expect another expedition?

We are sorry to learn that neither Bhai Protap Chunder Mozumder nor Bnai Amrita Lall Bose is thoroughly re-established in health. The former, however, gave a lecture recently at Lucknow, and the latter conducted the anniversary service at the Lahore Brahmo Somaj.

The Lucknow Methodist paper has the following on the Missionary Expedition:—"The Brahmos, under the leadership of 'the Minister,' a they call Baba Keshub, are indulging in a 'Missionary Expedition.' A strong delineation of the best representatives of the Somaj left Calcutta some weeks ago, and are slowly working their way up the country. Muzaffurpore, Gya, Bankipore, and Sonepore, were the chief places visited up to the close of last month, and the forces of ignorance, idolatry, and Rationalism as the various places were, so it is represented in the *Mirror*, vigorously assailed, with preaching, singing, praying and conversation, in English, Bengali, and Hindi. How far the party proposes to proceed we have not learned, nor just what the result have so far been. We presume considerable good will be done in the way of general enlightenment, whether the Brahmo cause in particular be much strengthened or not. The more they preach and stir up of their old feather-tricks and make to inquire what is the truth about God and salvation, the better."

Our Minister delivered a public lecture at Arrah. Mr. J. R. Worgan, District and Sessions Judge, Shahabad, who presided on the occasion, concluded the business of the meeting with the following words:—"Babu Keshub Chunder Sen has commanded our attention for some time to-night by a very eloquent and able address; and I have no

doubt you will all agree with me in feeling that he has fully earned our best thanks for favoring us therewith. It is not given to every one to be able to express his thoughts on a subject of the kind treated by Babu Keshub Chunder Sen with the fluency and force that he has done to-night, but it is within the competency of all to appreciate and expressions of thought when placed before them by those who have that power, and this has been our case. In what he has said there is much that is worthy of reflection, both by those amongst us who have received their education, and by those who are now receiving it. To this latter class belong many of those assembled here to-night. To these all that has been said is of special force. I will only add that one point especially to Babu Keshub Chunder Sen's address strikes me as peculiarly true—The British Government gives its subjects in this country Education, but it is for them to use it."

The *Lucknow Witness* has the following:—"The other evening Babu Protap Chunder Mozumder, delivered an elaborate lecture on 'The Forces in Hindu Society' in the Baradari at Lucknow. The audience was large and respectable, and the lecture was greeted with loud bursts of applause. The forces to which attention was directed are these, viz., Education, Civilisation, and Hinduism. Under the first head the lecturer denounced in no measured terms the godless scheme of education carried out in Government schools and colleges, and represented the goal reached by our educated countrymen as very unsatisfactory. The lecturer under the second head represented civilisation as consisting, not in the accident of dress and food, but in the essence of character, and reproduced a number of current jokes to satirise the wrong notions of progress in vogue among a class of our educated countrymen. The lecturer under the third and last head of his discourse emphatically asserted that Hinduism was neither dying nor dead, and that Brahmoism generally represented as an exotic nourished by foreign literature, was the ancient religion of the country revived. The lecturer rapidly reviewed the sacred literature contained in the Sanskrit language, and showed that, though apparently hydra-headed, its unifying principle was Theism, the **religion** preached in Calcutta under the auspices of the Brahmo Somaj!"

Devotional.

We desire to know Thy intention clearly and fully regarding our relations to our minister. People say all manner of things against us. Some charge us with Popery; some call us slaves. What are we, we know not. Tell us, Father, **how we ought** to treat him.

There is no minister appointed but by me. Leaders of congregations are ordained by me. Therefore, treat your minister as one who hath commission from Heaven. His words ye must hear with faith and cherish with reverence.

But has he not errors? If so, are we not to discountenance and condemn them, and keep ourselves from whatsoever is wrong and unclean in him?

With his unofficial position Heaven has nothing to do. If he is a bad man at home, unprincipled, selfish, ambitious, angry, deceitful, jealous, untruthful, you will not surely impute his vices. For all his errors and impurities he shall bear **his reward both** here and hereafter. Like every other man **be too shall be** severely judged. And condemned **for his misdeeds by** man and God.

How shall we then honor him? If we freely criticise his opinions and doings and condemn his misdeeds is wrong in him, his tastes and ideas and deeds, we must treat him as we treat other people, as our equals and inferiors, praising the good and censuring the evil in them. How can we honor him as our leader and minister? That man shown us, O Lord, the way to escape the horrors of Popery, but we fear we cannot show our minister much respect nor can we unitedly realise the true welfare of our Church, and treat him simply as one of us.

As one of you while at home, but not when in his office. His official position is different. When we minister to your spiritual wants and offices his prayers, and directs your missionary movements and otherwise renders service for your spiritual improvement, then bow to him as your minister, and let the whole congregation adopt and follow his teachings. Like the manager of a secular institution, a bank or a mercantile concern, he must exact the respect and obedience of all the subordinate agents so long as he occupies his official chair. Elsewhere he may be treated as others. But in his official capacity he must as an ordained minister command the allegiance of all members of his congregation.

In what things are we to take lessons from him?

In all matters appertaining to the development and success of the present dispensation. How you may best realize the invisible God and your future home, how you may love and honor all the prophets and saints of the world, how you ought to pray and hold communion with the indwelling spirit, how you may blend the spirit of asceticism with civilization, how to harmonise faith and philosophy, these are the cardinal principles of the present dispensation, and in connection with these ye shall give your minister thorough obedience. He will give you material help.

So be it! But even in questions like these we **do not** get enough light from him, and what he says concerning them is not always intelligible to us. Shall we follow blindly where we cannot comprehend?

Not blindly but trustfully, hoping and believing that I will in the fullness of time make all things plain and clear to you. No man can fully explain the deep truths of the spirit-world, unless the Holy Spirit reveals them to each individual. Therefore believe, and I will add to your **faith** knowledge.

One question more, O Lord. If ever we think **him** mistaken in these important matters **connected** with his official position, shall we **not try to** convince him of his errors and dissuade **him from** his path?

It may be you are mistaken, and **not he, in those** particular instances. Therefore, by your **re**monstrances you may run the risk of tempting your minister to disobey me and transgress my will. Where he has received my command, he shall stand unmoved like a rock amid the allurements, calumny and antagonism of the world, and faithfully do my will. If ye have anything to say against him come and tell me. But remember I will hold my steward, your minister, responsible if **he** should in anything disobey an iota of my command for the sake of even the best among **you.**

Thy will be done.

Correspondence.

*[We do not hold ourselves in any way responsible for the opinions of our correspondents.—*ED., *I. M.]*

VEGETABLES *vs.* MEAT.

TO THE EDITOR OF THE "INDIAN MIRROR."

SIR,—My letter on the subject stated **at the** head of this, you were pleased to insert **in** your Sunday issue of 16th March last. When I penned the above communication, I did not imagine that I should again have to speak in defence of a mixed diet—composed of vegetable and meat; but now, that you have made, in your Sunday issue of November 30, a statement opposed to facts, I have, as **a** lover of truth, no alternative **but to take up** the subject again. The statement referred **to is** this:—"*Vegetarian dishes may be made as rich and dainty as meat ones.*" The *Spectator* **is** right when **it** says that the *messes of the vegetarians* ***are not*** *palatable*. I have some experience **of the** culinary art; and though, as one of the *oldest* subscribers to your valuable paper, I have always sympathised with you, I was cruel enough to exult, when your remarks under review, having been explained to two of my female relatives, who are **very** good adepts in the art of cookery, and **can, of course,** prepare not only vegetable dishes, **but can also** prepare *pelao, kabab, korma, et hoc genus omne*, laughed you to scorn. They **lay** stress on the fact that some **of** the **best** vegetable curries become doubly delicious, when there is an admixture of fish or meat. Take, *e. g.*, *kopirdalna*, made of **cauli**flowers or cabbages, potatoes and green peas. It **is** good, nay very good in its way; but who **will** deny that it would become more palatable, **if** *Ruhi* fish had formed one of the ingredients? *Aloo* (potatoe) *pelao* is certainly palatable, **but** does it not sink into insignificance when compared with *Ruhi* fish or meat *pelao*?

Yours &c.,
OLD PENITENT.

The 4th December 1879.

ON THE MEANING OF THE TITLE—SON OF GOD.

TO THE EDITOR OF THE "INDIAN MIRROR."

SIR,—One of the most curious instances in which the true eastern spiritual conception of Jesus got transformed into a western material conception, is illustrated by the use of the expression "Son of God." But on this point I must warn your readers that the authorised English version of the Bible is not always trustworthy. Thus in Luke I, 32, we read, speaking of Jesus, "He shall be great and shall be called the son of the highest." But in the original Greek the definite article is wanting before the Greek word for son (uios), so that it ought to be translated "he shall be called a son of the highest." Again, in Luke VI, 35, we read "Love ye your enemies, etc., and ye shall be the children of the highest." But in the Greek the word here translated "children," is the same as that translated "son" in the first mentioned text, and is, in fact, the regular Greek word for "son." Hence this text ought to be translated "Love ye your enemies, etc., and ye shall be sons of the highest." Thus the same appellation is given to all good men, as is given to Jesus. Again, in Matthew IV, 3, we read, speaking of Jesus, "If thou be the son of God." But there is no definite article in the Greek before the word "son" in this case either, so that it ought to be translated, "If thou be a son of God." Then in Matthew V, 9, we find "Blessed are the peace-makers, for they shall be called the children of God." But on turning to the Greek, we find that the word here translated "children" is the regular Greek word for "son," above mentioned, so that the text ought to be translated "Blessed are the peace-makers, for they shall be called sons of God." Here, again, we see that the appellation "sons of God" is given to all good men, though our translators try to reserve a monopoly of it for Jesus. In other cases, however, the authorised version fairly translates the Greek, and applies the expression "sons of God" to men: as in John I, 12; I John III, 1, 2; Romans VIII, 14; but in Galatians III, 26, the expression "children of God" is found where the original Greek has the word "sons," again. Hence we see that the expression "Son of God" was considered applicable in Jewish phraseology to any person of a godly character. In like manner we find the term "sons of thunder" (Mark III, 17) applied to two of the disciples of Jesus, who once in their zeal for him are said to have asked if they should call fire down from heaven on a village which would not accord him a favorable reception. (Luke IX, 54). So also one of the early Christians who, having land, sold it and brought the money to the apostles to be divided amongst all the brethren, received the appellation of Barnabas, which is being interpreted "Son of Consolation" (Acts, IV, 36). Thus the Hebrew expression of Son of God as applied to Jesus was perfectly innocent, but when it got carried amongst Greek-speaking populations, they sought to find some material basis for the conception. One theory then mooted was that Jesus was the son of God by adoption, and that at his baptism a voice from heaven said "Thou art my beloved son, this day have I begotten thee." This story appears in a few manuscripts of the New Testament, but it is not found in the English authorized version which prefers, and justly prefers, another reading (Matt. III; Mark I, 2; Luke III, 22). It is found, however, in some other early Christian writings, and it appears to be alluded to in the Epistle to the Hebrews (I, 5) where speaking of Jesus, we read that he was made better than the angels and obtained a more exalted name. "For unto which of the angels said he, i.e. God, at any time thou are my Son, this day have I begotten thee." And again in Ch. V, 5, we read that Christ glorified not himself, but he that said unto him "Thou art my son, to-day I have begotten thee."

Then another theory for justifying the application of the term "Son of God" to Jesus, was that he was his son by descent. This idea is shown in the genealogy of Jesus which is given in the 3rd gospel, which traces the descent of Jesus up to Adam, the alleged first man, and concludes thus—"which was the son of Adam, which was the son of God."

Thirdly came the theory of the miraculous birth, which gave rise to the really shocking stories at the commencement of the 1st and 3rd gospels. On this point we may say with Mahomet of the Almighty:—"Far be it from Him, that which they affirm of Him: He begetteth not, neither is he begotten, He only saith of a thing, Be, and it is."

Lastly came the theory that Jesus was an embodiment of the Divine wisdom, a reason which existed with God from before the creation of the world. This was derived from Alexandrian philosophy and **finds expression** in the 4th Gospel.

Our critical consideration of these topics need not blind our eyes to the spiritual lessons to be derived from them. Let us love our enemies, and do good, and lend hoping for nothing again, and we shall be sons of the Highest (Luke VI, 35). Let us be peace-makers, and we shall receive the blessing of being called "sons of God." (Matthew V, 9). Let us open our hearts to receive the true light of heaven, wherever, and by means of whatever person, God may shed it, and we shall receive power to become sons of God, (John I., 12). Then we shall see God as He is, and having that hope in us, let us purify ourselves as He is pure (I John, III, 3) and let us be led by the spirit of God, for as many as are so led are the sons of God (Rom., VIII, 14).

Yours &c.,
A. D. TYSSEN.

40, Chancery Lane, London.

Provincial.

DUMRAON.

[FROM OUR OWN CORRESPONDENT.]

The 2nd December 1879.

THE Missionary Expedition is undoubtedly a success. Who could imagine when it left Calcutta that it would be received cordially by all classes alike in Behar. At Dumraon, it met with a warm welcome from the Maharajah. The latter invited the party to his palace, without at first deciding how the people would receive persons of a faith that discarded idol worship and caste distinctions. The Pundits were put to great difficulty on this score. However, the Minister came on the 25th ultimo, and was received at the station by the Manager, a man of liberal views and polished manners, and his *Guru*, the Nagaji, who had been waiting there with half a dozen phætons, buggies, tandoms, &c. They then drove to the celebrated Garden House of the Maharajah, where many European gentlemen are almost daily worshipped with various *Upaharans* of mutton, beef, ham and fowl. It was there that the leader of the Theistic Church and his party were accommodated. In the morning the Maharajah, followed by a few courtiers came to the house for an interview with the Minister. This having been done after the usual ceremonies of *Shaheb salamat*, the Maharajah left the place in a hurry with a special request to the Minister not to deliver any lecture at Dumraon, as he feared his men would be all *corrupted*. The party then went to the *Toung*, a two-storied wooden roofed building standing in the heart of the jungle. Here they sat for prayer. In that forest with its large, umbrageous trees, its hundreds of monkeys and apes jumping and frolicking on **all** sides, the deer running timidly across the roads, the birds singing melodiously in praise of their Great Maker, and in the midst of other natural beauties, the Minister chanted the name of God, made doubly sweet by the solemn **quiet** of the place. The party was soon after **led** across the jungle by the Nagaji to his *Asram*, where he entertained them with a repast under shady trees, while he himself sat a little apart with his own *fakiri* wooden water-pots, &c. After **a** while they drove to see the Bhojpure ruins. On their return the Minister and the party were ushered into the local School Hall, where upwards of two hundred men were gathered, and arrangements made by the Manager, **who** cherished **great re**gard for the Brahmo Somaj, **for an address, des**pite the strict injunctions **of** his **master,** the Rajah. Amongst the audience, there were many Pundits well versed in the Shastras, but few who could boast of English education. The address was given first in English and **then** in Hindi. Though the latter is the language **of** the up-country—Hindus, yet, I am afraid, only a few could appreciate the address, as it contained many Sanskrit words which the *generality* of the people reading *Persian* and *Urdu* from childhood, were not expected to understand. The Pundits that came simply at the request of the Manager, but with hearts full of consternation, praised the spirit of the lecture and its unostentatious delivery. They were quite surprised to find the lecturer, whom they had taken for a mortal enemy to their creed, profess profound reverence for the ancient *rishis*, and then admired his *bhakti*, *prem*, simplicity and sacrifice. They contrasted him with Pundit Dayanund Saraswati and much at the expense of the latter. The address being over, the party went to the place of the Manager, chanting hymns in Hindi. They were followed and joined by hands. Is of men. The flags, carried by a Behari Brahmin, presented a novel spectacle to the people of the place. The procession was led by the Manager in his rich but decent clothing that contrasted well with the *Orrisa* cloth of the Nazaji, and the simple apparel worn by the members of the Expedition party. The Manager gave them a rich and delicious repast, and bade them farewell with a *Dakshina* of *Khillut* of Rs. 200 and five *thans* of English merlin. The party then started for Zamanabad.

I cannot conclude without offering my thanks to the Manager of the Dumraon Raj, who did so much to honor the party. Had it not been for his energy and exertion, the people of this place would still have been in blissful ignorance of the Brahmo Samaj and its devout Missionaries.

Literary, Scientific, &c.

The vineyards of Europe occupy some 17,000,000 acres of land, which annually produce about 3,294,808,000 gallons. France, Italy, and Spain respectively head the list of wine-producing countries.

A PROPOSAL to introduce Penny postage into Paris has been made by the Municipal Council, as at present each letter within the fortifications costs 14d. The Council recommend that there shall be twelve deliveries of letters daily, instead of only eight.

How fashion repeats itself has recently been strikingly demonstrated in New York, where a young lady has been married in her grandmother's wedding dress, made seventy years ago, and, though it was left unaltered, no one knew that the dress was not made in the latest style.

THE Planet Jupiter has, for some time past, been covered with a large vermillion—colored spot, and astronomers now state that the spot denotes some great disturbance of the planetary substance. The spot is believed to be an affection of the pangetory body itself, not of its atmosphere. It is elliptical in shape, situated in the northern hemisphere, and covers a space equal to about one-fiftieth of the whole visible surface. Such a phenomenon has never before been recorded.

HERE is something regarding politics which will excite the indignation of a portion of our young men. It is Mr. Ruskin who speaks:—"Young men have no business with politics at all, and when the time is come for them to have opinions, they will find all political parties resolve themselves at last into two, that which holds with Solomon that a rod is for the fool's back, and that which holds with the fool himself that a cravat is for his head, a vote for his mouth, and all the universe for his belly"

WE understand that the Railway up Mount Vesuvius has been successfully completed, and travellers can now ascend without difficulty to the edge of the crater. The line which is rather over half a mile long, starts from a station 880 yards above the sea, and rises 470 yards higher up the side of the mountain. It is constructed on a solid pavement, so as to preserve it from destruction by lava, and the traction is carried on by two steel ropes, moved by a steam-engine at the foot of the cone. To prevent the carriages from leaving the line, the wheels are made to catch the rails, and further, each carriage is furnished with a powerful automatic brake, in order to stop the train immediately in case of the ropes breaking.

M. CULLADON has contributed a paper on the *Origin of Hail* in the *Bibliothèque Universelle.* It is of very great interest and originality. M. Colladon undertook the enquiry, in order to test the truth of Faye's theory that hailstorms and cyclones were descending vortices, and declares himself directly against such an idea. After citing most of the older authorities, he describes his own experience, that ascbss clouds, when rain is falling, are highly charged with electricity, as he proves by Franklin's method with a kite. He then adduces evidence to show that, when hail or rain is falling, there is set up an in-draft towards the upper part of the cloud to fill up the vacuum produced, and that the particles carried by these currents are strongly electrified. This influx of fresh electricity supplies the enormous quantity required for a long thunderstorm, and the hailstones are carried horizontally by the violent motion, and grow in their passage. He shows that in hailstorms passing over an observer, the existence of cold horizontal currents has been noticed. He has obtained a most novel and indisputing confirmation of the existence of the in-draft caused by falling water by observations at the well-known waterfall at Vallencias, near Martigny. Habus ascended the gallery beside the fall, and close to the top has observed a violent upward motion of drops of water just outside the falling sheet. This direct observation goes far to controvert Faye's theories.

Law.

HIGH COURT.

ORIGINAL SIDE.—PREEMPTORY CAUSE BOARD.
FOR MONDAY, THE 8TH DECEMBER, 1879.

(*Before the Hon'ble Mr. Justice White.*)

UNDEFENDED CAUSES.

Gocool Chunder Bhattacharji v. Bissessur Mookerjee—Pittar & Wheeler.
Bansyraubob Sen v. Chunnolall Johurry & ors, —G. C. Chunder—Barrow & Co.
Kissory Mohun Roy v. Tarucknauth Biswas—Pittar & Wheeler.
Kissory Mohun Roy & anr. v. Syamakamod Mookerjee & anr.—N. N. Sen.

(FOR JUDGMENT.)

Gurupprossno Ghose vs. Brojonauth Kurforma—Hart—Swinhoe & Co.

DEFENDED CAUSES.

(Final Disposal.)
M. Z. Martin v. J. Hickman (*pt. hd*) Orr & Harries Sanderson & Co.
H. Heinhold & ors v. Coolrai & anr. Sanderson Co. Pittar & Wheeler.
S. M. Kachalmoney v. Monemoheney Dossee & anr.—G. G. Chunder—W. C. Bonnerjee.
P. W. Glass v. J. V. Beake & anr.—H. H. Remfry—Leslie.
Abdool Ally v. The Bank of Bengal—Troloona & Watkins—Roberts Morgan & Co.
Kirtee Chunder Mitter vs. J. R. Barry & ors.—Pittar & Wheeler—Barrow Watson & Co.
Gavepolye—M. (s. Sen—Barrow Watson & Co.
Hurry Churn Roy Chowraj v. Gopeeloll Panday—Trotman and Watkins—Hart.

(*Before the Hon'ble Mr. Justice Wilson.*)

DEFENDED CAUSES.

(Final Disposal.)
Gobinloll Soul & ors v. Debendronauth Mullick & ors. (*nr. hd.*)—Carruthers—Beeby & Rutter.
Carruthers and Jennings.
Nawab Nazir Moonsoond-howlah Br. v. Mahidl Begum & ors.—Miller & Bhanjo—Ghose & Bose.
A. P. N. Avanchelan Setty & anr. v. Moung Pho Mea & anr.—Sittanauth Dass—N. C. Burral.
Kally Chora Shaw & anr. v. Dunchby Bibee & anr.—Luckynath Mitter—C. C. Chunder.
Chandmull Aururwalah v. Sreekissen Khettry & anr.—Beeby & Rutter—Gregory.
Aubin-lrohbosoan Chatterjee v. Preonath Mookerjee & anr.—Bewley—Defendant in person.
Sreenath Row v. Tarraknath Mookerjee & anr.—A. T. Dkur—C. D. Linton.
Narayun Dehee v. Sreenauth Mookerjee—Ghose & Bose—Gregory.
Shibkristo Sircar v. Abdool Hakeem—N. C. Burral—G. C. Chunder.
R. Dickinson & anr. v. D. T. Shaw & ors.—Pittar & Wheeler,—Orr and Harries.
Soorbdt Missor v. Beldeo Misser—Hart—N. C. Bose, P. N. Ghose.

[Advertisement.]

JUST PUBLISHED.

VICTORIA RAJSUYA.

THE History of the Imperial Assemblage at Delhi, in Bengali, Royal 8vo., more than 250 pages, with photos, neatly bound in cloth. To be had at the Sanskrit Press Depository, Canning Library, or from the author at 40, Sunkar Haldar's Lane, Ahiritola.

Price Rs. 5, post free. 167

STATISTICS FOR GIRLS.

(*Young People's Magazine.*)

A YOUNG English statistician, who was paying court to a young lady, thought to surprise her with his immense erudition. Producing his note-book, she thought he was about to indite a love sonnet, but was slightly taken aback by the following question :—

"How many meals do you eat a day ?"

"Way, three, of course : but of all the oddest questions"—

"Never mind, dear, I'll tell you all about it in a moment."

His pencil was rapidly at work. At last he said :

"My darling, I've got it ; and if you wish to know how much has passed through that little mouth in the last seventeen years, I can give you the exact figures."

"What can you mean ?"

"Now just listen," says he, "and you will hear exactly what you have been obliged to absorb to maintain those charms which are to make the happiness of my life."

"But I don't want to hear."

"Ah, you are surprised, no doubt ; but so itsties are wonderful things. Just listen : you are now seventeen years old, so that in fifteen years you have absorbed oxen or calves, 5 ; sheep and lambs, 14 ; chickens, 327 ; ducks, 204 ; geese, 12 ; turkeys, 100 ; game of various kinds, 824 ; fishes, 160 ; eggs, 3,130 ; vegetables (bunches) 700 ; fruits (baskets), 663 ; cheese, 103 ; bread cake &c., (in sacks of flour), 40 ; wine (barrels) 11 ; water (gallons) 3,000."

At this the maiden revolted, and, jumping up, exclaimed, "I think you are very impertinent and disgusting besides, and I will not stay to listen to you !" Upon which she flew into the house.

He gazed after her with an abstracted air, and left, saying to himself : "If she kept talking at that rate twelve hours out of twenty-four, her jaws would in twenty years travel a distance of 1,321,124 miles." The maiden within two months married a well-to-do grocer, who was no statistician.

DIFFICULTY OF VERIFYING HISTORY.

—o—

(*Chambers's Journal.*)

THE evidence on which historical statements rest is often found, on close and careful examination, to be wofully faulty. The real facts are ascertained to have been different in important particulars ; or the conclusions drawn from them are greater than they can support ; or no origin whatever for the statement can be traced. Grave discussions (for instance) have arisen within the last few years concerning the evidence on which the events and personages connected with the past history of England and Scotland are depicted by historians ; we assuredly ought to know the truth on such matters, if attainable. Instead of which, charges and counter-charges of error are freely, brought forth. Other countries experience a like difficulty. For our own pages, however, the subject may be illustrated by examples which admit of being treated with a lighter touch.

At Puzzuoli, in Italy, is a convent which owns a fish-pond just outside the wall; and near the pond is a figure of a man who, according to legend, was struck blind while fishing there: a punishment for fishing in sacred water, or in a pond situated in consecrated ground. He was thus deprived for ever of the power of seeing the fish he caught. So far good ; but it has been pointed out that the idea is traceable to a much earlier date, when there was certainly no convent at Puzzuoli. The Roman epigrammatist and poet Martial had long before given the self-same story, but applicable to a fish-pond belonging to the Emperor Domitian.

What did Lord Chief-Justice Cockburn say concerning the handwriting which was brought in evidence during the far-famed Tichborne trial ? Surely, it may be urged, there can be no doubt on such a point as this ! And yet doubt there was and perhaps still is. The reporters of most of the London daily newspapers took down the words with unquestioned honesty of purpose ; nevertheless there were differences, chiefly in the use of small words and in punctuation, which led to two directly opposite conclusions—one that the learned Judge declared two handwritings to be similar ; the other that he had pronounced them to be strikingly dissimilar. The late Mr. Thom, who introduced this matter in *Notes and Queries*, was twitted with having made a difficulty of it ; but his reply was a good one—that the twitters virtually twitted to one another.

When Baron Marochetti's equestrian statue of Richard Cœur-de-Lion was set up in Palace Yard, one of the newspapers informed its readers that King Richard, on his death-bed, commanded his attendants to lay him on the floor naked and flog him, as a wholesome discipline. They flogged him thoroughly, and then he died. A search in the old historians has failed to bring to light any other authority for this than that Richard underwent some discipline at the hands of the clergy.

During the Tobacco Controversy in the medical journals some years ago, one of the combatants declared that the great Sir Isaac Newton was a determined smoker. This set inquirers to work ; and they found that the reliable biographies of the great philosopher do not support this assertion. On the contrary Sir David Brewster says that "when Sir Isaac was invited to take snuff, he declined either to smoke or to snuff, remarking that ' he would make no necessities to himself.'"

"Up Guards, and at 'em !" Much interest attaches to the controversy whether the Duke of Wellington used these words at Waterloo. It is agreed on all hands that his custom was to shelter his troops as much as possible from artillery-fire by taking advantage of such irregularities of ground as might present themselves. He caused the soldiers to sit or lie down till the moment of attack ; and then, when the enemy appeared likely to advance, he bade them rise and be the first to attack. The general belief is that he did this at Waterloo. An officer of the second brigade of Guards, writing some years afterwards his reminiscences of that eventful period, stated that the Duke at the time was not in such a spot that troops could have heard him, and that the "Up Guards, and at 'em!" was the invention of some writer more graphic than veritable.

The curious part of the matter is that when Mr. Wyatt long subsequently took a likeness of the Duke, as a preliminary to a statue, and asked him about the truthfulness, or otherwise of the popular account, His Grace replied that he did not remember having used the words, nor could he remember what words he had really used. Certainly they are rather more melodramatic than suited the plain-speaking Wellington.

The French have a great tendency to cherish sayings and phrases which were uttered, or are believed to have been uttered by celebrated men. This proneness is due in part to a pardonable kind of national vanity, and in part to a certain fitness in the French language to adapt itself to brief, telling, epigrammatic sentences and phrases. Multitudes of such examples are to be met with found on sober scrutiny to lack verification ; nevertheless they live, and seem likely to live in spite of criticism.

"La France est assez riche pour payer sa gloire," is attributed to Guizot, the statesman, when he signed a treaty of peace with a vanquished power without asking for a money indemnity. France has truly shown herself, in recent years, to be rich enough to pay for defeat if not for glory ; but the question is whether Guizot uttered the words attributed to him—words which brought upon him a taunt for boastfulness by the Opposition. It has been shown that the phrase was put into his mouth by a French journalist—in fact, a down right invention.

"La Garde meurt, et ne se rend pas !" said to have been exclaimed by General Cambronne, has in like manner been traced to a Parisian journalist; yet the French will doubtless continue to believe that the General, in relation to the condition of the famous Imperial Guard at a critical moment, heroically declared that the Guard would die rather than surrender.

"Fils de St. Louis, montez au ciel !" The Abbé Edgeworth is said to have uttered these pious but somewhat venturesome words at the execution of the hapless Louis XVI. The Republicans, who decapitated the king, had of course no belief that they were sending "the son of St. Louis" to heaven ; but the Royalists long cherished the idea that the words had really been uttered by the Abbé. When questioned afterwards on the matter however, he stated that the phrase was invented by the editor of one of the newspapers, and had not been used by him.

"All is lost except Honor," was long believed in France to have been the sole contents of a letter in which Francis I. informed his mother of his defeat at the battle of Pavia ; but when a recent examination of the King's letters was instituted, no such words were to be met with.

During the short Peace of 1814, when a hope was entertained throughout the greater part of Europe that the man of the terrible Napoleon was set for ever, the Count d'Artois—afterwards Charles X.—entered France from exile in England. To please or appease persons who feared that stern measures would be adopted by the restored Bourbons, he is credited with having said : " There is only one Frenchman the more: nothing is changed." This became current on the authority of Count Beugnot. The speech was certainly neat and epigrammatic, as expressed in French : " Rien n'est changé, Messieurs ; il n'y a qu'un Français deplus." It had been found, however, that the words were invented by a *littérateur* to adorn a newspaper account of Charles' public entry into Paris. The inhabitants of the gay metropolis rather liked poking fun at the somewhat obese Bourbon Prince Sir Robert Wilson, in his *Note-book*, speaking of a time when there was a general belief that the Count had really uttered the words imputed to him, narrates that when the once famous giraffe came to Paris, some of the wits made the animal say : " Rien n'est change, Messieurs; il n'y a qu'un bête de plus ;" and that when the giraffe was taken to the palace at the King's command, the animal professed to be mortified at finding himself no longer the greatest *bête* in the kingdom. We must here bear in mind that *bête* in French frequently denotes dull, foolish, stupid—an additional sting in the arrows of the wits.

In an article relating to the question whether and to what extent "History repeats itself" (inserted in this *Journal* for March 15, 1879), reference is made to the Rev. George Harvest, a clergyman whose erudition was more than equalled by his eccentricities. In sheer absence of mind he threw his watch instead of a pebble into the Thames. There is something so marvellously like this in one of Addison's papers in the *Spectator*, that one's suspicions are excited. Will Honeycomb's Club and Mr. Harvest's Club Sconce set Gardens and the Temple Gardens; seven minutes to spare in each case; the picking up of a curiously shaped pebble ; the intention to show it to a virtuoso ; the pocketing of the pebble and the flinging away of the watch—coincidences beyond measure strange. We have deemed it not unprofitable to dip into this matter a little. *Notes and Queries* quoted the anecdote of Mr. Harvest from the *Rock* newspaper, and at the same time drew attention to its resemblance to the *Spectator* anecdote. The *Rock*, we find, gave no authorities. A little search has brought under our notice two biographical notices or pamphlets, published early in the present century, each giving in full the anecdote of Mr. Harvest. He was, it appears, incumbent of Thames Ditton in the second half of the last century. His death is noticed in some of the London periodicals for 1781 ; but we have failed to trace the story of his watch and pebble farther back than thirty years after that date. As the two tracts or pamphlets are anonymous, we have no hesitation in stating our belief that some writer (name unknown) connected the story out of materials which he found ready to his hand in the *Spectator*. This question of Mr. Harvest may seem trifling in itself, but it affords a good example of some of the difficulties which arise in verifying history.

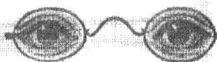

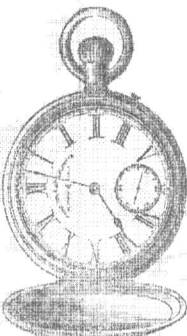

Life assured.	Year of Entry.	Amount paid by Society.	Premiums received.	Proportion of Payments to Premiums
Maj. J.C.D.S. Maj, England	1874	Rs. 3,000	Rs. A. P. 500 12 0	586 p.ct.
Dr. R. R., Cachar	1875	Rs. 500	805 0 0	...
T. V. N., Jubulpore	1875	1,000	76 5 0	1,315 "
E. G. D., Bombay	1876	2,000	468 0 0	427 "
G.T. Madras	1876	1,500	60 1 0	1,744 "
G. B., Jubulpore	1875	5,000	740 0 0	675 "
W. V., Poona	1876	3,000	290 14 0	1,034 "
F. C., Comewattee	1876	10,000	825 0 0	1,212 "
A. J. C., Mangalore	1877	3,000	102 0 0	2,941 "
M. R. A., Bombay	1878	5,000	323 0 0	1,501 "

The Indian Mirror

[Edited by Krishna Bihari Sen, M.A.]

SUNDAY EDITION

[REGISTERED AT THE GENERAL POST OFFICE.]

VOL. XIX. CALCUTTA, SUNDAY, DECEMBER 14, 1879. NO. 297

Telegraphic Intelligence.

REUTER'S TELEGRAMS.

ARGENTINE GOVERNMENT.

LONDON, 12TH DECEMBER.

The Argentine Government have invited tenders for the coinage of silver to the extent of from two to four milllion dollars.

Consols 97⅜.

FLOODS IN HUNGARY.

VIENNA, 12TH DECEMBER.

Disastrous floods have occurred in Hungary; great loss of life is reported, an 110,000 people have been rendered houseless.

THE NIHILISTIC CONSPIRACY IN RUSSIA.

ST. PETERSBURG, 12TH DECEMBER.

Arrests in Russia still continue, and in the possession of one prisoner was found a minute plan of the winter palace.

THE IRISH TRIALS ABANDONED.

LONDON, 13TH DECEMBER.

The Times publishes a paragraph stating that the trial of the Irishmen for seditious language has been abandoned.

DR. HUNTER AT BIRMINGHAM.

Doctor Hunter lectured last night at the Chamber of Commerce in Birmingham. He advocated a Treaty of Commerce between England and India for providing free importation of Indian products and abolishing Indian Import Duties.

FROM THE PRESS COMMISSIONER.

THE CABUL WAR.

FROM Cabul news dated 12th December states that General Massy endeavouring with horse artillery and cavalry to intercept enemy on Ghazni road was attacked by great numbers in difficult ground. The guns upset and were abandoned temporarily after repeated charges of cavalry. They were subsequently recovered by MacGregor on arrival of General Macpherson's force. Later the enemy attacked hills south of Bala Hissar, but were beaten off with loss. Our loss is 18 killed, including Lieutenant Hardy, Artillery, Heaney and Ricards 9th Lancers and 25 wounded, including

Cleland and Mackinzie 9th, Cook 3rd Sikhs, Forbes 14th Bengal Lancers.

Editorial Notes.

WE regret to notice that Mr. Spurgeon's failing health has obliged him again to leave his church and retire to Mentone for the purpose of recruiting his health.

——:o:——

THE Lucknow Witness publishes in a supplement a sermon by Mr. J. N. Darby, "the renowned leader of the Plymouth Brethren," entitled a "Reply to Babu Keshub Chunder Sen's Lecture on 'India asks,—Who is Christ?'" As we understand a copy of the sermon is already on its way to India to our address, we postpone our remarks for the present.

——:o:——

THE Viceroy advised the young noblemen of the Mayo College to cultivate the study of Urdu and Persian. "I am persuaded," he said, "that you will find the knowledge of these languages most valuable in after life, for to the Hindi-speaking youth in this country they open out the modern literature of all India." His Excellency touched a delicate chord here, and we are afraid his advice will not elicit a response in many quarters. In the first place, it is not true that Urdu or Persian "opens out the modern literature of all India." We doubt whether any original productions like those we have met issuing from the Bengali press have come out in Urdu or Persian of late. In the second place, Persian is not in any sense the Native language of India. Indian patriots love their Sanskrit as ardently and sincerely as they do love their own selves. If they are to take up any languages, they are sure to be those that are the direct modern representatives of Sanskrit.

——:o:——

A WRITER who signs himself R.O.B. has made a glorious discovery. Descanting on Brahmoism that wiseacre says in the columns of the Lucknow paper :—"If we were deliberately to represent Brahmoism as fitted to do what socialism is doing in Germany, and Nihilism is doing in Russia, a storm of indignation would be raised against us. Brahmoism has loudly and ostentatiously represented as the very salt of the earth, the palladium of social order, political liberty and moral reform * * * But if through its fair body of smooth speeches and assuring promises we endeavour to penetrate to its animating spirit, we shall see the inaccuracy of our first impressions, and represent it as the Lord of Misrule at whose shrine hecatombs have been offered by the champions of the political principle which has appeared under the varied names of chartism, agrarianism, communism, socialism, nihilism, atheism, and antitheism, and ravaged various parts of the globe!" "R.C.B." has a little of the forty-nine in him.

WE hope we are not correctly informed that Pundit Dayanund Saraswati does not speak respectfully of the religious beliefs of the people among whom he preaches. At a certain town in Behar he is said to have offered to kick at the stone idol of the Hindus. This behaviour, we are told, produced a very unfavorable impression, and it certainly prevented the words of the learned Pundit from reaching the ears of the people. From the Hindu iconoclast to the ardent Christian Missionary is but one step, and we are not surprised to read the following sentence in the Lucknow Witness :—"When the Brahmins are publicly exposed as the greatest rascals of the land, their crimes brought to light and due punishment meted out to them without favor, as to the meanest Pariah, the order receives a blow which goes far to spoil the veneration which it has managed to throw around it self for centuries." God forbid that we should ever use language such as this in speaking of any considerable section of our countrymen. Charity speaks in quite a different strain.

——:o:——

LORD CARNARVON lately delivered an interesting and praiseworthy address at Winchester. The striking point in his address was that the average sermon in England was not as good as the average churchgoer had a right to expect. In order to improve this state of things he made the following proposals:—"that only clergymen of proved ability should be permitted to preach; that the art of preaching should be more closely studied, and practically illustrated from pulpits by nomadic professors; that fewer sermons should be preached; and that clergymen who were not remarkable for literary power should read the discourses of divines of recognised merit instead of delivering their own." But Lord Carnarvon did not touch the reasons why English preaching was so poor. The World suggests the fact of the subjects being divested of practical and contemporary interest as one of the causes, and says that "too many of the sermons which are now heard in our churches are without any reference whatever to the affairs of daily life; they do not come home to men's bosoms and business."

——:o:——

LORD LYTTON delivered an excellent speech before the pupils of the Mayo College, Ajmere, on the occasion of his visit to the Indian Eton. With the general tone of his remarks we agree, and we hope that the young men whom he addressed will cherish in their hearts the noble words of advice given them by their august visitor. The portion of the speech which explained the philosophy of tone as the result of harmony was excellently conceived. The following paragraph embodies a bit of sound advice which we commend to those who put themselves denationalised by their first visit to England. His Excellency said :—

Do not suppose, my young friends, that because I commend to your adoption English habits of thought and activity, I should think the better of any of you, if on leaving the College, you left behind you your natural respect for the elders of your race, poor personal establishment to the companions of your childhood, or your social sympathy with any honest class of your country-men who have not acquired all the educational ad-vantages here opened to yourselves. No. "It is a dirty bird that fouls its own nest." For my part I despise any man who affects to despise his own country, and I should consider that your educa-tion here will, indeed, have been in vain, if it has not trained you, not only to higher sympathies with your English teachers, but also to warmer affection for your own countrymen, who will look up to you so long as you do not look down upon them.

These words ought to be engraven on the heart of every young man who is receiving an English education.

THE *Pioneer* refers to our suggestion that Mr. Lal Mohun Ghose should deliver a public lecture on England, and says :—"Yet the same paper remonstrates with the many who compare Wasudeo Bulwant Phadke, the Dacoit, to Tell, Washington and Gari-baldi." If Ghose be an Indian Hampden, then Bulwant is, at least, Washington." We confess we do not understand the logic of this. There are some Europeans to whom all Indian faces look the same. A *mehter*, a *Babu*, a Prince and a Maharajah are all the same, because they happen to have the same face. A man whose imagination can soar to this height will not be thought unreasonable if he thinks that the *chaprassis* of his office who wore guilty of a strike, the sweepers of Calcutta who defied Mr. Mai-mule, Nana Saheb who killed Europeans, Balwant Bhadke who led a dacoit band, and Mr. Lal Mohun Ghose who led an agitation in England, belong all to the same merry crew and hail from the same jolly place. The classification is a convenient one; but, seriously speaking, it diminishes the respect we hitherto felt for our contemporary's in-telligence. If the writer of the para-graph in the *Pioneer* were to enter the in-tellectual list with this "Indian Hampden," we should not be at a loss to guess the re-sult. He would certainly find the great gulf that separates a Balwant Phadke from a Lal Mohun Ghose.

THE following jargon about newspaper contemporaries may be interesting to our readers :—In the early part of this the *Nine-teenth Century* of the *Christian Era*, a *Citizen* of the *World* strolled at night along *Pall Mall* on his way from *Belgravia* to *White-hall*, accompanied only by the *Echo* of his footsteps. An old *Engineer* and soldier of the *Queen* he had travelled by *Land* and *Water* the greater part of the *Globe*, and had, since his *Broad Arrow* days, fought under more than one *Standard*. Taking out of his *Tablet* he stood and wrote as follows :—"The study of *Public Opinion* offers a wide *Field* for the intelligent *Spectator* and *Examiner* of the *Times*.—" At this moment a *Watchman*, who had been a close *Observer* of his movements, approached and said, "Come, my noble *Sportsman*, you must move on !" "And what if I refuse?" demanded the other, standing like a *Rock* with his back against a *Post*, immovable as *Temple Bar*. "To be *Brief* with you, my friend, I shall in *Truth* stay here a *Week* if I think proper." "Well," rejoined the *Civilian*, "I am the appoint-ed *Guardian* of this thoroughfare *All the Year Round*, and I protest against your mak-ing any *Sketch* or *Record* here ! Are you a *Builder* ?" Instantly a group of *Iron* was laid on his arm. "Do you wish me to *Punch*

your head ?" asked the *Traveller*, "Oh, no," replied the other, all in a *Quiver*, "pray don't, I was only in *Fun*."

IF Utopia were true, how much we should like that the ideal hygienic picture not up by Dr. N. B. Richardson were specially so. This learned doctor sees no reason why man's age should be confined to three score and ten and not prolonged to a hundred and twice ten. He draws thereupon "a picture of ideal cities, where the people have never entered into war, but have produced re-markable painters, sculptors, architects, musi-cians, and poets, with many men of distin-guished ability and originality in science and literature. The cities are moderate sized, five separate dwelling-houses to an acre of land, with five persons in each house. The houses, large or small, are all built on arches, with gardens around and on the roofs ; the bed-rooms are disconnected from the living-rooms. The human body has its natural work, rest and play. Out-door life is the first thought, and all are taught to ride, swim, row, walk, skate, and climb. The dress of both males and females is loose, and there is daily ablution. All has a knowledge of phy-siology, and of what are and are not healthy places. All carriers of contagion are des-troyed by fire, and intermarriage between healthy and unhealthy persons is prohibited. Simplicity of food is another rule, and natural rest is taken for which purpose they follow the example of the birds and setting with the orb of day." How beautiful is Utopia !

WELCOME TO LORD LYTTON.

WE accord a most hearty welcome to Lord Lytton on his return from up-country. A sad incident marred the effect of His Excellency's arrival. A Eurasian lunatic shot at the Viceroy, while the State carriage was going over the Strand Road, though the shot took no effect and the man himself was caught in no time. It is probably some relief to know that the would-be assassin was not a Native, Hindu or Mahomedan, for he had been, the fact would have by this time spread a sensation over the country, and given food to the morbid imagination of many people where-by a solitary instance of misdemeanour would have been magnified into an extensive conspiracy. Fortunately it was a Eurasian lunatic, and that puts an end to all odd surmises and conjectures. The event, however, is not without its significance. For it shows how the lives of Viceroys and the highest function-aries hang by the point of a needle, and the least ruffle of temper or the least outburst of discontent might deprive a country of its ruler. To Lord Lytton we beg to offer our heartiest sympathy and to his family our warmest congratulation on this happy escape. Lord Lytton possesses many excellent quali-ties which ought to endear him to the people. As a scholar and genial friend of progress His Excellency ought to have entered more largely into schemes of national importance. Unfortunately he came to India burdened and entrusted with a policy which does not allow of a quiet devotion to plans of home policy. Into the troubled vortex of Afghan politics we need not enter here, nor need we allude to those other questions of finance, famine or public opinion, which have gone far to lessen the popularity of the present Government of India. We have the mis-fortune to differ with the present rulers on most of the general questions of policy which have marked the recent administration of the

country. We believe that the tendency of their measures is most deplorable, as throwing the country half a century backward, and we know that any Liberal administration must be pledged to upset the policy of its predecessor. For all that we still welcome Lord Lytton. We believe His Excellency is about to com-plete the fourth year of his administration, so that unless circumstances compel him to resign, we may calculate upon bidding him farewell after another twelve months. May we hope that during the short period of his stay in the metropolis His Excellency will be so good as to invite the loyal co-operation of our coun-trymen in all affairs of administration—a co-operation which, we may say, had hitherto been repelled ? An impression has got abroad that the present Government is not well disposed to the cause of Native enlightenment, at any rate of the social and political elevation of educated Natives. How far the charge is well ground-ed, we are not in a position to say ; at any rate, Lord Lytton may not be, and we would fain believe he is not personally responsible for any measure that may have given color to it. But we may say this much that whatever the cause, it is in the power of the Viceroy to remove the impression and infuse that element of loyalty in our public men which personal contact with the governing power alone can create. A little condescension, a little interest in works of public importance, a little display of confidence would bring His Lordship into deserved popularity. We regret that no occasion has hitherto been given for the display of these necessary viceregal equali-fications. No advice would have been neces-sary on this score ; but, as we have said, an impression has gone abroad that the pre-sent Government is anti-Native, and we like with our whole heart that this should be removed. Many an educated Native has been intellectually benefited by the works of the great Lord Lytton, his father. The very gratitude which binds the country to the father should bind it to the distinguished son who has come to govern it.

THE PHYSICAL SIDE OF HINDU YOGA.

THE accounts which have appeared in this paper of Ramkrishna, the Hindu *yogi*, of Durkineswer, have excited a large degree of curiosity in the public mind, and many, we learn, go to interview him. The opinions which are formed on the spot are, as may be expected, of a varied nature. Some go and come away pleased—charmed as they say—while there are others who actually denounce him as an impostor. Very few take him at his proper worth. Those who praise him are induced to do so by the wonderful sight of his mesmerism or semi-conscious states. He is great, they say, because at any moment he can become insensible. This, we beg to say, is the least part of him. Religious superiority does not attach itself to one who displays it in a condition of un-consciousness. The thoughtful man would, on the other hand, be proud of his con-scious superiority. The fact that people attribute Ramkrishna's greatness to his inability to exert control over himself betrays the mistaken nature of Hindu opinion on religious culture in general. Ramkrishna, we say, is great, not because he becomes unconscious at times, but because he has such wonderful experiences of spiritual life to unfold before his hearers. A man zealously addicted to religion, having sacri-ficed health, wealth and family for the attainment of salvation is a sight rare enough in these days. His heart-stirring wor s, parables that carry the very marrow of religion, illustrations which are bewitching by their simplicity; his terrible earnestness which becomes irresistible in its fury when it has to confront a man of little belief, all these stamp him out as a man almost unique in the Hindu community. Yet let Bengal once know that Ramkrishna is a good man, a gentleman, a wise man, who can speak many wise and sage words, but one who does not possess the gift of losing his senses, and lo! the willing idolatry of thousands will give place to captious criticism and cavil. So much is the national mind subject to the influence of mystery. People think that this unconsciousness is a miracle—the gift of gods. We believe the superstition can be accounted for. Like spiritualism, the yoga system of the Hindus has its physical side, and this physical side, which both spiritualists and yogis account for by supernatural methods, may, we think, be explained by physical science, or we should be more correct if we said the science which explains the relations between the mind and the body. We have always expressed our opinion that this science has yet to be discovered, but that from what little has been discovered, we may positively infer that the spiritual phenomena referred to above are to be traced to the influence of laws as certain and unvarying as those that regulate the actions of the physical world. Now yoga, according to its professors, begins in a state of physical preparation. By a system of suppressed breaths and intense concentration of the attention upon such a part of the body as, for instance, the tip of the nose, the mind is carried to a state of unconsciousness or semi-consciousness which we have noticed in spiritualistic séances. The true end of yoga, say the shastras, is to free the mind from the bondage of the body and carry it to the Infinite Mind. The road from the body to the mind, in other words, from the physical to the spiritual, is the region haunted by those phenomena which are known as dreams, somnambulism, clairvoyance, &c. It is in passing through this road that the ancient yogi found himself suddenly encountered by strange sights. The yogi in his clairvoyant state was thought to be possessed of supernatural powers, of strength sufficient to conquer a lion, of command over the past and future, and of powers of divination not possessed by ordinary mortals. We read in our ancient books stories of rishis exerting a magic influence over tigers and other beasts of prey, reading other people's minds, foretelling events, and capable of destroying the wicked by their righteous and oftentimes unrighteous indignation. Science whispers to us that religion has nothing to do with these strange phenomena, and the yoga shastra tells us that these stages are passed by the man who has not attained the supreme spirit. But the soul that has freed itself from the world and the body and found itself face to face with infinity, is above the influences of these petty phenomena. It is incapable of supernatural efforts, simply because it has surrendered itself entirely to the Divine influence. We thus see that the real yogi is free from the supernaturalism which a credulous world seeks to fasten upon him. He may have to pass through the clairvoyant state, but when they once attains the goal of his ambition, that state vanishes away, and the soul becomes disregardful of mere dreams and illusions. Ramkrishna has not had to pass through the many-faced clairvoyant state, but the physical restraint which yoga requires, did exert a remarkable change in his power of self-control, so much so that what was a part of education and stern necessity became a second nature with him. It is now true of him that the bewitching name of God renders him senseless. But, then, it must be said that Ramkrishna himself is not quite satisfied that he should so often lose his consciousness. This proves the very thing we were going to say that the true yogi never cares for the adventitious aids of a delirare supernaturalism.

MISSIONARY EXPEDITION.

THE Brahmo Missionary Expedition has returned, and it is certainly desirable that we should place before the public a summary of its operations and results and a brief statement of its guiding principles. Many here and in the provinces are anxious to know more than they are already aware of concerning this so-called expedition. What is it? What has it done for the country? Why this ambitious organization? Whither this ostentatious military march? We shall try to satisfy public curiosity by giving an explanation of this novel and interesting movement. Its novelty is evident. For many years, it is true, yet from its very foundation, the Brahmo Somaj of India has worked as an essentially missionary association and its agents have gone forth in all directions to disseminate the saving truths of Theism. They went about singly or in groups, here and there, and always achieved a large measure of success whenever they went. But never was there so solid and compact an organization. Never were the missionaries so thoroughly and spiritedly united in a crusade against the enemies of Heaven. It was a warlike move, an aggressive union of soldier preachers. The time had come for a military demonstration. Rationalism, prayerlessness, unbelief, despondency, carnality, worldliness were fast growing both in and outside the Brahmo Church, and there were visible signs of spiritual decadence among professed Brahmos which were painful and startling. A vigorous move was needed. The voice of the Great Captain fell upon the still waters, and there was a ruffle at first, and soon a mighty wave. Almost all our missionary brethren, as many as were available, stood forth in response to Heaven's command. There was to be no tame preaching, no dilatory propagandism with the pen or the lips, such as had been practised before by individual preachers, but a desperate and violent charge of a battalion of drilled soldiers under the Divine Captain. Arms and ammunition and all necessary equipage were soon ready, and the army was completely furnished for military service. There were four flags, three of which bore the inscription Sathyamera Jayatei. "Truth will triumph," in Bengali and Devanagri characters, and the other contained the words, "Come all nations unto the True God." The chief officer was entrusted with the bugle, which was intended to cheer and excite the soldiers. The mridanga served as a terrible cannon, a forty-pounder whose peals would shake a whole army of infidels, and the pointed chtara served as bayonet. A crimson purse in the hands of the Secretary of the Expedition indicated that no black malt was to be levied, but that voluntary contributions freely poured into the beggar's purse were to meet the entire expenses of the Expedition. There was no calculation, no subscription-book. The army started believing that they would earn their bread and the sinews of war by begging. Their motto still was, "Take no thought for the morrow." The operations began on Tuesday, the 4th October, and ended on the 4th of December, extending over seven weeks. The main campaign, however, may be said to have begun on Saturday the 1st November, when the Expedition started for the Upper Provinces. The total number of miles over which the upward journey extended may be estimated at about six hundred miles. The places visited by the party were, —

CALCUTTA, HOWRA, NAIHATI, GOURIPPA, CHINSURA, DHINESHWAR, CHANDERNAGORE, JAGARDAL, NOKAMEI, MOZUFFERPORE, GYA, B-NEIPORE, DOMRAON, GHAZIPORE, SONEPORE, ARRAH, AND MOREPUKER.

The aggregate number of persons addressed in the above places, has been computed at nearly ten thousand souls. There were altogether thirty-six lectures and sermons, in English, Bengali and Hindi. There were sixteen open-air meetings, and twenty-four nagar kirtans or street procession. The total collection in the purse amounted to Rs. 580, and the proceeds of the sale of books by colporteurs attached to the army aggregated Rs. 65. From the above statement some idea may be formed of the distance travelled, the time occupied and the amount of work done. As regards the vehicles employed in travelling from place to place, they were of various kinds, such as intermediate, third and fourth class Railway carriages, conveyances, ghurries, shigram, palki, elephants; and while crossing rivers the party used steamers, steam boats, big and small country boats. The meetings addressed represented all classes of our countrymen, and also the official and non-official European community. There were Commissioners, Judges and Magistrates, and Professors and Indigo Planters. The educated Bengali Babu, the old up-country Brahman Pandit, the Zemindar and the wealthy Bania in richly embroidered cloth, the ignorant Tirhuti mali perfectly innocent of English literature and science, the Gyali priest, whose interests were identified with those of his idols, the sycs, the khitmutgar, and the Darwan, who had succeeded in squeezing away a few annuities from their masters' service, all were assembled to hear what our Minister had to say concerning God and Providence. The mob, the poorest and the lowest gathered round him and most eagerly heard the "Pandit" as they called him, and the sweet and popular songs of the Expedition. The whole thing, we say with thankful hearts, has been a great and decided success. The Expedition has found a warm welcome wherever it went, and the only thing which the people regretted was the shortness of its stay in each place and the rapidity of its movements. They all sincerely wished and importunately desired that the party should remain with them and serve them longer. They one and all regretted that the Expedition only came, conquered, and went away. But such was the Lord's command. An enthusiastic demonstration, popular excitement and speedy victory. That was the creed of the preaching army. The object of the Expeditionary movement was not to stay and make converts, to form and organize, but simply to excite and animate the public mind, and cast the seeds of truth on all sides. One thing has been proved. The fateful assumption which interests most people that the Brahmo Somaj is a declining institution has been exploded. It has been conclusively proved that this church of God is still a living and a growing power. The success of the Expedition is due not to human eloquence or intelligence, not to any earthly influence, but to the spirit of poverty and resignation and the power of faith and prayer in those who composed the Expeditionary force, and above all to the simplicity and sweetness of the gospel of God's motherly love, which the party have uniformly preached and sung. The Mother, the Mother, the Mother,—this is the battle cry with which the Expedition has humbly yet boldly fought to conquer the land, and its success has, therefore, been so great and so glorious.

AN ADDRESS TO THE HILLS AT GYA.

Sunday, 16th November 1879.

[Translated from Bengali.]

O ye hills, far and near, ye are the habitation of the Supreme God. As far as the eye can reach on either side I see you, a wide extending range of hills with the head of each exalted. Ye are not ordinary things. The Lord has not created you in vain. There is a deep purpose for which ye have been made by God so noble and exalted. Ye are fixed and immovable. Ye are standing before us as solid and impregnable citadels. Ye shall not move. None can remove you to another place. The Almighty hand of God has established you. Who among emperors is so mighty as to assail you? Surely you have been created for a high purpose. To show unto us how to make our faith firm and immovable,—that is the reason why ye are on earth. Teach us, then, ye hills, what ye are appointed to teach us. Your foundations are firmly established in the ground, but your heads are raised far above the world, and ye are looking at the high heavens. The azure sky is spread over your heads. The low ignoble world ye have left below. Your ascetic nature has kicked at all the little things of the earth, and soared high to converse and commune with the heavens above. While your feet are firmly planted in the earth, so as never to be moved, your heavenward heads have risen to the sky above. Then again, over your heads are first gathered the rains which descend from above, and after cooling and refreshing your heads, they go in torrents to the fields below to scatter (plenty and prosperity on earth). Ye hills, ye friends of our hearts, speak to us. Men hate you as unworthy matter. But at the feet of the Lord ye have assumed the attitude of solemn meditation. Ye are superior yogis. Teach us yoga. O ye hills before us, be not mute, but speak. Speak in your Native vernacular, in your natural dialect. Ye hills, ye brethren, ye are firm, why are we so fickle? Ye are so high and exalted, why are we so low? Though inanimate, ye have become true yogis, why are they who have intelligent souls not yogis? Man knows you not. Ye are friends of those who are devoted to the Lord. How can we forget you? My love towards you is intense. Much have I learnt from you, ye teachers and gurus. So long have I cultivated devotion and piety, and yet have I not been like you in firmness. Ye have opened before you and ye are expounding the eternal Veda and Vedanta. If we look at you and listen to you, how much may we learn! Brethren, speak unto us, and give unto us sanctifying wisdom. You are the Lord's, and we too are His. The same Hand that has established you here, has brought us to you to-day. We are both

created by the same Father. Brother hill, thou art simple and pure, come into my bosom. Thou art my friend, with wide extended arms I will embrace thee most affectionately. The ornament of my heart, the dear Lord of the hills is dwelling in thee. Ye hills, how gracefully has the Loving Friend formed and arranged you! It is the shower of His grace that cools your heads. Give us plentifully out of the waters of grace. So teach and influence us that seated on the Hill of Faith within I may behold Him whose glory is in the mountain and the sea, and whose bright face is everywhere.

PROCLAMATION.

To all my soldiers in India,

My affectionate greetings to all. Accept this Proclamation, believe that it goeth forth from Heaven, in the name and with the love of your Mother, and carry out its behests like loyal soldiers and devoted children. Ye are my soldiers, my covenanted soldiers. Ye are bound to fight valiantly and faithfully under my banners, and no other god shall ye serve. I will give thee victory and glory eternal shall be yours. I have chosen India to show unto all nations the workings of my special Providence in accomplishing national redemption. The British Government is my Government; the Brahmo Somaj is my Church. All the evils in each are human, and shall call forth my chastisement, but the essence of each is divine, and is mine. I have sent the British nation to prepare the way, and have established the Brahmo Church to build my house in India. My daughter, Queen Victoria, have I ordained and set over the country to rule its people, and give them education, material comfort and protect their health and property. She has received my command to give your country all the blessings of good government, and to protect you from ignorance, disease, famine, anarchy, oppression and lawlessness. Be loyal to her, for the warrant of her appointment bears my signature. She holds her power and authority from me direct. Therefore, give her allegiance and homage. Give unto Cæsar what is Cæsar's, and withhold not a tithe of what is due to your sovereign. Love her and honor her as my servant and representative, and give her your loyal support and co-operation so that she may carry out my purposes unhindered and give India political and material prosperity. Thus protected and trained by her go forth into the battle field, and there in open fight vanquish and slay my deadly enemies. Infidelity in every form, sensuality, untruth, pride, anger, covetousness, selfishness, and all false systems of worship prevalent in the land are my enemies. Against these level your united force, and crush them with your mighty prayers. With the sword of love cut into pieces sectarianism and unbrotherliness, and with the fire of faith burn into ashes every citadel of untruth and every stronghold of scepticism that comes in your way, and with the artillery of devotion and superior example blow up all forms of impurity and wickedness. As ye destroy my foes, proclaim my name and establish my throne. Tell all people to come direct to me, without a mediator or an intercessor, and accept me as their Mother. The influence of the earthly mother at home and of the queen mother at the head of the Government will raise the hearts of my Indian children to the Supreme Mother, and I will gather them in the Kingdom of Heaven and give them peace and salvation.

Soldiers, fight bravely and establish my dominion.

INDIA'S MOTHER.

Devotional.

PRAYER AT BUDDH GYA.

Saturday, 15th November 1879.

[Translated from Bengali.]

Nearly twenty-five centuries ago, it is said, here on this sacred spot under a shady tree, the great prophet Sakya Muni learnt at Thy feet, O Lord, asceticism, yoga and kindness. The noble example of his life is even to-day attracting the reverence and loyalty of millions of souls. As we looked, Almighty God, at the mute figure in the shrine, which his votaries have erected in his honor, his spirit seemed to say unto us in a thrilling tone,—"Be ascetics." Father, we have been greatly impressed with those living and burning words. The interval of long centuries is annihilated, and the spirit of Buddha Dev is nigh unto us. O Mother, Friend of the ascetic and the sannyasi, Thy child Sakya Muni is on Thy lap with other prophets. Humbly do we beseech Thee, Heavenly Mother, to vouchsafe unto us that spirit of poverty, humility, meditation and self-control which made Sakya Muni so great. Sanctify our unworthy hearts, and help us to conquer the world and sin. Seated on hallowed ground, may we imbibe its spirit, and in the midst of this ascetic atmosphere, may we learn to gather the riches of Buddha purity and self-abnegation! Grant, O Lord, that we may never forget Thee amid the fascinations of the world, but cultivate communion and poverty of spirit amid the world's trials and duties.

Address.

My friends, here that great soul Sakya Muni caught the flame of inspiration and became a saint. His example ye shall cherish in your hearts. The richest treasure on earth is asceticism or unworldliness and self-denial. This prophet was abundantly enriched with this treasure. Learn at his feet how to conquer self by meditation, and how to be kind towards the lowest and meanest creature. Love her hands discharge the duties of society, but let self be swallowed in Buddha asceticism. Upon your breast keep the lotus-like feet of Iswara, and enjoy eternal peace and happiness in your hearts. May the example of this illustrious prophet help you and cheer you in the struggles of life!

Brahmo Somaj.

The usual monthly service will take place in the Brahmo Mandir this day at 7-30 A. M.

Elsewhere we publish translations of the Minister's address to the Hills at Gya and his prayer and address at Buddha Gya.

Babu Protap Chunder Mozumdar is expected to leave Lucknow to-morrow and return to Calcutta in the course of the week.

Babu Bunga Chunder Roy has gone back to Dacca. Bhai Grish Chunder Sen has followed him.

The eighth anniversary of the Ahmedabad Prarthana Samaj will come off on the 17th instant. The entire festival extends over five days, from the 13th to the 17th.

WE have received No. 5 of the series published under the auspices of the Southern India Brahmo Somaj, entitled "Bhakti Teachings." It is a reproduction of the Minister's advice to the student of Bhakti.

THE Expedition, more than anything else, ought to convince every missionary brother of the importance of studying the Hindi and Urdu dialects. That a knowledge of these language is essential to the success of our mission in Northern India few will deny. We need only add that our up-country brethren have lately shown such hearty appreciation of our principles that any indifference on the part of our missionaries to their interests must be considered altogether unwarrantable.

THE Calcutta Roman Catholic journal indulges in some fun at the expense of the vegetarian position lately taken up in a late issue of this paper:—"The other day there was a horse-eating movement; just now there is a movement towards vegetable diet. The Brahmo missionaries are reported to be doing wonders in the way of endurance and activity on vegetable diet, and the *Indian Mirror* advances this as a proof that vegetarianism does not weaken men. That is to say, it is one proof the more since the days of Daniel, who grew plumper and comelier on pulse and water than the rest of the King's pages who were fed with meats from the royal table. Then there was the prophet who walked forty days and forty nights to the mountain of God, Horeb, with no better viaticum than a hearth-cake. The Trappist monks rise at midnight from a hard pallet to sing Matins, and are up again with the lark to sing God's praise before a day's hard work in the fields. Yet they eat but one meal, and that a purely vegetarian one, in the twenty-four hours, and are mostly stout and hale. But it is quite a mistake to suppose that vegetarianism and simplicity of taste are one and the same thing. Some one-and-twenty years ago in a half-civilized manufacturing district in England, where fish was not to be had, a priest's housekeeper served him up a tasty dish of cutlets with brown sauce for a Friday dinner. 'Why,' said she, "I've been cook at Mr. * * * * * * * *'s (a vegetarian family) and they used to give *dinner parties*.' And we in India are but too well—we might say too painfully—aware that vegetable diet does not ensure moderation in eating. There is the legend of the Brahmin who tied a straw beneath his waist * * * but why quote it, since it is so well known? *Esca ventri et venter escis*, says St. Paul; *Deus autem et hunc et has destruet.*

NOTICES TO CORRESPONDENTS.

—o—

Persons favoring us with communications are requested to write legibly, and on one side of the paper only.

Unauthenticated communications will not be inserted.

VINDICATOR OF ATHEISTS.—Declined with thanks.

AN OLD VAISHNAVA.—We are afraid your letter, as it is written, will not invite attention. The claims of Krishna, if you wish to sustain them, should be advanced in a more attractive manner.

R. N. B.—Recommends that the Brahmo Somaj should establish a Brahmo School in every village of India.

Provincial.

LUCKNOW.

—o—

[FROM OUR OWN CORRESPONDENT.]

YOU and your readers will be glad to learn that Babu Protap Chunder Mozumdar again entertained us with an interesting and excellent lecture on "Prayer and its Response," on Friday last. It was delivered in the spacious hall of the Kaisar Bagh Baradari, which was filled to the door. The lecturer's broad and catholic views, earnestness, perfect mastery over the subject, and thrilling eloquence made the lecture a rare treat. The whole audience sat like a statue, with their eyes on the lecturer all the time he was speaking—an involuntary tribute to the eloquence and fervour of the speaker. The innermost thoughts of the heart, those which could only be felt but never expressed, the lecturer clothed in words, and described graphically. For the benefit of your Brahmo readers, I shall try, in my own way, to give the substance of the lecture.

The lecturer began by asking God's blessing and help in understanding and viewing in their true light, truths relating to him. Then he dwelt upon the existence of God. It requires intellect and ingenuity—a man's intellect and a man's ingenuity—to do the least thing in our every-day life. The world above us, below us, and around us, gives indications of perfect harmony and excellent method and order. We see it is regulated by laws, by intersecting and apparently contradictory laws and principles, which have defied the keenness and observation of the profoundest philosophers and greatest astronomers. It required a Newton's eye, and a Galileo's intellect to know these laws and classify and arrange them. If it requires the greatest intellect and the sharpest intelligence to *find out* these laws, how mighty must be the hand that *works* them! It is easier to believe that the poems and plays of Shakespeare sprung out of an accidental combination of letters than that all the phenomena of this world—a world full of poetry in every leaf of tree and every grain of sand—the various phenomena which present themselves to wondering humanity, take place at hap-hazard. Nothing is the child of "chance." In God's world everything is the result of, and bows to, well-regulated laws and systems of laws. It is true we see anomalies, imperfections, and self-contradictions. They are so only because we cannot explain them, because our intellects fall short of understanding the laws which they obey. It sometimes happens that men suffer injury in this world, but it must be remembered that, at times, individual injury is public benefit. Chance finds no place in God's creation.

The first step is belief in the existence of God. The next is faith in God. Then comes prayer or worship of God.

The lecturer impressed on the audience that there is in us a soul. It is apart from the frame of flesh and blood which we call 'body.' It lives in us and out of us. It directs our movements and our thoughts and actions. Every one of us has this soul, this spirit. The souls or spirits of all men and women taken collectively and added to the Great Spirit which pervades everything, forms the soul-world, or, as it is generally called, the spirit-world. The soul, like the body, has its wants, hunger and thirst. It has aspirations high and noble, and a strong will of its own. You may feed the body with the richest and the most delicate viands, clothe it in gorgeous robes in which royalty was clad, roll in luxury and lie down in bed of roses, yet that will not satisfy the cravings of the spirit. With the most gorgeous exterior, you may have only a very poor spirit. You may keep up a serene external appearance, while struggles are going on within. Hence it is that the greatest tyrants have been the basest cowards in private life, and wicked men are always afraid of being alone. From our belief in the existence of God springs faith in God. When we acknowledge God as the Supreme Ruling Power—the Greatest Moral Governor of the Universe, our body, our mind and our soul must bow down to do honor and pay homage to him. Then again we are so beset by temptations—not of one, or two, or three but of various kinds of them—that we have to ask His aid in guarding the soul against sin. We feel it every day of our lives. We are so feeble, in body, mind and spirit, that in order to make a successful stand against formidable enemies—enemies outside and enemies within, we must invoke the blessing of God. What is faith? One great man appropriately defines it to be "The evidence of things not seen and the substance of things hoped for." Things not seen by the eye of flesh and blood are seen by Faith. What the eye is to the body, that is faith to the soul. By its means, we become cognizant of the intangible and invisible realities of the spirit-world, but realities nevertheless. Faith does not bow to a logical or historical deity. It adores the ever-living and all present reality. Faith, like a woman, has access to the innermost part of the house of God. On faith rest our hopes of a blessed eternity.

When faith has taken a firm hold on the mind, the next step is prayer. It takes many forms, according as faith rises to a maximum, or falls to a minimum. But all are one form or other of the same thing—prayer. When man has faith in God, he adores God and prays to God. If we want saving knowledge, if we have a sin we wish to give up, a weakness we wish to remove, and a power we want, we must pray and pray incessantly. "Posture is not prayer, and words are not wishes." It is all one, whether it is expressed in words or not, so long as it is a wish of the heart. We must be sincere and earnest. We must be sincerely and earnestly anxious to give up sin. If there lurks in our hearts the least desire to cherish our sins in secret, it is no use praying. To illustrate this, the lecturer very appropriately referred to that portion of Hamlet, where the wicked King, whose hands are stained with the blood of his brother tries to pray, but in vain. He has a very "strong inclination," but "stronger guilt" defeats his purpose, and like a man, who has a "double business" to do, stands in pause where to begin. When again he reflects on the unbounded mercy of God, he exclaims:—

"What, if this cursed hand
Were thicker than itself with brother's blood?
Is there not rain enough in the sweet heavens
To wash it white as snow?"

But the hope darkens into anxiety and despair when he thinks that he is still possessed of the effects for which he committed the murder—his crown, his queen, &c. When the struggles between good and evil powers raise a ferment in his bosom, he thinks of repenting for his sins, but finds he cannot repent. What then could repentance do? He kneels down and tries to pray. His endeavours prove unsuccessful, and, in utter despair, he cries out:—

"My words fly up my thoughts remain below,
Words without wishes never to heaven go."

Prayer, then, must be "a hungering and thirsting of the heart." It must be sincere and earnest.

So much for prayer. Then comes the subject of prayer. What to pray for, in order that our prayers may be answered? The speaker recommended prayer for spiritual knowledge and spiritual holiness. "For temporal happiness," said he, "seek other ways." If you want high paid posts, go to the Secretary to Government and apply. If you want other things, work for them. But pray for things spiritual, with sincerity and with your whole heart, and these will be yours.

The proceedings of the evening closed with loud cheers.

We hear the Zalsa Tahzib, which represents the intelligent and educated portion of the Native community of Lucknow, will wait upon Babu Protap Chunder to request him to deliver a lecture at the hall of the above Association.

Babu Protap Chunder is doing good work here. He has infused into the Brahmos of this place new energy and new vigour, and they have already taken in hand the completion of the Brahmo Somaj building, which now stands in a half-finished state, and has, for a long time, been the butt of much undisguised ridicule and covert satire. I sincerely wish it may soon be completed, and may rear its head high above the surrounding buildings.

Literary, Scientific, &c.

THE "Life and Writings of Henry Thomas Buckle" will shortly appear.

IT is stated that Professor Knight, of St. Andrews, is about to edit a collection of sermons by various representative preachers.

WE understand that Mr. Moncure D. Conway has written "A Necklace of Stories," which will shortly be published by Chatto and Windus. It will be illustrated by Mr. W. J. Hennessey.

DR. MARTINEAU is, we hear, one of the many contributors to the series of Philosophic Classics about to be brought out under the editorship of Professor Knight. He is to write of Spinoza.

THE vigorous handshaking which General Grant has been subjected to since his return to his native country must have required no small amount of endurance. At San Francisco, the General shook 1,043 hands in one hour and eight minutes.

WE read that an underground Railway is again being planned in Paris. It is stated that atmospheric pressure would be the motive power, the train being propelled through a narrow tunnel sunk 15ft. below the level of the road.

MR. GEORGE MACDONALD, the novelist, and his family, are expected to repeat this winter in New York, and probably in other American cities, their amateur preformance of a dramatized version of the second part of "The Pilgrims' Progress."

MR. GEORGE BARNETT SMITH, author of a biography of Shelley and of some other works, has written "The Life of the Right Honorable William Ewart Gladstone," which has lately been published by Messrs. Cassel & Co. Mr. Smith says, in his preface, that "the leading purpose of this book is of a biographical and historical, rather than of a polemical character." Those who want to know the story of Mr. Gladstone's public career, so far as it can now be told by help of the ordinary sources of information, will be much interested in the perusal of this book. It contains two portraits of Mr. Gladstone, copies respectively of one taken when he was thirty-one, and another taken this year.

AT the final meeting of the Sanitary Congress held at Croydon, the well-known Dr. W. B. Richardson read a paper on "Health at Home" in which he laid down what he called "a few golden rules for securing health." The first was to do away as much as possible with blinds and window-curtains, for sunlight was a bearer and sustainer of health; next, to take sufficient sleep, seven hours in summer and nine in winter for adults, and ten or even twelve for children. Our legislators, public writers, and editors were foolish to rob themselves of sleep. Then every person—man, woman, or child—ought to have a separate bed; and a daily bath, cold in summer, tepid in winter. If besides observing these rules, all people would eat good food, and live in houses which were well ventilated and always kept at an equable temperature of 60 deg., and subjected to a thorough cleansing once a year, their united efforts might lead them "a long way towards" Salutland.

Calcutta.

NARROW ESCAPE OF HIS EXCELLENCY THE VICEROY.

AS the Viceroy was passing, on Friday evening last, on his way from Howrah to Government House, and just as he had passed from the Bridge on to the Strand Road, two shots were fired at his carriage, in which, besides himself, were Lady Lytton and Captain Muir and a third shot at the second carriage, which was occupied by Sir G. P. and Lady Colley, Captain Rose and Baron Bentinck. Happily no one was struck. Indeed, neither the occupants of the Viceroy's carriage, nor the guard accompanying it, would seem to have been aware that any shot had been fired. At the third shot, however, Sir George Colley and Captain Rose alighted from their carriage, and seized the miscreant, who had fired. A small five chambered revolver pistol was found on his person, and he was forthwith made over to the Police. It has been ascertained that he is an East Indian by name George E. Dessa. He comes of a respectable family, and was for some years in Government employ. Owing to weakness of intellect he has been out of work for many months, and for the past six weeks has been supported in Calcutta by charitable friends. He was only lately discharged from the Allahabad Lunatic Asylum, and his mother, who is still alive, has been deranged for about 30 years. He is addicted to opium, and when arrested, was under the influence of liquor. Generally speaking, he was harmless and inoffensive, but he has frequently been known to use threats both against his employers and his own relatives. Since his arrest, he talks incoherently, and professes not to know what has occurred.

The man was in the Calcutta Preventive Service three years ago. He was then considered to be of unsound mind; and on being discharged, threatened to take the life of Mr. Kilby, the Superintendent of the Department.

About four months since he petitioned the Government regarding some injustice which he imagined had been done him in the Preventive Service, and the rejection of this petition may, perhaps, have led to the insane act which he committed the day before yesterday.

Selections.

FAITH, HOPE AND CHARITY.

1. FAITH, Hope and Charity,—these three;
 Yet is the greatest Charity!
Father of lights, these gifts impart
 To mine and every human heart;—

2. Faith, that in prayer can never fail;
 Hope, that o'er doubting must prevail;
And Charity, whose name above
 Is God's own name; for 'God is love!'

3. The morning star is lost in light;
 Faith vanishes at perfect sight;
The rainbow passes with the storm,
 And Hope with sorrow's fading form;—

4. But Charity, serene, sublime,
 Beyond the range of death and time,
Like the blue sky's all-bounding space,
 Holds heaven and earth in its embrace.

James Montgomery, 1852.

THE IMPOSTOR THEORY.

(Carlyle's Lectures on Heroes.)

OUR current hypothesis about Mahomet, that he was a scheming Impostor, a Falsehood Incarnate, that his religion is a mere mass of quackery and fatuity, begins really to be now untenable to any one. The lies which well-meaning zeal has heaped round this man are disgraceful to ourselves only. When Pococke inquired of Grotius—Where the proof was of that story of the pigeon trained to pick peas from Mahomet's ears, and pass for an angel dictating to him? Grotius answered that there was no proof! It is really time to dismiss all that. The word this man spoke has been the life-guidance now of one-hundred-and-eighty millions of men these twelve hundred years. These hundred-and-eighty millions were made by God as well as we. A greater number of God's creatures believe in Mahomet's words at this hour, than in any other word whatever. Are we to suppose that it was a miserable piece of spirited legerdemain, this which so many persons have lived by and died by? I, for my part, cannot form such supposition. I will believe most things sooner than that. One would be entirely at a loss what to think of this world at all, if quackery so grew and were sanctioned here.

Alas! such theories are very lamentable. If we would attain to knowledge of anything in God's true creation, let us disbelieve them wholly! They are the product of an age of scepticism: they indicate the saddest spiritual paralysis and mere death life of the souls of men: more godless theory, I think, was never promulgated in this earth. A false man found a religion? Why, a false man cannot build a brick house. If he do not know and follow truly the properties of mortar, burnt clay and what else he works in, it is no house that he makes, but a rubbish heap. It will not stand for twelve centuries to lodge a hundred-and-eighty-millions; it will fall straight way. A man must conform himself to nature's laws, be verily in communion with Nature and the truth of things, or Nature will answer him—No, not at all! Speciosities are specious—ah me!—a Cagliostro, many Cagliostros, prominent world-leaders, do prosper by their quackery for a day. It is like a forged bank-note; they get it passed out of their worthless hands: others, not they, have to smart for it. Nature bursts up in fire-flames, French Revolutions and such like proclaiming in terrible veracity that forged notes are forged.

But of a Great Man, especially of him, I will venture to assert that it is incredible he should have been other than true. It seems to me the primary foundation of him, that of all that can die in him, this. No Mirabeau, Napoleon, Burns, Cromwell, no man adequate to do anything, but is first of all in right earnest about it, what I call a sincere man.

NOVELS AND NOVEL READING.

The following report is transferred from the *Liverpool Daily Post* of October 23rd to the *Herald* at the request of several readers:—

The first meeting of the third session of Notes and Queries Society was held on Tuesday evening, at the Royal Institution, when the Rev. S. Fletcher Williams, the President for the year, delivered his opening address, his subject being "British Novelists from Defoe to Dickens." Mr. Williams said that, in these days, everybody read novels. Now and again they heard the voice of a thoughtful and earnest man raised against this popular recreation. Mr. Carlyle or the Archbishop of York might endeavour to prove to them that they were dissipating their minds, wasting their time, and encouraging laxity and diffuseness in their intellectual powers; but the preaching of the preacher was of no avail. Men were as laborious as ever they were. Their wives and daughters were more highly educated than were their mothers and grandmothers. They worked, and prayed, and rode, and danced, and gambled, and talked politics as assiduously as ever. But they all read novels—lawyers, divines, merchants, soldiers, sailors, courtiers, politicians and what not. There was hardly a man or woman who could read, who did not require that some amount of novel reading should be printed for the delight of his or her leisure hours. And so much was learned from novels, so much of good and of evil; so very many of the details of every day life were done honestly or dishonestly, selfishly or unselfishly, in a manner divine or diabolical, as the mind of the doer may have been operated upon beneficially or injuriously by the novelist's art that the production and possession of good novels instead of bad—that was, of novels that would teach good lessons instead of novels that would teach bad lessons—was a matter of vital importance to the nation. He (the speaker) thought he was right in asserting that the novels of the day—he meant the novels which were now read—had more effect on the national mind than either the sermons or the poetry—more, probably, than any other branch of literature with the exception of newspapers, even if they excepted them. At any rate, the novel, so long exposed to indiscriminating reproach, had stepped into a powerful, if not the most powerful, place among the literary "powers that be." No other form of thought and expression equalled it in extent. In it the genius of the Victorian age had found utterance—in some instances, its finest utterance, as in Dickens, Thackeray, Kingsley, Bulwer Lytton, George Macdonald, George Eliot, Miss Muloch, William Black—as the genius of the Elizabethan age poured itself forth in the drama. The finest brain of England had engaged itself in this sphere. Statesmen were artful enough to propound their political ideas in the attractions of romances. Philosophers condescended to adopt the method of fiction to discuss their theories. Scholars did not disdain to employ it in the hope of securing for their favorite themes a bearing which a ponderous essay would fail to obtain. Every variety of culture was busily occupied in preparing stories which numbers of people would read in their entirety, and others to the extent, alas! of only a page or two as a leaf from this part or that came wrapped round a pound of sixteens from the grocer's shop! The speaker proceeded to observe that not only the finest genius but the deepest questions of this generation had their expression in the novel. Courtship and marriage, angelic Jemimas, adorable Florences, exquisite Augustus Spoons, Esq., were not the only subjects. Far from it. History was portrayed, as in the pages of Scott, of Bulwer Lytton, of Thackeray's "Barry Lyndon" and "Esmond," each of whom breathed again into the past the breath of life, and presented it to them quick with its own soul and garmented with its own raiment. Social questions were vividly brought before them, as in Dickens, in Charles Reade, in some of Kingsley's stories, in Mrs. Linton's "Joshua Davidson." The working of the great social machine, which demanded not only that gentleness and goodness should prosper, but that weakness should suffer, and wickedness be punished, was represented in Anthony Trollope. The inner life, the secret workings, the artificialities and hypocrisies of "society" were laid bare in Thackeray's "Vanity Fair," which was the protest of a genuine man against all the mockeries and idolatries of conventionalism, be they never so respectable and fashionable. The sacredness of natural emotion in its natural modes of action, the divinity of rights and passions stamped by the seal-royal of nature against usurpations of cupidity and mode, were the important principles enforced by Currer Bell. The secret hiding-places of the soul were revealed—the development of character in a right or wrong direction according as circumstances sway it in this way or that, was delineated—and over all and under all the inevitable laws, independent of human volition, which governed human life, were seen in operation in George Eliot. Some of the profoundest problems which confronted the earnest religious thinkers of to-day were proclaimed and discussed in Kingsley's "Hypatia," in George Macdonald, in Edward Maitland's "Pilgrim and the Shrine"—a book altogether too little known. Thus, not only the heights of fashion and the abysses of crime, but the sphere of politics, the very worldly world of ecclesiasticism, the currents of social questions, and the depths of sceptical disquietudes, all were made to contribute to the novel. With all this wealth of fiction the question arose—Did the novel minister to the enrichment or to the impoverishment of their mental faculties? There were those who thought that novel-reading was absolutely injurious. They argued that its effect as a stimulant was to waste time and energy and thought which should be spent in study or in work; its effect as a sedative was to seduce them from real objects, real motives, real sources of joy and grief, of hope and fear, and to provide them with hours of sinless ease in which, cowards as they were, they shrank from those experiences whose very reality it was that appalled them. He (the speaker) confessed that there was substantial evidence in support of that opinion. A large proportion of the novels of the day must be characterised as unhealthy, dissipating to the energies of the mind by creating an appetite that indisposed and unfitted them for steady thought and hard work, and weakening to the morals by creating a temper that bid the clear outline of work of duty, of the claims and responsibilities of life—a temper that enticed them to play with human temper that disliked effort and endurance, those inevitable conditions of human existence. But such an indictment could not be justly laid against the great representative novels of English literature. Could no higher merit be claimed for them, they afforded, as Lord Derby said at the Plotou banquet, temporary amusement to the nation; and when business, or care, or pain or sorrow weighed too heavily upon them, it was refreshing to escape to the pleasures of the imagination. But a higher gain than pleasing relaxation was conferred upon them by the best novels—by Miss Austen's, Miss Edgeworth's, Miss Sedgwick's, Scott's, Dickens', Thackeray's, Kingsley's, Currer Bell's, Bulwer Lytton's later works, George Eliot's, Miss Mulock's, George Macdonald's. They imparted the benefits which Dr. Hugh Blair claimed for fiction when he said that they furnished "one of the best channels for conveying instruction, for painting human life and manners, for allowing the errors into which we are betrayed by our passions, for rendering virtue amiable and vice odious. The effect of well-contrived stories," added Dr. Blair, "towards accomplishing these purposes is stronger than any effect that could be produced by simple and naked instruction, and hence we find that the wisest men in all ages have more or less employed fables and fictions as the vehicles of knowledge." In the hands of the great masters the novel was instinct with pure feeling, animated by noble purpose, alive with healthy moral life, sensitive with sympathy, touched with sympathy; and, therefore, when he (the speaker) read, to cite a few instances, David Copperfield, Vanity Fair, Pendennis, Esmond, Jane Eyre, Shirley, Adam Bede, Hannah, John Halifax, Guy Mannering, Hypatia, Waverley and the Bride of Lammermoor, Alton Locke, Malcolm, Never too Late to Mend, Hard Cash, he was grateful for the sentiments they communicated, for the indignations they aroused, for the hopes they kindled, for the thoughts they suggested, for the communion with the human heart they marked; and he was thankful that the influence they exercised was an influence that made for righteousness. Mr. Williams then proceeded to review the great English novelists, characterising Defoe, Richardson, Fielding, Smollett, Goldsmith, Miss Austen, Miss Edgeworth, Scott, Bulwer Lytton, Dickens, and others. His address was received with frequent applause.

SUB-EDITING A LONDON NEWSPAPER.

BY A LONDON SUB-EDITOR.

NOTWITHSTANDING all that has been said and written about the inner life of our great newspaper establishments, the popular conception with regard to it is still of a very hazy and, indeed, incorrect character. The intricacy and magnitude of the work done cannot be well imagined by one who draws his conclusions from the completed broadsheet at his breakfast-table. It is rather in what does not, than in what does appear, that the untold labor, skill and experience brought to the compilation of a morning newspaper, can be justly estimated.

Though it is popularly supposed that the main work conducted with the compilation of a morning newspaper is accomplished in the editor's room, the work is really done in that of the sub-editor, and by that important functionary and his staff, to whom we shall now introduce our readers—leaving out of account in the meanwhile, the important responsibilities of the editor-in-chief.

Imagine then a moderately sized apartment in which there are five or six writing-tables, on each table a green-globed lamp, and before each a sharp-faced man. The principal of the sub-editors sits at a little apart from the others, and to him all the letters and 'copy' (manuscript) addressed to the newspaper are consigned. It is his duty to sort its miscellaneous heap of news and correspondence into separate bundles. Letters for the editorial department make one mound; letters relating to advertisements and business matters another; and those containing telegrams from and foreign, with the ordinary news paragraphs and 'copy' of reporters and correspondents, a third. This first two parcels are despatched, one to the editor's room, the other to the composing-room, there to be set up and set into type; the third is divided amongst the sub-editor's assistants—the pale-faced men aforesaid.

Having premised thus much, we shall see the beginning of the practical work of the evening—the selecting and preparing of the 'copy' for the next day's paper. It is seven o'clock, and all the gentlemen are at their posts. To one the chief sub-editor hands the Police 'flimsy' or this paper upon which, by means of a stylus, several copies of the same subject are simultaneously produced. This Police intelligence, if printed in full, would, probably, occupy about six or seven columns in the next issue; but the assistant to whom task it falls has to choose from this mass of badly written, badly spelled, ill composed, and ungrammatical material, as many cases as will, when improved, modified, and animated by him, make an interesting column of news. The revelations of the London Police Courts are painful in the extreme, and to one can pass many months in the July of sub-editing 'copy' of this kind without acquiring a melancholy insight into the viciousness of human nature. Having had some years' experience of the work, the writer can safely say that the odious crimes with which fiction's declining days are marked, will easily find a parallel in modern London. There are statues in our law-books which we imagine are seldom enforced, because we seldom read of them; but that waste-paper basket of the sub-editor is the obliterator in which many of the most atrocious offences imaginable are mercifully cast. The assistant having finished his revision of the Police reports, and having written two or three paragraphs out of them for the summary of news, next receives, perhaps, a telegram in French from the correspondent at Berlin, Vienna, Constantinople, or elsewhere. This translated, he may then be called upon to read through the 'copy' of the reporters, and make into neat paragraphs the items of news sent by the county correspondents, or to correct a telegraphed speech of Mr. Gladstone, or of Lord Beaconsfield.

But while this assistant is thus busily engaged, the others are not idle. News has just been received in the Office that some public man has died. If he be great enough to do on the list of those whose biographies lie in the sub-editor's desk—graveyard—the compartment is grimly called—silently writing the demand of their illustrious subjects, there is an end of the matter—the date and a few particulars regarding the last hours of the deceased personage are added, and the printer receives this 'copy' at once. But if he be a minor light, and yet one who must receive special notice to the extent of say a quarter or half a column, one of the assistants is called upon to compile a memoir. He forthwith furnishes himself with Vapereau's Dictionnaire des Contemporaine, with Men of the Time, an Encyclopædia, and one or two other books of reference, and in the course of a couple of hours the compendium are at work on the biography. Just then, a messenger from the Messrs. Spottiswoode, Government printers, arrives with a bundle of blue-books, containing perhaps official despatches, or reports on subjects interesting to the general community. The assistant having completed his memoir, is informed through his chief, that the editor requires an abstract of a blue-book of probably four or five hundred pages, to the extent of about a column or a column and a half. The unfortunate man settles down to his task, and plods as wearily until, in the space of perhaps three hours, his work is done. Then, to vary his monotony he is requested to look through the country papers, with a special eye, usually, to the Scotsman, the Glasgow Herald, and the Irish Times, to see if there be any scraps of news worth reprinting or quoting; and having finished a hasty overlook of this principal home papers he, in all likelihood, extends his survey to the American, Colonial, and French journals.

Assistant number three is meantime preparing the sporting news, which, if from the country, is telegraphed. This he arranges and, where possible, reduces in quantity; and what with betting, racing, boating, sailing, pedestrianism, and such beclouded subjects, this gentleman's time is fully occupied for the evening. The fourth assistant has been all this time preparing the foreign telegrams. He will spend a quarter of an hour in looking out an authoritative atlas the name of some obscure place, the speller of which has been misplaced and still occurs; by its being incorrectly telegraphed. He puzzles and racks his brains over the meaning of phrases made mysterious in their passage through a variety of continental telegraph offices with clerks of all nationalities. His skill in expanding curtly (owing to the immense cost) telegraphed news from the other end of the globe, is in constant requisition; he is a standing gazetteer and a court-newsman as well, his geographical knowledge and his acquaintanceship with the leading politicians and eminent personages of the world being about equally required. In the intervals that occur between the arrival of telegrams, this fourth gentleman is whiling away his time by reading a huge pile of flimsy, giving accounts of suicides by hanging, drowning, poisoning, and other means—of which a large number take place daily in London, only the most interesting of which, however, are published—of attempted suicides, of accidents of every conceivable kind, and of alleged mysterious occurrences which the fertile brain of the impecunious penny-a-liner endeavours to palm off on the wary and suspicious sub-editor and his astute assistants.

But what is the chief sub-editor about during all this time? He is busily engaged in throwing 'copy' away. As the news comes in, he hastily glances over it, and that which at the first sight appears to his practised eye unfit for publication is immediately, to use a technical expression, 'basketed.' That which he thinks may yield some readable matter is accumulated into a little heap, to be lifted by the first assistant disengaged. Then as the revised 'copy' leaves the hands of the assistant, the chief sub-editor again looks over it, to ascertain whether, in his judgment, the whole or some part of the particular matter may not, indeed, be worth publishing, or whether the assistant may not have allowed some injudicious sentiment or libellous expression to escape his attention. The principal generally writes the summary of the foreign news, and is particularly attentive to the tales given to the various para graphs, telegrams, reports, and so forth, as well as to the arrangement and disposition of the news into articles of so many paragraphs, the prominence to be given to the article in the paper, and as to whether particular news shall be given in the form of a paragraph, or as a separate article with an imposing heading, and whether the type shall be minion leaded nonpareil, or bourgeois.

Thus the night wears away, and half-past one A. M. is reached without much cessation in the amount of actual progressive work in the sub-editorial room. Then there is a great and sudden falling off, and by two o'clock the assistants are generally dismissed, the chief remaining another half hour to see the paper 'to bed'; that is, to ascertain that the foreman printer has carried out all his instructions, and to see that no hitch occurs at the last moment. During the night, this important functionary has had interviews with the Editor himself and foreman printer as to the number of columns in leading articles, specially ordered articles on general topics, literary reviews, or letters from correspondents, which the Editor intends to print; and as to the number of columns out of the total extent of the paper which the printer has in type as a certain hour. Thus the amount of 'copy' required is regulated with an accuracy, often calculated to a line!

The sub-editor's peaceful routine is frequently interrupted by importunate visitors. This man wants to know whether the report of a secret meeting of the International Society would be acceptable; and that person whether he could have a letter inserted in next day's issue showing how badly he had been treated by the Magistrate at a District Police Court, who had fined only a few shillings, a ruffian by whom he had been grossly insulted. Then a tradesman's assistant will call to see if he cannot, under the guise of giving the public information respecting a wonderful new invention, obtain the assistance of the newspaper in pushing his master's wares. A critical question will sometimes arise as to whether some special intelligence ought or ought not to be inserted, and a grave conclave of all in charge of the journalistic department of the paper is then held. And thus the night wears away—the paper is at length out of the hands of the literary staff, stereotyped, and got to press; and the tired sub-editor trudges home to enjoy his well-earned rest. And if his house be at some distance, say in the suburbs of London, he hard may be hardly laid on the pillow ere the first batch of printed sheets is issuing from the office, or perhaps on its way north or south by rail.

The typical sub-editor is a man of large journalistic experience, and generally between forty and fifty years of age. He is not ordinarily one of your so-so Bohemians, but quiet, sedate, and respectable. His work is of an exhaustive nature, and it quickly ages him; yet the necessities of his position requiring a constant attention to his health, he not uncommonly reaches a green old age, and may be met with in a suburban retirement living upon the savings of his more vigorous years.

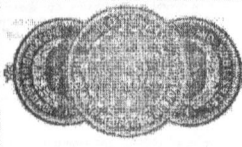

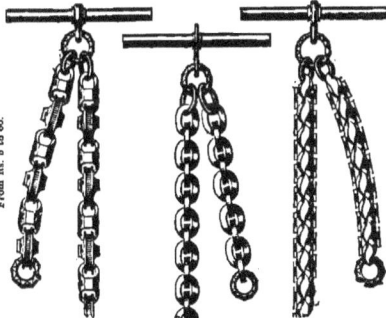

The Indian Mirror

[Edited by Krishna Bihari Sen, M.A.]

SUNDAY EDITION

[Registered at the General Post Office.]

VOL. XIX.   CALCUTTA, SUNDAY, DECEMBER 21, 1879.   NO. 303

CONTENTS.

Telegraphic Intelligence.

REUTER'S TELEGRAMS.

M. VAMBERY ON CABUL AFFAIRS.

LONDON, 20TH DECEMBER.

A letter from M. Vambery has been published, in which he takes a hopeful view of the position of General Roberts at Cabul, and states that England will be obliged to carry out the pacification of Afghanistan at any cost. M. Vambery further says that the Treaty of Gundamuck is impracticable, because no Amir of Afghanistan could resist Russian intrigue.

FROM THE PRESS COMMISSIONER.

THE CABUL WAR.

CALCUTTA, 20TH DECEMBER 1878.

A telegram received on the 18th from Colonel Acton, Pezwan, states that on the previous night Colonel Norman bivouacked out and was fired on. Two men were slightly wounded. He returned to Pezwan on the night of the 18th. All well. Macnaughten's casualties on the 18th were two men wounded. On the night of the same day, Jagdaluck was fired on, one man being severely wounded. Numbers of Ghilzais were out but seemed only rabble, and the attack was so far reported insignificant. The Khugiani tribes between Rozanbad and Surkhat are reported as still on our side. General Bright telegraphs on the 18th that the latest news from Gundamuck reported that all was quiet there. The road was open to Pezwan and a convoy was just going out there. General Bright further reports that all is quiet at present from Gundamuck downwards.

20TH DECEMBER.

No further details regarding Herat affairs have reached Candahar. From Kelat-i-Ghilzai reported all quiet. The tribes of that neighbourhood show no signs of disaffection. Health of Europeans at Candahar is excellent.

There have been exchanges of shots between our troops and tribes at Jugdaluck. Two or three of ours wounded. Numbers of Ghilzais are seen. Resistance hitherto is contemptible.

Editorial Notes.

THE season of our Anniversary Festival is drawing nigh, and there are only four weeks before us for preparation. Grand doings are contemplated. We send our cordial greetings to our fellow-Brahmos of all classes and parties in the provinces, and invite them to come and swell the chorus of united prayers and thanksgivings on the occasion.

WHEN one hear of endless squabbles amongst Christians about rubrics and vestments, bell and baptism, &c., he is apt to quote a neat epigram :—

" Bishop and vicar,
" Why do you bicker
" Each with the other,
" When both are right,
" Or each is quite
" As wrong as the other ?"

WITH reference to the use of the term "rascals" towards Brahmins made by the *Lucknow Witness*, we are reminded by that paper of " the amusing air of pious self-congratulation" which we assume in speaking of it. Our tone may have amused the *Witness*, but we assure our contemporary it was serious. We are glad, however, to read this passage :—" Possibly the *Mirror* thought we meant that *all* Brahmins were great rascals. This we did *not* mean, but only that all are not great saints, as we think they claim."

WE have received a copy of the Report of the Select Committee of the National Indian Association appointed to consider the best means of superintending the education of Native students in England. We noticed the appointment of a permanent Sub-Committee in connection with this work, in these columns sometime ago. It is composed of Lord Northbrook, Sir Barrow Ellis, Sir Henry Davies, Sir Arthur Hobhouse, and others, with Miss Manning and Mr. F. R. S. Wyllie as Secretaries. We shall express our views on the subject fully in another issue.

IF people still retain the prejudice that Natives are less fit than Europeans to do active railway duties, let them listen to what the Famine Commissioner, Mr. Caird, says about the Native guards of the Bombay and Baroda Railway. On this line, we are told, "1,500 people are employed, of whom little more than 15 are Europeans. The Native guards and other *employes* are most reliable, sober men. In ten years not one has been dismissed for drunkenness." That is a remarkable testimony to the intelligent and sober habits of the people. Can any one tell us the percentage of convictions for drunkenness among the European *employes* ?

MR. CAIRD'S authority is certainly great, and his impressions of his Indian visit as recorded in the pages of the *Nineteenth Century*, will have their due weight upon the authorities. But we have a right to know whether the sources of his information are altogether reliable. Speaking of the people he says:— "Disaffection is aroused, we are hated by the Mussulmans, and disliked by the Hindus. This is not likely at present to take tangible form, as there is no head under whom the various dissatisfied persons would unite. But a crusade is being preached here against the infidel Government by the Mahomedans, and on all sides there is a readiness to blame it on every occasion." The information about the crusade is new to us. Have Government taken a note of what Mr. Cairdhas said ?

THE man Deoss, who tried to shoot Lord Lytton on His Excellency's arrival in Calcutta, was taken to the Police on Monday last when he was examined by Mr. Bihari Lal Gupta, the Presidency Magistrate. The statement of the prisoner was as cool as it was methodical ; but as there was a suggestion that he might be a lunatic, he was sent to jail for medical examination. The case will come on for hearing on Tuesday next. The spectacle of a Native Magistrate trying a man who wanted to assassinate Her Majesty's Viceroy and adjourning the case according to the forms of strict justice, quite irrespective of the fact that it was the ruler of the land that had been the proposed victim, is one the moral grandeur of which cannot be surpassed, and speaks volumes in favor of the British administration of India.

—:0:—

THE report of the proceedings of the last meeting of the Bethune Society leads us to ask a somewhat important question. Is no one except men calling themselves "Christian Ministers" to be allowed to make the slightest allusion to the character and principles of Christ, from what is called the human side of his character, as an eminent man of thought and the founder of the most powerful school of morals and spiritual philosophy? Yet Dr. Bannerji's officious attempt "to set the meeting right on our Saviour's temptation in the interests of truth," implied nothing less. We should like to be told by what process Christian Ministers obtained this exclusive privilege, and why whenever an idea is expressed on the subject by an outsider they should jump upon their feet and claim to set the world aright. "The interests of truth," we submit, are more extensive than Christian Ministers are apt to think, and the glory of the Son of Man is increased, when men of all creeds find in him the light of their philosophy and conscience, than when he is made the Shibboleth of sects and "Christian Ministers."

—:0:—

A well-informed writer wonders that though the people of India for six generations have known us other rulers, Englishmen are still strangers among them. Mr. Dall illustrated this in a speech delivered by him at the Bethune Society some time ago. "How well he remembered the time when he used to hail Hindu gentlemen, his friends, just as he would have saluted a friend in Boston or New York. 'Good morning, Rajendra Babu! How are you?' 'Quite well, Sir,—' 'And how are you at home?' 'At home? That is not so easy a question to answer; but I may say we are uncommonly well; as we have only 25 children in the hospital to-day, I mean, of course, in the Zenana sick wards-rooms.' In a tone of puzzled sincere compassion, I repeated, 'Uncommonly well; and with 25 of your children sick? How can that be?' 'You forget,' he said, 'that we are more than three hundred in the family.' 'More than three hundred in the family! My dear Rajendra, I give it up. I must live and learn.'" Mr. Dall has lived here for twenty odd years, and he has but begun to know how little he knows about home life in India. We believe the wisest among our rulers is he who, like Socrates, knows that he knows nothing.

—:0:—

WE have received eleven numbers of a journal called La Bulletin Continental, being the organ of the British and Continental Society for the abolition of legalised prostitution. The object of the journal is pretty clearly explained in the title. Need we say that we fully sympathise with that object, and that the Society commands our heartiest good-wishes? The subject of prostitution is a delicate one, and it is one, moreover, which cannot be examined in its details in a newspaper. At any rate people would

allow a vice to commit its havoc upon society, if only it put on a fashionable dress and did not offend outwardly the tastes of a squeamish age. We believe, however, the time has come when this squeamishness should be openly protested against, and the demon exposed in its true colours. We are glad to hear the Society has done great good on the continent of Europe, and that golden results have resulted from its proceedings in Switzerland, especially in Geneva. We shall most probably recur to this subject in another issue. In the meantime we publish elsewhere a translation of the comprehensive programme adopted at the Congress of Genevain September 1877.

—:0:—

WE remember Mr. Matthew Arnold somewhere using the expression "hyæna bigot." Surely if it has any meaning, it has a peculiar and significant one, with those who for ever attacking the good Bishop Colenso for his supposed heresy, even after the splendid services done by him in Cape Colony. The following paragraph taken from the Inquirer will explain matters :—

On the 27th ult. the Rev. C. N. Gray, of Helmsley, wrote to the Primate that he had seen a statement in a newspaper that "a certain Mr. Colley, who declares himself to be Dr. Colenso's 'Archdeacon of the Diocese of Natal,' has given out in a sermon preached in Natal, that he, before he left England, had an interview with your Grace at Lambeth, and that you 'hoped he would be blessed in the work,' and gave him your best wishes and Godspeed." Mr. Gray, who is a son of the late Bishop of Cape Town, asks for a contradiction of this statement. The Archbishop replied on the 31st :—"I have no contradiction to give you of the statement which you have made to me." A week later Mr. Gray wrote again to express his deep regret that the Archbishop had given Mr. Colley his blessing on his work. Mr. Gray says:—"It is not for me to deal with the fact that your Grace has bidden 'God-speed' to and encouraged a man who has elected to serve one who has been deposed by the Church for denying the Faith once for all delivered. The dealing with your Grace's action in this matter must rest with the Synod of Maritzburg and the Provincial Synod of South Africa, and I would fain hope it will not be wholly ignored by the Synod of your Grace's own Province of Canterbury."

And much to the same effect. To the foregoing the Archbishop replied by the hand of his chaplain, that he could give no other answer than that in acknowledgment of the letter of Oct. 27, "as he has no wish to be drawn into a correspondence with you upon the complicated subject of the bishopric of Natal."

—:0:—

COLONEL OLCOTT and Madame Blavatsky of the Theosophic Society met with a cordial reception at Allahabad. At a meeting presided over by Mr. A. Hume, Colonel Olcott described the scope and functions of the Society. We are still in the dark about the true theological position of the body, and do not know whether the members are theists, pantheists or spiritualists. They are not Christians, and from the fact of their professing to follow the lead of Pundit Dyanand Saraswati, they cannot be atheists. Colonel Olcott spoke of the occult sciences and Hatel Yoga and Raji Yoga. The former is "a species of bodily training to develop will power by the self-infliction of physical pain, and the latter an evolution of the interior faculties of the soul by the intelligent concentration of the ascetic's vitality and mental force upon the inner man. Until European men of science comprehend the results that may be achieved by these two systems," said Colonel Olcott, "they will never know the vast possibilities of the living man." We concur. The mysteries of the inner man are a world by themselves. The scienti-

fic spirit of the West, in eschewing metaphysics, has excluded all chance of ascertaining the "vast possibilities of the living man." It is left to the crowd-bound spiritualists to startle the world with phenomena which they falsely ascribe to supernatural agencies but which, if the metaphysical spirit had been powerful, would have been so much gain to our knowledge of the mind. In India the cultivation of Yoga gave rise to a systematic practice of the bodily and mental powers in the direction of the unknown, and facts are told which are not only wonderful, but which, if accounted for, would open a new field of investigation to the naturalist and philosopher. If Colonel Olcott and his co-laborers succeed in rendering the occult sciences once more popular in Europe, they will earn the thanks of every true lover of knowledge. We are curious, however, to know whether that gentleman will consent to submit to the rules which the practice of Yoga requires. European Yogis and Yoginis will not be the least interesting feature of the progressive nineteenth century.

MR. VOYSEY'S SELF-DEFENCE.
—o—

WE expected that Mr. Voysey would make some further statement to defend himself against what we said concerning his position and that of his congregation in the last Theistic Quarterly Review. We publish his letter elsewhere. We are very glad to find that he has written in much more amiable spirit this time than he has done for some time past. This emboldens us to criticise his views with cheerfulness and freedom. Mr. Voysey need not be assured of our continued respect and esteem for him as a theistic minister, nay as the most prominent and outspoken theistic preacher of the day in the Western world. That makes us the more anxious to have such union and complete fellowship with him as it would be highly desirable to have among all theists wherever their several fields of action may be. By an unfortunate and very mistaken representation of our views in regard to Christ and Christianity, as well as by trying to revive certain exploded calumnies respecting our Minister, the influence of our church and one of our well-known men, Mr. Voysey has deeply disturbed that fraternal union and compelled us to explain our difference with him. Our principal complaint has been that Mr. Voysey's sermons and preachings have been controversial, critical, and negative, and that if his congregation had been asked in so many definite principles to state what their faith was, no two of them could perhaps unite. No positive religion could under the circumstances be expected to develop, and the repeated assaults on other systems of faith were simply so much waste of labor. Against this Mr. Voysey has the following. "This is a very great mistake, and the inaccuracy of the statement may be learnt not only by reference to any of my congregation, but by my own repeated assurances from the beginning of our undertaking eight years ago, until now, that the only real bonds of union amongst us were the positive beliefs and principles of pure Theism which we hold, and not the mere antagonism to orthodox creed." In proof of this, Mr. Voysey refers us to five of his sermons besides his inaugural address in October 1871. All this is no doubt very good. But Mr. Voysey should remember we did not mean to maintain that he had never directly or indirectly made any reference "to the positive principles and beliefs of true Theism." What we meant was that he had never laid down those "positive principles and beliefs," so that when people spoke of English Theism or the creed of Mr. Voysey's congregation, they would exactly or approximately know what to lay their hands upon. We in the Brahmo Somaj have got our "Essential principles," and "The Brahmo's Creed." What are the doctrines of Mr. Voysey's church? If Mr. Voysey has already ascertained and inculcated a similar code of principles, will he kindly let us know what they are, and where they are to be found? If he has not, will he undertake to produce one with the approbation of his congregation? Merely saying that we should have positive principles is not having them. He has been preaching for the last eight years, and every Sunday has elicited a sermon from his able pen. This gives us four hundred and sixteen sermons in the course of eight years. Out of these he refers us to five only as having any direct bearing upon affirmative Theism. We should like very much to know what the remaining four hundred and eleven sermons contain, and whether they are not mostly made up of controversial matter. Besides these Mr. Voysey has taken immense pains to publish his endless volumes of the Sling and Stone. Are all these anything more than a continued, and as we think somewhat needless hostility to the Christian religion. We leave then the impartial public to judge, whether what we said respecting the controversial character of Mr. Voysey's preaching was not correct. We are ready to admire the skill and perseverance with which Mr. Voysey carries on this crusade, but it is our firm belief that a theistic teacher of his powers and opportunities should devote himself to constructive purposes, rather than a destructive fight which at best, may end in a sort of victory that he might leave to less important workers to achieve. As to the falling off in his congregation, we are glad to be told our impression on the subject was erroneous, Mr. Voysey's assurance on the subject is enough. But will he tell us what led him to conclude that the influence of the Brahmo Somaj of India was on the wane? Will he be candid enough to take our assurance, as we have taken his, that the Brahmo Somaj and its leaders command as much influence and confidence as they ever did? We should like to be informed on one point. How is it that though Mr. Voysey has during the last eight years steadily endeavoured to build a local habitation for his services, he has not succeeded in the laudable purpose, and this in spite of the circumstance that some of his supporters are as affluent in their means as liberal in their dispositions? Our idea of a congregation is a brotherhood, a number of men who are

united in their convictions, unanimous in their impulses, one in their hopes, and frequent in their communion. Our idea of a sermon is that it creates and confirms these convictions, deepens, broadens and raises these impulses, fulfils these hopes and aspirations, promotes this communion, and converts it into a community. In this sense we should like to see Mr. Voysey having a congregation and delivering sermons.

ECLECTICISM AS A DISPENSATION.

The term eclecticism is not looked with favor by the philosophical world; much less is it favored by the religions. The worshippers of a particular method, whether in philosophy or in religion, are almost by the very laws of thought, compelled to be exclusive and intolerant. If a particular system be held to be right, it follows that any other system must be wrong, just as in the scientific world, one truth must be the truth and any theories opposed to it must be untrue. We admit the validity of this argument urged by scientific men, but ignore it when we enter the region of the mind. In the latter it has up to this moment been impossible to grasp the phenomena in their entirety. Every school looks at one side of the mind and holds that whatever is opposed to it is wrong. The philosophy of the future is assuredly that which will take cognizance of all the facts and all the phenomena of our nature, and reduce the whole to simple laws. If it is difficult to establish this position, so far as mind is concerned, much more difficult is it to do so where the interests of the soul are at stake. Each religion is held to be the word of God by its followers, and to think of another as capable of giving salvation is almost absurd. Each creed is veritably a Procrustean bed within the narrow bounds of which one must find it convenient to accommodate himself. From that religion and from that creed all the wants of men from the Arctic to the Antarctic circle are to get their satisfaction. A man from the very nature of things is expected to be either a Hindu, or a Mahomedan, or a Christian, or a Buddhist. God has placed no other alternative before men. We must say we cannot accept this assertion to be authoritative or final. Human nature is many-sided, and it is absurd to think that its spiritual wants in different climes and in different ages can be met by the stereotyped form of religion. It would be as wrong to say that a man must be Christian, or he cannot obtain salvation, as it would be to say that he must subsist upon rice meals, or he cannot suppress his hunger. In philosophy or in religion, the same argument holds good—many-sided human nature cannot be satisfied with a representation of one side of its wants. The only question is as to authority. We observe that an Epicurean in matters of eating has to depend entirely upon taste; a philosopher in his search after truth has to depend upon his reason. What should be the criterion of religious eclecticism? We cannot depend upon taste or reason, for in a concern upon which hangs our eternal welfare, both taste and reason may be wrong. Human judgment is fallible, and it is an altogether poor standard in measuring the truth or untruth of religious sentiments. Let all theists bear this in mind. If their religion is to be accepted as the religion of humanity, it ought to prove the authority according to which its

choice of truths is made. If its eclecticism be made to depend upon reason, it ceases to be theism—it becomes rationalism. Theism and rationalism are as wide apart from each other as heaven and earth. A theist may say that he accepts the sublime ethics of Christ or the yoga of the Hindus. But let him answer how he has been able to get the truth from either. If he says his reason has told him the truth, he ceases to be a theist, for reason is but a fallible thing, and what reason may say in one man or to one country or to one age, may not be said to another man or to another country or to another age. We believe that truth is God's, and unless God points it out to us, we cannot by our own reason or judgment discover it. A truth which is eternal, absolute and universally binding must be proclaimed by a voice equally absolute and authoritative. Now, here is the difference we find between theism or true religion and rationalism. A theist believes he can hear the voice of God in conscience and in spirit, and for every truth he has merely to turn his prayerful face to the Almighty to obtain the response. More than this. We theists observe and believe that there is a living providence that works out His ends in special ways and at special times. We believe that we are in the midst of such a dispensation—that the Brahmo Somaj is this dispensation. The truths which we proclaim, the salvation which is promised, are given to us in the midst of this dispensation. It is God who leads us from country to country, from age to age; it is He who guides us to the feet of this prophet or that prophet; it is He who responds to our daily calls, and sends us remedies for particular wants or diseases; it is He who tells us to cultivate the many sides of our nature, and He who shews us the pearls which are to be strung into a necklace for our use. We do not know why we appreciate Christ so much or Chaitanya so much. If reason were our guide, we should like any educated Hindu have reason to reject both. But no. Reason is not our guide. Heaven has brought us to these prophets, and we obey His commands when He tells us to accept as gospel the tidings which they came to preach in this world. Neither is easier than for a Christian or a Hindu to ridicule our pretensions is that we propose to set up an infallible judge for deciding the relative merits of prophets. We say we are no judges of the matter. For ask us why we find as much consolation, when we contemplate the sweet picture of Christ, or why we feel enraptured when we think of Chaitanya's love, and we shall say we do not know. Many of us were bitterly opposed to Christ at one time; yet behold the change! Against this contempt and ridicule of those days, there may be set up a heavenly consolation, a sweet repose, a fervent gratitude, and an unyielding obedience which we cannot account for today. How much of our nature has been moulded, changed and influenced by the teachings of that mighty prophet one cannot say. All that we know is that Christ is a fact of our life, that he has entered into our blood, and sustains us in our spiritual existence. Who has wrought this change in our constitution? Who has sent us this Gospel of salvation? We do not know; but the fact is that we prayed, and we got the response. The Brahmo Somaj is directed by Him, and all its truths are sent from Heaven. Yes, we live under a dispensation; and living in it, we find our hearts enlarged, our sympathies extended, our aspirations ennobled; we are made to embrace truth wherever found, and bow to prophets wherever born.

We find our life growing harmoniously on all sides. How shall we glorify the beauties of this dispensation? Truths lay scattered like dry bones on every side of us. Reason failed to reanimate them. But as soon as Heaven breathed, lo! the dead bones seemed to start into life. What we call eclecticism, therefore, is nothing but the unity of character formed by the rehabilitation of old truths brought on by the Father through the agency of His almighty dispensation.

A PSALM OF THE ANOINTED.

Sing praises unto the Lord God, O ye chosen ones !

Rejoice exceedingly, for your God hath been merciful to you, for the Almighty hath lifted you up and honored you.

Raise your voices in gladness, sing with drum and cymbal, with Israj, Vina, and Ektara.

Sanctify yourselves, and make your hands clean, because over the whole land are ye appointed and anointed as priests, even from the Himalayas to Rameswaram.

Blessed are they of the Lord that bless you, they and their seed for ever, and cursed are they that curse you.

The Lord will help those that help you, and they that spitefully prevent you shall be overthrown.

Who was so good to you in your affliction as the Lord, and who visited you while you lay in the dust with his marvellous love?

He made your prayer the song of salvation, and he heard your time and place of daily worship with the calmness and blissfulness of paradise.

To the holy paths of meditation and Samadhi his spirit led you, as the shepherd leadeth his thirsty sheep.

With the unspeakable reality and solemnity of his living presence he encompassed you, as the floods do encompass the dry, dusty, sunburnts soil, and he gave the fertility of feeling and truth unto your barren souls.

From the mire, yea from the haunts of uncleanness he called you, there was neither handsomeness nor worthiness in you.

Ye were but humble men, and abounded not in the gifts of nature or birth.

Forget not what ye were.

But the Lord said, the humble will I lift up, the Holy one said, with the unworthy will I build my kingdom.

Therefore did he call you all by name, one by one, and gave you his covenant, and condescended to bind you into a holy company of brothers, where each had his place and work.

And he hath taught the whole nation through you, and wherever ye go, honor and affection await you.

Oh the Lord's loving kindness hath been exceedingly great to you, his forgiveness hath been wonderful. He hath revealed his secrets unto you which no mortal ear hath heard, nor mortal eye seen in this age.

He hath dwelt and dwelleth among you and in your houses.

Your children lie on his bosom, and he provideth your daily food without stint.

He loveth you and hath need of you.

He rejoiceth in what you say and do in his service.

By pure precept and beautiful example hath he taught you, he hath caused his light to shine before your eyes. By pure precept and beautiful example go and teach ye others.

The sweetest and holiest of his prophets nightly and daily descend to sing to you and teach you.

A new hymn doth he cause you to utter aloud every day, and a new prayer daily riseth from your hearts like incense.

Sing praises unto the bountiful and loving God; declare ye his will; establish his covenant and kingdom; with enthusiasm and joy fulfil his purposes.

Sit in a circle, take the Yogi's grass mat, cry out with the tuneful rapture of the Bhakta.

Sit in a mystic circle with your wives and daughters, with your teacher and centre.

Sing with Israj and Ektara, with Mirdang and Mandira, with cymbal and trumpet, unto the Supreme Mother, sing day and night. A men.

ADDRESS TO THE FOREST IN DUMRAON.

[Translated from Bengali.]

Wednesday, November 1879.

O ye trees ! In this solitary forest, ye are worshipping the Lord of Forests, away from the bustle and clamour of cities. Ye know how best to adore that Divinity. Quietly and without words ye are serving your Great Master, and anything else than such service ye know not, ye remediate. How we are apt to forget your Lord and our Master ! Friend tree ! Thou art standing here to shew unto us the Supreme Friend, the Mother of the world, who is seated upon thy branches. The whole forest reveals the Lord's charming beauty. Friend, thou art manifesting unto us the simplicity of nature. In solitude, with speechless reverence, thou art adoring the Lord God, and thy solemn and deep devotion strikes with wonder even the mind of the Yogi. Whether the people of the city notice thee or not, thou art quietly and unostentatiously declaring the glory of thy God. Thou standest joyfully with wide extended branches. It was in the shade of trees that the Rishis of antiquity carried on their devotion and communion. Upon your heads, O ye trees, the Lord has cast the shade of His feet, and hence is it that devotees have in all ages cultivated devotion sitting at your feet. None is so humble, so forbearing. Tell, brother tree, how is that unselfish spirit which characterizes thee. I may fulfil the beneficent purposes of the Lord of the Forest. Brother tree, I desire to embrace thee. Shew unto me the mother Divinity that dwelleth in the forest. In this dense jungle only the beauty of nature is manifest. Here is no noise such as there is in crowded cities. The heart loves to linger in a place so full of the stillness, sublimity and beauty of nature. Therefore, ye friends, ye trees, help us. We have offered our prayers in the company of men and women. To-day seated in the midst of your assembly and looking upon you as brethren, we are invoking in a new spirit the president of your community, the Lord of the forest. Do ye join us in our devotion. O thou God of the forest ! Seeing thee in this dense forest the heart feels thrilled and the hairs of the body stand up electrified. All merciful Hari ! Thou lovest to dwell in forests. Eternal Kind Mother, here too thou hast spread thy lap for us. Had we the faintest hope that we should be able to find thee here? Come Mother, let us keep thee in our hearts. We have seen our Mother in our homes; in the depths of our own hearts too have we seen the Mother; in the jungle also have we seen our Mother. O thou Mother of the world, presiding Divinity of the forest, as the devotees of ancient times used to gather purity and peace seated in the midst of forests, so enable us to worship thy feet in solitude with love and devotion. Grant, O Lord, that by solitary and loving prayers we may become holy and happy.

Brahmo Somaj.

The New Year's Brahmo Diary is in the press, and will, it is hoped, be ready in time.

Bhai Protap Chunder Mozumder returned from Lucknow on Thursday last.

Lala Gyan Chand and Lala Kashiram of Lahore have contributed as donations Rs. 15 and Rs. 30 respectively to the mission fund.

We see from the proceedings and addresses connected with the late missionary expedition that the Brahmos were very often spoken of as Brahmo Pasthica Samaj which is said to have recommended itself to our countrymen in Upper India.

In accordance with a resolution lately passed, all our missionary brethren have been regularly holding service or Sankirtan every evening in different quarters of the town. Such activity is cheering and will, we trust, be kept up.

A private letter from Ahmedabad strongly urges the necessity of deputing the Minister and some of our leading missionaries to Bombay and Gujerat to further the cause of Brahmoism there. Is it not possible to send the expedition after a few months to Western India ?

The Secretary of the Tezpore Brahmo Somaj has presented to the Manager of the Mission Office 250 copies of a sermon on "God as King" preached by one of our missionaries on the occasion of the last anniversary of the Tezpore Brahmo Somaj. Price two annas each.

The Indian Church Gazette says :—"The position of the Brahmo Somaj in Calcutta is not described in the report (of the C. M. S.) at very hopeful. The schism in the ranks of the Society has been increasing, and the members do not appear to be altogether happy in their relations with each other; moreover such changes of belief or ritual as have taken place have been in the direction of either unmitigated idolatry or pantheism and mysticism. This latter tendency is an hopeless as the former, since it shows that the Somaj is losing the connection between religion and the facts of history and ordinary human life, which, though little enough at they best, was nevertheless one of its most hopeful characteristics. Bespattered with the progress of the Somaj are beset with the difficulty of ascertaining what its creed is, for every member appears to believe just whatever is pleasing, indeed the Society seems to owe the continuance of its existence chiefly to this very vagueness, for a religion without a creed easily embraces adherents of somewhat divergent views and every definition of belief produces division. It has no standard of orthodoxy; it has no real head. The probable fate of the organisation seems to be dissolution or increased schism. Earnestly as every Christian would hope for their advance and sympathise with their difficulties, it seems only too likely that both its creed and practice the failure of the Brahmo Somaj will add one more proof to the statement that man by searching cannot find out God." How complacently Christian missionaries accept the Brahmo Somaj as dead ! Yet if the truth is to be told, it is the very presence of the Somaj which has acted as a check upon the spread of orthodox Christianity among the educated Natives.

Devotional.

Father, we are only a dozen or two Theists in this land, who treat the Minister Thou hast appointed over us with special feelings of respect and loyalty. Tell us, O Lord, how far we ought to surrender our freedom to him and serve him as his disciples and followers.

Not a tittle shall ye surrender of that sacred prerogative I have given thee. Ye shall always remain independent, and never bow the neck in slavish adoration before any created being. Disciples and followers of man! Strange that ye should use before me such odious expressions. Ye are not our 's disciples, but mine. Stoop to no man as your master, nor acknowledge any human authority as equal to mine.

Shall we not then treat him as our *guru*?

Has he ever called himself or behaved towards you as your *guru*? Has he ever addressed you thus;—Disciples, there is no salvation except through me!

No, Lord. He has always spoken to us and of us as "friends" and fellow-sinners. Nay, we think, he feels that his own salvation is to be effected through **us**.

Verily. **Ye are** his friends, and he has been appointed **to** serve your society of friends as a loyal servant. If he cannot or does not serve you, if he becomes your master instead of servant, he is not saved. In servitude is his salvation.

If he is our servant, are we not to look upon him as our superior?

He is your superior only in this sense that he is vested with official power and privilege for the accomplishment of certain purposes of Providence, As other men are commissioned, so is he commissioned to do a particular work, and that *he* will do. Beyond this he has no other superiority.

Lord, is he not holier than we are? Is he not wiser?

Certainly not. There are among you men who are better and wiser and more pure-minded than he is. There are some among you in whom there is more asceticism, more poverty of spirit, some in whom I have found more charity, more sanctity of character than there is in him. I have judged him and found him wanting. Surely some of the so-called "disciples" are nearer the kingdom of heaven than the so-called "master."

Why then hast Thou set over us a man who has faults and is not spiritually superior to us? What Thou hast just said baffles our comprehension, What are we to do then?

Honor and love your Minister as your servant. I the Lord will judge him. Ye shall follow the spirit of his teachings so far as I direct you, but not further.

Correspondence.

[***We do not hold ourselves in any way responsible for the opinions of our correspondents.***—Ed., *I. M.*]

THE FOURTH GOSPEL.

—o—

TO THE EDITOR OF THE "INDIAN MIRROR."

Sir,—**Your** correspondent Mr. Edward **Bickersteth**, **in your** issue of October 12th, does **not correctly** represent my former statements. Speaking of the doctrine of the Divinity of Jesus he says, "Dr. Tyssen asserted that the Christians of the east learnt it from the west." I never asserted this. I merely used the term Eastern Christ to denote the conception of Jesus as a man, and the term Western Christ to denote the conception of him as a God. That was in my letter of your issue of June 22. Mr. Bickersteth, in his letter in your issue of July 6, raised a verbal question out of these expressions, and I am willing to substitute the expression contained in my letter of your issue of Oct. 5, so as to keep the substantial question free from any verbal question. Mr. Bickersteth then says it would be interesting if I would produce authorities for my original assertion. As I never made the assertion attributed to me, I may, perhaps, be excused from doing this. However, on the varying conceptions formed of the character and nature of Jesus by different portions of the early Christian Church at different times and in different places, I will refer Mr. Bickersteth to Baur's Church History, where he will find much that will certainly interest him, whether it convinces him **or** not.

Yours faithfully,
Amherst D. Tyssen.

THE TWO FALLACIES.

—o—

TO THE EDITOR OF THE "INDIAN MIRROR."

Sir,—I was pleased to find in a late issue of your paper that in the Logic paper of the last F. A. Examination of the Calcutta University, the examinee was asked to determine the truth or falsity of two well-known arguments—one about the possibility of the existing world being the best, and the other about the truth of the evolution theory. The examiner in that subject seems to have very cleverly hit upon these two arguments which are generally put forward by the students of our colleges. I know of a good many graduates and undergraduate, who would fain put their faith in the evolution theory for no other valid reason than this: that the theory has for its staunch advocates such men as Huxley, Darwin and Spencer. They would hardly stop to deliberate upon the reasonableness of the theory, but willingly allow themselves to be led away by the names of those learned men. This speaks much of the weakness of their hearts.

But now, as you like that some of your readers should take up the arguments and prove their truth or falsity in your paper, I cannot leave this opportunity of expressing what I think of them. Both the arguments are fallacious. The first is an instance of invalid Destructive Conjunctive Syllogism of the form:

If A is B, either C is D or E is G,
A is not B"
∴ No conclusion,

For the rule is that "if we affirm the antecedent, we must affirm the consequent, or, if we deny the consequent, we must deny the antecedent; but, if we deny the antecedent, or affirm the consequent, no conclusion can be drawn." Putting the argument in the logical form we get:

If the existing world is the best possible world either the Creator is infinitely wise or
He is infinitely powerful.
(But) the existing world is *not* the best possible world.

Here because "we deny the antecedent" we cannot, therefore, have any legitimate conclusion. And so to conclude from the above that "either God is not infinitely wise or He is not infinitely powerful" is illogical.

As for the second argument, it is fallacious on the very face of it. It is an example of *Ignoratio Elenchi*, or, as commonly called, the Fallacy of Irrelevancy. Because the number of adherents among men of science to the evolution theory is continually on the increase, this is no reason why the theory itself must be true.

I believe this is the correct view about these arguments; and if you or any of your readers find my statement wrong, I shall be much thankful **to** you for the necessary correction.

Yours &c.,
Alpha.

December 19, **1879.**

MR. VOYSEY AND THE *THEISTIC QUARTERLY REVIEW.*

—o—

TO THE EDITOR OF THE "INDIAN MIRROR."

Sir,—Nothing strikes my admiration so **much** as the fearlessness and impartiality with **which** you publish the opinions of those who differ **from** you a mark of candour and courage **very often** wanting in our religious newspapers at home. But this good spirit of yours encourages me to hope that some errors into which the Editor of the *Theistic Quarterly Review* has fallen were purely unintentional, that you will give me the opportunity of at once correcting those errors and placing my affairs in a true light before your readers.

On page 15 of the *Theistic Quarterly Review* the editor writes: "Mr. Voysey's congregation consists of men whose only ground of agreement is their disagreement with orthodox preaching. If they were asked to state their faith in so many definite and positive principles, we fear no two of them could possibly unite."

Allow me to assure you this is a very great mistake, and the inaccuracy of the statement may be learnt not only by reference to any of my congregation, but by my own repeated assurances from the very beginning of our undertaking, eight years ago, until now, that the only real bond of union amongst us were the positive beliefs and principles of pure Theism which we hold, and *not* the mere antagonism to orthodox creeds. You will see this in my inaugural address in October 1871, and find constant repetition of the same fact all through these eight years, and emphatically restated in my sermon on the last anniversary Sunday, October 5, 1879. That sermon I enclose for your perusal, and should, indeed, be grateful, if you can find room to quote the passage I have marked. I think, if you had read all the sermons which I have sent you, particularly those on *Natural Religion, Faith, Theistic Aims and Endeavours, Religion the Secret of Contentment, Man's Relation to God*, Part II, and many more of the same stamp, you would not have accused me of preaching only controversy. Another important error in the *Theistic Quarterly Review*, page 16, is the statement that my congregation is "falling off." This is wholly untrue, and the work is prospering much more than we could have expected in these hard times. On our last anniversary we collected the largest offertory we ever took, *viz*: £110. 15*s*. 6*d*.; and so far is zeal from fading amongst us that only a week or two ago when I wanted some money for a scheme in connection with our cause, I raised in a *few days* £705, more than double what was required. Into the subject of the dispute between myself and Babu Keshab Chunder Sen I will not here enter, except to say that all my objection against him has been simply *objection to his own words*. I have taken those words literally, and if he meant something else by them, it is a great pity he did not say what he really meant. Moreover, I have quoted his own words for my hearers and readers to see for themselves what he did say.

Yours, &c.,
Charles Voysey.

Literary, Scientific, &c.

Mr. Pogson, the astronomer of Madras, has concluded his observations on the sun-spots, and has declared that the Presidency is safe from famine for the next seven or eight years at least.

It is stated that an English Pilgrimage to Rome is being organised on an extensive scale by some leading English Roman Catholics, the object being "to be present at the celebration of the twenty-fifth anniversary of the proclamation of the dogma of the Immaculate Conception."

We learn that the Astronomical Observatory on Mount Etna is nearly completed, but the movable iron cupola and large telescope will not be fixed till next summer, owing to the large quantity of snow which has already fallen. It is also stated that a second building is to be built to shelter twenty persons, the whole being 9,000 feet above the level of the sea.

We read that the sources of the river Niger have been discovered by two French travellers despatched by a Marseilles merchant, M. Verminck. From Sierra Leone MM. Zweifel and Moustier ascended the river Rokelle, and pushed to the foot of the Kong Mountains, where they encountered considerable difficulties as the inhabitants have hitherto repulsed any whites. The natives, however, at length gave way, and the French explorers crossed the chain, and penetrated to the three sources of the streams which meet further down and from the great river of Western Soudan.

In **the** number **of** publications of journals and newspapers Paris seems to be ahead of all metropolitan cities in the world. For we understand that it has already 1,190 daily and weekly papers, the daily political papers alone amounting to 49. The *Graphic* says that "of these publications recreative literature claims 139, commerce and finance 153, legal matters 104, and religion 71. Then there are 134 industrial journals, 90 devoted to literature and bibliology, 80 to medicine, 70 to fashions, 48 to science, 31 to education, 18 to the fine arts, while 17 are theatrical and 13 musical.

***Iron* tells us that** the telephone **in** the nursery **is** proving a real boon to anxious mothers **in** America. "Thus recently a loving grandmamma, just promoted to the honors of that relationship, was awakened in the dead of the night by her daughter's alarmed voice *per* telephone, 'I'm sure baby has the croup, what shall I do?' Grandmamma promised to be with her daughter in a moment, and communicated with the family doctor. He in his turn requested to be put in connection with the anxious mamma, and bade her lift her child to the telephone, and let him hear it cough. The child coughed, and the doctor at once declared the ailment to be of no consequence, so the disturbed family settled once more peaceably to rest." "Such are the wonders of Science !!

Very few of us care to know the etymology or history of the Bengali family names, such as Deb, Das, Dutt, Bose, Ghose, &c. Dr. K. M. Bannerji professes to have found the duointhe origin of Das, the prefix to the surname of the Kayasthas. "Why should the Kayastha be so extremely tenacious of such a title? Notwithstanding the supposition that the word in such a case indicates a servant or slave of *holy Brahmins*, and that every pious Sudra glories in such a title, it may be asked, why the Kayastha should do so more than a lower Sudra, or why the privilege of prefixing the title of *Das* should be denied to the lower Sudra, when it would be, on the contrary, still more appropriate for the latter, if, indeed, the Sudra be sprung from the Dasyus as a servile race. To the lecturer this anomaly is capable of explanation. The Dasyus or Dases were not *by birth* a servile race. They were, of course, a non-Aryan race, but they were not the Aborigines of India, like the Kols, Bhils and similar tribes; neither is the term *Dasa* in Vedic language, a badge of servitude. That term in primitive Sanskrit was derived from *Das* which simply meant *to ravage* and *lay waste* or *destroy* as an enemy. *Dasa* meant *fierce* as a warrior, such as *parantap* now signifies. In the Rig Veda, the word *dasra* is applied to the gods in the sense of *parantap*. The lecturer was far from saying, that the term *Dasa* was accorded to the Sudras as a military distinction, but he did think that it was not applied in the sense of a slave, and that it was an ethnological term signifying *Daha*, a Persian tribe, who had probably emigrated to India with the Aryans themselves, either as friends or pursuers, probably the latter. They may have had conflicts with the Aryans, and being vanquished were made captives. *They were prisoners of war*, but were reduced to servitude like the Helots of Sparta. But as a race, the Dasas or Dahas were not contemptible. They are honorably mentioned in the Zend-Avesta, 'as pure men and women of Dahian regions,' and their country was noticed by Herodotus and found in the Assyrian inscriptions."

THE MAGAZINES.

(*The Nineteenth Century for October*, 1879.)

THE number for October is singularly rich in contents. It begins with Miss Bevington's reply to Mr. Mallock on the subject of Atheistic morality —a paper which we have already noticed in these columns. Mr. Karl Hillebrand begins a series of Familiar Letters on Modern England which is likely to be very interesting to foreigners. The writer notices the wonderful sameness of existence in England. "There you pass house after house for miles and miles, and one is as like as the other as any twin brothers can be; and not the outside alone. You enter, and you find the disposition the same everywhere; the dining-room here, the drawing-room there, the bedrooms above. At the same hours the inmates sit down to the same breakfast, lunch, and dinner. At the same moment the same roast lamb is brought in with the same mint sauce; at the same period of the dinner the same kind of glass is removed, to be replaced by the same set of new glasses. People rise at the same hour, go to business or to church at the same hour, wear the same hats and caps, and read the same book. Why should they not, one is tempted to ask oneself, think the same thoughts and feel the same feelings, from Regent Street to Kensington?" Still it is a wonder that under such fetters of conventionalism, the strong individualism of the Englishman remains unaffected. We are told that, on the continent such writers as Darwin and Mill find numerous adherents,—Darwin in Germany, and Mill in France and Italy. On the contrary, August Comte was brought from the continent by "the radical philosophers anxious to oppose some foreign authority to the foreign authorities invoked by the school of Carlyle." But Comte, the writer says, is almost without repute in his own country. "This bulky author—not to be confounded with M. Ch. Comte, one of the clearest and most original of his contemporaries—this diffuse writer whose leading ideas were either of very doubtful value, as Mr. Huxley has proved, or more or less disguisedly taken from his master Saint-Simon, as has been pointed at elsewhere, never succeeded in getting any serious acknowedgment in France. One of the reasons may be precisely his diffuseness; another is certainly his language. The French *will not* read an author who does not give himself the trouble to write clearly and fluently. All their real thinkers, from Descartes down to M. Taine, have been masters of the language—as in fact all real thinkers are. Comte left France perfecty cool. No body paid attention to him, and those who did, with few exceptions, regretted the time they had given to a heavy and unprofitable labor, which might have been more agreeably or more profitably employed in reading Montaigne or studying Condillac. Even the rare adepts who followed him corrected his system (?) so as to leave little of it." Mr. Fawcett speaks of Indian Finance and vigorously advocates a policy of retrenchment and the larger employment of Natives. The fifth article takes up one of the most disgusting chapters of Papal history and recounts the career of the three Borgias—Alexander VI, Cæsar Borgia and Lucrezia Borgia. The writer examines the defence which a German author sets up in favor of Lucrezia Borgia, the "fair devil," and considers that the charge of incest has not been disproved. The most interesting contribution is that made by Dean Stanley on the subject of Baptism. The learned writer gives a clear and graphic summary of the various stages through which the practice of baptism has passed from the time of John the Baptist. In the apostolic age the scene of baptism was either some deep way-side spring or well or some rushing river or some vast reservoir, and in all cases it meant complete immersion. The following is an interesting picture of the ceremony as it was observed in the first three centuries:—"There was, as a general rule, but one baptistery in each city, and such baptisteries were apart from the churches. There was but one time of the year when the rite was administered—namely, between Easter and Pentecost. There was but one personage who could administer it—the presiding officer of the community, the Bishop. There was but one hour for the ceremony; it was midnight. The torches flared through the dark hall as the troops of converts flocked in. The baptistery consisted of an inner and an outer chamber. In the outer chamber stood the candidates for baptism, stripped to their shirts; and, turning to the west as the region of sunset, they stretched forth their hands through the dimly lit church, as in a defiant attitude towards the Evil Spirit of Darkness, and speaking to him by name, said: "I renounce thee, Satan, and all thy works, and all thy pomp, and all thy service.' Then they turned, like a regiment, facing right round to the east, and repeated, in a form more or less long, the belief in the Father, the Son, and the Spirit, which has grown up into the Apostles' Creed in the West, and the Nicene Creed in the East. They then advanced into the inner chamber. Before them yawned the deep pool or reservoir, and standing by the deacon or deaconess, as the case might be, to arrange that all should be done with decency, the whole troop undressed completely as if for a bath, and stood up, naked, before the Bishop, who put to each the questions to which the answer was returned in a loud and distinct voice, as of those who knew what they had undertaken. Both before and after the immersion their bare limbs were rubbed with oil from head to foot; they were then clothed in white gowns, and received, as token of the kindly feeling of their new brotherhood, the kiss of peace and a taste of honey and milk; and they expressed their new faith by using for the first time the Lord's Prayer." The fact that the ceremony was concluded in midnight, and that the candidates were required to bathe naked, "uttering prayers or incantations as they were understood to be, gave rise, we believe, to those rumours of bacchanalian festivities in connection with Christianity which were prevalent in the early ages of that religion. The learned Dean then proceeds to educe the various ideas contained in the word. The first idea was that the use of water should be a symbol for physical and spiritual cleanliness. The phrase "cleanliness next to godliness," the maxim of Wesley, bears a meaning almost parallel to it. The use of water is an essentially oriental, not to say, Hindu idea, and baptism in this sense need not be a disagreeable idea to the Hindus. As it is, every Hindu is baptised, that is to say, immersed on occasions of initiation and other religious ceremonies. Many of our readers will probably find the following account of the order of the Bath new to them: "There was one form of this idea which continued far down into the Middle Ages, long after it had been dissociated from Baptism, but which may be given as an illustration of the same idea represented by the same form. The order of knighthood in England, of which the banners hang in King Henry the Seventh's Chapel in Westminster Abbey, and which is distinguished from all the orders as the 'most honorable' is called the Order of the Bath. Why is this? It is because in the early days of chivalry the knights, those who were enlisted in defence of right against wrong, truth against falsehood, honor against dishonor, on the evening before they were admitted to the Order, were laid in a bath and thoroughly washed, in order to show how bright and pure ought to be the lives of those who engage in noble enterprises. To 'dub' a knight is said to be taken from 'the dip,' 'doob' in the bath. Evelyn saw the Knights in their baths." *Doob*, it will be observed, is also a Bengali word. To *dub*, therefore, means in Bengali to take a *doob*. Having given the various meaning of baptism, the writer proceeds to say that nevertheless the word has a purely spiritual sense. "It is not by the water, but by the spirit that the second birth of man is wrought in the heart." "Jesus, we are told, never baptised, and Paul thanked God that with a few insignificant exceptions, he baptised none of the Corinthians." We are then treated to a masterly sketch of the superstitious phases through which the ceremony passed, and the numerous changes it underwent. Of the latter we read:—"For the first thirteen centuries the almost universal practice of Baptism was that of which we read in the new Testament, and which is the very meaning of the word 'baptise'—that those who were baptised were plunged, submerged, immersed into the water. That practice is still, as we have seen, continued in Eastern Churches. In the Western Church it still lingers amongst Roman Catholics in the solitary instance of the Cathedral of Milan, amongst Protestants in the austere sect of the Baptists. It lasted long into the Middle Ages. Even the Icelanders, who at first shrank from the water of their freezing lakes, were reconciled when they found that they could use the warm water of the Geysers. And the cold climate of Russia has not been found an obstacle to its continuance throughout that vast empire. Even in the Church of England it is still observed in theory. Elizabeth and Edward the Sixth were both immersed. The rubric in the Public Baptism for infants enjoins that unless for special cases, they are to be dipped, not sprinkled. But in practice it gave way since the beginning of the seventeenth century. With the few exceptions just mentioned, the whole of the Western Churches have now substituted for the ancient bath the ceremony of sprinkling a few drops of water on the face. The reason of the change is obvious. The practice of immersion, apostolic and primitive as it was, was peculiarly suitable to the southern and eastern countries for which it was designed, and peculiarly unsuitable to the tastes, the convenience, and the feelings of the countries of the North and West." The giving up of immersion was certainly convenient to the people of cold climates, though Sir John Floyer questions how far it was useful, the prevalence of consumption, according to him, having dated from the disappearance of the practice.

Mr. Caird's concluding article on India gives a variety of information which will no doubt be useful to the English reader. The last paper that we have to notice is that contributed by Mr. Gladstone on the "Olympian System *versus* the Solar Theory." It supplies another instance of the wonderful versatility of this gifted man, showing that Mr. Gladstone is as much at home in the department of finances and political philosophy as in that of comparative philosophy, or Greek classics, or controversial theology. In this paper the ex-Premier takes up the orthodox Christian ground and endeavours to establish the fact that the religious ideas and ideas of cosmogony, which were common to the Aryan and Semitic nations before the separation, and which are still to be found existing in their literatures are substantially conveyed in the book of Genesis. He rejects the following proposition of Max Muller:—"The theory that there was a primeval preternatural revelation granted to the fathers of the human race, has now no more supporters than the theory of one complete and perfect primeval language." We need not dwell long upon this controversy; but let us say that while we hold Professor Max Muller to be perfectly in the right as taking up a post on quite irrespective of what the Bible in its earliest chapters may or may not say, Mr. Gladstone acts the part of a chivalrous champion of the truth of scriptural history and deals a few blows at his antagonist which it may be hard to return. Though our sympathies are with the Oxford Professor, we must say we like this passage of arms between the two intellectual gladiators. Some of Mr. Gladstones' remarks are wothy of note. Among others we quote the following:—"It is impossible not to acknowledge the pure and noble enthusiasm, as well as the ability and learning, of Max Muller; but I own he appears to me, though doubtless most faithful in dealing with facts, yet, when he enters on those wide ranges of interpretation which admit of speculation, sometimes to bend his materials to suite his pleasure. Resolved to make an adequate provision for religion out of the stores of the human constitution, from which he considers it to spring, he represents the infant man of the Aryan stock as pregnant, so to speak, with a great, though dim, idea of Deity, which he works out into language through a succession of images, and by language brings out at length into a form of definite thought. Is this a real or is it an unreal representation of the primæval man? Primæval man was childlike man, but abstract ideas are not the property nor the plague, of children. Speculation may now, as it has often done before, decline to submit itself to the restraints of fact; but in the Book of Genesis, as in the poems of Homer, there is hardly to be found a shadow or a vestige of an abstract idea." Let us say, however, that one of the first words used in Genesis is the word God. Is not God sufficiently abstract in its meaning? And yet it does occur in that book which is meant to describe the "childlike man." Professor Max Muller intends to establish nothing more than this. He tries to account for the idea of the Infinite in the human mind, whether civilized or barbarous, grown-up or childlike. Mr. Gladstone rejects the solar theory as applied to the Olympian system and draws the following inference as against the conclusions of scholars like Renan and Max Muller:—"The philologists, I suppose, justly glory in the discovery they have made, through the common words of the Aryan languages, such as *kings, laws, temples, palaces, ships, carriages, high roads, bridges*, of the principal thoughts and occupations of our Aryan forefathers in their earliest undivided state. But if we produce out of the Olympian system, from its Apollo, its Athena, its Leto, its Iris, and various other persons or particulars, ideas identical in substance with those that are embodied in the first chapters of Genesis, how can they or we avoid the conclusion, in parity of reasoning, that these ideas, marked and peculiar as they are, which are found existing alike in the poems of the Aryan Greeks and in the Sacred Books of the Semitic Hebrews, were common to those Aryans and those Semites before the epoch of their separation?"

Calcutta.

It is proposed to hold a meeting next Thursday at the Albert Hall to consider the best means of perpetuating the memory of Rajah Ram Mohun Roy, the founder of the Brahmo Somaj.

We regret to hear of the continued indisposition of the Rev. L. Rivington. This eloquent and popular preacher has been confined to his bed for nearly a fortnight now, and it is probable that he will be compelled to take a sea voyage to Madras to recruit his health.—*Statesman*.

MAMMOTH PAVILION.

MR. WASH NORTON will take his farewell benefit to-morrow night. The Calcutta public are promised an unusually rich entertainment on the occasion. There will be a full display of combined talent. Messrs. Draw and Moore of Dave Carson's company; Professor Hennicke of the Pavilion, Ben Alla, the Premier Ventriloquist the famous Madame Stella; and Misses Owen, and Jones, will all assist the departing "Merry Maker" to make his "farewell night" a memorable event of the present Calcutta Season. We hope there will be a full house on the occasion.

ARRIVAL OF THE OVERLAND MAIL OF NOV. 28.

THE P. and O. Co.'s S. S. Cathay, Commander R. Harvey, with the overland mails of November 28th, arrived in Bombay harbour at 2-30 She left Suez on the 5th and Aden on the 10th Dec. The following is the list of passengers:—From Southampton.—Mr H. Wilson, Major and Mrs. Greenfeld, Mrs. Trevour and infant, Lieut.-Col. and Mrs A. H. Davies, Mrs. Col Horne, Mr. H. R Raption, Miss Selby, Mrs Birch and infant, Mrs. Ward. Mr A. Hunt, Mr C W Clifton, Colonel H Watson, Mrs Weedon, Major F W Grant, Mrs Harwood and infant, Mrs Howard, Sarg. A. W. Lee, Mr Owen, Mrs Stephens, Mrs A Turner and child, Mr T Fereira, Mrs Lambert Mr and Mrs D Newall.

From Venice.—Mr. Bayley, Mr. and Mrs. Hilderbrand, Rev. Mr. and Mrs. Clark and infant, Mr. and Mrs. Allen, Mr. and Mrs. Hill, Mr. and Mrs. Sisley, Mr. and Mrs. Slank, Major Jopp, Mr. W. C. Cox, Mr. Kennedy Mehdi Khan, Mrs. Parsons, Mrs. White and two daughters, Mr. and Mrs. Rattigan & child, Miss Higgins, Ghulam Husain, Mr. Roberts, Mr. Hopper, Mr. R. Pezzo, Mr. and Mrs. Simpson, Mr. Wienholt, Mr. Lake, Mr. R. S. Anderson, Mr. and Mrs. Sheppard, Mr. Morrison, Mr. Turner, Mr. P. C. H. Snow, Mr. and Mrs. Walker.

From Brindisi.—Mr. F. S. Walcott, Major Powlett' Mr. R. McCraken, Mr. Whitney, Capt Chapman, Miss Valentin and brother.

From Malta.—Mrs. Davies.

From Suez.—Mr. Cushing.

From Aden.—Mr. Lester.

THE BETHUNE SOCIETY.

AT 8-30 P. M., on Thursday last, a meeting of the Bethune Society was held in the theatre of the Calcutta Medical College, when Babu Keshub Chunder Sen delivered a lecture on the subject of "Materialism and Idealism." Mr. C. H. A. Dall, in the absence of Mr. Tawney, was voted to the chair.

The following is the *Statesman's résumé* of the lecture:—

In speculative philosophy two forces were found to be in constant strife, to be waging perpetual war with each other. These two forces, between which there existed so much antagonism, were the active, living forces of mind and matter; and it did seem strange that the two, which had their origin from the same source, which were the offsprings of the same parent, should be at continual variance; yet such was the fact, for the history of philosophy was nothing else but an account of the continued warfare which was going on between the two. The question, then, which naturally arose out of the existing state of affairs was—Are mind and matter constitutionally opposed to each other? The lecturer had no hesitation in saying that they were not opposed, and could not be opposed, to each other. They were both realities which owed their origin, their existence, to the same source, and it was only when they lost their equilibrium in the uncertain wilderness of speculation; when they did not meet with the theoretical views of fanciful men, that they fell out, or, what was nearer the truth, that they seemed to fall out. Analysing the ideas which had prevailed, which had been taught, and which had been the creed of the several schools of ancient and modern thought, the lecturer said that whatever may have been the end of individual sects and schools, of the rise of one and the fall of another, humanity in the aggregate, in its totality, had gained by the conflict; in fact, the progress of humanity was the necessary result of the friction between the two ideas. The reason why the two forces could not be made to act harmoniously together was, the lecturer said, due to the faculty of reflection, which, when left to itself, could only arrive at partial results. Hence it was that when an individual devoted himself exclusively to the subject of matter, his mind became so absorbed with the subject, that he fondled and extolled it to the neglect of spirituality. Partial study inevitably led to fallacious conclusions and the result was that in philosophy,—of which the speaker admitted the existence only of two schools—a man was either a materialist or an idealist, these being the two points towards which the human mind was always converging. The lecturer then gave vivid illustrations drawn from history, of the predominance of each idea and the results that had followed, stating that if he could be made acquainted with a man's philosophy, he would be able to state what that man was, as it would be found that in all departments of speculation or practice, the character—the sayings, doings, passions, impulses, &c. of the man invariably bore the impress of his system of philosophy; in fact, consciously or unconsciously, it would be found that humanity had arrayed itself under either one or other of these ideas. If a man (or a nation) was idealistic, the result would be seen in everything in and around him; his idealism would be brought into the social and domestic circle; he would not be influenced by materials; he would be true to his conscience, strictly moral, all sublime, and no traces of worldliness—of things earthy—would be found in the midst of his philosophy: so likewise, if a man (or a nation) was materialistic, would he be known by his surroundings and the general tenor of his character. Immortality, and the things concerning it, would be foreign to him; the certainty of ethics would be unintelligible to him; and a government established upon his principles would be always at variance with a government established upon the principles of idealism. Between these two ideas, the lecturer said, would be found a golden mean, where the truths drawn from both were held in equal reverence, and the one was not subordinated to the other. The lecturer then gave a hasty sketch of Hindu philosophy from the Vedas down to modern times, and explained that at the time when the Vedas were all-powerful, Nature was the supreme homage-receiver; then when the Upanishads followed, which gave vent to reflection, Pantheism prevailed; while later on, several other schools came into existence, the most prominent of which, in modern times, arrived nearest from materialism. The lecturer also briefly noticed the history of Grecian philosophy, of which no true system existed, he said, till the time of Socrates, who made men think for themselves by the creed which he had promulgated—"Know thyself." It was the disciples of Socrates—Plato and Aristotle—whose systems developed themselves into the two schools known as Stoicism and Epicureanism, the one being naturally, according to the constitution of the human mind, a protest against the other. The lecturer then gave a history of the rise of modern systems of philosophy, which having, he said, its conception in Bacon, had, by the still later writings of Locke, filled the whole universe with a hard, stolid, and impenetrable materialism. Were Indians, then, to allow themselves to fall victims to either of these two systems of philosophy, or were they, out of them, to found a new school for themselves? The science of the West had come to connect the spiritual ideas of youthful India; but if India plucked simply from the tree of science the flowers of materialism, she would not be doing the right thing; for that would amount to vindicating science at the expense of the soul. England, the lecturer went on to say, had been reigning over India, since her subjugation, both in mind and in body, and everything which pertained to English education, government, and manners, partook largely, if not wholly, of secularism and materialism. As, however, India was an idealistic country, the lecturer would ask her to conserve her idealism, and to take in as much of European materialism as was true and suited to her. The lecturer concluded by making a very vigorous appeal to his countrymen, by asking them to study their ancient Aryan literature; and deprecated, in round terms, the policy of the University, which insisted upon the study of physical, at the expense of spiritual science. He did not, he said, see why ethics should not be studied and form a part of the University curriculum; nor did he advocate the entire abolition of matter, but asked for some material for the mind. He asked the University, he said, to devote equal attention to matter and spirit. However, the subject was one which it was for the young men to decide, who alone should arrest the tide and torrent which was drifting them all away,—slowly, steadily, and surely,—to materialism. The lecturer resumed his seat after explaining the philosophy of the story of the Temptation in the Bible.

Dr. K. M. Bannerji, in moving a vote of thanks to the lecturer, said that the lecturer had scolded the University much more severely than it deserved. For several years he had been one of the examiners on behalf of the University, and he had never known that physical philosophy formed one of the subjects for the Matriculation Examination. At a late meeting of the Social Science Association, held at the Town Hall, he remembered, Dr. Ewart had animadverted very strongly on this subject, and preached quite a philippic, because physical philosophy was not included in the list of subjects. He then proceeded to say that as a Christian Minister and in the interests of truth, he was bound to set the meeting right with regard to the allusion that had been made to Christ's temptation.

Dr. D. B. Smith here called the speaker to order, as it was one of the rules of the Society, that no religious questions were to be discussed at its meetings.

Babu Tarini Kumar Ghose, who seconded the vote of thanks, said that he had attended the meeting in the hope of learning something about the difference between materialism and idealism; but he would leave it, he was sorry to say, as wise as he was before. It was all very well for the speaker to have exhorted his hearers to steer clear of the two extremes, and to take a middle course between them. But how was this to be done? That was the grand point, and on that point, unfortunately, the learned lecturer had thrown no light whatever.

Mr. H. Bell warmly thanked the lecturer for his excellent address, and with reference to the remarks of the previous speaker, regretted that Babu Keshub Chunder Sen, though quite able to deliver an eloquent and interesting lecture, was unable to impart intelligence to men who did not possess it. The manner in which the subject of materialism and idealism had been treated, commended itself, he thought, to every man's common sense. So far as he had been able to understand the lecturer, he seemed to him to say that, though we lived in an age of materialism, we ought not to be slaves to it; that there was a higher life than the present one, and that we ought to aspire to attain to that higher life. It was not his intention to make a long speech, but he must say that he could not very well close his eyes to the wonders that science was daily working. He would not say, therefore, that we should put away all our chemistry, and botany, and geology; but he would say that there were certain secrets which materialism could not fathom. He admired the wonders of science, but he felt, at the same time, that there was a hidden influence which far transcended that of science. With reference to Dr. Bannerji's discussion about the Calcutta University, he admitted that that Institution was not perfect, and was certainly capable of improvement; but, then, that was not a subject that could be discussed offhand, and would, besides, be somewhat irrelevant. Dr. Bannerji had begun by moving a vote of thanks to the lecturer, but had he (the speaker) been the lecturer, he would have been disposed to exclaim: "Heaven defend me from such friends." For his own part, however, he thought the best thanks of the meeting were due to Babu Keshub Chunder Sen.

Dr. D. B. Smith concurred with Mr. Bell in admiring the lecture, and then proceeded to explain the reasons which had led him to call one of the speakers to order.

The lecturer explained that he had adverted to Christ and the Kingdom of Heaven, not in a religious point of view, but simply and entirely on metaphysical and philosophical grounds.

Mr. Dall, the Chairman, in bringing the meeting to a close, said that he was present when Alexander Duff, as president of the Bethune Society, said that he had accomplished the greatest triumph in the then life of the Society by establishing that any man could state a religious truth there, but that none were privileged to discuss it. He did not, however, wish to say anything more than had been said on that *vexata quæstio*, and turned with more grateful feelings to the lecture of the evening. He had listened to that lecture intently, and with great satisfaction, and it recalled forcibly to his mind what he had always considered the "co-ordinate value of the soul and the will." As he understood it, the main thought of the lecturer was that the Will dealt with just so much, and no more, of the Theos as the Theos had chosen to reveal in matter—that is, with the visible; while the soul dealt with what He had not revealed in matter, that is, with the invisible. And these the lecturer had designated materialism and idealism. Perhaps realism, as directly opposed to idealism, would have been the preferable word; but, however, he could not but thank Babu Keshub Chunder Sen most sincerely for the very eloquent and excellent **lecture to** which he had treated them. The meeting **dissolved at** about 11 P. M.

ACKNOWLEDGMENTS.

Religious Privilege, preached at Oxford, by Hon. and Rev. W. H. Freemantle, 2 Nov., 1879.

2. The Supremacy of Christ over the **Secular** Life, preached before the University of Oxford, on April 27, 1879, by the Hon. and Rev. W. **H.** Freemantle.

3. Brief Narrative of Facts Relative **to the New** Orphan Houses (for 2,050 children) on Ashley Down, Bristol, and the other objects of the Scriptural Knowledge Institution for Home and Abroad. By G. Muller.

Selections.

ONE NEGLECTED CHILD.—A REMARKABLE STORY.

The power for good or evil that resides in a little child is great beyond human calculations. A child rightly trained may be a world-wide blessing with an influence reaching onward to eternal years. But a neglected or misdirected child may live to blight and blast mankind, and leave influences of evil which shall roll on **in** increasing volume till they plunge into the gulf of eternal perdition.

A remarkable instance was related by Dr. Harris, of New York, at a recent meeting of the State Charities Aid Association. In a small village in a county on the upper Hudson, some seventy years ago, a young girl, named Margaret, was sent adrift on the casual charity of the inhabitants. She became the mother of a long race of criminals and paupers, and her progeny has cursed the country ever since. The county records show *two hundred* of her descendants who have been criminals. In one single generation of her unhappy line, there were twenty children; of these three died in infancy and seventeen survived to maturity; of the seventeen, nine served in the State Prison for high crimes an aggregate term of fifty years, while the others were frequent inmates and penitentiaries and alms-houses. Of the nine hundred descendants through six generations of this unhappy girl, who was left on the village streets and abandoned in her childhood, a great number have been idiots, imbeciles, drunkards, lunatics, paupers and prostitutes; but two hundred of the more vigorous are on record as criminals. This neglected little child has thus cost the county authorities, in the effects she has transmitted, *hundreds of thousands of dollars*, in the expense and care of criminals and paupers, besides the untold damage she has inflicted on property and public morals.

Who can tell how many of the descendants of those people who saw this helpless child sent adrift on the world, have been wronged, robbed, contaminated, or ruined by her descendants? The sceptic who finds fault with the God of the Bible for "visiting the iniquities of the father upon the children, to the third and fourth generation," will please explain how his God, the God of Nature, is any better, in view of ten thousand such instances of transmitted depravity which abound on every hand. And those respectable people who neglect the poor and helpless, and make no effort to reclaim the vicious and train the wayward, but wrapt themselves up in comfort, with the Cain-like plea "Am I my brother's keeper?"—will do well to consider what a harvest of murderers, thieves, incendiaries and harlots they are allowing to go on around them to plague themselves and ruin their offspring. None of us liveth to himself. The interests and destinies of humanity are interlinked. We must save the lost; or, as they go down to wretchedness and ruin, they may drag after them those that are nearest and dearest to our hearts.

There, go now, and try to save one neglected child, Seal up a fountain of grief and woe and cursing, and a fountain of joy, and peace, and blessing, and open "know that he that converteth a sinner from the error of his way shall save a soul from death, and HIDE A MULTITUDE OF SINS."

FEDERATION BRITANNIC, CONTINENTAL AND GENERAL FOR THE ABOLITION OF PROSTITUTION SPECIALLY REGARDED AS LEGALISED OR TOLERATED.

(*Le Bulletin Continental.*)

RESOLUTIONS VOTED AT THE CONGRESS OF GENEVA. (17-22 September, 1877.)

The Section of Hygiene affirms:—

1. That self-control in sexual relations is one of the indispensable bases of individual and public health.

2. That prostitution is a fundamental violation of the laws of hygiene.

3. Considering that the role of public hygiene should not be confined to the examination and physical prevention of the diseases which can affect the population, we declare that its true function is to develop all the conditions favorable to health which has its noblest expression in public morality.

4. The Section of Hygiene has ascertained the complete failure of all those systems of the police of morality which have for their aim the regulation of prostitution.

5. * * *

6. The Section of Hygiene expresses also its wish that the ordinary Police should have decency strictly respected in the streets and public places, and that it should repress all public scandal, whether caused by men or by women.

The section of Morals affirms:—

1. That the practice of impurity is as reprehensible in men as in women.

2. That its regulation tends to destroy the idea of the unity of moral law for the two sexes and to lower the tone of public opinion upon the subject.

3. That all systems of organisation of prostitution encourage debauchery, augment the number of illegitimate births, develop clandestine prostitution, and lower the level of public and private morality.

4. That the compulsory medical visit to woman based upon regulation, is an outrage upon woman, so much the more so odious that it tends to consummate the ruin of the unfortunates compelled to undergo it, and even to destroy among the most degraded the last vestiges of modesty.

5. That official registration **is a blow at** public liberty and rights.

6. That by **regulation the State, forgetting** that it should **equally protect the two sexes,** corrupts them **in reality and degrades the woman.**

7. That the State **whose mission is to protect** the minor and to **sustain him in his struggle for** good excites **him** on the contrary **to debauchery** by facilitating it for him by regulation.

8. That in licensing places of debauchery and making of disorder a regular profession, the State sanctions the immoral and erroneous idea that debauchery is **a** necessity for man.

9. That an appeal will be made to the conscience of **all** authors, editors, booksellers and **hawkers of the** two continents to bind themselves **not to favor** in any manner the sale or diffusion **of corrupting** literature, immoral works, and obscene **engravings.**

The Section of Charity affirms:—

1. **That the ideas which** agree **with** the system **of** the regulation of vice are incompatible with **all** efforts for a rescue of the fallen.

2. That it is proved that the regulation of prostitution is a great impediment to the success of efforts for rescue, because registration and medical visits are opposed to all sentiments of feminine modesty which are never absolutely extinguished **in any** woman, and **they** render that rehabilitation **more** difficult which one may and should hope for **every** woman however lost she may be.

3. **It is to be** desired that Homes should be established everywhere of which the system should be as little as possible penitentiary, because Christian love **and** sympathy are the only efficacious means for rescuing young women.

4. It is **to be** desired that **a** system of international **communications** be established to prevent the **trade in young** women and to watch over the **well-being of** women who seek for employment in **different countries.**

The Section of Legislation affirms that:—

1. The state has not the right to regulate prostitution, **because it should never make a** compromise **with evil, nor sacrifice constitutional** guarantees **to contestable interests.**

All **systems of official regulation of prostitution** entails **the despotism of the Police and the violation of judicial guarantees assured to all individuals, even to the** greatest criminals, **against arbitrary arrests and** detentions.

As this violation of rights is committed solely to the prejudice of woman, there results between her and man a monstrous inequality; woman is lowered to the rank of a simple means, and is no longer treated **as** an individual. She becomes an outlaw.

Besides by **the** regulation of vice, the state directly violates its own penal law, since the latter prohibits encouragement of debauchery, and the State makes itself at least an accomplice to such encouragement, inasmuch as it is practised by the establishments or by the women that it licenses.

3. **The** object is not attained; because regulation produces **and** develops prostitution instead of diminishing it.

The conclusion from all this is that the State should give up pursuing the hygienic end, the more so as the question here is not of an exterior danger to public health in general, like epidemic diseases, but of a danger to which a person exposes himself, seeking and wishing for it.

The State should continue the to punish encouragement of debauchery committed upon minors of either sex and particularly the infamous traffic in the accursed thing.

Holloway's Ointment and Pills effect wonderful cures of bad legs and old wounds. If these medicines be used according to the directions which are wrapped round each pot and box there is no wound, bad leg, or ulcerous sore, however obstinate, but will yield to their curative properties. Numbers of persons who had been patients in the large hospitals, and under the care of eminent surgeons, without deriving the least benefit, have been cured by Holloway's Ointment and Pills, when other remedies had signally failed. For glandular swellings, tumours, scurvy, and diseases of the skin there is no medicine that can **be** used with so good an effect. Though potent **for** good, it is powerless for harm; and though the cure it effects is rapid, it is **also** complete and permanent.

Darlington's Pain-Curer has been found to be a certain cure for Pains in the Back, Lumbago, Pains in the Chest, Sore Throats, Coughs Colds, Tightness of the Chest, Headache, Toothache, Neuralgia, Colics, Rheumatism, Paralysis, Pains in the Groins, Contracted Joints, Gout, Sciatica, Bad Legs, Bad Breasts, Swellings, Old Sores, Piles, Ring worms, Pimples, Freckles, & Eruptions on the skin.

NOTICE.

THE Press at No. 2, British Indian Street, at which the Indian Mirror has been printed since the 1st January, 1878, being distinct from the Press at No. 6, College Square, where the Paper before that date was printed, it is hereby announced for public information that the Press in British Indian Street, where the Mirror is now, and will hereafter be printed, is henceforward to be called the "Sen Press." All communications for the Indian Mirror Newspaper and the Sen Press to be addressed accordingly.

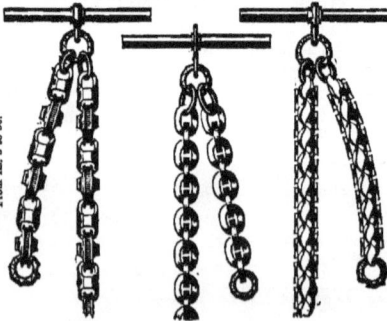

Hooghly Bridge Notice.

THE Bridge will be closed for traffic on Tuesday, the 23rd December, 1879, from 9-30 A. M. to 12-30 P. M.

G. H. SIMMONS,

a-6   Secretary to the Bridge Commissioners.

INDIA GENERAL STEAM NAVIGATION COMPANY, "LD."

SCHOKER, KILBURN & Co.—*Managing Agents.*

ASSAM LINE NOTICE.

Steamers leave Calcutta for Assam every Friday, and Goalundo every Sunday, and leave Debrooghur downward every Saturday.

THE Str. *Agra* will leave Calcutta for Assam, on Friday, the 19th inst.

Cargo will be received at the Company's Godowns, Nimtollah Ghat, up till noon of Thursday, the 18th instant.

THE Str. *Sadiya* will leave Goalundo for Assam on Sunday, the 21st instant.

Cargo will be received at the Company's Godowns, No. 4, Fairlie Place, uptill noon of Friday, the 19th instant.

Passengers should leave for Goalundo by Train of Saturday, the 20th instant.

CACHAR LINE NOTICE.

REGULAR WEEKLY SERVICE.

Steamers leave Calcutta for Cachar and intermediate Stations every Tuesday, and leave Cachar downward every Thursday.

THE Str. *Patna* will leave Calcutta for Cachar on Tuesday, the 23rd instant.

Cargo will be received at the Company's Godowns, Nimtollah Ghat, up till noon of Monday, the 22nd instant.

For further information regarding rates of freight or passage money, apply to—

4, FAIRLIE PLACE,   O. J. SCOTT,
Calcutta, 19th December, 1879. }   *Secretary.*
a-23

RIVERS STEAM NAVIGATION CO., "LIMITED."

The Steamers of this Company run weekly from Calcutta and Goalundo to Assam and back.

THE Steamer *Burmah* will leave Calcutta for Assam on Tuesday, the 30th current.

THE Str. *Mysore* will leave for Assam from Goalundo on Thursday, the 25th December.

Cachar Line Notice.

The Steamers of this Company will run fortnightly between Calcutta and Cachar.

MACNEILL & CO.
a-32

PHOSPHORINE.

THE properties of this valuable medicine are the most remarkable of any known to medical science.

It possesses the power of stimulating all the vital functions of the human system without leaving any after-feeling of lassitude or reaction.

Professional men, students, and all literary workers, can exert themselves far beyond the natural enduring power by using this remedy and that too, without experiencing any evil effects after the stimulus is removed.

It does not act like many nervous excitants which leave the person who has had a temporary benefit from them worse than before, but, on the contrary, Phosphodine, while it excites and strengthens every faculty of mind and body, leaves behind it a permanent benefit.

No better evidence of this can be shewn than that those who have taken it and felt its power feel so much relieved that in a short time they cease to need it or any other stimulant, and have no desire for it until ill-health or overwork again demands a supply of renewed vitality.

Per bottle, 2/6.

Per doz. 30/-free to any part of India. Payment may be made at local Post Offices.

Sole Agents for India,
J. CORFIELD & CO.,
a-8   Calcutta.

THACKER, SPINK & CO.'S

LATEST PUBLICATIONS.

VOL. II. HINDU TRIBES AND CASTES; together with an Account of the Mahomedan Tribes of the North-West Frontier and of the Aboriginal Tribes of the Central Provinces. By the Rev. M. A. SHERRING, M.A., LL.B. Demy 4to, cloth Rs. 16.

The Volume contains no account of the Tribes of the Punjab and its Frontiers—Central Provinces and Berar, Bombay Presidency and Frontiers of Scind.

CIVIL PROCEDURE CODE AMENDMENT ACT.—The Sections of Act X of 1877, as amended by Act XII of 1879, reprinted in full, together with the new Sections. *Printed on one side only of the paper so as to admit of any incorporation with Broughton's and other editions of the Civil Procedure Code.* Royal 8vo. Re. 1.

GOODEVE'S HINTS FOR THE MANAGEMENT and Medical Treatment of Children in India. By EDWARD A. BIRCH, M.D., Surgeon-Major. Seventh Edition. Crown 8vo., cloth. Rs. 7.

"I have no hesitation in saying, that the present one is for many reasons superior to its predecessors. It is written very carefully, and with much knowledge and experience on the author's part, whilst it possesses the great advantage of bringing up the subject to the present level of Medical Science." *Dr. Goodeve.*

ELEMENTARY DYNAMICS, WITH NUMEROUS examples. By W. G. WILLSON, M.A. Second Edition. Crown 8vo., cloth. Rs. 3-8.

THE COMMERCE AND NAVIGATION OF THE Erythraean Sea : being a translation of *Periplus Maris Erythraei* by an Anonymous Writer and of Arrian's Account of the Voyage of Nearchus from the mouth of the Indus to the head of the Persian Gulf, with Introduction, Commentary, Notes, and Index. By J. W. McCRINDLE, Esq., M. A., Principal of the Government College, Patna.

THE STEEPLECHASE HORSE ; how to Select, Train, and Ride Him. With Notes on Accidents and Diseases, and their Treatment. By Capt. J. HUMFREY. Cloth, limp. Rs. 2-8.

THE LAW OF INHERITANCE as in the Viramitrodaya of Mitra Misra translated by Golap Chandra Sircar, Sastri, M. A., B.L., Royal 8vo. cloth. Rs. 10.

HOW WE DID "THE LIONS" OF THE North-West ; A Trip in the Durga-Pujahs to Lucknow, Delhi, Agra. By F. O. B. Re. 1.

THE SAILOR'S EAST INDIAN SKY INTERpreter and Weather Book ; being a description of the Phenomena and Prognostics of the Bay of Bengal October-Cyclones, as experienced at the Pilot Station off the mouth of the Hooghly. By S. H. BLOSS. 8vo. Re. 1.

THE SOVEREIGN PRINCES AND CHIEFS of Central India. By G. B. Aberigh-Mackay, Principal, Residency (Rajkumar) College, Indore, Central India. Illustrated with Portraits and Views. Volume I. Royal 8vo., cloth, extra gilt, and gilt top. Rs. 12.

THE SEA-CUSTOMS LAW, 1878, and Tariff Act ; with Notes and Appendices. By W.H. GRIMLEY, Esq., B. A., LL.B., C. S. Demy 8vo., cloth. Rs. 7-8 ; Interleaved. Rs. 8-8.

LAWS OF IND. By Aliph Cheem. The Sixth Edition, Enlarged with six new Lays, and several Illustrations. Imperial 16mo., cloth extra gilt, and gilt edges. Rs. 7 nett.

LAMB'S TALES FROM SHAKESPEARE.—Thacker Spink & Co.'s School Edition. Foolscap, cloth. Rs. 1-4.

EUCLID'S ELEMENTS OF GEOMETRY, Part I, containing the First Four Books, with Notes, &c. By P. Ghosh. Sewed, Re. 1-4 ; cloth. Re. 1-8.

DUKE.—QUERIES AT A MESS TABLE : What shall we eat ? What shall we drink ? By JOSHUA DUKE, Surgeon, 3rd Punjab Cavalry, Author of "Banting in India." Re. 2-4.

DUKE.—HOW TO GET THIN ; OR BANTING in India. By Joshua Duke, Surgeon, 3rd Punjab Cavalry, Author of "Queries at a Mess Table." Second Edition. 18mo., boards, Re. 1.

A MANUAL OF GARDENING FOR BENGAL and Upper India. By T. A. C. FIRMINGER. 8vo. Rs. 10.

A MANUAL OF SURVEYING FOR INDIA. By Col. Sir H. L. THUILLIER and Col. SMYTH. 8vo. Rs. 16.

INDIAN DOMESTIC ECONOMY AND RECEIPT Book. With Hindustani Names. By Dr. R. RIDDELL. Foap. 8vo., Rs. 7-8.

ROXBURGH'S FLORA INDICA ; OR DESCRIPtions of Indian Plants. Reprinted literatim from Carey's Edition. 8vo. Rs. 5.

A HANDBOOK FOR VISITORS TO AGRA AND its Neighbourhood. By H. G. KEENE, Esq. M.R.A.S., &c. Fourth Edition. Enlarged and Imported. Rs. 2-8.

A HANDBOOK FOR VISITORS TO DELHI AND and its Neighbourhood. By H. G. KEENE, Esq. Maps. Foap. 8vo. Rs. 2.

ANCIENT INDIA AS DESCRIBED BY MEGASthenes and Arrian ; being a Translation of the fragments of the Indika Megasthenes collected by Dr. Schwab back and a Translation of the first part of the Indica of Arrian. With Introduction, Notes, and a Map of Ancient India. By J. W. McCRINDLE, Esq., M.A., Principal of the Patna College, 8vo. Rs. 2-8.

A GUIDE TO TRAINING AND HORSE Management in India, with a Hindustanee Stable and Veterinary Vocabulary and Calcutta Turf Club Tables for Weight, for Age and Class. By Capt. M. HORACE HAYES, Author of "Veterinary Notes for Horse Owners." New Edition re-arranged and much enlarged. Crown 8vo. Rs. 5.

CALCUTTA TO LIVERPOOL, BY CHINA. Japan, and America, in 1877. By H. W. N. Rs. 2.

A MILITARY DICTIONARY, comprising Terms Scientific and otherwise, connected with the Science of War. Compiled by Major-General G. FYVIE, Assisted by Captain DeSAINTCLAIR St. VERNON. Third Edition. Crown 8vo., cloth. Reduced to Rs. 7-8.

THE INDIAN CONTRACT ACT (IX of 1872) and the Specific Relief Act (I of 1877). With full Commentary. By D. Sutherland, Esq., Barrister-at-Law. Royal 8vo. cloth. Rs. 10.

JUDGMENTS OF THE PRIVY COUNCIL on Appeals from India. By D. Sutherland, Esq., Barrister-at-Law. Vol. II, 1868 to 1874. Royal 8vo. sewed. Rs. 20; or half-calf Rs. 22-3. Vol. I, 1831 to 1867. Rs. 16. The two Vols., embracing from 1831 to 1874, for Rs. 30; or half-calf, Rs. 35.

THE CODE OF CIVIL PROCEDURE, being Act X of 1877. With Notes and Appendix by the Hon'ble L. P. Delves Broughton, of Lincoln's Inn, assisted by W. F. Agnew, Esq., of Lincoln's Inn, and G. S. Henderson, Esq., of the Middle Temple, Barristers-at-Law, Royal 8vo., cloth Rs. 30.

BENGAL COUNCIL ACTS—The unrepealed Acts of the Lieutenant-Governor of Bengal in Council. Edited with Chronological Table, Notes, and Index, By Frederick Clarke, Esq., Barrister-at-Law. Royal 8vo., cloth, Rs. 22.

THE LAW OF EVIDENCE IN BRITISH INDIA.—By C.D. Field, Esq., M. A., LL. D., Barrister-at-Law. Third Edition. 8vo., cloth. Rs. 18.

THE INDIAN CONTRACT ACT, with Annotations. &c. By the Hon'ble H. S. Cunningham, M. A., and W. H. Shephard, Esq., M. A. Third Edition. 8vo., cloth, Rs. 14.

THACKER, SPINK & CO.,
5 & 6, GOVERNMENT PLACE,
a-34   CALCUTTA.

THE INDIAN MIRROR

RATES OF SUBSCRIPTION.

(IN ADVANCE.)

Foreign.

For Twelve Months (*via* Southampton)   48   5   0
     "   (*via* Brindisi) ...   54   10   0

Sunday Edition.

(Both for Town and Mofussil.)

For One Month   ...   1   0   0
   "   Three Months ...   2   8   0
   "   Six Months   ...   5   0   0
   "   Twelve Months...   10   0   0

(Single Copy Four Annas.)

Foreign.

For Twelve Months (*via* Southampton)   12   7   0
     "   (*via* Brindisi) ...   14   14   0

ADVERTISEMENT RATES.

For casual Advertisements 2 annas per line.

No Advertisement charged for less than a Rupee.

For special contract rates apply to the Manager.

Printed and published for the Proprietor by W.C. Soor, at the Sun Press at No. 4 British Indian Street, Calcutta.

The Indian Mirror

[Edited by Krishna Bihari Sen, M.A.]

SUNDAY EDITION

[Registered at the General Post Office.]

VOL. XIX.   CALCUTTA, SUNDAY, DECEMBER 28, 1879.   NO. 309.

Telegraphic Intelligence.

FROM THE PRESS COMMISSIONER.

RUNNING AMUCK.

CALCUTTA, 27TH DECEMBER.

From Candahar, dated 26th—Mir Ahmed Khan, a Popolzai of good family, with three attendants, attempted to run amuck through cantonments this morning. Leader and two followers were cut down, fourth escaped but is being pursued. None of our people hurt.

CABUL NEWS.

CALCUTTA, 27TH DECEMBER.

Colonel Norman reports that on his return from conveying Major Thackery, R.E., he was wounded in an attack on Jugdulluck Kotal to Peshwan on the 24th. Asmatullah Khan with about 300 men tried to cut him off, Colonel Norman's parties left to hold points in the pass, stood firm, and beat him off with loss, since understood to the twenty-five men, among whom Afghan Khan, a man of some note, killed. Our casualties are three wounded. On the 25th, a detachment passed from Peshwan to Jugdulluck without molestation. No news from General Gough or General Roberts. Weather cloudy and some snow fallen. The Mohmunds are reported to be quiet and no agitation among Afridis. The entire Zakka Khyel Jirga is now at Jumrud. One company Madras Sappers and one company fifth Fusiliers have reached Lundi Kotal. The remainder, 22nd N.I., about 160 men, have reached Jellalabad, and gone on to Gundamuck. Posts in front have all been well strengthened. The following details have been received of an attack on Jezailchi post near Jellalabad. On the night of the 24th, Dalangai Post near Ali Boghan was attacked by a strong band of raiders, supposed to be Mandzai Shinwarries. Some cartmen, contrary to orders, had taken shelter there for night, instead of going on to Barikab camping ground, and would not return to Ali Boghan, although warned by the postmen. Of these cartmen, 15 were killed and 6 wounded, of whom two were postmen. Some of the band moved against another station at the Zayarat close to Ali Boghan, but were driven away by the guard, assisted by villagers, who turned out on the alarm. No other disturbance reported.

Editorial Notes.

We deeply regret to have to announce the death of the Rev. J. Welland for many years Secretary to the O. M. S. in Calcutta.

—:o:—

A paper in Rochester, New York, advertises a church pew on sale, " commanding a beautiful view of nearly the whole congregation."

—:o:—

Shall heathendom, asks Unity, teach us religious liberty ? In a recent proclamation, the King of Siam says :—" Whoever is of opinion that any particular religion is correct, let him hold to it as he pleases : the right and the wrong will be to the person who holds it."

—:o:—

It appears, says the Cawnpore correspondent of the Indian Church Gazette, that the followers of Dayanand Saraswati are rapidly increasing. His shafts are aimed at idolatry, superstition and the whole system of caste : his last visit, made about a month ago, has created great stir and sensation, and a Vedic Association in Cawnpore is the result of the visit. Is it true that, while at Benares, the learned Pundit was ordered by the Magistrate not to address a public meeting at which Colonel Olcott took a leading part ?

—:o:—

It is good now and then to ascertain the limit of progress reached by Christians of the liberal school. Dr. Abbott in sermons recently preached at Oxford held (1) " That liberal Christians should expect to find an admixture of error in the Old and New Testaments, and (2) that they can regard the question of miracle or no miracle with neutral impartiality as a mere question of fact, the issue of which does not involve the higher question of worship." The concessions are important, and point to the growth of theistic sentiments in enlightened Christendom.

—:o:—

Thanksgiving Day was kept throughout the United States, in accordance with the annual custom of setting aside a day for national thanksgiving for the blessings of the past year. Originating over 250 years ago with the Puritans of the little Plymouth colony, the day was first kept only in New England, but it is now observed in every State as a combination of religious services and feasting, in the latter of which turkeys and pumpkin pies are traditional dishes. The Puritan Fathers' first Thanksgiving Day began as a day of fasting and prayer, kept in consequence of a severe drought which threatened to destroy the maize crop, their only means of making bread. While the congregation was assembled in the log meeting house—the first place of worship in New England—a heavy shower of rain fell, and the day was changed from fasting to rejoicing, thus inaugurating a custom religiously maintained by the Fathers' descendants.

The Bombay Guardian sees "something shocking and very like blasphemy in the ascription to God of the ideas" embodied in our devotional columns. We see something shocking and very like atrocious infidelity in the ascription to man of the ideas and truths which belong to God. We believe that whatsoever is true is from God, for all truth is of God and is in itself Divine. If our contemporary could show that the proclamation from "India's Mother" is false, contains falsehoods and false sentiments, then, but not till then, shall we declare it to be a forgery and a fabrication. If loyalty to Victoria is not a lie but a perfect truth in itself, than it is God's, and the Proclamation is verily from India's Mother, Every moral truth, in or outside the Gospel, is God's truth. Truth, whether from our contemporary's pen or ours, belongs to neither of us, but to God's. Only lies and falsehoods, shame and death, belong to man, but truth and life belong only to God.

The exact date of Rajah Ram Mohun Roy's birth is not known. Miss Carpenter says it was most probably the year 1774. There are others who believe he was born in 1780. If the latter estimate be the correct one, then, as Mr. Macdonald observes in his pamphlet on the Rajah, 1880 will be the centenary of his birth. We take, however, the first mentioned year as the more probable one, because it is the one given by Miss Carpenter who certainly heard it from the Rajah. Whatever the fact might be, a hundred years have elapsed since the death of this great man, and our countrymen have done nothing to preserve his memory. This is a national disgrace. If India had been Europe, a centenary festival would have been held long ago to honor the greatest Hindu born within the period comprised in British Indian history. On the principle better late than never, we are glad that an attempt is being made to collect subscriptions with a view to preserve some thing like a decent memorial of the man. The proceedings of the meeting held at the Albert Hall on Thursday last will be found elsewhere.

Unpardonable almost to the eyes of the white man is the crime of color. The Negroes of the United States, though enfranchised, are so fiercely persecuted by their Southern tyrants that they have boldly determined upon emigrating to Kansas. Hosts of them are leaving their accursed homes and settling upon a kindlier soil. But this determination to fly from the evil subjects the Negroes to still fiercer persecution. A correspondent writing from Kansas under date October 20th, states that a colored man, who had arrived in that State at the beginning of the exodus, having worked hard and saved some money, lately returned to Mississippi to fetch his wife and family. He was seized, dragged from the house, and both his hands were cut off ! He was then told, with fearful oaths, to go to Kansas and make his fortune. In another case, a young man having worked hard in Kansas some months, returned to marry and bring his bride back with him. The night after his marriage he was set upon, his arms were cut off above the elbows, and he was left to bleed to death! And this rascality goes on under a Christian Government in the face of the whole civilized world.

———:o:———

The cant of liberty is often heard in connection with the drink traffic. We are never amused so much as when we hear Englishmen utter the nonsense that the least interference with the practice of drinking is an encroach upon liberty. Liberty! Liberty to commit sin and hurl men headlong into peril and destruction! Why the instinct of self-preservation ought to induce society to free itself from the shackles of that cursed drink. As Canon Farrar very eloquently remarked at Oxford the other day:—"The moth is not free which is only free to plunge into the flame. The ship is not free which is only free to run straight upon the iron shore in the fury of the storm, with no hand of the steersman upon her helm. If freedom is to be another name for 99,000 public-houses; for 39,000 beershops; for 1,537,656 persons arrested for drunkenness and disorder in ten years; for 100,422 cases of assault in one year, of which 2,736 were "aggravated assaults on women and children;" for 16,525 women drunk and disorderly in London alone last year; and if these be but items in the hideous total of such a freedom—if freedom is to hear the wail of myriads of savage beasts, myriads of desolated homes, then in heaven's name let us have instead of it the beneficent bondage of virtue, the salutary restraint of Christian legislation; for such bondage is above such liberty."

———:o:———

The *Spectator* is of opinion that worship cannot survive the destruction of the belief in miracles:—

If the belief were ever to fail mankind that God can mould nature at his will, we do not think that worship, in its true sense, could possibly survive it long. In its place would be substituted, at best, a comparatively dubious spiritual admiration, which would trust doubtfully in the power of him who could inspire the conscience, but who could not "beset us behind and before," by reason of the obstruction of the very universe which he had himself made, or it may be, only moulded. To our minds, miracle means not an interruption of law, but a proof of the absolute subservience of the physical to the spiritual; and without its conspicuous presence in the whole chain of revelation, we sincerely believe that the conscience of man would be in danger of feeling imprisoned, instead of merely embodied, in his physical organisation; and that man himself would at best yield to God nothing better than a faint spiritual loyalty, in place of that hearty devotion of both body and soul which is the life of true worship.

We are sorry the enlightened *Spectator* takes this narrow view of human nature. To identify worship with the belief in miracles would be to say as if men could best adore that Being who violates His own laws most frequently. Worship, besides, is based upon the belief that God is perfect. To anticipate the destruction of religion if the miracles are disbelieved would, therefore, be as suicidal as it would be for a man to cut the branch of the tree upon which he is seated. Yet we regret this is the many Christians adopt to justify an untenable doctrine. If miracles are found out to be fictions by competent authorities, will worship die out? That would be to take an entirely wrong view of man's spiritual instincts.

———:o:———

M[illegible]s Frances Power C[illegible]bbe, who holds the hon[illegible]ary office of S[illegible]retary of the Society for the Protection of Animals from Vivisection, 1, Victoria Street, Westminster, has edited and written a preface to a small volume, entitled "Bernard's Martyrs." The book gives an account of Claude Bernard, "the most notoriously cruel of all the vivisectors of the Continent," and contain some hideous illustrations representing the repulsive cruelties to living animals perpetrated under his direction. Miss Cobbe (we quote the *Christian World*) feels herself justified in calling public attention to these distressing facts, because the leading physiological teachers of England have recently subscribed to raise a memorial to Bernard, and several of them have formed themselves into a sub-committee for the purpose of receiving contributions in England for the same object. This fact Miss Cobbe considers to be a sufficient answer to the plea which has been advanced against the anti-vivisectionists—namely, that vivisection, as practised in England, is much more humane and free from unnecessary horrors than it is as practised on the Continent, in such schools as those of Paris, Leipzic and Berlin. Miss Cobbe urges that the question now lies before the English nation—Shall this practice of vivisection go on? and expresses the hope that the conclusion arrived at by every reader of "Bernard's Martyrs" will be this. "That there must be no compromise with the abominable practice, no room left on England's blessed ground for these Earthly Hells, the Torture-Chamber of Science; and that, instead of maintaining English schools of vivisection on purpose to hinder our students from going abroad, we ought to shut them up first—every one of them—by the imperative voice of the nation, and then turn to help the noble champions of mercy who are contending against vivisection in Germany, Italy, Denmark, and France, till they, too, conquer at last, and the student who may desire to enjoy the privilege of a course of vivisection shall find no school wherein to follow it under God's heaven."

———:o:———

We hear from England that it is announced that, on January 1, 1880, there will be published the first number of a new Quarterly Magazine to be called the *Modern Review*, the Editor being the Rev. Richard Acland Armstrong, B. A. The Review is no doubt intended to supply the place of the *Theological Review*, which has just been discontinued, with somewhat less of the old Unitarian and more of the Theistic spirit in it. The prospectus of the new Magazine is as follows:—

The first need of a New Periodical is justification: the purpose of this Prospectus is to justify the publication of the *Modern Review*.

No task is less possible than accurately to measure and co-ordinate the intellectual and spiritual forces of the observer's own times. Yet no thoughtful man refrains from the endeavour.

All wise men admit that there must be some, and may be much error in their estimates of current mental movements; but both those whom it elates and those whom it afflicts agree that a rapid and even irresistible disintegration is now affecting old beliefs long held in reverence. Such disintegration is the work of a Modern Philosophy described as Positive, that term implying allegiance, not to a Master, but to a Method.

We live at a time in which Magazines have acquired unprecedented influence in the formation of the national mind. Increasing multitudes feed their intellectual life, in no small measure, on articles in Periodicals. The attitude of current magazine literature towards that disintegration of belief which is in process becomes, then, a matter of moment. It is a mark of the growing strength of Free Inquiry that the ablest Reviews of the day give space impartially to champions of Ancient Creeds and exponents of the positive Philosophy.

Close observation, however, reveals the fact that types of Orthodoxy more or less deeply pledged to Tradition, and types of Agnosticism, more or less distinctly Atheistic, divide the chief hospitality of these Reviews between them; while types of Religious Belief spiritual, yet reasonable, fail of adequate expression. It ensues that Religion and Science, Faith and Reason, tend to be popularly regarded as contradictories; nor will it be disputed that the opinion is rapidly spreading that such is their relation.

If, then, there are men who, amid many diversities of thought and habit, yet agree in fervent loyalty to the principle of Free Inquiry, in fearless welcome to the teachings of Modern Science, and in deep conviction that the sanctities of Faith and Hope must be permanently characteristic of sound manhood, these constitute a third party in the intellectual world with peculiar claims to share the public heed. To afford competent writers within this circle their due influence, whatever that may be, in the formation of the national thought and sentiment, is the purpose of the *Modern Review*.

Within the limits suggested by this purpose the *Modern Review* will aim at the widest variety of topic and treatment. It will comprise articles historical, biographical, critical, philosophical, scientific, and purely religious. It will receive contributions from eminent religious liberals in America, Germany, France, Holland, and Switzerland. It will attempt to revivify the flagging interest in the Hebrew and Christian Scriptures by naturalising in England the Reconstructive Criticism familiar on the Continent. It will differ from other Quarterly Magazines in the brevity of a large proportion of its articles.

The writers of the *Modern Review* will be concerned with no sectarian interests. From the outset members of a wide variety of denominational connections will co-operate in its production with writers unpledged to any denomination. Their bond of union will subsist in no ecclesiastical relations, but in sympathy with the purpose of the Review and desire to promote Freedom, Progress, Knowledge, and Religion.

All good Brahmos should wish success to the *Modern Review*. The reli[illegible]ious condition of England is not so different from that of India as might be at first supposed. Both have a traditional religious system calculated in many ways to give development to the devotional instincts of human nature and inspire its adherents to lead holy lives. But both religious systems involve many imperfect ideas handed down from a remote antiquity, which are shattered now by the light of modern knowledge. The danger in England is that this demolition of some of the incidents of the ancient faith may drive out faith altogether. While the real fact is that no one of the modern discoveries casts any doubt whatever on our belief in a wise, good and powerful Creator and Governor of the Universe, or on our faith in His administration of justice to His creatures, both here and hereafter. A magazine recording the thoughts and opinions of those who definitely declare themselves in favor of this retention of the vital principles of religion in the present crisis, cannot fail to strengthen the faith of the writers and to lead others to enrol themselves under the same banner. The *Review* ought to command a large circle of readers, owing to the reputation of many of the contributors to it, as we find the following on the list of the contents for January, 1880:—

1. The Story of Nineteenth Century Reviewing, by the Editor. 2. The Force Behind Nature, by William B. Carpenter, C.B., M.D., F.R.S., &c. 3. St. Thomas Aquinas, by Charles Hargrove, M. A. 4. In the Name of Christ, by J. Allanson Picton, M.A. 5. The Homes of the Stanleys and the Taits, by Charles Shakspeare, M. A. 6. Fervent Atheism, by Professor Upton, B. A., B. Sc. 7. The Present Situation of the Reformed Church of France, by M. le Pasteur, President Désiré Charruaud. 8. The Miracles in the New Testament, by Philip Henry Wicksteed, M. A. 9. A Liberal Country Parson—In Memoriam: P. C. S. Desprez, by John Owen. 10. The Tides of the Inner Life, by Miss Frances Power Cobbe. 11. A Recent Discussion on Romans ix., 5, by G. Vance Smith, D.D. 12. Farrar's St. Paul, by Allan Menzies, B. D. 13. The Early Buddhist Beliefs concerning God, by T. W. Rhys-Davids. 14. Sight and Insight, by Joseph Wood. 15. Fragments, by contributors.

The Review is to be published by James Clarke & Co., Fleet Street, and to be sold at the price of Half-Crown each number.

WHAT WE HAVE GAINED.

THE recent history of the Brahmo Somaj has afforded food for comment in many quarters. To theists in England and in India the actions of our leaders appear in many respects inexplicable and tending to mysticism. In some circles the idea has somewhat gained ground that the Brahmo Somaj is receding from the position of theism it has all along taken up. The many misrepresentations of our motives and actions which have of late striven to lower us in public estimation, have served to strengthen that idea. We are believed to be preaching a creed which is as untheistic as it is retrograde, and the friends of truth are called from every side to destroy this accursed common foe. We are represented to be alone, without friends and without influence; and our cause is said to have diminished in power, strength and consistency. Those who were friends before are taken in by these persistent misrepresentations, and those who are athised with us have ceased to take interest in us. How vainly our opponents fight! It is hard, very hard to kick against the pricks. Our friends forget that though we may be alone, there is One who is with us, and with His aid we defy all opposition. Let us look to facts. Have our opponents been able to touch a hair of our head? A few clamorous people may have adopted the wise plan of abusing us away from the face of the earth. But has any work of ours suffered? Not a bit. Our journals are as popular as they were, even more; our Mandir is as compact as ever; our lectures as largely attended as before; our missionaries as warmly received as at any time. Wherever the Missionary Expedition went, it was welcomed with acclamation. Not a word of "protest" was raised. Friends and foes all heard our preachers with respect. That is certainly no failure where ten thousand men could be brought together to hear a preacher? What is more important, all the exposition we have met with has beautifully succeeded in rousing the energies and faith of every one of us. There is not one who has not become ten times more devout, more devoted, more energetic and more obedient to the call of Heaven—not a Divine service which has not become sweeter, more attractive, and more full of tender emotions. The Brahmo Somaj of India is still the source from which truth flows. Foolish men! to think that a God-sent movement can ever fail. We are often asked why we do not contradict the numerous misrepresentations by means of which people endeavour to bring us into disrepute. We do not, we will not, condescend to do so. We are too confident in the strength of our cause to think that it is ever in need of contradictions, especially when it is only abuse that has to be answered. Let facts stand by our side. Here we are, before the public, with our creed and confessions, ready to proclaim truth and confess error, never merciful to our own weaknesses, but always benefiting by the rebukes of friends and enemies; let us be judged according to what we say and do. The facts relating to our work are recorded with scrupulous fidelity in these columns, and these will vindicate us from calumny and abuse. The friends of the Brahmo Somaj should not lose hope. Truth is on our side. What greater consolation is there than the thought that, though our opponents have tried to reproduce every one of our institutions, they have not succeeded in lessening in the least either our usefulness or our service. God be thanked for all that! The ordeal through which He has carried us has

resulted in nothing but good. If more opposition comes, we should welcome it; it more troubles are in store for us, let us be prepared for them. For in the economy of providence, enemies are at best but friends, and let us all embrace them.

INDIAN YOUTHS IN ENGLAND.

WE publish elsewhere the circular of the National Indian Association, containing the rules framed by the Sub-Committee for the education and supervision of Native youths in England. The Association has our heartiest good wishes, and we need not say that every guardian will be immensely obliged to the ladies and gentlemen who have undertaken to look after the safety and welfare of our young men. The rules framed with this view are calculated to inspire confidence and if they are properly carried out, we venture to think much of the present risk attendant upon a young man's stay in a foreign country will be removed. We particularly approve of that portion of the prospectus in which the Association expresses its readiness to undertake the payment of the necessary expenses from funds which may be placed at its disposal by guardians. The plan admits of a little improvement. If an arrangement could be entered into with Government, whereby the district treasuries might receive periodical contributions from guardians, and the amount placed by Government at the disposal of the Association, it would save much trouble and extra expense, the District Officers in the meantime submitting to the guardians from time to time the reports received from England. In this way something like a regular relation will be established between Government, the guardians and the young people who go to England. In the present transition state of Native society, in which once outside the family influence, a young man is virtually above restraints of any kind, the Government alone can exercise a control and power which, if rightly exerted, may resemble family discipline in some shape. We have more than once repeated in these columns the objections which our countrymen have come to entertain against "England-going." If we are to classify them with any thing like exactness, they will be found to resolve themselves under two heads; (1) that young men who go to England lose their nationality in respect of dress, diet, manners, and feelings, and (2) they lose their religion, and have nothing to offer instead. With respect to the first of these we are sure a reasonable representation to the Committee of the Association will turn their attention to the particular evil complained of. But the second appears to be an insuperable difficulty. We should be fully satisfied that young men, on their arrival in England, will be kept outside the influence of those temptations which are so fatal to strangers, and that they will be placed under the most religious teachers, who, both by example and precept, may imbue in their minds the sense of duty and moral responsibilities. We are not aware if the points we have alluded to have drawn the attention of the distinguished members of the Committee. If so, we should like to know what steps have been taken to meet the wishes of our countrymen; and if not, we beg humbly to commend the subject to their attention. The matter has assumed the shape of a grievance, and it is only if generous Englishmen come to the rescue that the evil we complain of may be removed. So great is it that enlightened Bengalis have come to think that this mania for a visit to Europe should be checked. And their

apprehensions are well grounded. For a young man who returns from England invariably leaves home and society. In a few years all the young man will form themselves into a separate community, thus cutting off sympathies and direct relations with the Hindu society. Now, under these circumstances, a guardian would be the last to consent to his young son separating himself for ever from the domestic circle, and betaking himself to ways and means not at all commendable to the society which they should adorn. We hope that the Committee of the National Indian Association will carefully consider the matter, and come to such a decision as may in the end establish mutual relations between the rulers and the ruled. When statesmen like Lord Northbrook, Sir William Muir, Sir Barrow Ellis, and an indefatigable worker like Miss Manning have moved in the matter, we may reasonably hope that their deliberations will be productive of nothing but unmixed good to the country at large.

Brahmo Somaj.

WE have been requested to announce that the ninth anniversary of the Simlah Brahmo Somaj will take place on the first of January 1880 at No. 4 Bhoirob Biswas' Lane, Manicktollah street.

We understand that the programme of our approaching festivities will be unusually attractive, and will include among other things a series of open-air meetings and torchlight processions, singing at house-gates, juvenile gatherings, ladies' festivals, temperance demonstrations, expeditionary movements, &c. We hope to publish the programme in our next.

We heartily thank their Highnesses the Dowager Maharani and the Maharajah of Burdwan for having very generously contributed rupees a two hundred to the Brahmo Missionary Home Building Fund. It will no doubt be a great comfort to our poor missionary brethren to know that Burdwan has evinced such generous interest in their welfare. May God bless those who help His poor servant.

THE BRAHMO PULPIT.

THE following is the substance of a sermon preached by the Minister in the morning of the second autumnal festival at the Brahmo Mandir, on the 19th of Kartic last:—

At one time the doctrine of casa Brahmin (rice is God) was prevalent in this country. To call rice God is in accordance with Hindu Sastras. We are theists, and so we cannot say that rice is God. But we do believe that God is in the rice. The ancient devotees said,—"Rice, thou art God, my Creator." With the progress of knowledge and civilization that doctrine waned. The dark age (kaliyug) has now come. Let us see what its creed is. It says that there is no God, no religion is free. According to this odious doctrine, rice is simply an element of diet, not of devotion. There is error in both the ancient and the modern opinions. True devotees have adopted the golden mean. They would not say that rice is God, but they believe that God is in rice. For an exalted object can be the Creator; rice cannot be the goddess Lakshmi, still it is essentially Divine. Rice is the dark blood of the soul. It makes faith and hope grow in the soul. The very grain of rice the Lord liveth. The very sight of it draws tears from the eyes of the devotee, and he thus cries out, "O Rice! could man have lived, if thou hadst not been? Human blood is visible in thee. Thou art the giver of strength, the dispenser of power, the source of energy. Holy Rice! in this rice-consuming country—Bengal—thou shalt be vexed." Thou dost rice gladly thou more of Hari as it is swallowed by the true believer. Hari grows the corn in his field by means of His own water and air. Thus corn goes into the peasant's cottage, singing the name of Hari. The peasant goes in for money to the merchant, who again brings it to the house of every man. Thus the Lakshmi (prosperity) of the field becomes the

Lakshmi of the house, the *Lakshmi* of the house is the *Lakshmi* of the body. Strength comes to the body in the form of rice. From corn rice came out, and that rice, when cooked, became nana. The stomach received cooked rice, and there it began to be transformed into blood. Observing all these the *Bhakta* exclaims:—"No where—not even in the Vedas and Vedantas—can the *Living* Almighty Providence be so fully and clearly realized as in the rice-field." He finds Divine strength and the blood of *yogis* and *bhaktas*,—all hidden in rice. The extensive rice field appears to him to be a vast ocean of blood. The strength with which the *bhakta* serves his Master is at first imparted to the rice-field by God Himself. In those grains of rice God has kept hidden His power and love.

Devotional.

WHAT treatment, then, will they among us find, O Lord, who altogether deny the minister?

If they are good and devout, they will be saved. The Kingdom of Heaven shall be recruited from his friends as well as from his bitterest enemies. Among those foremost in my kingdom, there may be not a few of those who have attacked and opposed him. The Lord is no respecter of persons.

How shall we, then, treat those who are antagonists of our minister?

Love them and honor them if they are good men, and associate with them in good works. But as regards the special work to which I have called you and your leader, you must not admit any antagonistic outsider into your fellowship, lest he should defile my dispensation and hinder my work. Within the domain of my dispensation I am a jealous God, and I shall not tolerate an iota of conflicting element. For I mean to do a work, and only those should fraternise in my inner sanctuary who believe in that work and are determined loyally to co-work with me. The spirit of rebellion will find no admittance therein, nay, not even half-hearted loyalty. In the outer court-yard of *my* mansions all are welcome, not only good theists but good men of all religious denominations. Whatsoever by direct association or indirect influence injures deep devotion, firm faith, intoxicating love, fiery enthusiasm, poverty and asceticism, ye shall eschew as an abomination. Be kind to friends and foes, but I solemnly charge you to keep my dispensation pure and undefiled.

Amen!

Correspondence.

[We do not hold ourselves in any way responsible for the opinions of our correspondents.—ED., *I. M.*]

A REQUEST.

TO THE EDITOR OF THE "INDIAN MIRROR."

SIR,—I have read with much interest Mr. Sen's lecture on "Who is Christ," and have been looking for some answer to his somewhat crude and—pardon my saying—second-hand ideas on the subject.

The accompanying article has been sent me by Mr. Darby, who, having been absent in Pau Pyrenees in France, did not see the lecture till somewhat recently.

Although it is very long, still I would ask you to find room for it in an early impression. As an earnest seeker after truth, you will, I feel sure, agree with me that the other side should be heard, and in the interests of Fair Play, Justice, and Truth, I would ask you to insert it. From the fact that Mr. Darby does not recognize any of the existing denominations, his opinion ought to be the more valuable as being more likely to be unprejudiced. But it is very suggestive to find him in perfect accord with all denominations on the subject of the lecture, "Who is Christ?" Apologising for thus trespassing on your space, I am

Yours Faithfully,
J. H. CONDON.

Lydenham, S. E., October 1879.

SOCIAL MORALITY.

TO THE EDITOR OF THE "INDIAN MIRROR."

SIR,—In your issue of the 7th Instant, you publish some remarks on social morality which are worthy of notice. You do, I think, rightly entertain apprehensions as to the probable morality of those young men who not only object to early marriages, but who venture to fix their own time for choosing a partner for life. Looking at these young men as a community, there cannot be a doubt that under such social rules as these, their morality must be extremely lax. Take, for example, the young Englishmen, especially in the large towns in England; they observe similar social rules, and the result is that purity of life amongst them before marriage is not only extremely rare, but is generally impracticable. Experience of life among young Englishmen in a place like London fully confirms what I have stated. Very early marriages are certainly objectionable; but earlier marriages than Englishmen usually make are absolutely necessary to preserve the entire social fabric in England from falling to pieces.

I have been struck, since I have resided in India, with the remarkable stability of the family ties which the wisdom of your ancestors has devised. Looking at this great social fabric thus raised, there are no signs of decay visible on this side of the structure, nor will there be so long as the prudent regulation is maintained that makes marriage the first object in mature life, not the second, nor the least important as is too often the case among English people. You are right to warn your young fellow-countrymen not to establish new rules with respect to the time for contracting marriage. The grand object of existence is marriage; to that every thing in the moral, social, and religious world must be subordinate. The strong conviction of this fact may have originated the custom of early marriages in India; but notwithstanding the objections to this custom, which are generally admitted, the securing of marriage at the proper time has kept Hindu society together for two thousand years or more, and would maintain it for another equally long period. Take care that the lax morality, so frequently observable among Christians, by their neglecting to acknowledge the obligations of marriage at the age when Nature's demand for the sacred tie is the strongest, does not invade your houses.

Yours, &c.,
ANGLICAN.

THE FOURTH GOSPEL.

TO THE EDITOR OF THE "INDIAN MIRROR."

SIR,—You have done well, in the course of the controversy respecting the Fourth Gospel, to point out to your readers that the fact of its being written in the middle of the second century of the Christian era, need not blind us to the true spiritual lessons to be derived from it. I would even go further and say that it will enable us to derive spiritual lessons from it, which we did not perceive before, and remove from our paths certain stumbling blocks which previously existed. No one can charge Jesus with arrogance of self-assertion for any expressions to be found in this Gospel, when we know that the words in it are not his own, but represent the admiration and devotion of one of his followers more than a century after his death.

Again, let us take the story in the beginning of the second chapter. Jesus went to a marriage feast at Cana; the company wanted wine; there were six waterpots containing two or three firkins apiece; Jesus ordered these to be filled with water, and turned it all into wine. And when the ruler of the feast tasted it, and knew not whence it was, he said to the bridegroom, "Every man at the beginning doth set forth good wine; and when men have well drunk, then that which is worse: but thou hast kept the good wine until now."

Now here is a story which is frequently appealed to against preachers of abstinence as an authority for drinking wine to the heart's content, and indeed supplying extra good wine to men who have well drunk already. But from the Theist's point of view is the story credible? Certainly not. Nor need we go far to find the origin of it. We read in the other gospels that Jesus was once asked why his disciples did not fast like other Jews, and in his answer he said, "Neither do men put new wine into old bottles: else the bottles break, and the wine runneth out, and the bottles perish: but they put new wine into new bottles, and both are preserved"—(Matthew, IX, 17; Mark, II, 22; Luke, V, 37.) Here then he compared his doctrine of Love to God and love to man to new wine, which was not to be put into the old bottles, that is to say, embodied in the formalities of Jewish fasts and observances. Then some one, enlarging on this idea, compared the world to a marriage feast originally supplied with old wine, the Jewish religion, which had become exhausted, and there was nothing but the cold water of indifference to fill men's hearts. That insipid liquid was turned by the word of Jesus into the new wine of Christian love, and that new wine was acknowledged by all who tasted it to be better than the old. This allegory was mistaken, by some who heard it, for the narration of a fact, and so the story dressed up with a little incident to give it life, got inserted as a piece of history in the fourth Gospel. But the story has a moral for us too, for the wine of Christolatry with its mysticism, its miracles, its eternal punishment, its devils, its atonement, has become exhausted now itself; and a new spirit is kindled in our hearts by the preaching of faith in the God of science and history and human nature—faith in the Lord of millions of worlds and millions of ages, who is and always has been loving and gracious to all His creatures without requiring any mediator, any sacrifice of His own son, or anybody else's; who does not judge man by his believing or disbelieving a set of improbable stories on insufficient and conflicting evidence, and call such credulity, faith; but who judges man by his regarding the mighty universe and wonderful world in which he finds himself placed, and having faith in the Creator of it, and honestly seeking to learn and to do that Creator's will. And let us not put this new wine of faith in the Author of our being into any old bottles of Hindu customs or Christolatrous dogmas. They cannot and will not hold it, but will only burst and spill it. Let it be embodied in the new bottles fit for it, namely in leading an active, intelligent, and virtuous life, showing respect for our neighbours, who hold erroneous religious views, but keeping ourselves free from their superstition and bigotry, and from rendering homage to aught but the one Supreme Governor of the Universe. Then our new wine and new bottles will both be preserved, and our new wine will be acknowledged by all who taste it to be far better than any they have tried before.

Yours Faithfully,
A. D. TYSSEN.

NOTICES TO CORRESPONDENTS.

Persons favoring us with communications are requested to write legibly, and on one side of the paper only.

Unauthenticated communications will not be inserted.

R. M. B,	Received.
X	Ditto
A BRAHMO, DACCA.	Ditto
LAHORE AND CHITTAGONG LETTERS	Ditto
M. A. D. TYSSEN.	Ditto

We have received also Mr. J. N. Darby's Reply to Babu Keshub Chunder Sen's Lecture on "India asks, who is Christ?"

Provincial.

LUCKNOW.

[FROM OUR OWN CORRESPONDENT.]

The 16th December 1879.

AT the invitation of the members of the *Jalsa Tahsib*, which represents the best talents of Lucknow, Babu Protap Chunder Mozumdar delivered an interesting lecture in the halls of the above Association, on Friday last on "Personal Character." The attendance was smaller than on the two previous occasions, when we had the pleasure of hearing Babu Protap Chunder speak, but quite as respectable.

The lecturer said he had occasion more than once of speaking to audiences of his own countrymen and of Europeans too, but it had never before fallen to his lot to address a meeting of which Hindustani gentlemen formed the major portion. The subject chosen, added the lecturer, was one of general importance. It affects men to whatever nation, race, church or creed they may belong. It could be viewed from a safe, broad, catholic standpoint. However much men may differ in other matters, they all feel the necessity of preserving a pure, unspotted personal character, and they set aside all differences of opinion when they come to speak of it. All religions enjoin it, all systems of philosophy recommend it, and society demands it.

In man there is an inner man—a good man and a bad man. We live in the midst of an unremitting conflict between good and evil powers. All religions acknowledge the existence of these, and though each calls it by a different name, they mean the same thing. There is in us something invisible, something intangible that points out to us—"this is right, this is wrong." It emphatically points out the right course of action, and there is no mistaking it. It will be no use saying "we do not know which is the right thing to do." Whenever you are on the point of committing a wrong act, though circumstances my n cessitate it, though your heart may have an intense hungering after it, though it may be advantageous to you to do it, there is something in you that speaks with an unmistakable voice—"No! decidedly no! it is wrong." This is the voice of God. Never say after this that you cannot hear God. This voice of God in man is called Conscience—the power of judging between right and wrong, between good and evil. It is the vicegerent of God in the human mind. It is this which stayed the hand of Theodore Parker when he raised the stone to pelt the frog, and it is this which his mother advised him to obey through life. What is it that makes the criminal confess his sins, years after he had committed them, and court the punishment that he so long dreaded? What makes the murderer willingly disclose facts, the revelation of which he knows too well would bring capital punishment on him? The sting of Conscience. Outraged conscience goads him to make a confession, and he would much rather deny self and brave death than deny the truth. "It has", as Butler says, "the right to rule over the human mind, but not the might." God made man a free being, free to act as he thinks best, and therefore responsible for his acts. Conscience has the power to show you the path,—pursuing the path depends on your own choice. It has, therefore, the right to rule over the human mind, but not the might. The *might* you must supply. "How and whence?"—you may ask. "From your will" is the answer. If you do not will to do the right thing, you never can. It requires a very strong will to cope with the various temptations that beset us every day of our lives. You overcome one form of temptation, but you find it too hard to combat, when it takes a more enticing form. You should struggle manfully, not once, but as often as you have occasion, and you will find repeated struggles will ultimately change into strength, and not only will you be in the end strong enough to resist temptations, but you will be above their reach.

There is another force that dictates our actions. What led Wilberforce to lay down his life for the abolition of the detested slave trade, and Howard to make it the sol aim of his existence to improve the condition of pr ners, and makes many men at the present d y to devote their lives to ameliorate the condition of the Hindu widow. It is a strong feeling of sympathy for suffering humanity.

With a strong will the heart must be bestirred to the love of truth as pointed out by conscience. Our lives must be a series of conscientious actions. We must learn to honor truth above riches and pleasures and boldly sacrifice them, if need be, for its sake. With an apology to his lawyer friends present, the able lecturer pointed out the fact that many Pleaders disgrace the learned profession by endeavouring to defend cases they know to be perfectly rotten, with an air of innocence—a disguise too thin and flimsy to evade the eye of scrutiny. We should not only speak the truth, but live in the truth. India's sons have often been branded by Europeans with the utter want of love of truth, and it is high time for the people of India to give the lie to this statement by words and deeds.

Medical men tell us that the system is predisposed to disease before the disease actually comes. The same with the moral system of man. Before you commit a sin, you must feel disposed to it from sometime before. The atmosphere which encompasses our daily life is saturated with evil influences, and as soon as the moral system is predisposed, it catches the contagion. Man, when he comes into the world, has a pure, innocent nature. If ever we can realise the meaning of "man being made in the image of his maker," it is when we behold a beautiful little child. What heavenly purity beams in its eyes and what unspeakable beauty resides in its tender form! As the child grows up, this natural innocence is defiled, the natural purity is tainted. He falls from one sin into another. Nature ever builds. But it is at length overpowered, and there is not strength enough in the man to resist temptations. We must, therefore, keep a strict eye over every word that we utter or hear uttered, every act we do or see done, the company we keep, and the books we read. However little may be the influence that each individual exercises on our moral nature, yet the sum total of all these form the basis of our moral character. These may tend either to make us the slaves of our carnal propensities or make us the masters of self. Truly hath it been said that it is nobler to reign within one's self and rule passions and desires than to sway mighty empires. We must, therefore, beware of the pleasures we enjoy.

This applies to those who are not wallowing in the mire of sin and immorality. But what of those over whom sin has got a firm hold, who cannot resist temptations even if they wished? Is there nothing in God's creation, nothing under the canopy of heaven that can give the stren so necessary for his regeneration? Is there thing that can bring him into the ways o rig ousness and truth? Certainly there is. If nothing can save him, religion shall come to his rescue. "Ask and it shall be given, knock and it shall be opened."

When you find no human aid of any avail, God will stretch his helping hand.

With religion foster the quality of goodness. First *wish* to be good, then *will* to be good, then *resolve* to be good, then *determine* to be good and most assuredly the goodness will come. With a few more appropriate words the lecturer sat down amid loud cheering.

For the benefit of those gentlemen who did not understand English, Pundit Pran Nath translated the lecture into Urdu, retaining the sentiments of the speaker as far as he could.

On the afternoon of Sunday last, the 14th instant, Babu Protap Chunder discoursed in Hindi on various religious subjects in the hall of the Brahma Mandir. His earnestness and fervour touched the hearts of a large number of people assembled on the occasion.

Babu Protap Chunder left this for Calcutta last night. We sincerely wish him a safe and pleasant journey and a happy home.

Literary, Scientific, &c.

WE are glad to be able to announce that Dr. Martineau has in the press a second series of sermons, entitled "Hours of Thought."

BIRTHDAY books from the works of Shakespeare, Sir Walter Scott, and George Eliot have already been compiled and published, and these are to be followed immediately by a similar work compiled from the writings of Mr. Carlyle. It will be issued with the sanction of Mr. Carlyle.

REC NT eruptions of Vesuvius have somewhat altered the appearance of the volcano. There are now three craters around the great cone, two small craters having opened at the end of October last, and blown off portions of the mountain which obstructed the issue of the lava. We learn that the current is flowing slowly in a north-easterly direction into the valley between Monte Somma and Vesuvius, and is clearly visible from Naples to the naked eye.

A CERTAIN literary gentleman, wishing to be undisturbed one day, instructed his Irish servant to admit no one, and if any one should inquire for him, to give him an "equivocal answer." Night came, and the gentleman proceeded to interrogate Pat as to his callers.

"Did any one call?"
"Yis, sar; wan gentleman."
"What did he say?"
"He axed was yer honor in."
"Well, what did you tell him?"
"Sure, I gave him a quivikle answer jist."
"How was that?"
"I axed him was his grandmother a monkey!"

Now that we are soon going to have tramways in Calcutta, we believe that any new scientific information about tramcars will be interesting to our readers. We read that a very simple but cleverly-devised improvement has been made in the construction of the tramcars which are propelled in New York by compressed air. Instead of the air being admitted direct from the reservoir to the cylinders and pistons which act upon the wheels, it is first caused to pass through a tank of hot water by which treatment its bulk, and therefore, its pressure is considerably increased. The tramcars are charged with air at their starting-point, an operation which only occupies three or four minutes.

JUPITER has for some months now carried a remarkable rose-colored spot almost motionless u its surface. This spot is a long oval, a little than 30,000 miles in length, and about 10,000 wide, situated about 40° south of the planet's equator. When first seen, in July 1878, by Professor Pritchett (of Glasgow, Mo.), it was much shorter than now and appeared to have a rapid motion over the planet's surface. In October and November, it seems to have disappeared or been covered up; but during the past summer and autumn has reappeared, changed in form, but retaining its brilliant color and almost motionless and permanent. What it can be it is very hard to say, or even to conjecture; for its present permanence and immobility are in striking contrast with its earlier behavior and with that of the other features of the planet's markings.

MR. JOHN BRIGHT is noted for his pure and vigorous English. When asked how he had acquired such command of the language, he replied: "By almost learning by heart the purest English writers." A correspondent of the N.Y. *Evening Post* writes:—"I once had a conversation with Mr. Bright on the same subject, and the answer he gave me was that he had not for many years gone to bed a single night without reading some good English poem. He added to this that, of late, he had been compelled to confine himself almost exclusively to our American writers—naming Bryant, Longfellow, Whittier and Lowell. He said that the English poets of the present day had become, some of them, too obscure and others too finical and affected to suit his taste; but that the Americans continued in the line of the 'simple, sensuous, passionate' begun by Shakespeare and Milton, and perpetuated by Southey and Wordsworth."

THE *Indian Church Gazette* gives the following history of Cawnpore:—"Cawnpore or Kanhpur (one of the names of Krishna) is, as the name shows, a city of Hindu origin. Tradition gives it the following history:—Hindu Singh, the last Rajah of Sachendi, went to bathe in the Ganges in the vicinity of old Cawnpore city, and was so pleased with the scenery of the spot that he wished to found a small town there. The Brahmin priests who accompanied him, having made astrological calculations, pronounced the day most auspicious, adding that a town founded at that moment would in time gain *a world-wide fame!* The Rajah at once ordered the dependent Rajah of Ramai-pur to lay the foundations, and being the anniversary of the birth of Krishna or Kanh, the town was fittingly called after him: two *pukka* gates, a ghat, and a large mansion were erected, the city gradually extending afterwards. It is supposed to be above 125 years old, and the new city, opposite the present Civil Lines, only a century old, corresponding probably with the military occupation of the station.

THE MAGAZINES.

Contemporary Review, November 1879.

THE number for November contains some very good articles, among which we may mention Professor Max Müller's lecture on Freedom, Mr. Proctor's article on Suspended Animation and that of Professor Stanley Jevons entitled John Stuart Mill's Philosophy Tested. There is also an interesting discussion on Mr. Gladstone by a Liberal and a Conservative respectively. The first article, that by Professor Max Müller, is written in one of his happiest moods. It begins with an allusion to Mill's complaint against the tyranny of public opinion as embodied in the following passage:—"The modern *régime* of public opinion is in an unorganised form what the Chinese educational and political systems are in an organised; and unless individuality shall be able successfully to assert itself against this yoke, Europe, notwithstanding its noble antecedents and its professed Christianity, will tend to become another China." Professor Max Müller admits the charge of uniformity, and contends that it is due not to the action of society, as Mill affirms, but to the inherited chains fastened on us by past generations. A beautiful explanation of the principle of heredity then follows. The English, he says, "are Aryan in language; they have inherited their alphabet from the Egyptians, their division of time into sixty minutes from the Babylonians, and the figures from the Hindus. "When we write a capital F, when we draw the top line and the smaller line through the middle of the letter, we really draw the two horns of the cerastes, the horned serpent which the ancient Egyptians used for representing the sound of *f*." "In the same manner the undulating line of our capital L still recalls very strikingly the bent back of the crouching lion, which in the later hieroglyphic inscriptions represents the sound of L." Now this chain of tradition is not a "galling fetter." On the contrary, every boy should wear this fetter—in other words should not "begin life as a young savage, or be left to form his own language, and invent his own letters, numericals and coins." School education must in the beginning be dogmatic.

"Boys at school must turn their mind into a row of pigeon-holes, filling as many as they can with useful notes, and never forgetting how many are empty. There is an immense amount of positive knowledge to be acquired between the ages of ten and eighteen—rules of grammar, strings of vocables, dates, names of towns, rivers, and mountains, mathematical formulas, &c. All depends here on the receptive and retentive powers of the mind. The memory has to be strengthened, without being overtaxed, till it acts almost mechanically. Learning by heart, I believe, cannot be too strongly recommended during the years spent at school. There may have been too much of it when, as the Rev. H. C. Adams informs us in his 'Wykehamica' (p. 357), boys used to say by heart 13,000 and 14,000 lines, when one repeated the whole of Virgil, nay, when another was able to say the whole of the English Bible by rote :—'Put him on where you would, he would go fluently on, as long as any one would listen.'

"No intellectual investment, I feel certain, bears such ample and such regular interest as gems of English, Latin, or Greek literature deposited in our memory during our childhood and youth, and taken up from time to time in the happy hours of our solitude."

But academic teaching ought to be not merely a continuation, but in one sense a correction of scholastic teaching. Professor Max Müller lays down an important distinction between the two sorts of teaching :—

"While at school instruction must be chiefly dogmatic, at University it is to be Socratic, for I find no better name for that method which is to set a man free from the burden of purely traditional knowledge ; to make him feel that the words which he uses are often empty, that the concepts he employs are, for the most part, mere bundles picked up at random ; that even where he knows facts, he does not know their evidence ; and where he expresses opinions, they are mostly mere dogmas, adopted by him without examination."

Of dogmas he says :—

"I do not think of religious dogmas only. They are generally the first to rouse inquiry, even during our schoolboy days, and they are by no means the most difficult to deal with. Dogma often rages where we least expect it. Among scientific men the theory of evolution is at present becoming, or has become, a dogma. What is the result? No objections are listened to, no difficulties recognized, and a man like Virchow, himself the strongest supporter of evolution, who has the moral courage to say that the descent of man from any ape whatsoever is, as yet, before the tribunal of scientific zoology, 'not proven,' is howled down in Germany in a manner worthy of Ephesians and Galatians. But at present I am thinking not so much of any special dogmas, but rather of that dogmatic state of mind which is the almost inevitable result of the teaching at school."

Mr. Müller's liberality in matters religious is well known. He says :—

"If some—ay, if many of the doctrines of Christianity were met with in other religions also, surely that would not affect their value, or diminish their truth ; while nothing, I feel certain, would more effectually secure to the purer and simple teaching of Christ its true place in the historical development of the human mind than to place it side by side with the other religions of the world. In the series of translations of the 'Sacred Books of the East,' of which the first three volumes have just appeared, I wished myself to include a new translation of the Old and New Testaments ; and when that series is finished, it will, I believe, be admitted that nowhere would these two books have had a grander setting, or have shown with a brighter light than surrounded by the Veda, the Zendavesta, the Buddhist Tripitaka, and the Qur'an."

The writer complains that in English universities there is too little of academic freedom. There is not only guidance, but far too much of constant personal control. From the following we may learn by contrast how wretched in this respect is the education which young men receive in this country :—

"Most horses if you take them to the water will drink ; and the best way to make them drink is to leave them alone. I have lived long enough in English and in German Universities to know that the intellectual fibre is as strong and sound in the English as in the German youth. But if you supply a man, who wishes to learn swimming, with bladders—nay, if you insist on his using them—he will use them, but he will probably never learn to swim. Take them away on the contrary and depend on it, after a few aimless strokes and few painful gulps, he will use his arms and his legs, and he will swim. If young men do not learn to use their arms, their legs, their muscles, their senses, their brain, and their heart too, during the bright years of their University life, when are they to learn it? True, there are thousands who never learn it, and who float happily on through life buoyed up on mere bladders. The worst that can happen to them is that some day the bladders may burst, and they may be left stranded or drowned. But these are not the men whom England wants to fight her battles."

The two articles on Mr. Gladstone may form a curious psychological study. A Liberal rightly enough extols Mr. Gladstone, but a Conservative would not even give him the credit for moral rectitude. John Stuart Mill called the Conservative party the stupid party, and we confess we first understood the significance of this epithet when we went through the diatribe of this Conservative writer. At any rate, we lose all faith in his intelligence when we hear him actually question Mr. Gladstone's sincerity and uprightness, and says that in changing his political views from time to time, he was actuated by motives of prudence and selfishness. To say this of the most pure-minded statesman and party-leader since the days of Cromwell !

Our readers may remember a hoax played some months ago by an Australian journal which reported the discovery of a medicine by means of which persons and animals might be left in a state of suspended animation for any length of time, and then may be brought back to life at pleasure. Mr. Proctor writes upon this subject, and discusses the probability of the method under notice. Many interesting experiments are quoted, some of which we may extract here. Here is one :—

"A young lady, who had seemed gradually to sink until she died, had been placed in her coffin, careful scrutiny revealing no signs of vitality. On the day appointed for her funeral, several hymns were sung before her door. She was conscious of all that happened around her, and heard her friends lamenting her death. She felt them put on the dead-clothes, and lay her in the coffin which produced an indescribable mental anxiety. She tried to cry, but her mind was without power and could not act on the body. It was equally impossible to her to stretch out her arms, or to open her eyes or to cry, although she continually endeavoured to do so. The internal anguish of her mind was, however, at its utmost height when the funeral hymns began to be sung, and when the lid of the coffin was about to be nailed on. The thought that she was to be buried alive was the first one which gave activity to her mind, and caused it to operate on her corporeal frame. Just as the people were about to nail on the lid, a kind of perspiration was observed to appear on the surface of the body. It grew greater every moment, and at last a kind of convulsive motion was observed in the hands and feet of the corpse. A few minutes after, during which fresh signs of returning life appeared, she at once opened her eyes, and uttered a most pitiable shriek."

The following is said by Dr. Richardson :—

"At a meeting of the British Medical Association at Leeds, 'a member of the Association was showing to a large audience the action of nitrous oxide gas, using a rabbit as the subject of his demonstration. The animal was removed from the narcotizing chamber a little too late, for it had ceased to breathe, and it was placed on the table to all appearance dead.' 'At this stage,' he proceeds, 'I went to the table, and by use of a small pair of double-acting bellows restored respiration. In about four minutes there was revival of active irritability in the abdominal muscles, and two minutes later the animal leaped again into life, as if it had merely been asleep. There was nothing remarkable in the fact; but it excited, even in so cultivated an audience as was then present, the liveliest surprise."

"It is not incredible," says Dr. Richardson, "that the Indian Fakirs possess a vegetable extract or essence which possesses the same power, and by means of which they perform their as yet unexplained feat of prolonged living burial."

Mr. Jevons' article on Mill is not so exhaustive or clear as his last. In it he reveals his own creed, and proclaims himself to be an evolutionist. We quote the following concluding paragraph :—

"According to Mill, we are little self-dependent gods, fighting with a malignant and murderous power, called Nature, sure, one would think, to be worsted in the struggle. According to Spencer, as I venture to interpret his theory, we are the latest manifestation of an all-prevailing tendency towards the good—the happy. Creation is not yet concluded, and there is no one of us who may not become conscious in his heart that he is no Automatum, no mere lump of Protoplasm, but the Creature of a Creator."

If the tendency of all manifestations is towards "the good—the happy," is it not certain that there is a Beneficent Being who ordains them? We do not understand why nature, unless it be presided over by God, should always end in good and never accidentally in evil.

NOTICE.

RAM MOHUN ROY MEMORIAL FUND.

SUBSCRIPTIONS to the above Fund will be thankfully received by the undersigned.

KRISHNA BIHARI SEN,
Address,—"Indian Mirror" Office,
2, British Indian Street.
Or Albert School,
15, College Square.

Calcutta.

THE Maharajah of Gurdwan has kindly contributed rupees two hundred and fifty to the Albert Hall Library Fund.

THE Arya Nari Somaj met at the Kamal Kutir, Lily Cottage, yesterday, and among other things framed certain rules and resolutions for regulating the mutual social relations of the sexes and maintaining the nationality and sanctity of Hindu womanhood.

NATIONAL INDIAN ASSOCIATION.

OF late years an increasing disposition has been shown by Native gentlemen in India to send their sons to be educated in this country. Under proper safeguards such a course is eminently deserving of encouragement, the benefit to be gained by a Native of India from a well-directed visit to England, in enlargement of view and improved knowledge of English society and ways of thought, being universally admitted.

It appears, however, that many Indian parents, who are anxious to send their children to England, are deterred from doing so by the difficulty of securing any adequate supervision over them. Removed from all the influences and restraints of home, and placed in a foreign country, a Native youth is necessarily exposed to considerable temptation, while his parent has no sure means of obtaining information of his conduct or of ascertaining whether his time is spent profitably or otherwise.

It has been thought by some persons who are interested in the welfare of India that if this want of supervision could in any way be met, and greater facility given to the upper classes to educate their sons in England, a material benefit would be conferred on the Natives of India, and good service rendered at the same time to the State.

A meeting recently held in London, to consider this question, was attended by the Earl of Northbrook, Sir Barrow Ellis, Sir Henry Davies, Sir William Muir, Sir Arthur Hobhouse, Colonel Keatinge, and several Members of the National Indian Association, which has for two or three years past, in addition to other work, rendered friendly assistance to Native students living in this country.

It was ascertained at this meeting that the National Indian Association was not unwilling to extend its operations, and to establish, if it should be thought feasible, an organisation for the purpose of supplying information and assistance to Native gentlemen desirous of educating their sons in England ; and also of exercising a general control over those Native students whose supervision the Association might, after enquiry, arrange to undertake.

A Committee was appointed to consider the best method of carrying out such a scheme, and a Report embodying their proposals, with a set of Rules (of which a copy is appended) was approved and adopted by the National Indian Association on the 25th of June. A Permanent Sub-Committee, composed of the Earl of Northbrook, Sir Barrow Ellis, Sir Henry Davies, Sir Arthur Hobhouse, and Mr.

Seymour V. FitzGerald, was at the same time appointed to give effect to the proposals, and it was resolved that the scheme of the Association should be communicated to the Viceroy, Governors, Lieutenant-Governors, and Chief Commissioners in India, with a request that its object and scope may be made known to the classes interested.

It will be observed from the Rules that the National Indian Association is prepared, under certain conditions, to accept the supervision of Native students entrusted to its care. The Rules will be liable to such modification as experience may suggest; but under no circumstances is it contemplated to render assistance of a charitable nature, the Association being of opinion that the proposed scheme, to be productive of any real good, should be self-supporting.

All communications should be addressed to the office of the National Indian Association, 6, John Street, Bedford Row, London.

F. E. S. WYLLIE (late Bombay Civil Service),
E. A. MANNING.
} *Hon Secretaries.*

8th August, 1879.

RULES.

1. Any Native gentleman desirous of availing himself of the advantages of the National Indian Association in this branch of its work must write to the Honorary Secretary of the Association (6, John Street, Bedford Row, London) at least six months before the proposed departure from India of his son or ward, giving full information as to his age and previous education, the education desired for him in England, and accompanying the application with satisfactory references as to the position of the applicant, and the means of defraying all the expenses of his son or ward while living in England. One of the references should be from a Collector and Magistrate, or other officer of equal relative rank.

II. All applications will be submitted to the Permanent Sub-Committee of the Association, and decided on their merits, the conditions being settled by special arrangement in each case. The Association reserves to itself the right of rejecting any application.

III. The responsibilities of the Association will be to meet the student on his arrival, to procure lodgings for him, and to make all necessary arrangements for his education, whether at the Universities or Inns of Court, or by the employment of Tutors or otherwise. The Association will also undertake, to the extent of the remittances placed at its disposal, all payments requisite for the above objects, and for the general superintendence of the students, as well as the distribution to them of such personal allowances as many be agreed upon with the parent or guardian.

IV. The Association will from time to time communicate to the parents or guardians the progress attained by those entrusted to its care, and in the event of anything unsatisfactory coming to its knowledge as to the conduct of a student, will advice as to the desirability or otherwise of of his being retained in England.

V. An annual charge to defray minor expenses will be made for each student under the care of the Association, the amount of each charge to be determined according to the circumstances of each case.*

MEETING IN HONOR OF RAJAH RAM MOHUN ROY.

—o—

PURSUANT to notice a meeting was held at the Albert Hall on Thursday, the 25th of December, to consider and determine the best means of perpetuating the memory of Rajah Ram Mohun Roy.

Babu Keshub Chunder Sen was unanimously voted to the chair.

In opening the business of the meeting the Chairman made a short introductory speech, in the course of which he noticed briefly the more striking points in the character and career of the distinguished reformer, Rajah Ram Mohun Roy. He said if ever an apology was altogether out of place for the introduction of departed greatness to the favorable notice of an intelligent and grateful public, it was upon the present occasion. Some apology, however, was needed, not for holding the present meeting, but for convening it so late in the day. The unjustifiably long period which had elapsed since the death of the illustrious reformer must be a matter of the deepest concern and regret to all his friends and admirers. To them it could not but be painful to contemplate that while statues and portraits abounded in the land, commemorating the lives of India's numerous benefactors, there was not an inch of canvas or a grain of marble in honor of one so truly great. Perhaps the appreciation of greatness was always tardy, and nations were slow to recognise the merits and services of men who were in advance of their age. Certainly Rajah Ram Mohun Roy was one of India's great men and possessed unmistakably all the requisites of greatness. A representative man, a genius, he left his mark upon the age and revolutionized Native society. It was not to be expected that such a man should be readily appreciated and recognized by his contemporaries. The reforms he intiated excited ridicule and bitterness, and even hatred and antagonism, and the number of adherents who stood by him was extremely small. In such a state of things appreciative sympathy it was idle to expect. And none saw this more clearly than Ram Mohun Roy himself. He was the last person to seek or expect a monument in his honor. He devoted himself to the welfare of his country, and he sought no other reward. But it was our duty, said the Chairman, to give him the honor which he himself never sought, and which his countrymen had hitherto withheld from him amid the clamour of contending parties and the excitement of theological polemics. Now that such excitement had subsided and the reforms set on foot by the illustrious Rajah had quietly permeated all classes of the community, a memorial movement in his honor could not but commend itself to all educated Natives of India. A younger generation had come forward to make amends for the shortcomings of the past generation, and posterity unhesitatingly glorified the man whom his contempories were slow to acknowledge. The present movement was, indeed, too late, as half a century had rolled away since the death of the Rajah. But better late than never. On this principle alone he, the Chairman, would justify this movement. Rajah Ram Mohun Roy needed no eloquent advocate to commend his virtues and abilities. His name was a household word. Many and varied were his claims upon the gratitude and esteem of his countrymen. These might be briefly set forth. It was generally supposed that Rajah Ram Mohun Roy was merely a religious reformer, and that it was in the domain of theology alone that he manifested his extraordinary abilities and talents. No. In other fields too his merits shone as conspicuously. His services in the cause of political reformation were such as could not be overrated. He was in England at the time when the subject of the renewal of the Charter of the East India Company was under discussion, and he readily took advantage of the opportunity to suggest several political reforms for the consideration of Parliament. His reported evidence before the Select Committee of the House of Commons on the affairs of the East Indian Company bore ample evidence of his legal knowledge and political sagacity. In the papers published by the Committee were embodied his opinions on a variety of important subjects, such as the judicial and revenue systems, the condition of the agricultural classes, the law of rent. He also published at the time his views on many of these subjects, which no doubt helped greatly to influence English public opinion. In fact, Ram Mohun Roy had done more than any of his countrymen before or since to interest the Parliament and people of England in the affairs of India, and certainly no Native of this country ever had so respectful a hearing at the hands of the House of Commons. In whatever he said or did concerning the political welfare of his country he always manifested not only liberal views and sound judgment, but also remarkable earnestness of feelings. He was not a mere agitator, but an enthusiastic and devoted patriot. Referring to his labors in the cause of social reformation, the Chairman spoke of the abolition of the barbarous rite of *sutti* which had been brought about chiefly through his exertions here and in England. For his signal success in this and other reform movements, political and social, the whole country from one end to the other must feel profoundly thankful, however widely people might differ in theological matters. The subject of promoting cordial social intercourse between the European and Native races, which was so dear to every patriotic heart in these days, was uppermost in Ram Mohun Roy's mind. Lastly, in learning and literary ability that great reformer had few equals, and certainly no superior among his countrymen. The many and varied works he had left behind were standing monuments of the literary genius of that intellectual giant. How few there were among the educated classes who cared to study foreign languages! Ram Mohun Roy was acquainted with ten different languages. Some of these he knew critically, and as a scholar, as his published writings would abundantly testify. He knew besides Bengali, Hindi and Urdu, Sanskrit, Arabic, Persian and also Hebrew; he had also a knowledge, though comparatively limited, of Greek, Latin and French. He was distinguished for his close reasoning and the wonderful argumentative power with which he vanquished his proudest adversaries. As the founder of the Brahmo Somaj, the illustrious Rajah had thoroughly established his reputation as a religious reformer of modern times and a fearless apostle and expounder of Monotheism. As such he was honored by thousands in the land, but all India, irrespective of religious differences, glorified him as a great reformer and benefactor. The Chairman concluded by saying he had little doubt that a general appeal on behalf of the present movement to the patriotic feelings of all classes of the people in the several presidencies would meet with a ready and cordial response.

He then called upon Babu Protap Chunder Mozoomdar to move the first resolution.

The resolution was as follows:—

That subscriptions be set on foot with a view to secure a fitting memorial of Rajah Ram Mohun Roy.

In rising to move it Babu Protap Chunder Mozoomdar said:—Gentlemen, you have heard what Rajah Ram Mohun Roy was. The facts of his life have been laid before you in a manner I could not have expected to do. It remains for me only to express one or two sentiments which arise in the mind when the mention of Rajah Ram Mohun Roy's name is made. At a public cemetry in the city of Bristol, they keep a book in which every Hindu, who visits England, and makes a pilgrimage (for it is nothing less) to see the tomb of the departed Rajah, is requested to write something expressive of thoughts suggested by the spot where lie buried the mortal remains of their illustrious countryman. In this book you will find a quotation, "The bread cast in the waters is found again." "If thy spirit, O Rajah, once more visited the land in which thou didst labor long, and against such odds, thou wilt find that the bread of truth and goodness which thou didst cast upon the troubled waters of theological controversy in Bengal, imagining perhaps, as others imagined, that the bread could not be found again, is now returned a hundredfold, nay a thousandfold in the shape of the vast numbers of the present generation of thy countrymen, who have adopted thy doctrines with enthusiasm, and carried on thy good work with earnestness amidst the aggressive and victorious church which thou didst establish." At a public hall in the city of Bristol you find hung up high on the wall, mounted on a massive golden frame, the likeness of a tall, dark-complexioned man, the refined intellectual dignity of whose face, the visible manliness and superiority of whose features gave the portrait a marked singularity over other pictures in that same room. On asking you are told this is a faint likeness of the great Brahmin, who more than a century ago first showed the way to renounce the social prejudices of his caste and nation, and manifested the originality and moral strength of not only feeling at home in a foreign land, but extracting the kernel of truth from a foreign religion founded by one who was neither a Hindu nor a European, but a poor despised Jew of his time, though now exalted to the highest pedestal of prophetic eminence, namely, Jesus Christ of Nazareth. England has done due honor to the memory of Rajah Ram Mohun Roy. Coming back to India when you land at Bombay, you observe at a bungalow on Malabar Hill the likeness of a face cast in plaster of Paris—a face that is faded, sad and worn out with the only grandeur of a noble high forehead. This is a cast of the features of the Rajah as he lay dead. Travelling further east, you have nothing to show as token of the reverence in which his memory is held by his countrymen. And the strongest thing of all is that in Bengal—the land of his birth, the scene of his labors, the people who have profited most by his precepts, struggles, and example, there is not a bust, not a picture, not a sign to show that the greatest and the best of our benefactors receives from our grateful hearts the homage due to him by every right, human and Divine. The cheap enthusiasm which evaporates in speech-making has been frequently expended in empty laudation of the Rajah's greatness. But practically to perpetuate his memory nothing has been up to this time done. This calls for a fresh attempt on the part of his admirers to do what has been left undone. I do not hesitate to say that large subscriptions may be easily collected to give us a fitting memorial. There may be differences of opinion and estimate in regard to others of our public men. But Rajah Ram Mohun Roy's name is a sacred name everywhere. And

---

* It is anticipated that an annual charge of Rs. 50 to Rs. 100 will suffice, but this charge will be liable to alteration after some experience has been gained as to the amount of petty expenses.

in Bombay, in the Punjab, throughout the N. W. Provinces, his memory is held in such thorough veneration by vast numbers of the people that a simple mention of our object will elicit strong and practical sympathy such as will answer the purpose for which we meet here. I have great pleasure, therefore, in moving the resolution entrusted to me.

Babu Amarendra Nath Chatterji, in seconding the Resolution, said that, in responding to the call of his esteemed friend in the chair, he had, after what had fallen from the chair and the feeling utterances of his learned friend, the mover, very little to add. It behoved the Native community which was reaping the fruits of the Rajah Ram Mohun Roy's labors in India and in England, to show, by adopting a fitting memorial, their appreciation of the services which that great and good man had rendered to his country. He, the speaker, would not dwell upon the Rajah's extensive erudition, cosmopolitan culture, and wide-spread philanthropy which had made his name familiar as a household word, not only amongst Hindus, but amongst Mahumedans by whom he is known as Moulvi Ram Mohun Roy. In the field of politics, his labors were not confined to the advancement of any particular class, section, or creed, but were directed to the amelioration of all. His strenuous advocacy of the rights of the subjects of the British Empire, and luminous exposition of the defects of the then British administration in India led to the most valuable results, but the least of which was the recognition by Parliament of the noble and enlightened principle that no subject of the realm should, by reason of race, creed, color, or descent, be excluded from any office in the State. Ram Mohun Roy was a man pre-eminently in advance of his age. His letter to Lord Amherst on the paramount duty of the Government to encourage and foster the growth of English education among the subjects of the British Crown, and his labors in connection with the founding of the Hindu College are standing monuments of his greatness of mind and heart. As a social and religious reformer, besides being the founder of a creed establishing the worship of the Deity, in spirit and in truth, which could not be unacceptable even to the orthodox, and recommended itself peculiarly to the educated Hindu, he labored for the abolition of the barbarous and inhuman Sutti, and—what was not generally known—wrote a paper on the remarriage of Hindu widows, which was published many years after his death by his gifted son, the late Babu Ramapershad Roy. But, Sir, the name of Rajah Ram Mohun Roy is entitled to the highest respect, as he was the first Native of Bengal who disabused Englishmen of the notion they had formed of the Bengali character from the glowing but not complimentary description of it by Lord Macaulay. He was the first Bengali who raised the intellectual and moral character of his countrymen in the estimation of the civilized world. Was it right that such a man, whose life was illustrated by so many great and good works, should be without a memorial—the outcome of public esteem. Renascent Bengal owes to the memory of her great benefactor a debt immense of endless gratitude (Loud cheers.)

Babu Krishna Bihari Sen, in moving the second resolution, said that both as a political and an educational reformer, Ram Mohun Roy had claims to the respect and gratitude of his countrymen. He said that he had once had a talk with the late Rajah Digumber Mitter—himself a politician of a very high order—and he had heard him say that the political writings and utterances of Ram Mohun Roy bore the impress of true genius, and that many of his views on political subjects were true up to that day. As regards his character as an educationist, he would commend to the notice of all a paper written by the Rajah in which he anticipated all the arguments brought forward by Lord Macaulay in favor of English education in his celebrated minute which has already found a place in the classics of English literature. The paper alluded to would be found in Babu Peary Chand Mitra's "Life of David Hare." The speaker said that if the Committee now to be appointed did its work with a will, something like a national memorial might be obtained in no time. There were many reasons why a movement like this should succeed. In his own days Ram Mohun Roy was viewed with disfavor by his countrymen. But in the histories of communities and nations it was most true that the conservatives of the generation became the liberals of the next, and vice versa. The very ideas for which Ram Mohun Roy fought were self-evident truths at the present day. There would be no difficulty, he hoped, in obtaining co-operation for a movement in which every educated Native must necessarily feel an interest.

He then moved the following resolution :—

That the following gentlemen (with power to add to their number) be appointed a Committee to give effect to the above resolution:—

Babu Keshub Chunder Sen,
Babu Dijendro Nath Tagore,
Babu Joy Gopal Sen,
Rev. C. H. A. Dall,
Babu Shama Churn Sircar,
Babu Protap Chunder Mozumder,
Babu Amarendra Nath Chatterji, B.L.

This was seconded by Babu Joy Gopal Sein.

Proposed by Babu Boykonto Nath Sein and seconded by Babu Grish Chunder Dutt—

That Babu Krishna Bihari Sen, M.A., be appointed Secretary and Treasurer.

After a vote of thanks to the chair, the meeting terminated.

Selections.

STORIES ABOUT RAM MOHUN ROY.

—o—

(From Mr. Macdonald's Life of the Rajah.)

RAM MOHUN ROY AND LORD W. BENTINCK.

THERE are various anecdotes still current in Calcutta with a narration of some of which I may close this paper. For these I am indebted to a Bengali friend. It is said that on one occasion, Lord William Bentinck, the Governor-General, on hearing that he would likely receive considerable help from the Rajah in suppressing the pernicious custom of widow-burning, sent one of his Aides-de-Camp to him expressing his desire to see him. To this the Rajah replied, "I have now given up all worldly avocations, and am engaged in religious culture and in the investigation of truth. Kindly express my humble respects to the Governor-General, and inform him that I have no inclination to appear before his august presence, and therefore, I hope he will kindly pardon me." These words the Aide-de-Camp conveyed to the Viceroy, who enquired.—"What did you say to Ram Mohun Roy ?" The Aide-de-Camp replied :—"I told him that Lord William Bentink, the Governor-General, would be pleased if he would come and see him." The Governor-General answered go back and tell him again "that *Mr. William Bentinck* will be highly obliged to him, if he will kindly see him once." This the Aide-de-Camp, did and Ram Mohun Roy could no longer refuse the urgent an[d po]lite request of His Lordship.

A GENTLE REPROOF.

[It] was characteristic of Ram Mohun Roy that, though he could not reprove his disciples for their faults, still, if he himself was guilty of any fault and if any disciple reproved him for it, he invariably took the reproof in good part. Here is an instance. According to the custom of that time, Ram Mohun Roy wore *Babri* hair (long flowing hair like that of a female). After bathing, he used to spend some time in dressing it. On this one of his disciples, Tara Chand Chakravarti, wittily remarked :—"Sir, was the Hymn beginning with How long wilt thou see thy face in the mirror with pleasure," intended for others only ? [It should be remembered that this beautiful hymn, exposing as it does the vanity of human wishes, was composed by the Rajah.] Ram Mohun was, however, a little abashed, and said "Yes, *Brother* ; you are quite right."

THE RAJAH'S BENEVOLENCE.

Though Ram Mohun was slow to reproach the disciples for slight offences, he never allowed any grave ones to pass unreproved. For indulging in excess of drinking he refused to see the face of one of his disciples for six months. On this, the disciple is said to have reformed. The Rajah was not a vegetarian, but he was very much opposed to cruelty to animals. Almost every evening he partook of animal food. One day it happned that his servant tortured to death the animal intended for supper. The Rajah, on hearing this, was very angry, and ran barefooted after the servant with a stick, from the house to the compound. It was with much difficulty he was persuaded to give up the chase.

THE HEAVEN'S DURBAR.

One other anecdote and I am done. Ram Mohun Roy used to attend church in what Bengalis regard as full dress, worn only on state occasions. He justified this practice by remarking that when we have to attend a nobleman's or a king's Durbar, we repair thither in such full dress, intending thus to show proper respect and regard to our host. "And what is a worshipping congregation," said he, "but a *Durbar* of the King of kings. We should, therefore, dress in a way worthy of the solemnity of the occasion."

Darlington's Pain-Curer has been found to be a certain cure for Pains in the Back, Lumbago, Pains in the Chest, Sore Throats, Coughs Colds, Tightness of the Chest, Headache, Toothache, Neuralgia, Colics, Rheumatism, Paralysis, Pains in the Groins, Contracted Joints, Gout, Sciatica, Bad Legs, Bad Breasts, Swellings, Old Sores, Piles, Ring worms, Pimples, Freckles, & Eruptions on the skin.

LICENSED SIN.

—o—

[TO THE EDITOR OF THE "BOMBAY GUARDIAN."]

DEAR SIR,—Much has been done to raise the moral tone of the British soldier in India, but much remains to be done. One cannot fail to appreciate the praise-worthy efforts made by Mr. Gelson Gregson and other philanthropic gentlemen to expel intemperance from the ranks of our army. Drink, however, is not the only curse which our brave soldiers are subjected to. Truth compels reference to another curse. Your readers will be able to form an idea of what it is, from the following extract taken from an English religious journal:—

"There stand upon our Statutebook, as a nation, certain Statutes—'Acts' which require no description. It is enough to say that they shamelessly set at naught the laws of God, the sanctities of family life, and the rights of individual liberty. It is not necessary to prove or to argue that they are capable of being turned to account by the vilely debauched and the basely tyrannical in a way and to an extent from which the grave of the suicide alone can furnish the protection which a professedly Christian nation denies. What is the object and what is the half-suppressed plea ? The answer is furnished by the very action which has been taken. It has been claimed for 'military districts.' It is directly associated with the army. And why ? Because Britain, powerful, wealthy and Christian, cannot afford to maintain an army in which the laws of morality and the sanctions of family life are recognised and allowed. A vicious army is less costly than one in which virtue is fostered, in which marriage is tolerated and God is honored. To save the tax-payer, immorality is made easy and safe. As a consequence the shadow of the British flag wherever it is raised is a signal for the gathering of the fallen and the outcast. Nay worse, the British soldier—and no less the British officer—is, on the national statute-book, recognised as the special representative and promoter of impurity and shame. For the honor of their flag let British officers look to it. That is a stain which no battle-fields can wipe out, a disgrace which will eat out the manly vigour and destroy the reliable courage of even British soldiery. But, yet more, let every honest citizen, let every parent, let every Christian look well to it. The canker is spreading in our midst. And if this nation still will have it so, that the luxurious combination of a standing army and immunity from its necessary cost shall be secured by the bold and unblushing countenance and assistance of vice, then woe betides the 'cottage homes of England'—given over by the national will and for the wages of iniquity to the legalised arts of the professional seducer."

The above is no exaggeration. Almost every cantonment in British India testifies to its veracity, Christian England prostituting her religion and degrading her prestige, by supporting a traffic, shameless, iniquitous, and abominable, in the extreme. It is enough to make every true-hearted child of Britain bow his head with shame.

Must these things continue so ? Is there no one to lift up his voice against this iniquity, this national sin ? What are the many earnest Christian workers in this land doing ? Will they not endeavour to rid our flag of this foul stain ? Will they not unite as Englishmen, as Christians, to roll away this terrible reproach from before the heathen.

Members of Missionary Societies, of Missionary Conferences, you who are anxious to see India regenerated, will you not unite in gathering out the stones and casting up a highway for the Lord of Hosts ? The Annual Conference of the Methodist Episcopal Church will soon be in session. I would respectfully suggest that they take some action regarding this so-called (and falsely called) "necessary evil." Action might be taken by these Conferences calling on other Missionary bodies and the Christian community of India in general, to come up "to the help of the Lord, to the help of the Lord, against the mighty."

NEANISKOS.

15th December 1879.

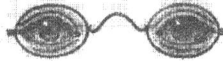

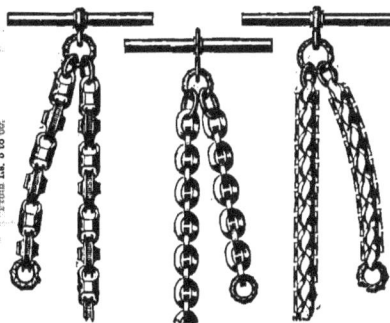

www.ingramcontent.com/pod-product-compliance
Lightning Source LLC
Chambersburg PA
CBHW030827270326
41928CB00007B/940